75 YEARS OF FORMULA ONE

F1 RACING

THE ULTIMATE COMPANION

This updated edition first published in 2025
First published in Great Britain in 2024 by
Michael O'Mara Books Limited
9 Lion Yard
Tremadoc Road
London SW4 7NQ

EU representative:
Authorised Rep Compliance Ltd
Ground Floor
71 Baggot Street Lower
Dublin D02 P593
Ireland

Copyright © Michael O'Mara Books Limited 2024, 2025

All rights reserved. You may not copy, store, distribute, transmit, reproduce or otherwise make available this publication (or any part of it) in any form, or by any means (electronic, digital, optical, mechanical, photocopying, recording or otherwise), without the prior written permission of the publisher. Any person who does any unauthorized act in relation to this publication may be liable to criminal prosecution and civil claims for damages.

A CIP catalogue record for this book is available from the British Library.

Papers used by Michael O'Mara Books Limited are natural, recyclable products made from wood grown in sustainable forests. The manufacturing processes conform to the environmental regulations of the country of origin.

For further information see www.mombooks.com/about/sustainability-climate-focus
Report any safety issues to product.safety@mombooks.com and see www.mombooks.com/contact/product-safety

UK ISBN: 978-1-78929-823-9 in hardback print format
US ISBN: 978-1-78929-800-0 in hardback print format

1 2 3 4 5 6 7 8 9 10

Designed and typeset by Luke Griffin
Picture research by Paul Langan

Cover photographs: All © Motorsport Images
Front cover: Top: Daniel Ricciardo, Monaco Grand Prix 2016 (Zak Mauger)
Bottom: Lewis Hamilton, Singapore Grand Prix 2019 (Andy Hone)
Spine: Michael Schumacher's helmet 2005 (Sutton)
Back cover: Top left: Jeddah Street Circuit, Saudi Arabia Grand Prix 2023 (Sam Bloxham)
Top right: Circuit de Monaco, Monaco Grand Prix 2022 (Steven Tee)
Left: Oscar Piastri, Azerbaijan Grand Prix 2023 (Simon Galloway)
Right: Start of the Spanish Grand Prix 2022 (Sam Bloxham)
Bottom left: Mick Schumacher, Austrian Grand Prix 2022 (Andy Hone)

Printed and bound in China

www.mombooks.com

75 YEARS
OF FORMULA ONE

F1 RACING

THE ULTIMATE COMPANION

BRUCE JONES

Michael O'Mara Books Limited

CONTENTS

Introduction   8

Europe   10

Americas   138

Austria	12	Monaco	81	Argentina	140
Belgium	22	Netherlands	88	Brazil	150
Czechia	34	Poland	98	Canada	162
Denmark	34	Portugal	99	Chile	173
Finland	35	Russia	104	Colombia	174
France	38	Spain	108	Mexico	175
Germany	52	Sweden	120	United States of America	180
Hungary	64	Switzerland	122	Uruguay	194
Ireland	65	Turkey	123	Venezuela	195
Italy	66	United Kingdom	124		
Liechtenstein	80				

Above left: Monte Carlo remains the jewel in Formula 1's crown.

Above: The Circuit of the Americas has been the home of the United States GP since 2012.

Above right: Fireworks light the night sky as Max Verstappen crosses the line at the 2023 Abu Dhabi GP.

Above far right: Riccardo Patrese powers his Williams around Kyalami in the 1992 South African GP.

Right: Melbourne's Albert Park circuit is located just a short tram ride from the city centre.

Following page: Lewis Hamilton blasts through Las Vegas on F1's return.

Asia and the Middle East 196

Azerbaijan	198	Saudi Arabia	220		
Bahrain	200	Singapore	222		
China	202	South Korea	224		
India	204	Thailand	225		
Indonesia	206	United Arab Emirates	226		
Japan	207				
Malaysia	216				
Qatar	218				

Africa 242

Morocco	244
Zimbabwe	246
South Africa	247

Oceania 228

Australia	230
New Zealand	240

Index 254

Picture credits 256

INTRODUCTION

Ferrari has been a constant since the first year of the World Championship in 1950, but everything else has changed and keeps on changing, as teams, drivers, circuits and F1-hosting countries come and go. One of the glories of Formula One is that no two races are alike. F1 fans now enjoy twenty-four grands prix every year and more than seventy circuits have hosted a Grand Prix, each presenting a distinct challenge to drivers and a unique spectacle for F1 fans. Those circuits have played host to more than 750 drivers from dozens of nations, as the sport has expanded to become a global phenomenon.

The classical motorsport nations of France, Italy, Germany, the United Kingdom and the United States have all produced world champions. They have also offered a varied array of circuits. In recent decades, they have been joined by newcomers with little or no racing history but with an undeniable appetite for the sport, like countries in the Middle East.

In this globe-trotting guide to Formula One, you'll find entries on every country to have hosted a race or produced a driver in the World Championship. Some have become fixtures on the Grand Prix calendar without ever producing a home-grown driver, while, at the other end of the scale, there are nations that have managed to produce Grand Prix winners or even world champions despite having no top-level circuits within their borders. Take Finland as an example, with Keke Rosberg, Mikä Hakkinen and Kimi Räikkönen all being forced to head overseas to refine their youthful talents. Those drivers who grew up in the United Kingdom, France and Italy in particular are lucky, as there are enough circuits available on the home scene for their national single-seater series to be worthwhile. Further up the single-seater ladder, though, and all drivers know that they must travel to be seen.

The motor-racing heritage of some countries stretches back for the best part of a century. A handful of circuits even hosted Grands Prix before the World Championship was launched in 1950, but such is the make-up of the F1 calendar that these gems are used alongside circuits that have been tailor-made in the past two decades or laid out on urban plots. Comparing the best circuits with the duds, the modern and the almost forgotten is part of F1's rich history.

Throughout this book you will see that many a circuit has been dropped because of no longer matching up to safety requirements, while long-term survivors like Monza, Silverstone and Spa-Francorchamps, even Monaco, have had to have a nip and tuck or two to remain current. Others have fallen off the F1 map because the host country can no longer afford to pay the hosting fee, while some have been replaced as the World Championship organisers look to make the sport's reach more global. The only golden lining to COVID was that it introduced F1's new fans to some great circuits when regular circuits, particularly in South-east Asia, were ruled out because of travel restrictions. This meant that a handful of great circuits were either given a chance to welcome F1 back, like Istanbul Park, or to welcome F1 for the first time, like the Algarve International Circuit and Mugello.

This book is a celebration of Formula One and racing history, not just of the world's great circuits, both past and present, but also of the greatest drivers and teams that each country has produced, and the famous and sometimes infamous races. A gaggle of countries are queuing up to host a Grand Prix, so expect new treats in store.

– Bruce Jones

Right: Four of F1's champions in 1986: Ayrton Senna, Alain Prost, Nigel Mansell and Nelson Piquet.

EUROPE

Europe is the birthplace of motor racing, with the first race being a blast along public roads from Paris to Rouen. This was in 1894 and was the start of the special and diverse sport that we know today.

France continued to lead the way by holding the first Grand Prix near Le Mans in 1906 and the sport expanded from there. When F1 began in 1950, the inaugural World Championship kicked off at Silverstone, followed by Grands Prix in Monaco, Switzerland, Belgium, France and Italy. Nominally, the United States' Indianapolis 500 was part of the show, but there was no crossover and F1 remained a Eurocentric sport until the end of the decade.

As well as hosting a Grand Prix, most European countries opened a range of circuits and developed their own national series. There was even internal rivalry as circuits fought to have the honour of hosting their nation's Grand Prix, with Silverstone and Brands Hatch in the UK, Reims and Rouen in France and the Nürburgring and Hockenheim sharing the race. Until the 1970s, there were also a number of non-championship F1 races that gave lesser circuits – think Oulton Park and Snetterton in the UK or Modena and Syracuse in Italy – the chance to get a taste of the sport's ultimate drivers and machines.

Time and fashion have forced a change in venues, but some, like Paul Ricard, were reinvented to have a second spell as part of the World Championship as the sport continues to reinvent itself.

AUSTRIA

Austria has punched above its weight by producing two champions from its ranks, but it can also claim Formula One's most picturesque track.

Austria is a country of two halves, with the western end mountainous and the eastern end offering wide plains around Vienna. Yet the World Championship has only ever visited the western end where all but the first Austrian GP at Zeltweg have been held on a circuit laid on a mountainside. This is the Osterreichring, which was truncated to become the A1-Ring and then renamed the Red Bull Ring.

Zeltweg was a temporary circuit laid out at a military airfield. First used in 1958, it followed the Aspern airfield circuit which hosted a non-championship Grand Prix in 1961 by having one of its own in 1963. Zeltweg then had a one-off World Championship Grand Prix in 1964 and was used for sportscar racing until 1968, but its surface was incredibly rough and it rattled cars into submission.

Austrian fans had a huge boost in 1969 when not one but two permanent circuits were opened, taking racing to a new level in Austria. One was the Salzburgring and this was popular with F2, touring cars and motorbikes. The other was the Osterreichring, just a kilometre or so up the side of the valley near Zeltweg. This was the country's jewel, as the circuit had a tremendous flow up and down the slope. It was opened just in time to let rising star Jochen Rindt show the skills that would make him world champion and would go on to provide a perfect playing field for Niki Lauda and Gerhard Berger in the years ahead.

Opposite: Lorenzo Bandini's Ferrari survived the bumps in 1964 to win the only Austrian GP at Zeltweg.

Below: Max Verstappen leads the field into Turn 3 at the Red Bull Ring in 2022 en route to victory.

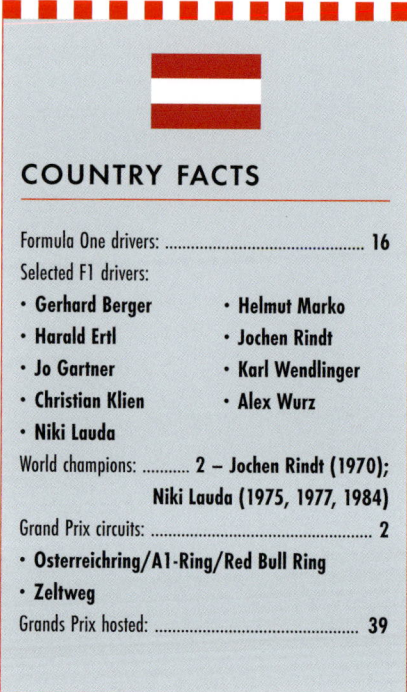

COUNTRY FACTS

Formula One drivers: 16
Selected F1 drivers:
- **Gerhard Berger**
- **Helmut Marko**
- **Harald Ertl**
- **Jochen Rindt**
- **Jo Gartner**
- **Karl Wendlinger**
- **Christian Klien**
- **Alex Wurz**
- **Niki Lauda**

World champions: .... 2 – Jochen Rindt (1970); Niki Lauda (1975, 1977, 1984)
Grand Prix circuits: 2
- Osterreichring/A1-Ring/Red Bull Ring
- Zeltweg

Grands Prix hosted: 39

Niki Lauda

Niki appeared to be a capable driver rather than a superstar as he took a loan to pay for an F2 campaign and his F1 debut came in his home Grand Prix in 1971. However, his strength was his intelligence and after making strides with March and BRM, he was picked to join Ferrari for 1974. The team was in disarray, but he and Luca di Montezemolo gave the team focus and he was a winner on his fourth outing. In 1975, he went better still and landed the title. He might have done so again in 1976, but he suffered a fiery accident at the Nürburgring. Incredibly, Niki bounced back to be champion again in 1977. A move to Brabham brought just one win, then he took time out to form his own airline before returning with McLaren in 1982 and going on to pip teammate Alain Prost to the title in 1984.

DRIVERS

Jochen Rindt won the 1970 title, although he died before he knew it, then Niki Lauda became Austria's other world champion, taking three.

Jochen Rindt

He was Austria's first racing superstar, winning wherever he pleased in F2 from 1964 on. Jochen (pictured below) would also make his World Championship debut that year, having rented a car from Rob Walker Racing Team for his home event. Cooper ran him in F1 for the next three years, but it was in decline, so he moved to Brabham in 1968, then Lotus in 1969. Despite Jochen's fears that Lotus cars were as fragile as they were fast, he took his breakthrough win in the 1969 US GP then won five races in 1970, only to be killed in a crash at Monza, although he would still be crowned world champion.

Gerhard Berger

Although he took ten F1 wins to Rindt's six, albeit in over three times as many races, Gerhard would never become world champion. He was seen as quick but wild when he made his F1 debut for ATS in 1984. Coming sixth on his second outing helped Gerhard land a ride with Arrows in 1985, but it took a move to Benetton in 1986 for him to land his first win. Then Gerhard joined Ferrari and he finished third behind McLaren's dominant duo in 1988. He ranked third for McLaren in 1990 and third for Ferrari in 1994 before finishing his F1 career with a win in 1997 for Benetton.

Alex Wurz

Alex was a top BMW rider, who then shone in F3, leaving Ralf Schumacher in his wake in 1994. He raced touring cars for Opel in 1996, but his calling card came when he won the Le Mans 24 Hours at his first try. Alex stepped up from Benetton's F1 test team in 1997 when Gerhard Berger fell ill. A third-place finish on his third outing (at the British GP) landed Alex a seat for 1998 and five fourth-placed finishes impressed, but it took until 2007, when he had joined Williams, for his second podium finish. Alex then moved to sportscars and won at Le Mans again in 1999, for Peugeot, before racing on with Toyota.

AUSTRIA

CIRCUIT

Flowing in its original format, the Red Bull Ring is still blessed with a fabulous backdrop and two tricky corners.

Osterreichring/A1-Ring/Red Bull Ring

Austria is a country that has always loved its motor sport, but it didn't have much to offer its rising stars. When Jochen Rindt was ascending the racing ladder, all it could offer him was the bumpy airfield circuit at Zeltweg and another at Tulln-Langenlebarn near Vienna.

Fortunately, plans were in place for a permanent venue and this was opened in the Steyr region near Zeltweg in 1969 and the Osterreichring, as it was called, really upped the ante: it was purpose-built and its gradient changes and sweeping corners provided drivers with a real challenge.

Its first Grand Prix came in 1970, with Rindt leading the title race and drawing in 100,000 fans on race day to see if he could win again for Lotus. As it happened, the Ferraris dominated and Rindt's engine failed when third. Alas, he would never race there again. A year later, Niki Lauda made an inauspicious F1 debut there, but he became Austria's next great and soon, in turn, drew in the fans. He finally won his home race in 1983.

The Austrian GP continued until 1987, when the narrowness of its start/finish straight probably contributed to two start-line shunts, and so it was dropped.

It took a decade for it to return and the circuit had more than just a new name – the A1-Ring – as it had been chopped down to size largely in a bid to cut speeds to make it safer, with the first corner now a tighter right about three-quarters of the way to the original first turn. The flat-out blast uphill through the meadows was also gone and the famed Bosch Kurve at which the circuit used to start its descent of the slope was also removed. The final parabola onto the main straight was made more abrupt and turned into two corners, bringing the lap down from 5.94 to 4.32 km. The track was back on the F1 calendar from 1997 and remained a fixture until 2003.

A second name change came in 2008 when it was retitled the Red Bull Ring after the energy drink manufacturer gave the facilities a make-over and it returned to the F1 calendar to host the first Austrian GP since 2003.

Opposite: Benetton duo Gerhard Berger and Teo Fabi make the most of BMW turbo power as they sweep through the chicane in 1986.

Following pages: Ferrari used blatant team orders in 2002 to request Rubens Barrichello (right) to pull over so that Michael Schumacher could win, even though it was only the sixth round of the year.

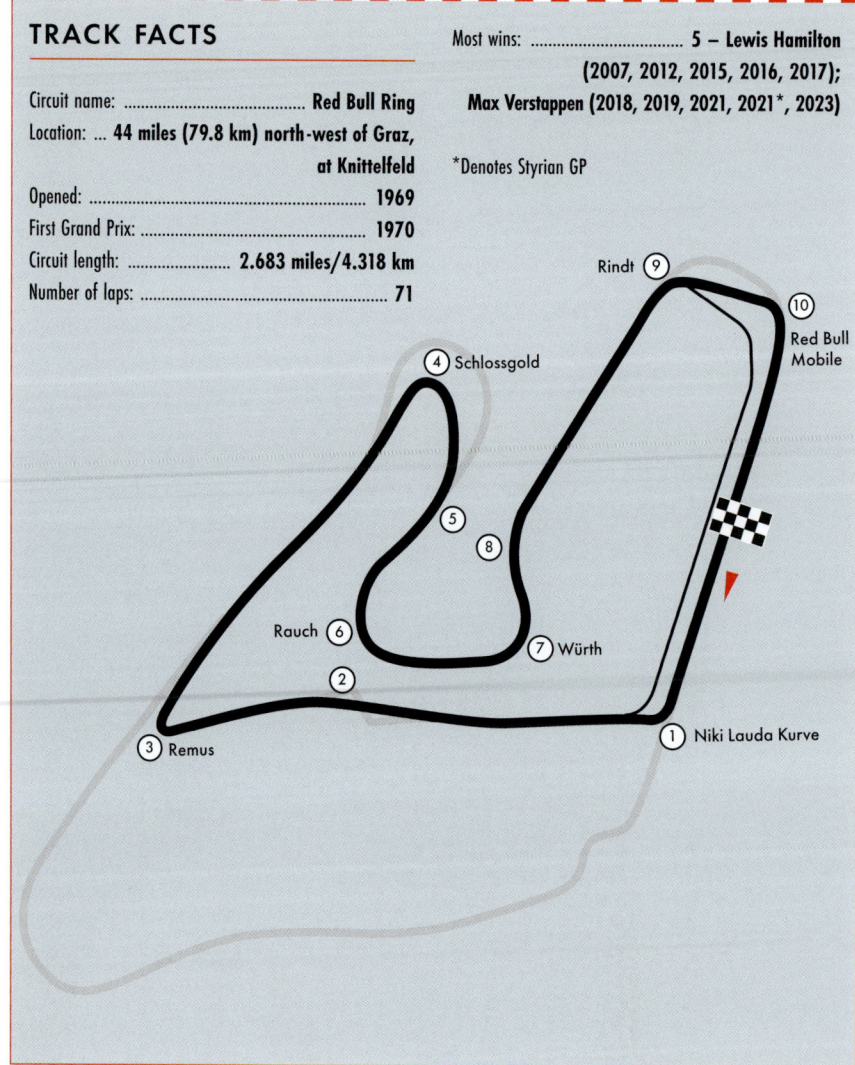

TRACK FACTS

Circuit name: .... Red Bull Ring
Location: ... 44 miles (79.8 km) north-west of Graz, at Knittelfeld
Opened: 1969
First Grand Prix: 1970
Circuit length: .... 2.683 miles/4.318 km
Number of laps: 71

Most wins: .... 5 – Lewis Hamilton (2007, 2012, 2015, 2016, 2017); Max Verstappen (2018, 2019, 2021, 2021*, 2023)

*Denotes Styrian GP

16 | AUSTRIA

AUSTRIA | 17

MOMENTS

Team orders, torrential rain, limping home out of fuel and managing not to be shaken apart are themes of Austria's magic moments.

Stuttering but holding on to win

The 1982 season was extraordinary, with no one driver able to put their stamp on the campaign. By the time the thirteenth round arrived at the Osterreichring, nine drivers spread between four teams had tasted victory. This was expected to be a race for the turbo-powered cars, but soaring temperatures accounted for the Brabhams that had led away from the front row. Then, with five laps to go, Alain Prost's Renault failed and this left Elio de Angelis in front in his normally aspirated Lotus, but he was being caught by Keke Rosberg's Williams. Then, with his first win in sight, de Angelis's car began to stutter, short on fuel, and yet he held on by 0.050 seconds... Rosberg, though, would go on to be champion.

Shake, rattle and roll

The first World Championship Grand Prix held in Austria was at the Zeltweg circuit in 1964, but the rutted concrete surface was so bumpy that many cars began breaking in practice, with Jim Clark having steering arms fail on his Lotus. Graham Hill qualified on pole for BRM, but it was Ferrari's John Surtees and Brabham's Dan Gurney that pulled away, with Lorenzo Bandini third in the second Ferrari while Clark worked his way back to fourth after a poor start. Then Surtees' suspension collapsed and Clark passed Bandini to chase after Gurney, only for his driveshaft to break. Then Gurney's suspension failed and Bandini was left all on his own, with Richie Ginther's BRM the only other car on the lead lap.

Ferrari asks the unaskable

Team orders do have an occasional place in motor racing, but only in the final few rounds when a championship title is in the balance. Yet Ferrari, with Michael Schumacher having already won four of the 2002 season's opening five rounds and with twelve Grands Prix still to run, chose to ask Rubens Barrichello to move aside. The Brazilian, who had led from pole, was infuriated but eventually agreed and pulled over on the final lap. The crowd, even the tifosi, booed the outcome and even thick-skinned Schumacher felt uneasy about the podium ceremony, signalling Barrichello up to the top step. Ferrari team boss Jean Todt was unrepentant, saying that racing was a business, but all F1 fans were upset.

Opposite: Vittorio Brambilla mastered the rain in 1975 for his only win, then promptly crashed.

Below: Elio de Angelis resists a late-race challenge from Keke Rosberg's Williams in 1982 to hang on to win for Lotus by just 0.05 seconds.

Victory, celebration, accident

Vittorio Brambilla was always an all-or-nothing driver, earning the nickname 'The Monza Gorilla' for his robust style. His bravado meant that he often shone when conditions were at their worst, and the 1975 Austrian GP was definitely an extremely wet race. Niki Lauda led from the start, but the rain became heavier and James Hunt hit the front for Hesketh. When he was delayed by his teammate, Brambilla seized the moment to put his March in front. Then, suddenly, the chequered flag was shown early as cars were aquaplaning and Brambilla fired both arms aloft in celebration, but his car snapped away from him and wiped its nose off against a barrier. It was to be his only F1 win.

BELGIUM

Having been part of the World Championship since its first season in 1950, Belgium has played a leading role in motor-racing history.

Belgium was an early adopter of motor racing, with a road course in the Ardennes hosting its first race in 1902 and Spa-Francorchamps being opened in 1924. Two years later, Belgium got its second circuit, when the temporary but very high-speed road course at Chimay was opened near the border with France.

In 1965, a third circuit, Zolder, was added to its ranks, then in 1971 another, Nivelles, both of which would fleetingly become home to the Belgian GP. However, they only ever really had the race on loan while Spa-Francorchamps was being modified, shortened and made safer.

Belgium has always had a strong national racing scene, with touring cars and GTs always featuring strongly, both in national series and at the annual 24 Hours of Spa-Francorchamps.

Spa-Francorchamps was a staple of the Grand Prix scene from when it first hosted the Belgian GP in 1925, with the fast but tricky track one of six European circuits to host rounds of the inaugural World Championship season in 1950, along with Silverstone, Monaco, Bremgarten, Reims and Monza.

With its generous lap length and the challenge until the 1970s of running into the next valley, Spa-Francorchamps has also featured in all the leading sport-prototype series of the day and it is currently one of the leading circuits to host a round of the World Endurance Championship. Not only is the track a challenge in itself, but changeable weather has almost always been a factor, especially in the longer races in which it has more time to strike.

Opposite: The descent past the old pits from La Source to Eau Rouge is one of F1's iconic sectors.

Below: Emerson Fittipaldi won both Grands Prix at Nivelles, for Lotus in 1972 and then McLaren in 1974.

COUNTRY FACTS

Formula One drivers: 24
Selected F1 drivers:
- Lucien Bianchi
- Thierry Boutsen
- Johnny Claes
- Jérôme d'Ambrosio
- Paul Frère
- Bertrand Gachot
- Olivier Gendebien
- Jacky Ickx
- Roger Laurent
- Willy Mairesse
- Patrick Nève
- André Pilette
- Jacques Swaters
- Eric van de Poele
- Stoffel Vandoorne

World champions: 0
Grand Prix circuits: 3
- Nivelles-Baulers
- Spa-Francorchamps
- Zolder

Grands Prix hosted: 69

DRIVERS

Belgium has yet to produce a world champion, although Jacky Ickx ended the season as championship runner-up in both 1969 and 1970.

Jacky Ickx

It would seem strange to racing fans in the 1960s that Jacky's career would be best remembered for his success in the Le Mans 24 Hours, as he was the coming man in single-seaters. After winning three Belgian motorcycle racing titles, Jacky landed the national saloon car title then went straight into F2. In 1967, he shocked everyone when he qualified his F2 Matra third for the German GP. Although F2 cars were made to start at the back, he climbed to fourth before his car broke. Ferrari snapped him up for 1968 and Jacky rewarded them by winning the French GP. He was also starring in sportscars and sponsor Gulf moved him to Brabham for whom he won twice, to be runner-up to Jackie Stewart, before returning to Ferrari in 1970 for whom he was runner-up again. Yet, his forte was long-distance racing and he won Le Mans six times between 1969 and 1982.

Olivier Gendebien

Although his major successes came at Le Mans, this aristocratic racer gave F1 his best shot. In fact, Olivier started with Ferrari. This was in 1956 after he had had a run of second-place finishes in long-distance road rallies. Ferrari wanted him principally for its sportscar team, but he came fifth in Argentina on his F1 debut. After winning at Le Mans with Phil Hill in 1958, Olivier's best F1 season came in 1960 when he came second in the French GP. The year marked the second of his Le Mans wins for Ferrari and he added two more with Hill in 1961 and 1962.

Paul Frère

Although a motoring journalist first and a racing driver second, Paul was good enough to finish second behind fellow Ferrari driver Peter Collins in the 1956 Belgian GP. Paul sprung to prominence when he landed a drive in an F2 HWM at Chimay in 1952 and recovered from a setback to win. HWM then gave him his World Championship bow at his home race and he advanced to fifth. After coming fourth in his home race for Ferrari in 1955, he went two places better in 1956. He loved Le Mans and finally won it in 1960 when he shared a Ferrari with Olivier Gendebien.

Willy Mairesse

Better known for his accidents, of which there were many, than his race results, Willy was rapid, as shown when he finished third in the Italian GP for Ferrari in 1960, his first year in F1, albeit in a race boycotted by most of the teams. He came second in the Le Mans 24 Hours the following year, sharing a Ferrari with Mike Parkes, then won the Targa Florio road race around Sicily in 1962. Sadly, his career came to an end when he suffered a major accident at Le Mans in 1968. This left him with head injuries and, depressed, he took his own life the following year.

Thierry Boutsen

Jacky Ickx noticed Thierry's pace in Formula Ford and helped him into F3 in 1979. In F2, he won races for March then Spirit and that helped him into F1 with Arrows in 1983 and his four years with the team peaked with second at Imola in 1985. Two years with Benetton followed before he joined Williams and the 1988 season proved to be Thierry's most successful, as he ended up fourth in a season dominated by McLaren's Ayrton Senna and Alain Prost. It was only after joining Williams in 1989 that Thierry took his first win, adding two more before moving on to Ligier.

CIRCUITS

Multiple Belgian circuits have hosted Grands Prix but by far the most revered is Spa-Francorchamps, a circuit worshipped by Formula One fans around the world for the testing challenge that it provides.

Spa-Francorchamps

Spa-Francorchamps can be seen as having a two-part history with the second period starting in 1979 when the track was halved in length as its passage through the neighbouring valley between Malmedy and Stavelot was truncated. This was done in the name of safety and the quest even for the newer, safer circuit to remain safe continues to this day, something that has been highlighted by two drivers being killed in recent years in the Eau Rouge/Raidillon complex.

The original circuit was more than nine miles long when it opened with a largely triangular-shaped course linking the village of Francorchamps with the towns of Malmedy and Stavelot. The original start line was on the drop between La Source and Eau Rouge. When the track crested the hill, it kept going over the top to dive into the neighbouring valley. What followed was an all but flat-out blast along the valley, with the Masta Kink being its most fearsome challenge. At Stavelot, there was a hairpin and then the drivers came back up through the woods through a series of corners taken in top gear all the way back to La Source. One mistake or one mechanical failure and the cars would fly into the trees. Fatalities were not uncommon.

After BRM driver Pedro Rodríguez's winning average speed in the 1970 Belgian GP almost hit 150mph (241.4 kmh) and then Rodríguez and Jackie Oliver averaged 154mph (247.8 kmh) in the following year's Spa 1,000kms, it was decided that the speeds had become too high and that something had to be done.

So, the track went under the knife and a linking section was inserted from what is now the Les Combes esse down the hillside to rejoin the original return leg three quarters of the way up its climb. This took the track length down from 9.236 miles to 4.317 and, bar a few tweaks, it has remained much the same to today. Any talk of emasculation was soon forgotten as, even in its second form, the lap contains the challenge of Eau Rouge/Raidillon, the overtaking opportunities up the Kemmel Straight plus the tricky downhill double left at Pouhon and the high-speed sweep at Blanchimont.

Opposite: BRM racer Pedro Rodríguez leads Chris Amon's March into Eau Rouge in 1970 en route to winning with an average speed of just under 150mph.

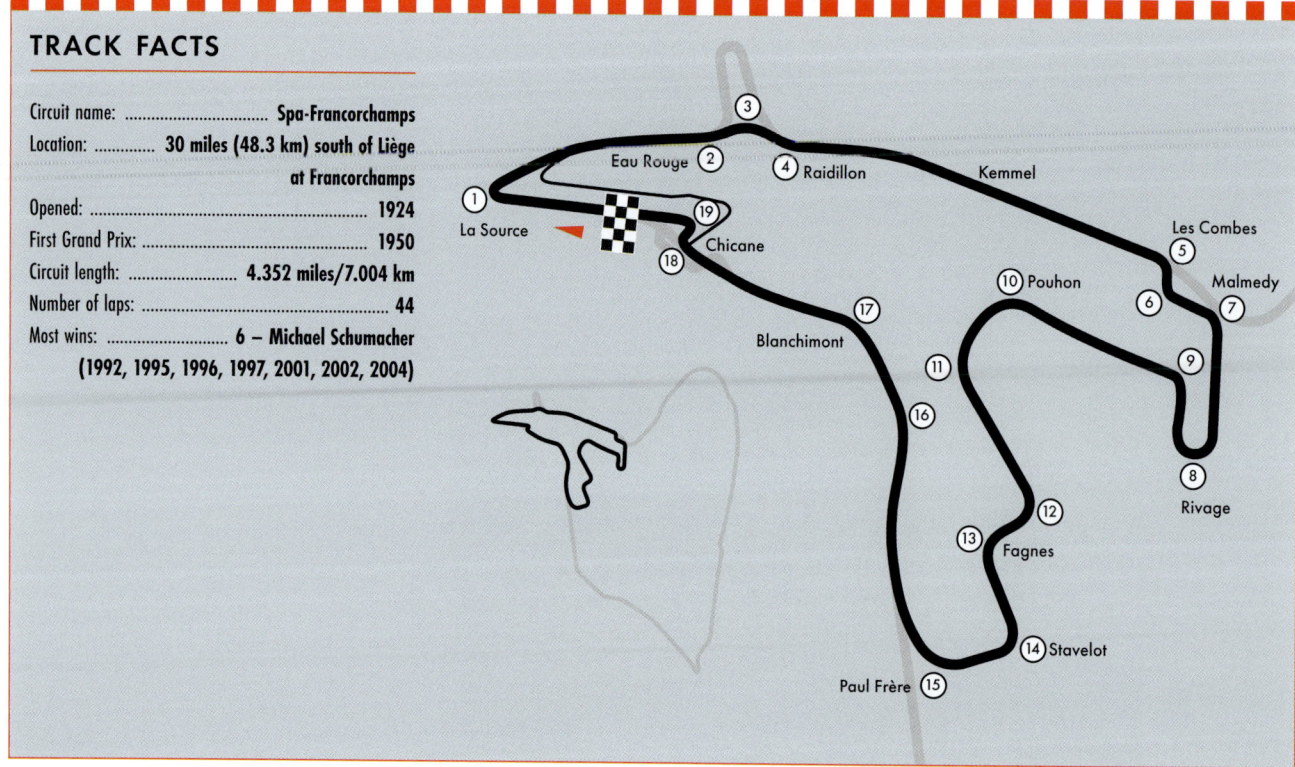

TRACK FACTS

Circuit name:	Spa-Francorchamps
Location:	30 miles (48.3 km) south of Liège at Francorchamps
Opened:	1924
First Grand Prix:	1950
Circuit length:	4.352 miles/7.004 km
Number of laps:	44
Most wins:	6 – Michael Schumacher (1992, 1995, 1996, 1997, 2001, 2002, 2004)

Zolder

Situated on flat terrain 35 miles (56.3 km) to the east of Brussels, Zolder offered a very different challenge to the established, upcountry track at Spa-Francorchamps. There was no majestic landscape, just a narrow course through wooded land with heavy braking into several of its tighter corners breaking the flow. However, it was welcomed, as it provided a second permanent venue for drivers in the national championship to enjoy. Six years later, those championships were offered a third permanent venue when the Nivelles-Baulers circuit opened to the south of the capital but, although it hosted two Grands Prix, it closed its gates in 1978.

A lap of Zolder begins with a run down to an open left-hander followed by a long, dropping right towards the lap's lowest point, the straight alongside a canal. From there, a right-hander feeds the track behind the paddock, with a chicane added in 1973 to what was originally a fast left. After cresting a gentle rise, the track drops to what was the first of a pair of quick right-handers.

Still running through the woods, the track arcs to the left then tightens to the left at Bolderberg. From here to the pits is a run of swerves and a final chicane that was added in 1996.

Zolder hosted the Belgian GP for the first time in 1973, with Jackie Stewart winning for Tyrrell, but the subsequent races seldom stood out for the right reasons and the circuit will always be associated with Ferrari driver Gilles Villeneuve, beloved in F1 for his sheer bravado, as he was killed in qualifying there in 1982. He was caught out on a flying lap when he came upon Jochen Mass's March and the contact threw the French-Canadian from his car, killing him.

F1 returned one more time, in 1984, using a chicane inserted to slow speeds into Terlamenbocht, but Zolder's diet ever since has been topped by touring car and more recently GT events.

Left: The Ferraris of Michele Alboreto and René Arnoux are split by Renault's Derek Warwick at Zolder in 1984.

Following pages: Lewis Hamilton gets it wrong at Les Combes on lap 1 in 2022 and his Mercedes flips up after clipping Fernando Alonso's Alpine.

TRACK FACTS

Circuit name:	Zolder
Location:	35 miles (56.3 km) east of Brussels
Opened:	1965
First Grand Prix:	1973
Circuit length:	2.648 miles/4.262 km
Number of laps:	70
Most wins:	2 – Niki Lauda (1975, 1976)

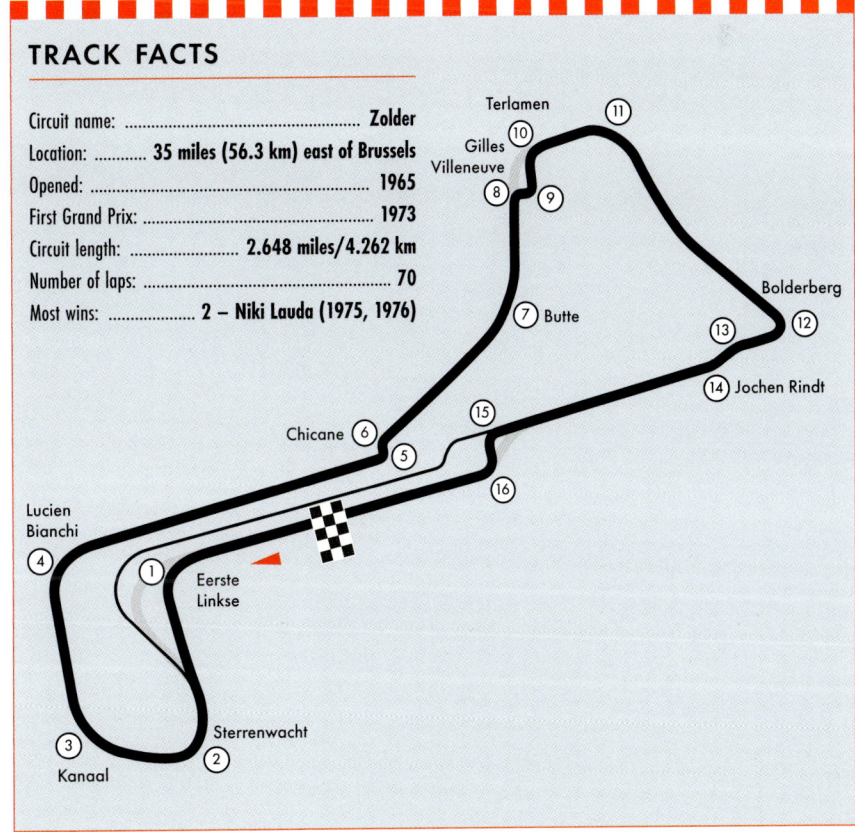

BELGIUM | 29

MOMENTS

Spa-Francorchamps is a circuit tailor-made to provide not just thrills and spills but great racing too, and so it has proved since 1950.

Lewis Hamilton gets tipped up

La Source, the hairpin that starts the lap, has long been a place at which a driver can make up places on the opening lap. Alternatively, it has long been a place at which drivers can have their race wrecked within 100 metres of the start. Once through there, drivers can breathe a sigh of relief. Then they have to focus on the next likely passing spot, into Les Combes at the far end of the Kemmel Straight. This is where Lewis Hamilton's Mercedes was assaulted in 2022 by Fernando Alonso's Alpine and tipped him high into the air as they fought over second. Alonso continued, Hamilton did not, while Max Verstappen roared up from the back of the grid to victory.

Opposite: One year on from his F1 debut, Michael Schumacher triumphed for Benetton in 1992.

Below: Eventual winner Emerson Fittipaldi chases after Ferrari's Clay Regazzoni in the second Belgian GP held at Nivelles in 1974. Niki Lauda follows in third.

Michele Alboreto wins last Zolder race

Michele Alboreto was smiling after qualifying for the 1984 Belgian GP as he had finally claimed a pole position in his fourth year in F1, beating Ferrari teammate René Arnoux by 0.5 seconds. In the race, Derek Warwick immediately got ahead of Keke Rosberg, who failed to get his Williams off the line and then took his Renault past Arnoux into the first corner, but he had no answer to Alboreto's pace. Stretching his advantage with every lap, Alboreto went on to beat Warwick by forty-two seconds, while Rosberg came from stone last to third, then ran out of fuel on the last lap to drop back to fourth. This was the Italian's third F1 win and also the last time that Zolder hosted a Grand Prix.

Emerson Fittipaldi triumphs at Nivelles

A low point for the Belgian GP was its two visits to Nivelles when Spa-Francorchamps was dropped from holding the race on safety grounds after its winning average speed in 1970 was almost 150mph. This short and bland circuit was hated by the drivers, but Emerson made the best stab at it, winning on both visits, for Lotus in 1972 and McLaren in 1974. On the first occasion, the Brazilian qualified on pole but had to overcome Ferrari's Clay Regazzoni, catching, passing him and going on to win at a canter. Belgian ace Jacky Ickx was frustrated by being kept back in third, with teammate Regazzoni not letting him by. Later, his fuel injection failed and then Regazzoni retired after hitting a spinning Tecno.

Michael Schumacher takes first win

One year on from his impressive debut for Jordan, Michael Schumacher looked to be on course to make it six podiums in twelve rounds, but nothing more than that. Then at two-thirds distance, the wet track began to dry. Nigel Mansell led from Williams teammate Riccardo Patrese ahead of Schumacher and Martin Brundle. Then Michael ran wide at Stavelot but noticed on rejoining that his teammate's rear tyres were blistering and pitted immediately. This was a masterstroke, as Brundle lost so much time on the next lap that he was behind Schumacher when he rejoined. Williams waited longer to pit and Schumacher's fast laps on his new tyres meant that he was leading when Mansell rejoined and the German went on to take his first F1 win.

CZECHIA

There has been just one Czech driver in F1, Tomáš Enge, but its rich racing history deserves to have produced more.

COUNTRY FACTS

Formula One drivers: 1
World champions: 0
Grand Prix circuits: 0
Grands Prix hosted: 0

Czechoslavakia, as it was in the 1930s before the subdivision into the Czech Republic (later Czechia) and Slovakia in 1992, had one of the most epic road circuits of all.

This was the Masaryk circuit, more than 18 miles (29 km) of twists and turns to the north-east of Brno. Opened in 1930, it was a happy hunting ground for Louis Chiron who won three years running. Then Hans Stuck, Bernd Rosemeyer and Rudolf Caracciola won the last three Grands Prix here for Auto Union and Mercedes before racing was ended by Hitler's invasion in 1937.

The track was chopped to 11 miles in 1949 and the direction of flow was reversed. Later truncations followed, sometimes chopping out sections through villages, but it was used until 1986 by the European Touring Car Championship. Then, in 1987, Brno's purpose-built circuit opened, hosting FIA GT races in the early years of the twenty-first century.

Czechia's other circuit is a smaller one near Most in the north-west of the country.

Tomáš Enge's father Bretislav raced in those European Touring Car Championship races and Tomáš got his F1 break in 2001 when Luciano Burti was injured.

DENMARK

Denmark produced the greatest Le Mans winner of them all, nine-time champion Tom Kristensen, but perhaps a lack of circuits has held it back.

COUNTRY FACTS

Formula One drivers: 5
World champions: 0
Grand Prix circuits: 0
Grands Prix hosted: 0

Denmark has never had many circuits to its name. By far the most important of these is Jyllandsringen. This circuit 25 miles (40.2 km) west of Aarhus, is built on flat ground that at least affords spectators a view of most of the track from the surrounding banking.

It had a forerunner in the Roskilder Ring, which was built in a bowl near to the capital, Copenhagen. This was operational from 1956 until the 1970s, when it was adjudged no longer safe and, as there was little space to extend into, it was shut. Its heyday came in the early 1960s when it held the non-championship Copenhagen GP in 1961 and 1962, won by Stirling Moss and Jack Brabham.

Ring Djursland was next to open, but this was only suitable for the lowest formulae of single-seaters and saloons and invariably plays second fiddle to Jyllandsringen.

As a consequence, aspiring Danish racers like Jan and then Kevin Magnussen largely headed around Europe in order to rise through the junior single-seater ranks. Kristensen reached the fringes of F1, but it appears that the nation's best hope of future F1 involvement will be 2023 F2 race winner Frederik Vesti.

In recent years, Padborg Park opened on the Jutland peninsula, which has provided more variety.

FINLAND

Finland is principally a rallying nation, but its lack of circuits didn't stop F1 champions Keke Rosberg, Mika Häkkinen and Kimi Räikkönen.

The first Finnish GP was a sportscar race on a circuit of public roads at Munkkiniemi in 1932 and this was followed by races at Eläintarha near Helsinki in the late 1930s, but most early competition was down dirt roads through forests or on frozen lakes.

Finland's rallying pedigree was what it was best known for in the 1960s, with Timo Mäkinen redefining what could be done. Then, at the start of the World Rally Championship in the 1970s, it gave the world Hannu Mikkola, then Ari Vatanen, who became the dominant drivers. In time, they were followed by Marku Alén, Juha Kankkunen, Tommi Mäkinen and Marcus Grönholm. Finland's round of the WRC, the 1,000 Lakes Rally, was famous for its high-speed blasts down gravel tracks through forests with occasional huge jumps. With this illustrious roll call and miles of forest tracks, it's understandable why most young Finns thought only of going rallying.

Trying to go racing was not so simple until the Hämeenlinna circuit was built in 1967, complete with a crossover. It hosted one non-championship F2 race that year, but only national championship categories after that. Other circuits followed, with Keimola opening in 1967 followed by Kemora, a street circuit at Seinäjoki and another track at Alastaro.

Yet, all the Finnish drivers who went on to F1 knew that they had to head overseas to get noticed, and this is precisely what Keke Rosberg did, followed by JJ Lehto, Mika Häkkinen, Mika Salo, Kimi Räikkönen, Heikki Kovalainen and Valtteri Bottas.

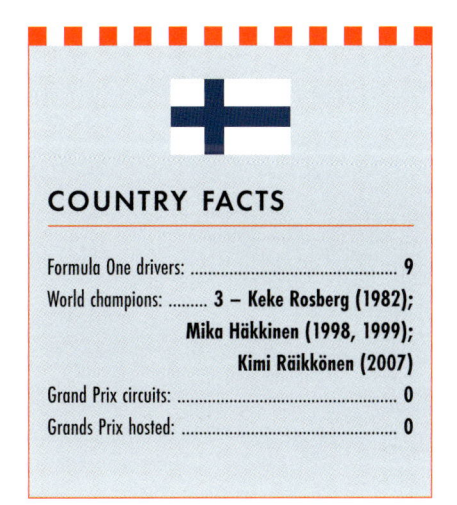

COUNTRY FACTS

Formula One drivers:	9
World champions:	3 – Keke Rosberg (1982); Mika Häkkinen (1998, 1999); Kimi Räikkönen (2007)
Grand Prix circuits:	0
Grands Prix hosted:	0

Below: Mika Häkkinen became Finland's second world champion in 1998 when he beat Ferrari's Michael Schumacher at Suzuka to land the first of his two titles for McLaren.

DRIVERS

The fact that Finland can claim a trio of F1 world champions is remarkable considering that only nine Finnish drivers have raced in F1.

Mika Häkkinen

Healthy backing from Marlboro helped Mika to vault his way with insouciant ease through the GM Lotus Euroseries and F3 and then straight into F1. Wins came easily to Mika and he impressed when he made his F1 debut with Lotus in 1991. Strong form in his second campaign made him a driver in demand, and McLaren snapped him up when it seemed that Ayrton Senna might not race in 1993. Near season's end, Michael Andretti was dropped and Mika got his chance at Estoril, immediately outqualifying Senna. McLaren weren't competitive until 1998 and Mika landed the F1 crown, followed by a repeat in 1999.

Keke Rosberg

There was a time before he got to F1 that Keke was seldom off an aeroplane. Having won three Finnish karting titles and been a champion in Formula Super Vee, Keke spent 1978 racing Formula Pacific in New Zealand, F2 in Argentina, Formula Atlantic in the USA plus a season of F2 in Europe and, after winning the non-championship International Trophy race at Silverstone, a full F1 season too. A move to Fittipaldi brought a third place in 1980 and a move to Williams his first win in 1982, when he landed the title. Keke raced on with Williams until 1985 before a final year with McLaren.

36 | FINLAND

Kimi Räikkönen

Kimi's route to F1 took him just twenty-three races from stepping into single-seaters to starting the 2001 Australian GP for Sauber. Sixth place first time out silenced those who said that having experience in only Formula Renault was insufficient. Kimi was fourth twice and landed a seat at McLaren for 2002. His first win came at Sepang at the start of 2003, and he was Michael Schumacher's challenger for the title. Kimi joined Ferrari and became 2007 world champion at the final round, pipping the McLaren drivers. After taking time out to go rallying and try NASCAR, Kimi came back for more in 2012 and stayed on until 2021.

FRANCE

This is the country where it all began, with the first road races then first Grand Prix, and it's played a leading role ever since.

The first-ever motor race was from Paris to Rouen in 1894. Things moved on quickly though and so did the speeds, often startling members of the public who may never have seen a car before. As a result, it was decided that it would be safer to close off public roads and the first Grand Prix was held on a 66-mile (106.2-km) loop of roads near Le Mans. This was in 1906 and motor racing as we know it was born.

France had set the ball in motion and the rest of the world gradually followed, but it also started another trend, for endurance racing, with the Le Mans 24 Hours being held for the first time in 1923. In pre-World Championship days, the French GP moved around, largely being held on street circuits, although the banked Montlhéry circuit near Paris was an exception.

When the World Championship started in 1950, Reims was France's chosen venue, but the challenging Rouen-Les-Essarts track soon moved into an alternating pattern with it. Then, in 1965, the twisting and undulating Charade circuit near Clermont-Ferrand was given a go. With safety concerns mounting, France looked for a new venue and one was built in the south of France, the almost futuristic Circuit Paul Ricard that opened in 1970. The smaller, more old-school Dijon-Prenois circuit was also used occasionally, but both were replaced in 1991 when Magny-Cours was given a massive upgrade to become the race's home for the next seventeen years before the French GP returned to a revamped Paul Ricard in 2018.

Although the French GP was long one of F1's staples, it has, like the German GP, been dropped from the F1 calendar, even though Liberty Media has boosted it to twenty-three or even twenty-four Grands Prix per year. Not long ago, that would have been unthinkable.

Opposite: Clermont-Ferrand provided a challenge for drivers and great viewing for fans as they watch Jackie Stewart leading Jacky Ickx in 1972.

Below: Ferrari's Charles Leclerc leads out of Camp corner on lap 1 in 2022, but it wasn't to be his day.

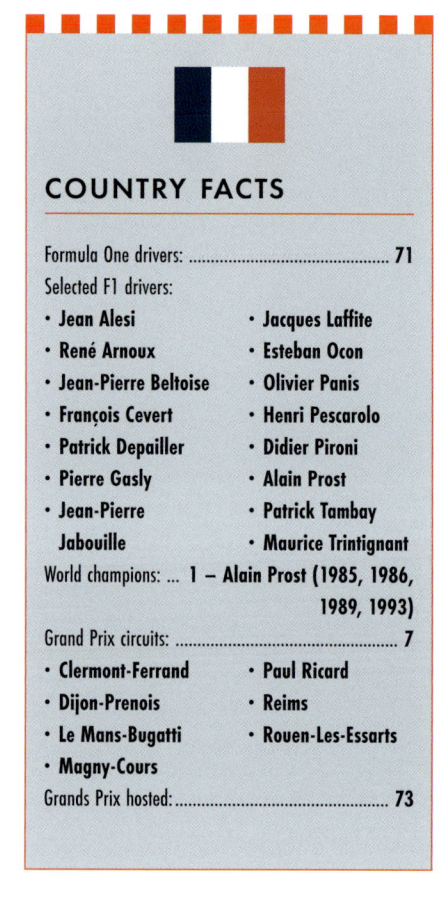

COUNTRY FACTS

Formula One drivers: 71
Selected F1 drivers:
- Jean Alesi
- René Arnoux
- Jean-Pierre Beltoise
- François Cevert
- Patrick Depailler
- Pierre Gasly
- Jean-Pierre Jabouille
- Jacques Laffite
- Esteban Ocon
- Olivier Panis
- Henri Pescarolo
- Didier Pironi
- Alain Prost
- Patrick Tambay
- Maurice Trintignant

World champions: ... 1 – Alain Prost (1985, 1986, 1989, 1993)
Grand Prix circuits: 7
- Clermont-Ferrand
- Dijon-Prenois
- Le Mans-Bugatti
- Magny-Cours
- Paul Ricard
- Reims
- Rouen-Les-Essarts

Grands Prix hosted: 73

Marlboro
MARTINI
DUBONNET
BOSCH
CARAVANES
Sterckeman
BARDAHL

Alain Prost

Alain was not only ultra-rapid in everything he raced but had a calculated approach that helped him to extract every bit of performance from both his team and his car. This is why he won three junior single-seater titles en route to F1. Starting with McLaren in 1980, he finished sixth in an uncompetitive car on his debut, but a move to Renault in 1981 produced his first win, fittingly at the French GP. After being runner-up to Nelson Piquet in 1983, Alain went back to McLaren which had been reinvented, and the wins began to flow. Pipped by teammate Niki Lauda in 1984, Alain landed the first of his F1 titles in 1985 and the second in 1986. Ayrton Senna's arrival in 1988 rocked the boat and Alain left for Ferrari after winning the title in 1989. His final title came after a year's sabbatical, when he was given the tools for the job by Williams.

DRIVERS

It is peculiar that only one French driver has become world champion, but at least Alain Prost found the formula to win the crown on four occasions.

René Arnoux

Diminutive, shoulder-shrugging René was the quintessential French racer. His fans also loved the raw pace he showed in Formula Renault and F2 when he was pipped to the 1976 crown by Jean-Pierre Jabouille before bouncing back to win it in 1977. Then the little Martini team stepped up to F1 in 1978 and he was its driver. It took a move to Renault to show his true form, with his first wins coming in 1979. They kept coming, but never enough for a title, so he joined Ferrari in 1983 and pushed Nelson Piquet hard. After losing his focus, René raced on without success at Ligier until 1989.

Didier Pironi

Despite three Grand Prix wins, Didier's was a wasted talent, as he could have been France's first world champion. A race winner in F3 and F2, Didier got his F1 break with Tyrrell in 1978, a year in which he also won the Le Mans 24 Hours. Two thirds in 1979 landed him a drive with Ligier and he took his first win at Zolder before moving to Ferrari in 1981. The relationship soured in 1982 when he ignored team orders to beat Gilles Villeneuve at Imola. Didier didn't have long as Ferrari's number-one driver as he hit Alain Prost's Renault at Hockenheim and suffered career-ending injuries.

Maurice Trintignant

Many drivers in the post-war years were way older than today's twenty-something F1 drivers, but Maurice looked even older than his thirty-two years in the first year of the World Championship. That he raced on in F1 for a further thirteen years proved that looks could be deceptive, as he became a two-time Grand Prix winner. The first came at Monaco in 1955, when he won for Ferrari in a race made famous by Alberto Ascari ending up in the harbour. The second, also at Monaco, came in 1958, when he triumphed in a Rob Walker Racing Team Cooper.

Jacques Laffite

When Ligier broke into F1 in 1976, this very French team was led by this very French driver. Jacques, who had starred not only in F2 but F1 as well, finished second in the 1975 German GP for Frank Williams. The dumpy Ligier was effective enough for Jacques to be second in Austria then win in Sweden in 1977. The start of 1979 was a surprise to all as Ligier started the year from the front, with Jacques winning easily in Argentina and Brazil, but that was a high point and, bar two years with Williams, he saw out his career with Ligier in 1986.

CIRCUITS

Multiple venues in France can boast Grand Prix heritage, chief among them Paul Ricard, which was the most modern circuit in the world when it opened in 1970, and again when it made its F1 return in 2018.

Paul Ricard

It would have been hard when the Paul Ricard circuit opened in 1970 ever to imagine it falling from grace, and yet, even the most modern safety standards in the world weren't enough to keep it on the World Championship roster.

The drinks industry was a lucrative one and Paul Ricard, the person behind the Ricard pastis brand, helped to finance a new circuit to enable the French GP to move on from outmoded Reims, Rouen-Les-Essarts and Clermont-Ferrand as well as from the uninspiring Le Mans-Bugatti circuit that hosted the French GP in 1966.

Built on a plateau inland from Toulon, Paul Ricard was built with a modern pit and paddock complex that could not have been further from the ramshackle and stony paddock at Clermont-Ferrand. Furthermore, the crash barriers and tyre walls were positioned much further away from the edges of the track than at other circuits of the day, offering a level of safety of which lone safety campaigner Jackie Stewart would have approved.

One key feature stood out: the mile-long Mistral Straight and, best of all, the corner at its far end, Signes, was a hugely fast right-hander at the crest of the incline that provided a real challenge for the drivers. The remainder of the lap was a long right-hander followed by a series of swerves into a tight corner onto the start-finish straight.

With the area's gentle climate, Paul Ricard was the go-to venue for winter testing. Sadly, Paul Ricard wasn't as safe as had been thought, as Elio de Angelis inverted his Brabham here in 1986 and was killed. This led to a drastic remedy and the 3.6-mile (5.8-km) lap was chopped by a third, with a cut-through from just past the pits to halfway up the Mistral Straight, but this wasn't enough to prevent the French GP moving on to Magny-Cours in 1991.

Paul Ricard was given a second shot at hosting the French GP when it was put back onto the World Championship calendar in 2018 after a ten-year break and it was safer still, with the barriers moved even further back and broad bands of ever more abrasive painted lines beyond the edges of the circuit to slow errant cars.

With the loss of the World Championship after its 2022 race, partially due to terrible traffic management that blighted recent events, Paul Ricard remains a popular circuit for a host of international sportscar series and French national championships.

Opposite: Ivan Capelli looked to be heading for a surprise victory for Leyton House in 1990, but was passed by Ferrari's chasing Alain Prost.

TRACK FACTS

Circuit name:	Paul Ricard
Location:	20 miles (32.2 km) north-west of Toulon
Opened:	1970
First Grand Prix:	1971
Circuit length:	3.630 miles/5.842 km
Number of laps:	53
Most wins:	4 – Alain Prost (1983, 1988, 1989, 1990)

6 L'École
Camp
7 Sainte Baume
5
4
3
9
1
2 Esse de la Verrerie
8
Ligne Droite du Mistral
14 La Tour
Signes
10
12
Virage du Pont 15
13 Village
Le Beausset 11

FRANCE

FRANCE | 43

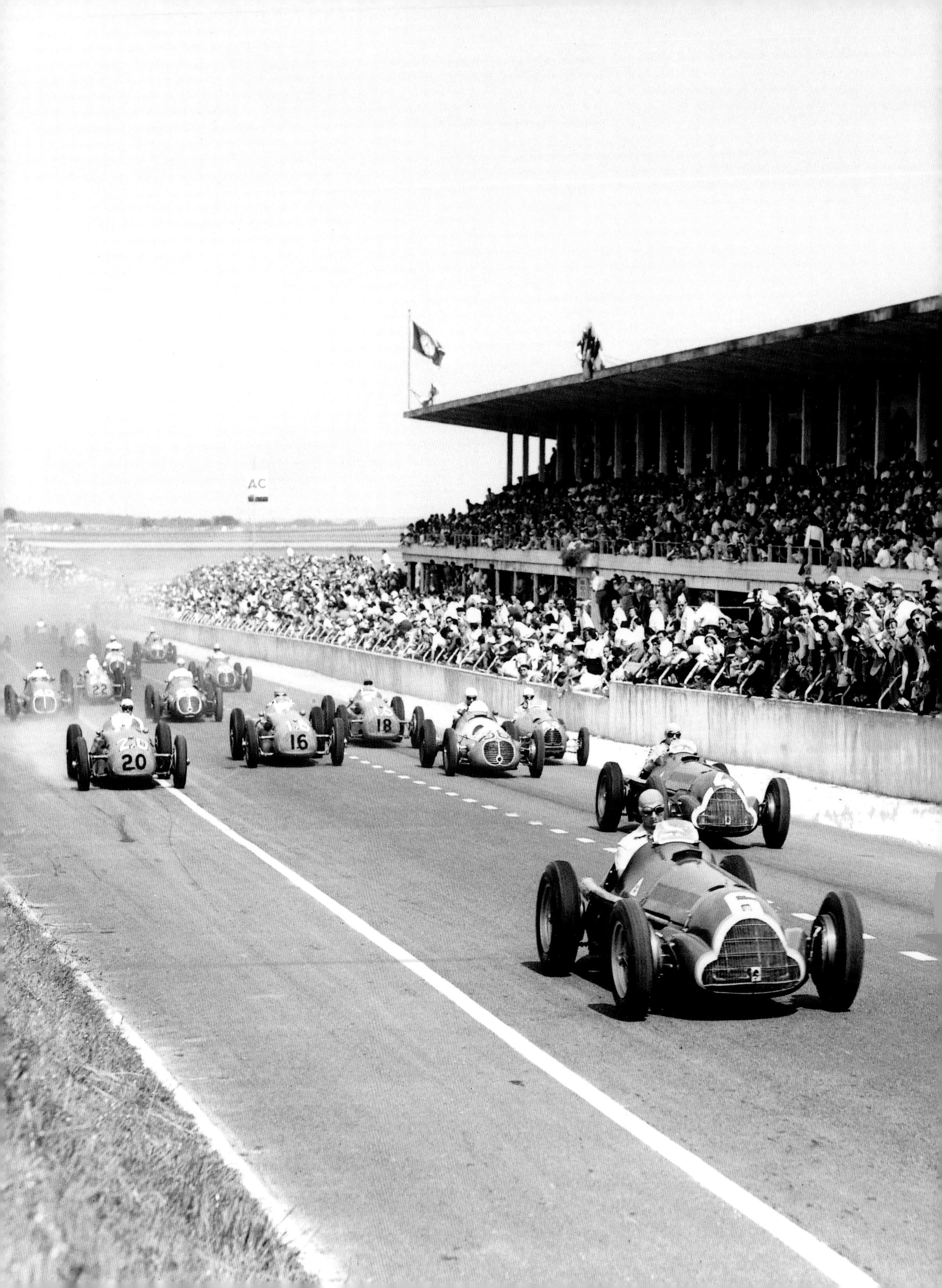
AC
20
16
18
22

Reims

The old pit buildings still stand alongside the Reims circuit, marooned on an otherwise unremarkable stretch of French country road, yet these overlooked one of the most exciting stretches of tarmac used by the World Championship from the 1950s to the mid-1960s.

The Reims circuit first hosted the French GP back in 1932 when Tazio Nuvolari won for Alfa Romeo. Its lap through the open fields west of Reims in the Champagne region was just under five miles as it ran a basically triangular course through the village of Geuex, before cutting through more fields to reach Route Nationale 31, the main road between Reims and Soissons. Turning right, the cars would run flat-out along the Thillois Straight down to Thillois corner where they would brake heavily and heave their cars through a 140-degree right-hander onto the home straight where they would try to get close enough to a rival's car to do the same again. Slipstreaming was rife here and multi-car battles were commonplace.

When the World Championship had its inaugural campaign in 1950, Reims was one of the six tracks chosen to host rounds and Juan Manuel Fangio led home Luigi Fagioli in an Alfa Romeo one-two.

There was a major change for 1953, when the first corner was brought closer to the start line both to make it less sharp and to bypass Gueux village. Then, cutting across the leg to the RNL31, the revised layout took the cars up an incline and past some woods to a righthand hairpin called Virage de Muizon further along the Thillois Straight. With its tighter entry and extra 50 per cent in length, it made the importance of getting a tow down to Thillois all the greater.

Financing the circuit became an increasing problem and it closed in 1970, with national standard drivers far happier to take fewer risks and go racing on purpose-built circuits instead.

Left: Juan Manuel Fangio (left) races away alongside Alfa Romeo teammate Giuseppe Farina in 1950.

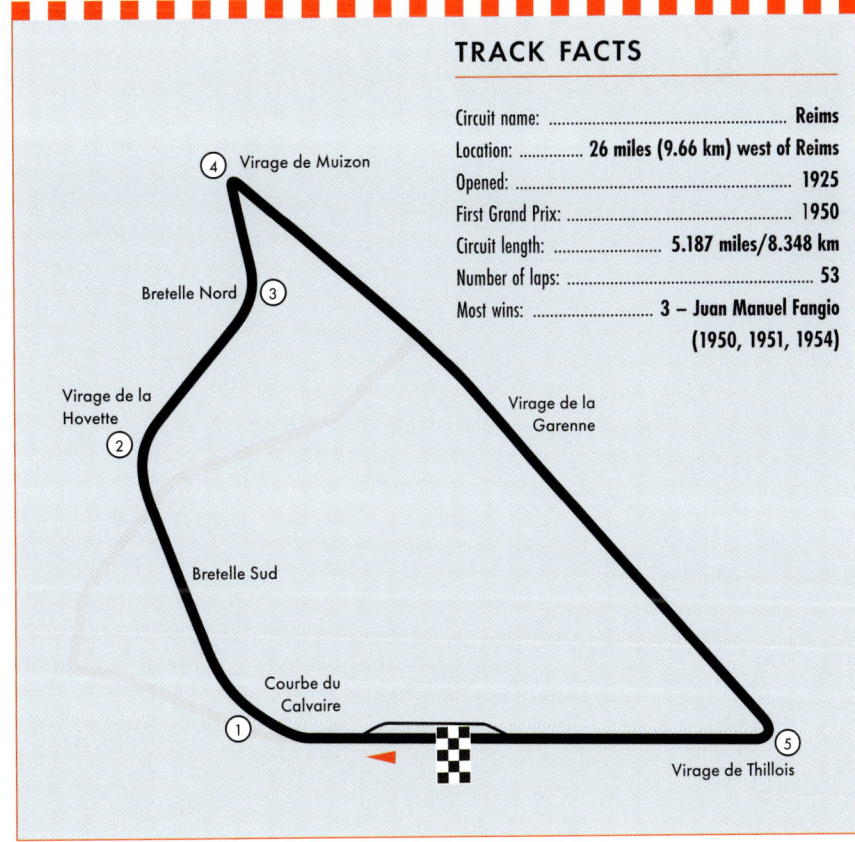

TRACK FACTS

Circuit name:	Reims
Location:	26 miles (9.66 km) west of Reims
Opened:	1925
First Grand Prix:	1950
Circuit length:	5.187 miles/8.348 km
Number of laps:	53
Most wins:	3 – Juan Manuel Fangio (1950, 1951, 1954)

FRANCE 45

Magny-Cours

Such was the lowly status of Magny-Cours when news broke in the late 1980s that it was being redeveloped to host the French GP that few outside the French club racing scene would have been able to place it on a map. So, why was it chosen for such an upgrade? Because President Mitterand, who had long been very pro motor racing and had guided investment towards the Ligier F1 team, came from the opposite end of the political spectrum to the right-wing party supported by the likes of industrialist Paul Ricard and he was keen that the French GP should be moved away from Ricard's track. Added to this, Mitterand was also a friend of Guy Ligier who was looking to base his F1 team here and plans were laid down for Magny-Cours to become the hub of the French motorsport industry and so bring both jobs and life to the incredibly rural region near Nevers.

Strings were pulled and purses opened, *et voilà*, a gem of a circuit was suddenly to be found in the heart of France.

The circuit had opened in 1961 and it was just 1.24 miles (2 km) long, but this was soon changed as the lap length was boosted to nearly 2.4 miles (3.86 km) in 1971 by a loop being added from its lowest point up to its highest point at a tight right called the Adelaide hairpin.

When the Grand Prix deal was clinched, further changes were made, firstly with its start line being moved from what is now the slope down towards the final corner and a new pit building being erected to make it a far cry from the rudimentary originals. A further change followed in 1992 when a chicane on the exit of the Adelaide hairpin was removed.

Not everyone liked the track when F1 turned up, but the engineers loved its smooth surface and the drivers learned how to get a rapid exit from the unusually long Estoril corner to try to catch a tow or even break a tow on the climb up to Adelaide.

The downhill chicane on the drop from Adelaide to 180 hairpin also shuffled the pack, with the uphill Imola esse another spectacular corner.

Right: Jordan's Heinz-Harald Frentzen leads Michael Schumacher's Ferrari and Olivier Panis's Prost in 1999 in one of Magny-Cours's wettest ever races.

Following pages: Dan Gurney takes the flag at Rouen-Les-Essarts in 1964 to take Brabham's first win.

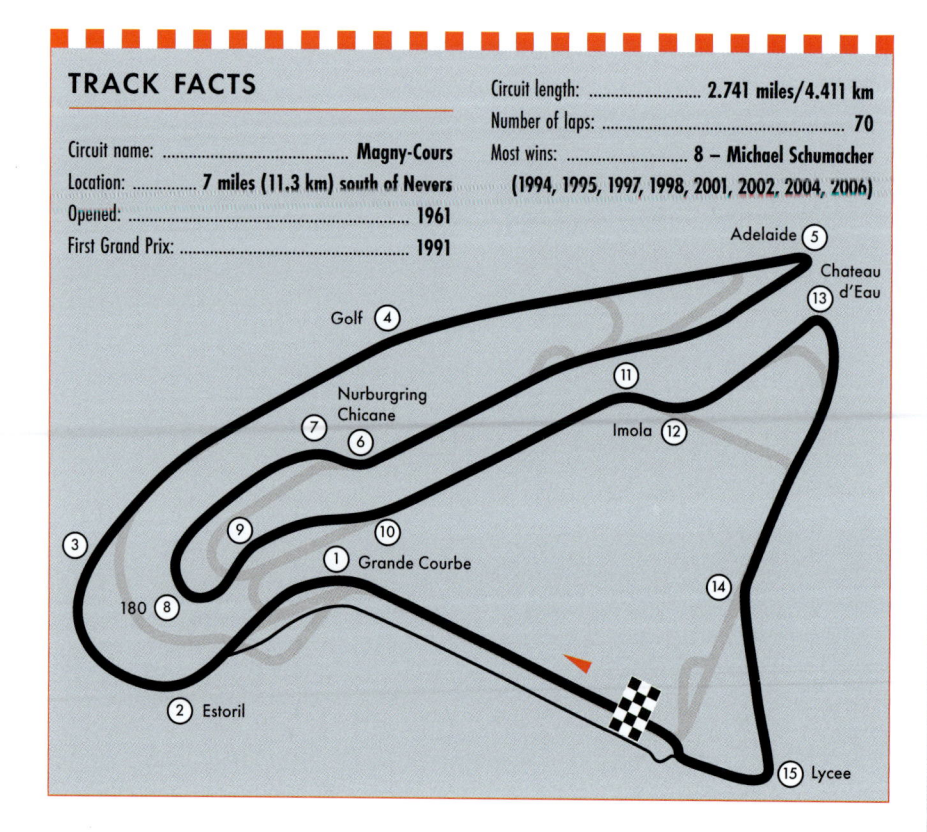

TRACK FACTS

Circuit name: .... Magny-Cours
Location: .... 7 miles (11.3 km) south of Nevers
Opened: 1961
First Grand Prix: 1991
Circuit length: .... 2.741 miles/4.411 km
Number of laps: 70
Most wins: .... 8 – Michael Schumacher
(1994, 1995, 1997, 1998, 2001, 2002, 2004, 2006)

BUZZIN HORNETS
MasterCard
PEARL
PEARL
8
PlayStation
PlayStation

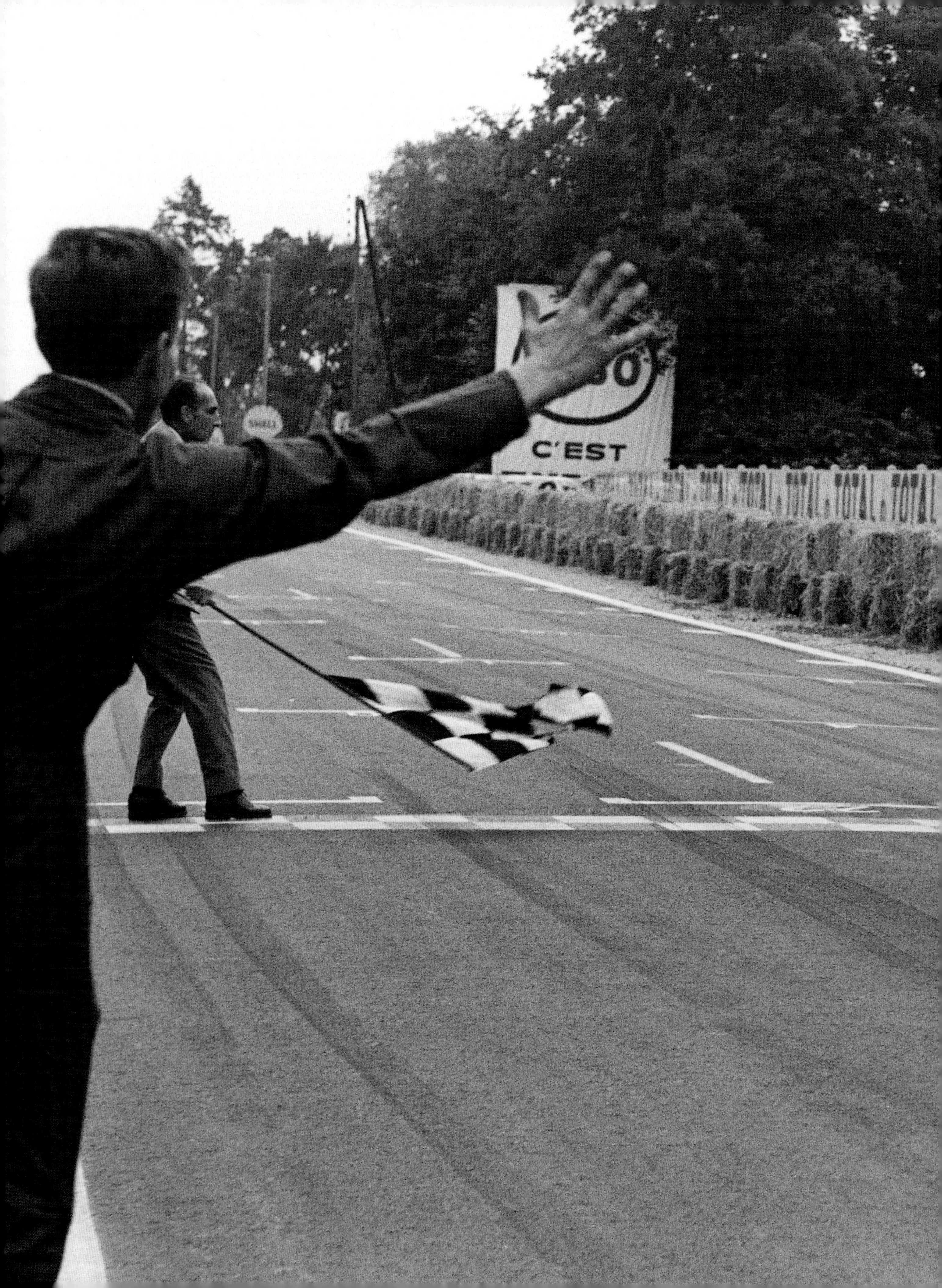
C'EST
TOTAL TOTAL TOTAL

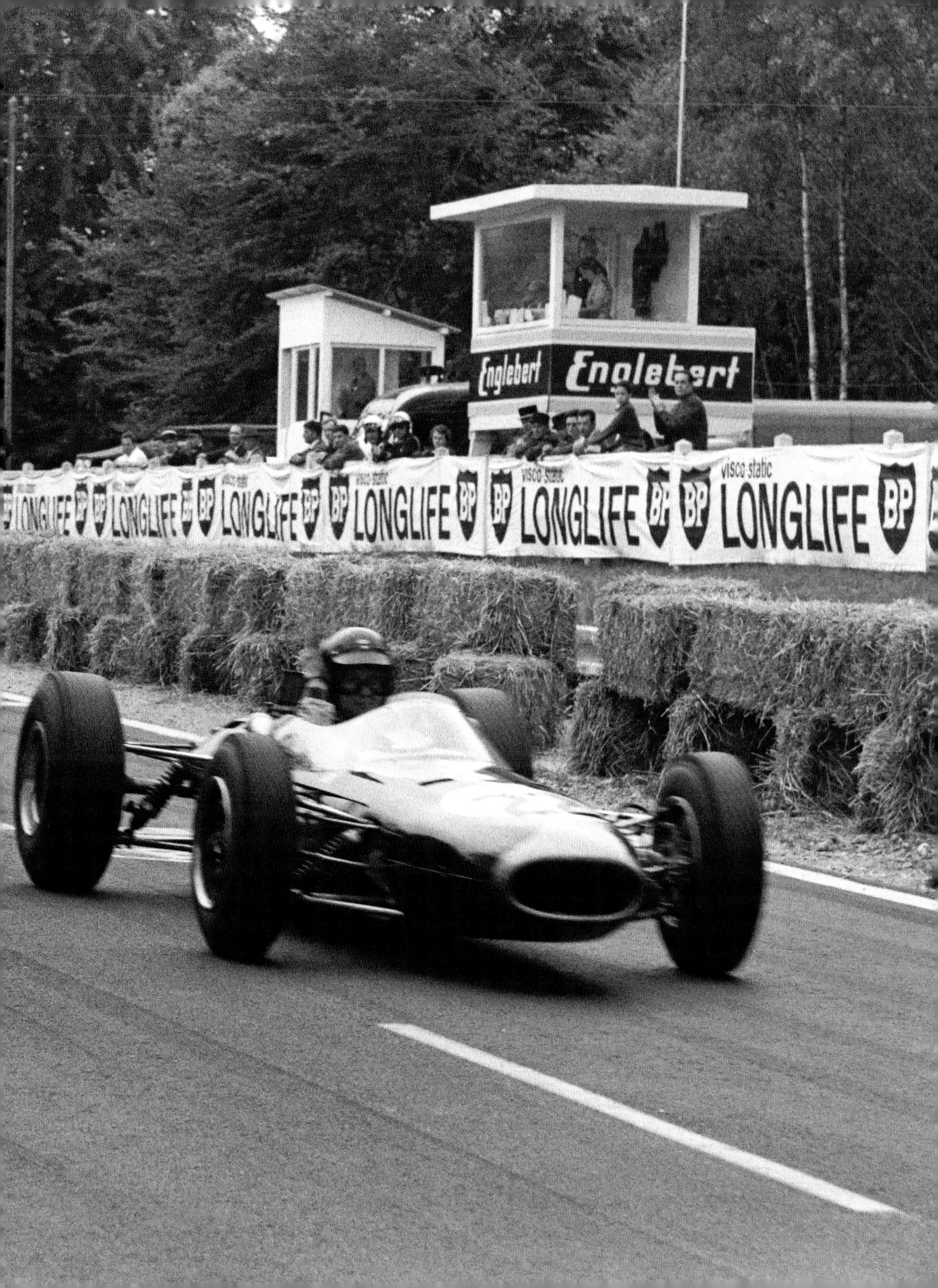
Englebert
Englebert
visco static
LONGLIFE
BP

MOMENTS

The differing circuits that have hosted the French GP all have their own character and they have produced a diverse range of great races.

Gurney races to victory at Rouen

Dan Gurney joined the young Brabham team in 1963 and outscored team founder Jack Brabham. This would have both pleased and infuriated 'Black Jack' and the pattern was repeated in 1964. However, all was forgiven at the French GP when the American gave the team its first World Championship victory. He had been heading for victory at the previous round in Belgium, but his BT7 ran out of fuel with a lap to go. At Rouen-Les-Essarts, he qualified on the front row, but Lotus's pole starter Jim Clark opened out a lead of a minute before his engine broke. This put Brabham first and second and Gurney raced on to victory while Brabham was caught and passed by BRM's Graham Hill.

Mike Hawthorn wins Reims slipstreamer

British drivers were desperate for success and the 1953 French GP at Reims was where the turnaround began. Having impressed in his maiden year of F1, when he came third in the British GP, Mike Hawthorn was signed by Ferrari and he struck a blow for the young guns. José Froilán Gonzáles' decision to start with a half fuel load enabled him to lead, but the pit stop wasn't fast enough. So, entering the final stages, it came down to Hawthorn against Juan Manuel Fangio's Maserati, with the latter enjoying more power, the former superior handling. Then it became clear that Fangio couldn't engage first gear, and this hampered him out of the final corner, which was all Hawthorn needed to secure a famous first win.

Capelli leads Prost at Magny-Cours

Seldom has a team found form in such a marked way as Leyton House did midway through 1990. In a flash, having righted a wind tunnel modelling anomaly spotted by outgoing designer Adrian Newey, by introducing a new diffuser and undertray, the team's CG901s went from non-qualifiers at round six to challengers at round seven. The upturn came at Paul Ricard, with Ivan Capelli and Maurício Gugelmin not only qualifying in the top ten, but also Capelli leading until three laps from the finish when a fuel pick-up problem set in and Ferrari's Alain Prost nipped by. Gugelmin had been holding third place in the sister car until engine failure forced him to park up. Nonetheless, the turnaround had been remarkable.

Opposite: Ferrari's Gilles Villeneuve holds onto second place under considerable pressure from Renault's René Arnoux at Dijon-Prenois in 1979 in what was one of F1's all-time great scraps.

Below: Mike Hawthorn (left) pulls his Ferrari alongside Juan Manuel Fangio's Maserati at Reims in 1953.

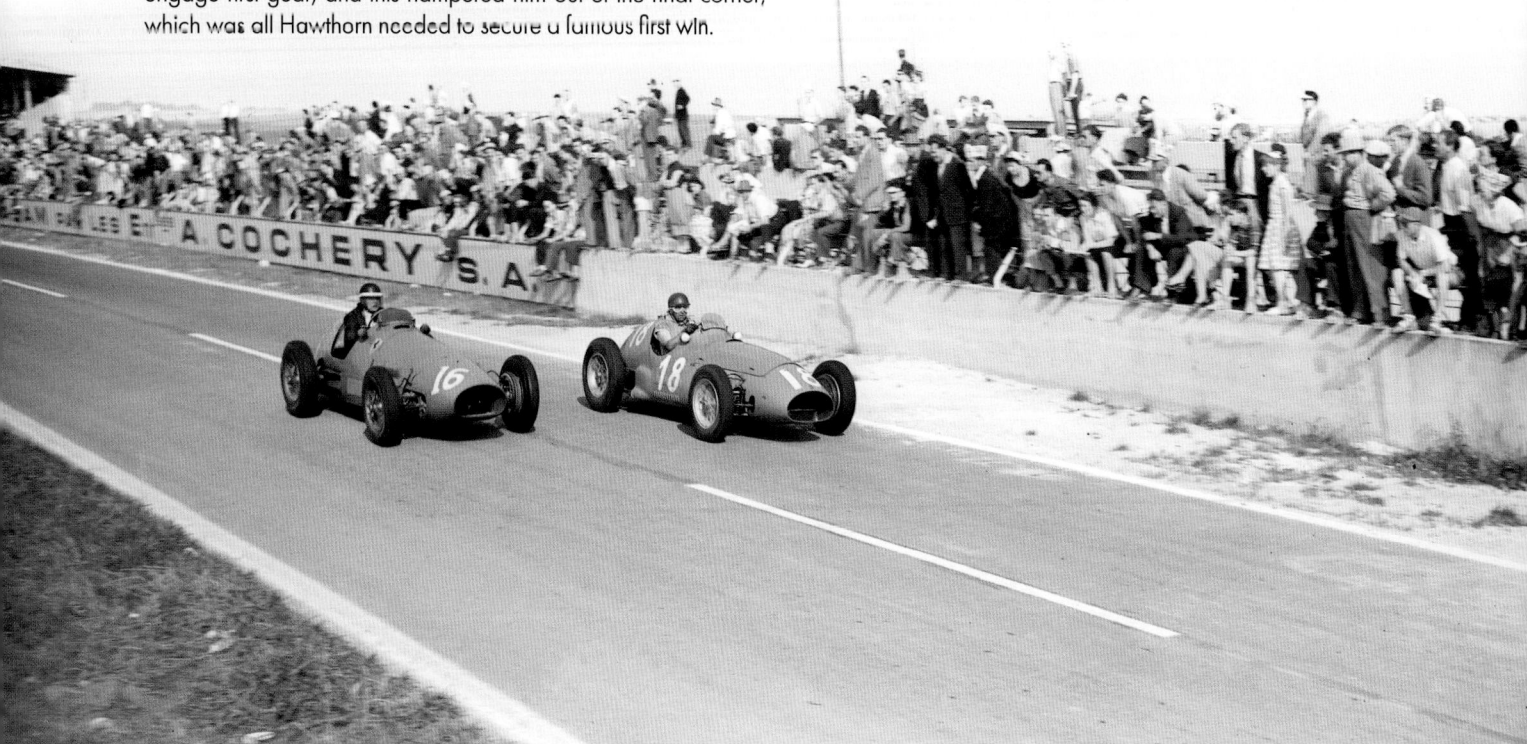

Arnoux and Villeneuve have ultimate battle

The Dijon-Prenois circuit was never thought to be very exciting. Then along came the 1979 French GP and some of the ultimate F1 fireworks were produced in the closing laps. It was already set to be a remarkable result as Jean-Pierre Jabouille was heading for Renault's first F1 victory. Yet, it was what happened in his wake that made people blink. His teammate René Arnoux and Ferrari's Gilles Villeneuve had the most remarkable battle through the last three laps, banging wheels, running wide and changing position at almost every corner. It was mesmeric, as Villeneuve, his tyres destroyed, fell to third but fought back time and time again and somehow came home second.

GERMANY

Germany has produced three world champions (Schumacher, Vettel and Rosberg), but amazingly now doesn't even host a Grand Prix.

Germany set the standards in Grand Prix racing in the 1930s, when the state funded Auto Union and Mercedes in its quest for national glory. It also paid for the Nürburgring to be built to help its automotive industry test its cars.

This mighty track first hosted the German GP in 1927 and it showed the Silver Arrows, as the works Auto Unions and Mercedes were known, in their pomp as they swept all before them. Its undulating 14-mile (22-km) lap, dotted with 170-plus corners, made it a daunting place, especially with rain and mist often coming in.

The Nürburgring Nordschleife, the North Loop, is peppered with classic corners as it rises and falls through the forest but, in time, the drivers began to consider it dangerous. They talked of boycotting the 1976 German GP, but relented, and an accident nearly cost Niki Lauda his life.

So that was that and the German GP transferred to Hockenheim instead in 1977. This flat circuit could not have been more different, twisting between giant grandstands before heading out into a loop through a forest, with its flat-out blasts interrupted only by a trio of chicanes.

To regain the Grand Prix, the Nürburgring chopped off more than 11 miles (17.7 km) off its lap and welcomed F1 again in 1984, but it could not have been more different or unloved in comparison.

The only other circuit to host a German GP, in 1959, was the Avus circuit that ran up and down an autobahn, with a huge, banked corner at one end.

Opposite: Ferrari's Tony Brooks runs high around Avus's Nord Kehre en route to victory in 1959, chased by the Coopers of Stirling Moss and Masten Gregory.

Below: Nico Rosberg had it all under control for Mercedes in 2014, racing from pole to victory.

COUNTRY FACTS

Formula One drivers: 57
Selected F1 drivers:
- Stefan Bellof
- Christian Danner
- Heinz-Harald Frentzen
- Nick Heidfeld
- Hans Herrmann
- Nico Hülkenberg
- Karl Kling
- Jochen Mass
- Nico Rosberg
- Michael Schumacher
- Ralf Schumacher
- Rolf Stommelen
- Hans-Joachim Stuck
- Sebastian Vettel
- Wolfgang von Trips

World champions: .... 3 – Michael Schumacher (1994, 1995, 2000, 2001, 2002, 2003, 2004); Sebastian Vettel (2010, 2011, 2012, 2013); Nico Rosberg (2016)

Grand Prix circuits: 3
- Avus
- Hockenheim
- Nürburgring

Grands Prix hosted: 79

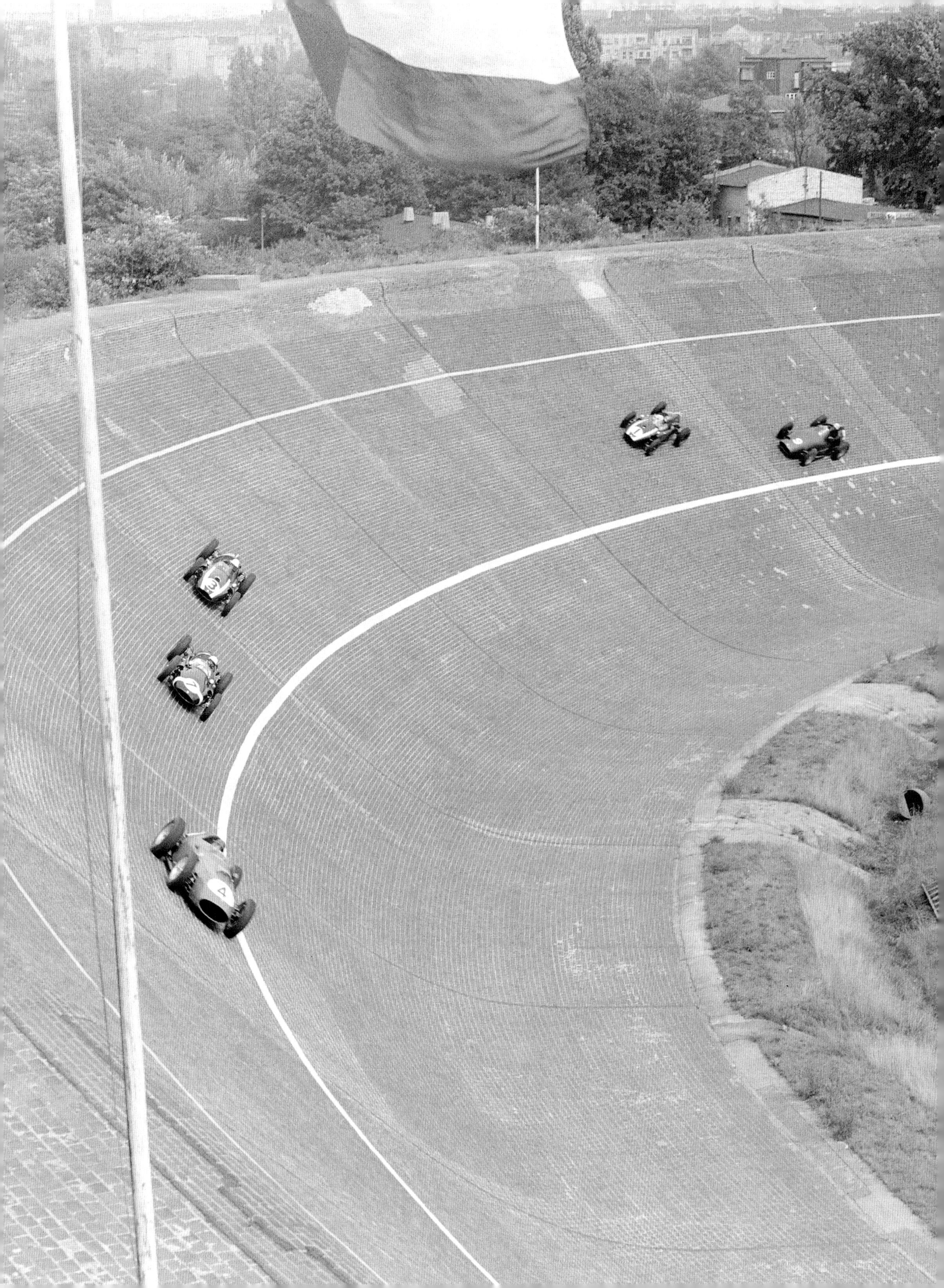

DRIVERS

Michael Schumacher gathered seven F1 titles, Sebastian Vettel four and Nico Rosberg one, but only four other Germans have become Grand Prix winners.

Nico Rosberg

Son of 1982 F1 world champion Keke Rosberg, Nico spent his youth racing karts, often with Lewis Hamilton as a teammate. In fact, he reached F1 before the British driver, in 2006, after becoming the first GP2 champion. His F1 break came at Keke's old team, Williams, and Nico would stay for four years before joining the Mercedes team when it was formed from Brawn GP for 2010. He outraced the returning Michael Schumacher and became a winner in China in 2012. Being partnered with Hamilton was a challenge, but Nico peaked by landing the 2016 title and then retired from racing.

Ralf Schumacher

Michael's younger brother was a very different character. Although he shone in German F3 before landing the Formula Nippon series in Japan when he was twenty-one and earning an F1 ride for 1997, Ralf never had the hard edge that Michael had and would end up a Grand Prix winner but never a world champion. Pipped for victory by Jordan teammate Damon Hill in the 1998 Belgian GP, Ralf joined Williams in 1999 and ranked sixth, then fifth in 2000 when the team got BMW power and fourth in 2001 when he scored the first of his six F1 wins.

Wolfgang von Trips

This aristocrat could have been Germany's first world champion, but he was killed in an accident in the 1961 Italian GP when he clashed with Jim Clark's Lotus. With wins at Zandvoort and Aintree plus two second-place finishes, 'Taffy' was the title favourite. Instead, on his death, it went to Ferrari teammate Phil Hill. He made his name with strong performances in sportscars for Mercedes, Porsche and Ferrari. This earned him a full F1 campaign in 1958, helping Ferrari teammate Mike Hawthorn to win the title. He shone in sportscars again for Porsche in 1959 before rejoining Ferrari.

Sebastian Vettel

With a startling record in the junior single-seater formulae, Sebastian was destined to reach F1, but he did it sooner than expected when he was given his debut in 2007 after Sauber's Robert Kubica was injured. After scoring on his debut, aged just nineteen, he landed a ride with Scuderia Toro Rosso. Then in 2008, not only did he qualify on pole at a wet Monza but he went on to win. Red Bull Racing signed him for 2009 and then, in 2010, he won the first of his titles after a four-way battle. Three more followed between 2011 and 2013, then Sebastian drove for Ferrari and Aston Martin, ending up with fifty-three wins.

Michael Schumacher

Fast, driven and ruthless, Michael was the most exciting driver out of Germany since Stefan Bellof in the 1980s. He landed his F1 break just as his money was running out, grabbing an opening at Jordan when Bertrand Gachot was jailed. Benetton pounced. In return, Michael won two F1 titles for the team, the first of which was completed with a robust move on Damon Hill at Adelaide, the second, a year later in 1995, achieved with the spectre of having used illegal traction control. However, Michael's reputation was made when he turned around struggling Ferrari in 1996, took a failed tilt at the title in 1997, was held back by a broken leg in 1999 then won the title from 2000 to 2004. After retiring in 2006, Michael returned with Mercedes in 2010, but failed to win in three years before retiring for good. Sadly, he suffered brain injuries in a skiing accident in 2013.

CIRCUITS

Germany boasts two of the most storied circuits in F1 history in Hockenheim and the Nürburgring, which has held races since 1926 and its undulating course of over 170 turns per lap remains one of racing's ultimate challenges.

Nürburgring

The original Nürburgring is a circuit that could never be built now. This isn't just because Germany's Green Party would block its construction, but because no one builds tracks this long any more.

Clocking in at 14 miles (22 km), the full Nürburgring Nordschleife was a monster, with trees close to the track's edge and points at which the cars could take off. The nature of the track was revealed early in its lap, through the dropping and twisting Hatzenbach curves. Then the lap opened out before tightening at tricky Aremberg, opening out again at fearsome Fuchsröhre, diving into tight Adenau Bridge, rising again and becoming very fast before the climb to Karussell, the first of the lap's two banked corners. Hohe Acht marks the highest point with Brünnchen and Pflanzgarten major tests before the drivers pulled onto the long homeward straight. Added to these challenges, the circuit's lofty altitude and forest location creates a microclimate that produces its own rain and fog, just like at nearby Spa-Francorchamps.

By 1976, though, the Nordschleife was considered too dangerous for F1 as the drivers threatened to boycott it. They relented and it almost cost Niki Lauda its life just before Bergwerk. That was that for F1, but the full circuit continues to be used to this day, ever more as an antidote to the safety-first circuits used by F1 today. Its major race is its twenty-four-hour race for GT cars and this typically attracts up to 150 cars, with drivers coming from all over the world to take up its challenge.

After the loss of its place in the World Championship, the lap was chopped in 1984 so that it could host F1 events again, with a new Grand Prix circuit being laid out beyond the original first hairpin. With gravel traps, broad verges and barriers set well back from the track as the new circuit dropped down to a hairpin, many critics said that this modern layout was the Nürburgring only in name. The track then rose back up to the level of the pits then plunged behind it, went through a chicane and then turned right to rejoin the pit straight rather than left towards Hatzenbach.

Opposite: Jackie Stewart leads François Cevert to an utterly dominant one-two finish for Tyrrell in 1973.

TRACK FACTS

Circuit name:	Nürburgring
Location:	35 miles (56.3 km) north-west of Koblenz
Opened:	1926
First Grand Prix:	1951
Circuit length:	3.196 miles/5.144 km
Number of laps:	60
Most wins:	3 – Juan Manuel Fangio (1954, 1956, 1957); Jackie Stewart (1968, 1971, 1973); Michael Schumacher (1995, 2000, 2001)

GERMANY

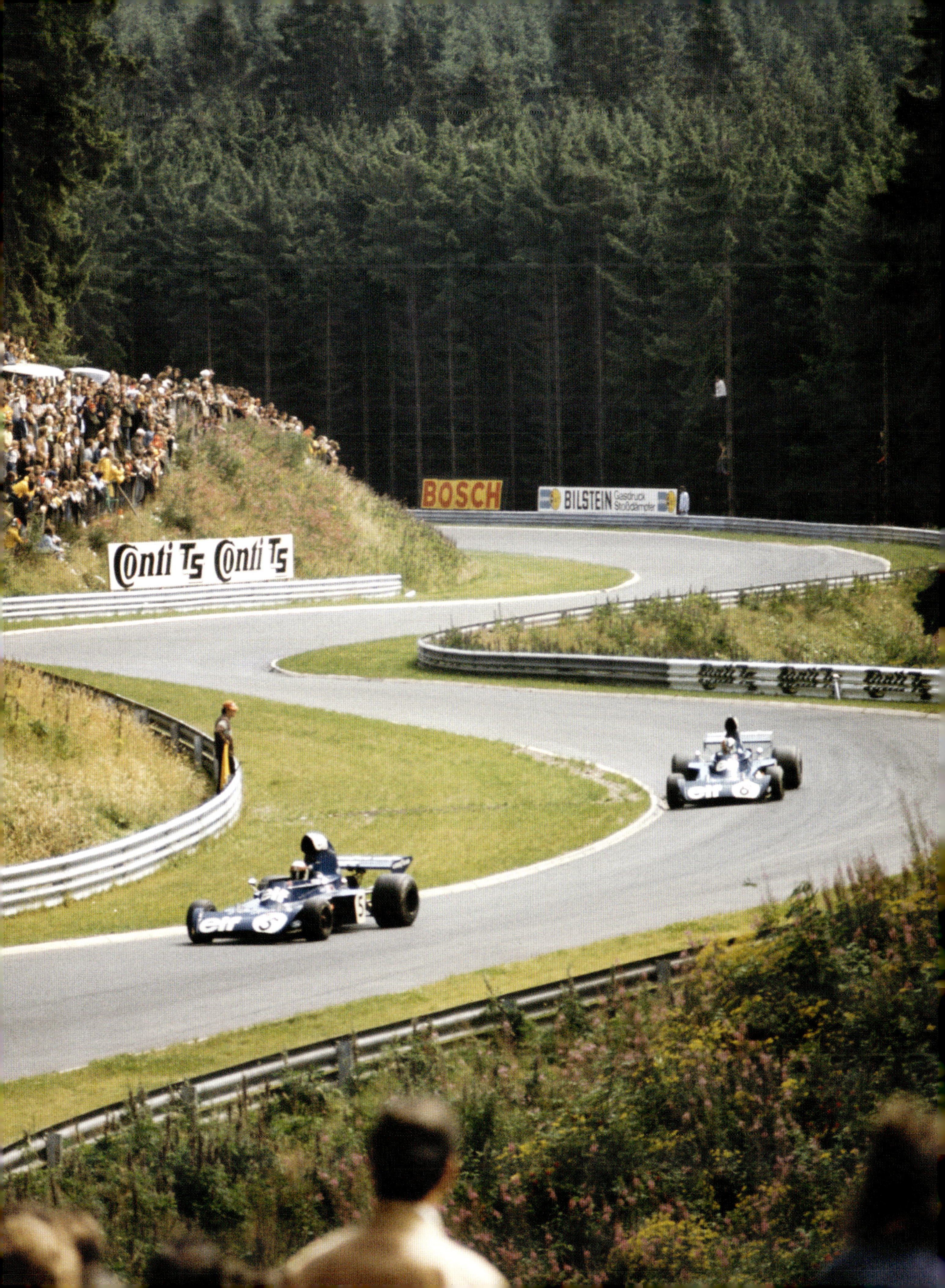
BOSCH
BILSTEIN Gasdruck Stoßdämpfer
Conti TS Conti TS
elf

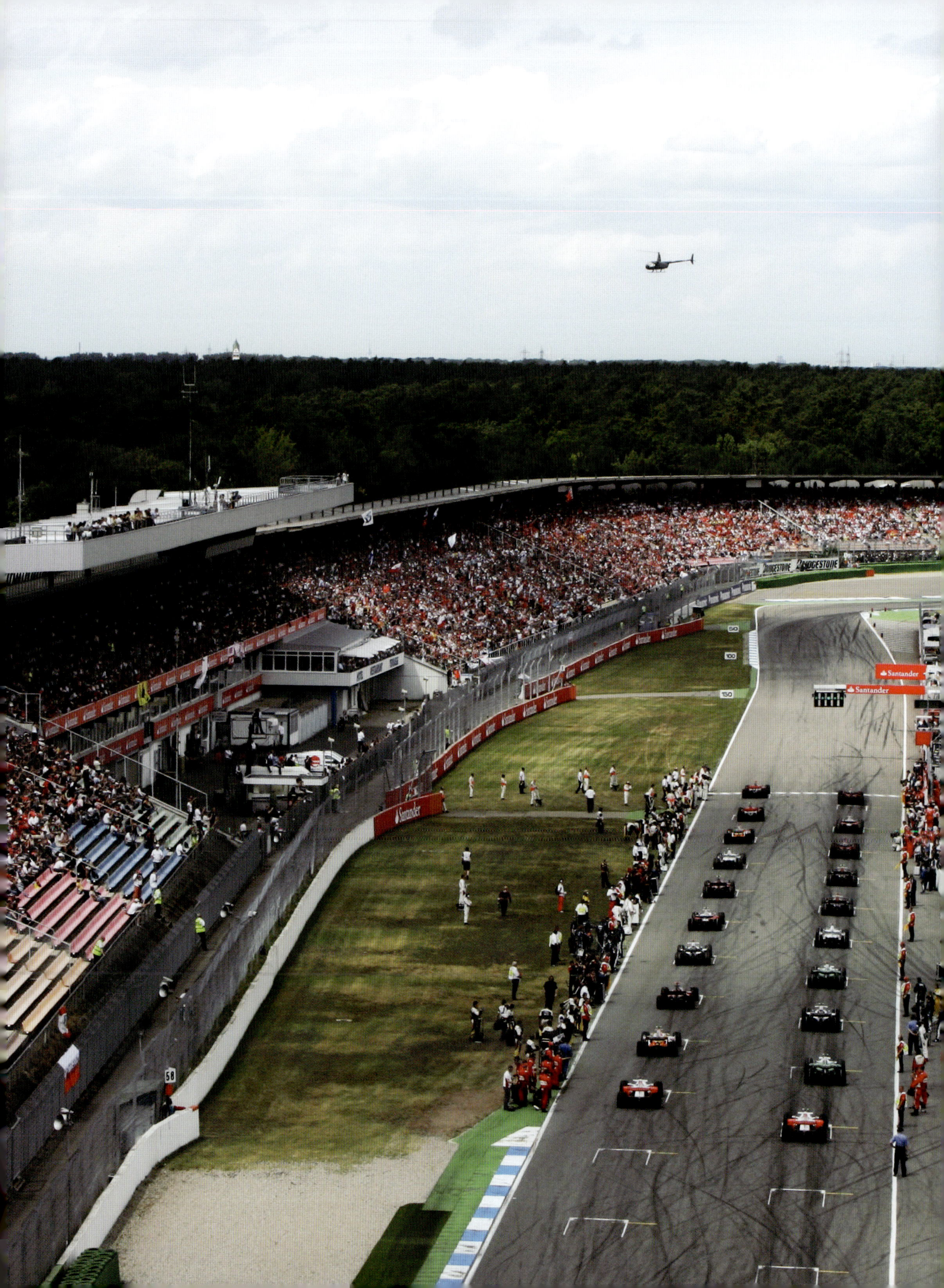
Santander
Santander
BRIDGESTONE

Hockenheim

As well as a one-off Grand Prix run at the hairpin-shaped Avus circuit near Berlin in 1959, there used to be non-championship races held at the 7-mile (11.3-km) Solitude circuit near Stuttgart until it closed in 1965. After that, though, it was the more modern Hockenheim circuit near Heidelberg that was best suited to take over from the Nürburgring.

Hockenheim actually hosted the German GP in 1970 when the Nürburgring took a year out for upgrading work. However, it was from 1977 on that the true Hockenheim era began.

Opened in 1929, just three years after the Nürburgring, Hockenheim was a very different facility. It too ran most of its lap through a forest, most of it taken at full throttle, but the circuit was level and the corners far less frequent on its 4.8-mile (7.7-km) lap. This was cut back in 1966 to make space for an autobahn, but any love for the place as a venue that offered great slipstreaming both going out to the Ostkurve and back again was extinguished when a driver thought to be the best of all, double world champion Jim Clark, died in an F2 race there in 1968. However, the regular visits by the F1 brigade began to earn it a little popularity as it produced some great racing and the atmosphere was added to when the cars returned from the loop through the forest and burst back into the arena.

The track was modified by the insertion of chicanes, two in 1970, one on the outward leg and one on the return, and a third in the middle of the Ostkurve in 1982 after Patrick Depailler was killed when he crashed there in testing in 1980. The circuit's major change came in 2002, however, when the forest loop was all but removed, with a sharp right being made a third of the way to the first chicane, with the track then curving up to the site of the third chicane. From here, a hairpin turned them back towards the pits, with a twisting section before arriving into the arena again.

Left: The grandstands along the pit straight and at Nordkurve are packed before the 2008 German GP.

Following pages: Red Bull Racing's Sebastian Vettel leads the way out of the first corner in 2013.

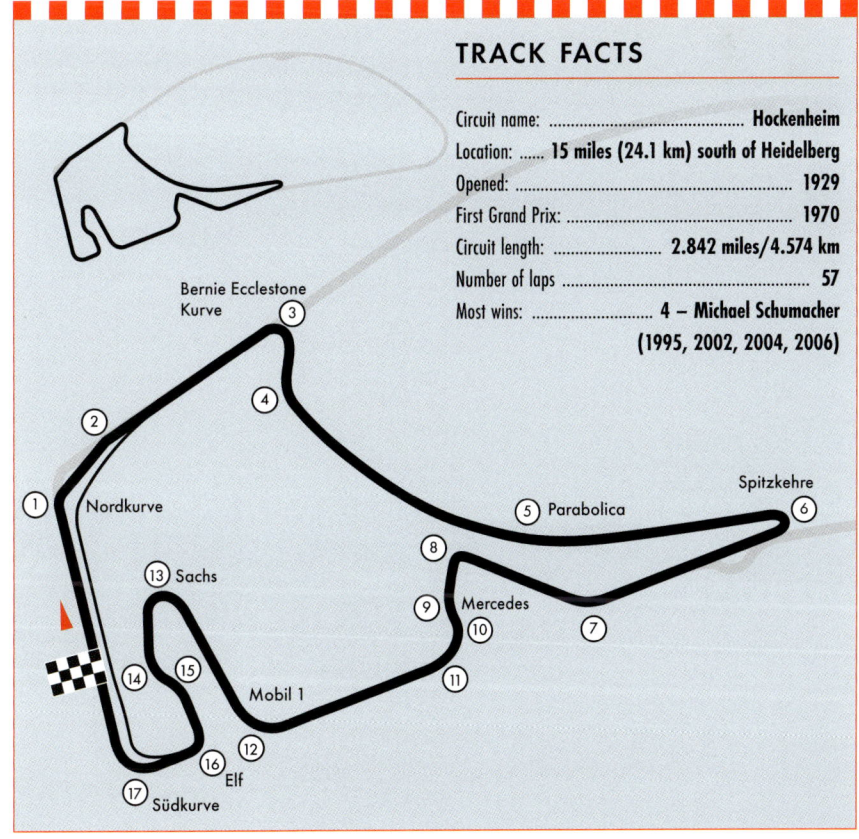

TRACK FACTS

Circuit name:	Hockenheim
Location:	15 miles (24.1 km) south of Heidelberg
Opened:	1929
First Grand Prix:	1970
Circuit length:	2.842 miles/4.574 km
Number of laps:	57
Most wins:	4 – Michael Schumacher (1995, 2002, 2004, 2006)

GERMANY | 59

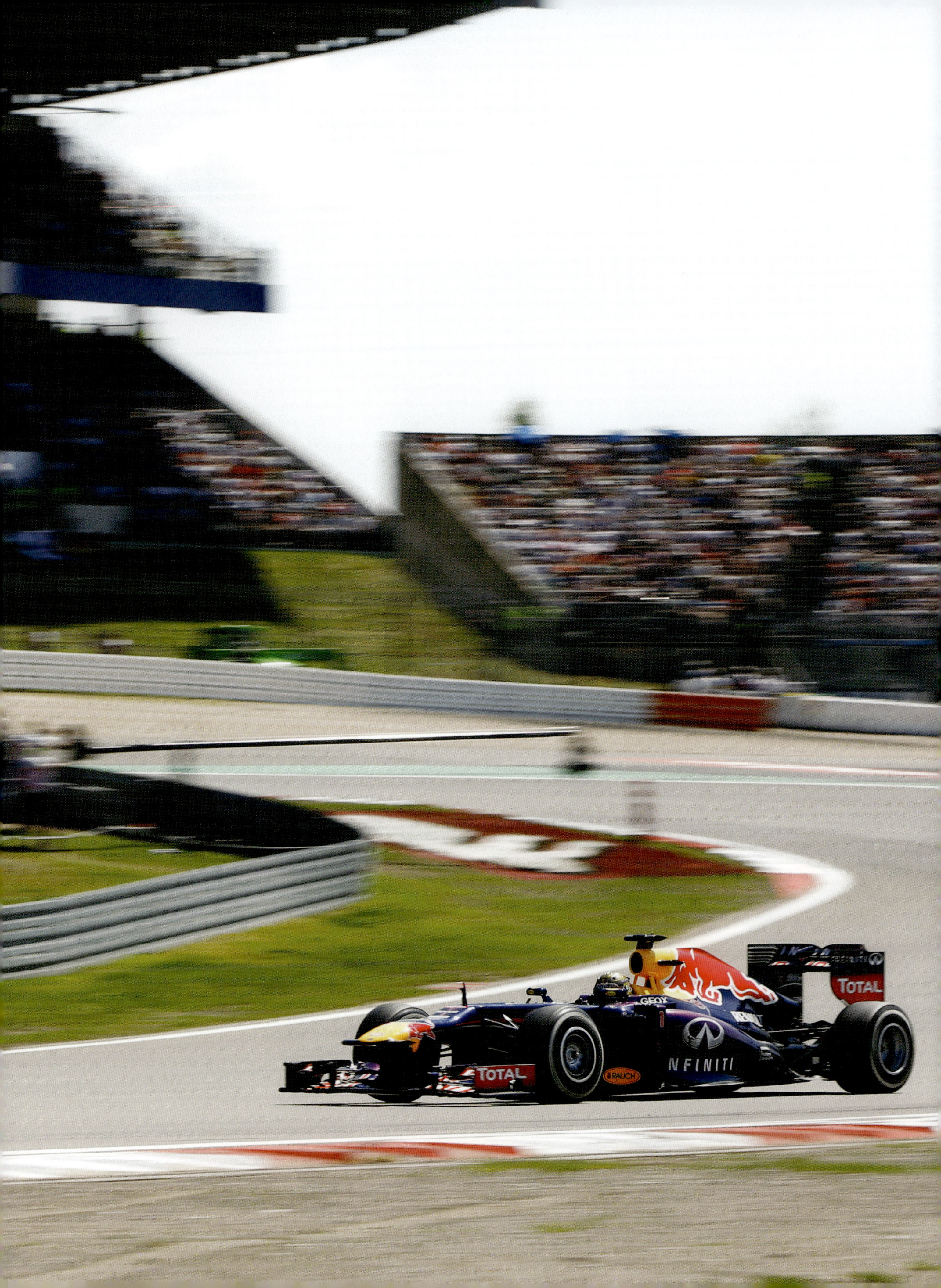
TOTAL
GEOX
TOTAL
RAUCH

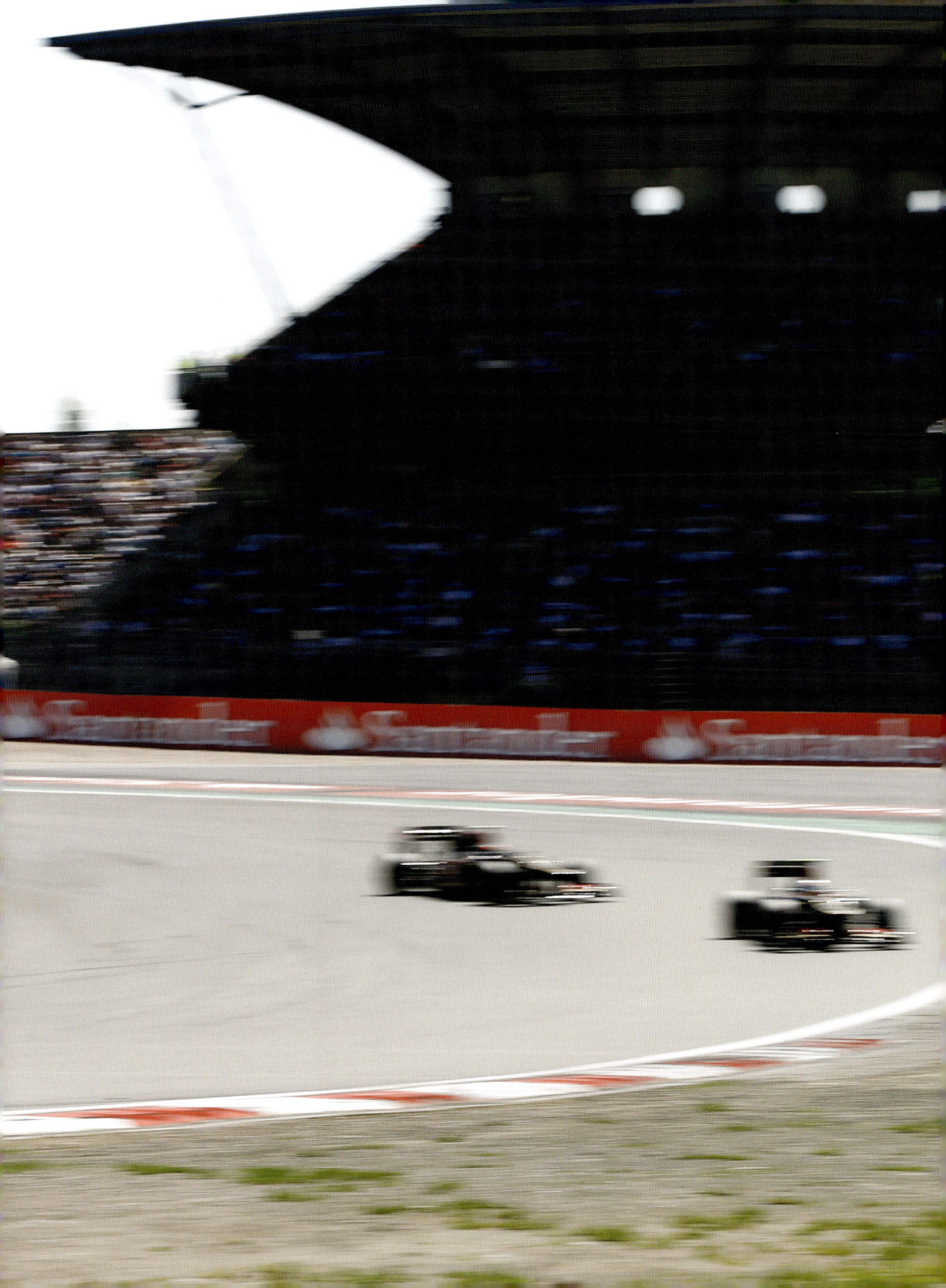

MOMENTS

A circuit as challenging as the original Nürburgring was always going to produce great races, but the modern, shorter version has too.

Fangio passes the Ferraris to win

Juan Manuel Fangio was fully forty-six years old when he arrived at German GP in 1957, but he was at the peak of his prodigious career and made to race as he'd never raced before when he gambled on making a pit stop for fresh tyres in his Maserati, when such an enterprise wasn't done in the blink of an eye, as it is now. Ferrari had decided that its cars would go non-stop and Fangio would later describe driving every lap 'as though it was a qualifying lap' as he set off after Mike Hawthorn and Peter Collins. He broke the lap record ten times as he made up a full minute and hit the front with just one lap to go.

Opposite: Michael Schumacher leads away from brother Ralf at the start of the 2002 German GP.

Below: Johnny Herbert raced to a surprise victory for Stewart GP at the Nürburgring in 1999.

Brooks conquers Avus' banking

This one-off turn at hosting the German GP in 1959 offered the drivers the unusual challenge of racing at Avus and, especially, on the forty-three-degree banking of the North Curve. Tony Brooks put his Ferrari on pole ahead of Stirling Moss' Cooper. Due to concerns about tyre life, the Grand Prix was run as two thirty-lap heats, and Brooks had a slipstreaming battle with Masten Gregory's Cooper and Ferrari teammate Dan Gurney. Phil Hill won the second heat in another Ferrari, but Brooks prevailed and the win was notable not only for being the final F1 win for a front-engined car but also for the death of former Ferrari F1 driver Jean Behra in a supporting sportscar race when his Porsche flew over the top of the banking.

Herbert takes shock win for Stewart

Rain did not spoil play when the European GP was held at the Nürburgring in 1999. Firstly, it shuffled the order, with Heinz-Harald Frentzen snatching pole for Jordan. The race started in dry conditions and there was immediate trouble at the first corner when Alex Wurz's Benetton hit Damon Hill's Jordan and flipped. Frentzen led the McLarens of Mika Häkkinen and David Coulthard when the safety car withdrew. Then the rain arrived, but not enough and Häkkinen pitted to soon. Then Frentzen lost power, Coulthard slid off when more rain fell, Ralf Schumacher took the lead, but had to pit again. Giancarlo Fisichella then slid out of the lead, Schumacher had a blow-out and Johnny Herbert came through to give Stewart its only win.

The Schumacher brothers fill the front row

Older brothers can often be quite unkind to younger brothers and the 2002 season was marked by Michael Schumacher cutting Ralf, younger by six years, very little slack. German fans were excited when the pair filled the front row at Hockenheim, but any hopes that Ralf might have had that his pole-starting Williams might take him to victory were ended immediately as Michael's Ferrari made the better start. This was the first year of the shortened layout and so there were fewer chances for Ralf to catch a tow. In fact, his escape was made easier as teammate Rubens Barrichello latched onto Ralf and then, late in the race, soaring engine temperatures forced Ralf to pit, thus ending all hopes of a fraternal one-two.

HUNGARY

The first racing in Hungary started in the 1930s, but then there was a gap of fifty years before the next new circuit, the Hungaroring.

The announcement that the Hungaroring would host a Grand Prix in 1986 came as a shock to the racing establishment, as Hungary was still a communist country, where F1 would have been seen as a capitalist pursuit contrary to government policies. However, it went ahead and awoke memories that the country had hosted international races before the Second World War. Indeed, even after it became a communist state in 1949, racing continued, albeit in a restricted way.

The country's first circuit made its bow with a sinuous temporary layout in Budapest's Népliget Park in 1936. Its one major event, the first Hungarian GP, produced a surprise result as Tazio Nuvolari kept his Alfa Romeo ahead of the mighty Silver Arrows from otherwise dominant Auto Union. The circuit then wasn't used again until the 1960s, after a short-lived spell using a circuit laid out at the Ferihegy airfield, with touring cars and Eastern European single-seater series racing there until 1972.

The Hungaroring took racing in Hungary up the international ladder and suddenly Eastern Europe had a modern racing facility of its own. With 200,000 turning up to see Nelson Piquet win its inaugural Grand Prix in 1986, it was clear that this gamble had been a good one. In the late 1990s, its grandstands used to be filled with Finnish fans, cheering on Mika Häkkinen, as this was their closest F1 circuit. However, local fans have only had Zsolt Baumgartner to cheer on, with Jordan in 2003 and with Minardi in 2004.

A new circuit, Balaton Park, opened for business to the west of Budapest in 2023.

COUNTRY FACTS

Formula One drivers:	1
World champions:	0
Grand Prix circuits:	1
• Hungaroring	
Grands Prix hosted:	39

Below: Esteban Ocon exits Turn 7 on his way towards an unexpected victory for Alpine in 2021.

Hungaroring

With the start-finish straight sitting on one side of a valley, the circuit plunges into a dip, kicks up onto the opposite side, runs through a series of turns and then dives back into the dip for the return leg, with a tight combination of corners to be negotiated to bring the cars back past the pits. Best of all, most grandstands offer a view of several points of the track.

The lap is largely medium speed and overtaking has always been a challenge.

There have been a couple of layout changes, with the first coming in 1989 when what had been a right-left-right combination after the current Turn 3 were removed in a change that offered the chance to get a faster run to Turn 4, transforming it into the trickiest corner of the lap.

The second change came in 2003, when Turn 12 was changed from a sixty-degree turn to the right into a ninety-degree turn further up the paddock side of the valley.

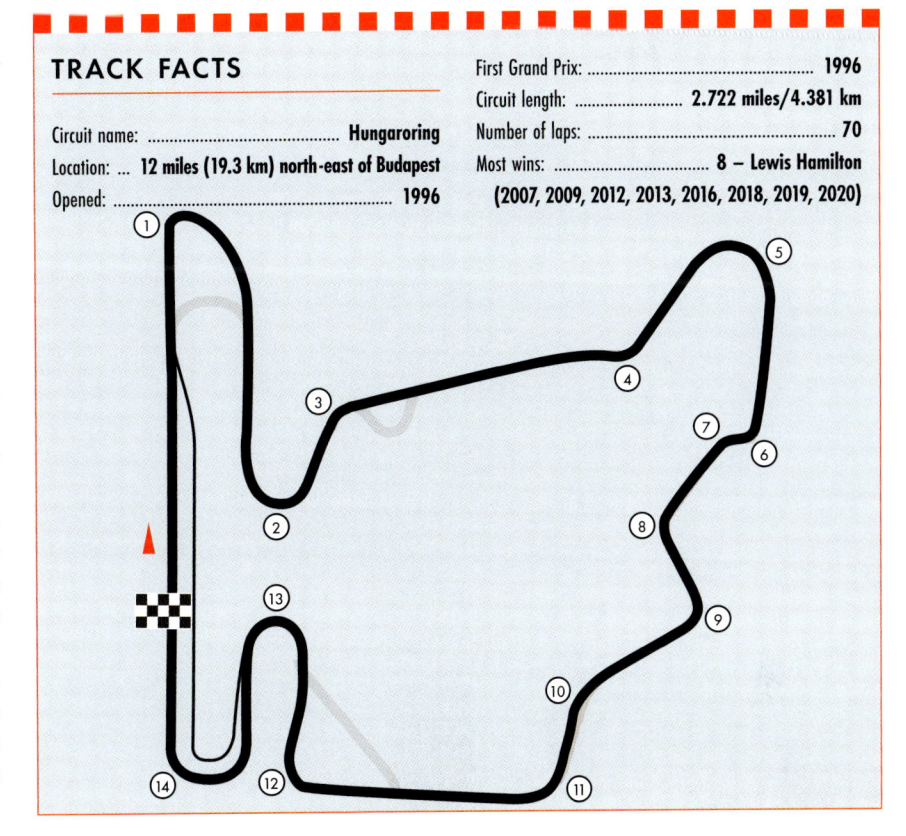

TRACK FACTS

Circuit name: .... Hungaroring
Location: ... 12 miles (19.3 km) north-east of Budapest
Opened: 1996
First Grand Prix: 1996
Circuit length: .... 2.722 miles/4.381 km
Number of laps: 70
Most wins: .... 8 – Lewis Hamilton
(2007, 2009, 2012, 2013, 2016, 2018, 2019, 2020)

IRELAND

There's always been a strong racing scene in Ireland, based chiefly at Mondello Park, but also at Dublin's Phoenix Park in the past too.

COUNTRY FACTS

Formula One drivers: 4
World champions: 0
Grand Prix circuits: 0
Grands Prix hosted: 0

Ireland hosted the first international race meeting in the British Isles when it held a Gordon Bennett Trophy race on a road course near Athy in 1903. This was at a time when road racing was banned in Britain and Northern Ireland later held road races until the 1950s on the testing Ards and Dundrod road courses around Ulster's fast but dangerous public roads.

All the up-and-coming drivers from the Emerald Isle, from both sides of the border, will have cut their teeth racing in the national championships centred on Mondello Park. From 1929 until the 1980s, their diet would have included once-a-year races around Dublin's Phoenix Park, but that was ruled out on safety grounds and Mondello Park, Ireland's only purpose-built circuit, was duly lengthened and modernised in the late 1980s thanks to financial input from Martin Birrane.

Located just outside the town of Naas, 20 miles (32.2 km) from Dublin, Mondello Park, opened in 1968, is where Tommy Byrne, Derek Daly and David Kennedy all cut their racing teeth before heading across to England where the competition in Formula Ford and Formula 3 was much more intense, as did their Northern Irish counterparts including Kenny Acheson and Martin Donnelly.

HUNGARY / IRELAND   65

ITALY

Italy set the pace in F1 through Alfa Romeo, Ferrari and Maserati in the 1950s, but now it only has Ferrari at the front.

Italy and motor racing seem to go hand in hand. For starters, Italians have Monza and, better still, they have Ferrari, the world's most popular and legendary team.

Italy also has a Grand Prix that dates back to 1923 plus two of the world's most revered road races, the Mille Miglia around Tuscany and the Targa Florio on Sicily.

Fired up by huge success in the 1920s before being thrashed by Auto Union and Mercedes in the 1930s, Italy emerged from Second World War as the pre-eminent motor-racing power and so began the World Championship in control when it started in 1950. Mercedes fought back and the little British teams made the established manufacturers look slow of thought as they reinvented F1. Yet, through all this, the Italian fans always had Ferrari, some years competitive, others less so. Also, because it was allowed to host the honorary San Marino GP at Imola in addition to its regular Grand Prix at Monza, Italy has hosted more Grands Prix than any other country.

Their Grands Prix haven't only been held at Monza and Imola, though; once it was held on the Pescara road course and, due to COVID, once at Mugello too.

The Italian racing scene has always been a busy one, using circuits in addition to Monza and Imola ranging from Mugello in the heart of Tuscany to Misano on the Adriatic Coast to Vallelunga near Rome and Enna-Pergusa on Sicily, all of which have attracted international visitors across the decades.

COUNTRY FACTS

Formula One drivers: 71
Selected F1 drivers:
- Michele Alboreto
- Alberto Ascari
- Giancarlo Baghetti
- Lorenzo Bandini
- Vittorio Brambilla
- Elio de Angelis
- Giuseppe Farina
- Giancarlo Fisichella
- Luigi Musso
- Alessandro Nannini
- Riccardo Patrese
- Ludovico Scarfiotti
- Piero Taruffi
- Jarno Trulli
- Luigi Villoresi

World champions: .... 2 – Giuseppe Farina (1950); Alberto Ascari (1952, 1953)
Grand Prix circuits: 4
- Imola
- Monza
- Mugello
- Pescara

Grands Prix hosted: 106

Opposite: Juan Manuel Fangio races his Maserati around Pescara's high-speed rural course in 1957.

Below: Ferrari's Charles Leclerc got the tifosi excited when he led away from pole at Monza in 2022 but he had to settle for second behind Max Verstappen.

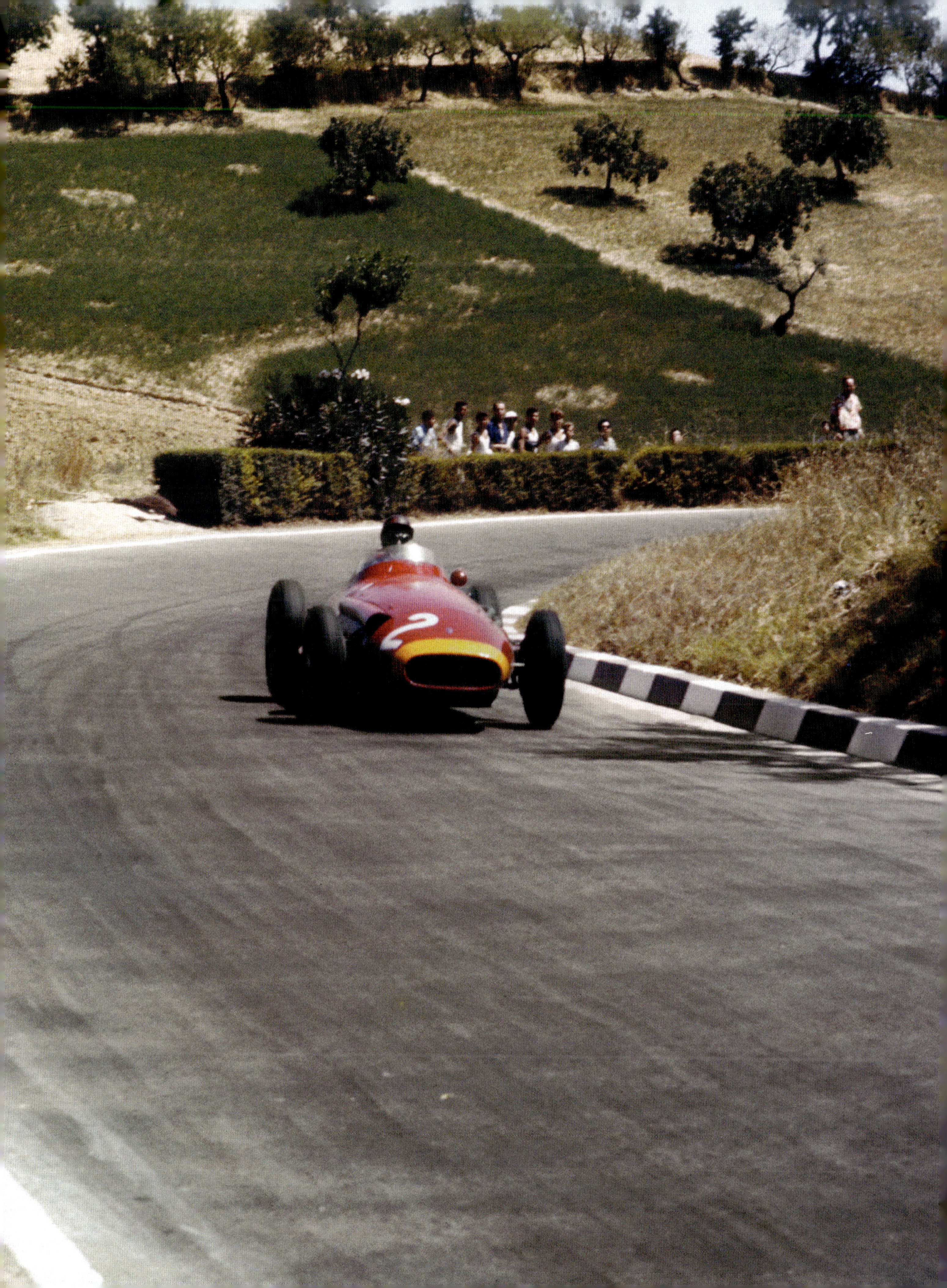

Riccardo Patrese

It took an evolution from perhaps an overconfident F1 rookie for Riccardo to become the seemingly unflappable driver who went on to win six Grands Prix before he finally quit F1 seventeen years later with a then record 256 Grands Prix to his name. After a debut year with Shadow then four years with Arrows, Riccardo joined Brabham in 1982 and scored his first win in a chaotic race at Monaco with a second victory following at Kyalami in 1983. Then came two years with Alfa Romeo and a return to Brabham before five years at Williams that included a final win at Suzuka and a swansong with Benetton.

DRIVERS

Italian drivers won three of the first four F1 titles but have not won one since, which is an extraordinary record.

Giuseppe Farina

Giuseppe became the sport's first world champion when he led Alfa Romeo's attack in 1950. He hospitalised himself on his hill-climb debut in 1932, then decided that circuit racing might be safer. As it happens, Giuseppe had many more accidents, but he learned from Tazio Nuvolari and began winning Grands Prix for Alfa Romeo. Then came the Second World War. Alfa Romeo returned to action for the first year of F1 and wins at Silverstone, Bremgarten and Monza landed him that first crown. He was then overshadowed by Juan Manuel Fangio, so moved to Ferrari for 1952 when Ascari did the same.

Michele Alboreto

Michele had a shot at becoming Italy's third world champion when he raced for Ferrari in 1985, but he was beaten by McLaren's Alain Prost. Michele was European F3 champion in 1980 and Tyrrell gave him his F1 break, with his first win at Caesars Palace in the 1982 finale. In 1983, he became the last driver to win with Ford's DFV engine. Then Ferrari signed him and he stayed for five years, finishing second in the World Championship in 1985. After leaving F1 in 1994, he found success in sportscars, winning the Le Mans 24 Hours in 1997, but he was killed when testing for Audi at the Lausitzring in 2001.

Giancarlo Fisichella

Giancarlo was able to pounce when opportunities arose and so he ended his fourteen-year F1 career with three wins to his name. After landing the 1994 Italian F3 title, Giancarlo raced touring cars for Alfa Romeo, made his F1 debut for Minardi in 1996, then had a boost when he moved to Jordan for 1997. Benetton snapped him up and he raced for them for the next four years, but it took a return to Jordan for that first F1 win to come, in Brazil in 2003. He then won the 2005 season opener for Renault with his final win coming at Sepang in 2006.

Alberto Ascari

This second-generation racer cleaned up for Ferrari when the World Championship ran to F2 regulations in 1952 and 1953. He started off racing motorbikes, but changed to cars after the Second World War, quickly becoming one of the leading names. At the start of the World Championship in 1950, Ferrari were overpowered by Alfa Romeo, but Alberto was able to win at the Nürburgring and Monza in 1951. Then came the rule change for 1952 and Alberto was all but untouchable, winning all six rounds and then the first three rounds of 1953 to claim both titles. Changing to Lancia for 1954 was a disaster as the car wasn't ready. However, it was competitive at the start of 1955, but just days after crashing into the Monaco harbour, Alberto was killed when testing a Ferrari sportscar at Monza.

CIRCUITS

Monza is one of the pillars on which the legend of motor racing has been built: a constant since the 1920s and home to the world-famous tifosi. But Imola and Mugello can also boast recent F1 pedigree.

Monza

The description of Monza as 'The Temple of Motor Sport' is absolutely fair, as it has been at the heart of the sport now for just over a century, operating at the sport's highest level and producing some of the most exciting races, year in year out.

Built within the walls of a park, the beauty of the place is that you can feel the history at every turn. The circuit has been given nips and tucks, safety modifications and had its infrastructure changed, but it is still identifiably the circuit that opened its doors in 1922.

The original circuit had what is the current Grand Prix track with a special addition, in that the lap also continued past the pits before turning right onto a banked oval and doing a tour of that before cars were fed back onto the start-finish straight, making the lap 6.2 miles (9.98 km). Without the loop, it was, as it is now, 3.6 miles (5.79 km) long.

The Grand Prix circuit didn't change much until the last corner, Vedano, was made more flowing in 1957 and this really helped the multi-car slipstreaming battles that were waged down the long straights. After an epic finish to the 1971 Italian GP, though, and numerous accidents in junior events, chicanes were inserted at three points around the lap to keep speeds in check. The shape of the first chicane has been changed several times since then, but Monza is still very much Monza, still high-speed and still requiring precision as well as bravado.

On a clear day in spring, the view down the main straight past the old control tower to the snow-capped Alps beyond remains one of the classic views in racing, usually when the World Endurance Championship visits. The Italian GP is always held in autumn, though, often when the title race is hotting up, and the atmosphere is phenomenal as the tifosi make it absolutely clear that they are wanting only one thing: a Ferrari win. These have been in relatively short supply, except for occasional Ferrari purple patches, like in the early 1960s or when Michael Schumacher was dominant in the first decade of the twenty-first century.

In 2023, Ferrari's fans nearly had their wishes granted again, when Carlos Sainz Jr led away from pole. However, the outcome was the same as nearly all the other races of the season as Max Verstappen came through to score yet another win for Red Bull Racing.

Opposite: Ferrari's fans craved a home win especially in 1988, at the first Italian GP after the death of founder Enzo Ferrari, and Gerhard Berger delivered when he led home teammate Michele Alboreto in the only race that year not won by McLaren.

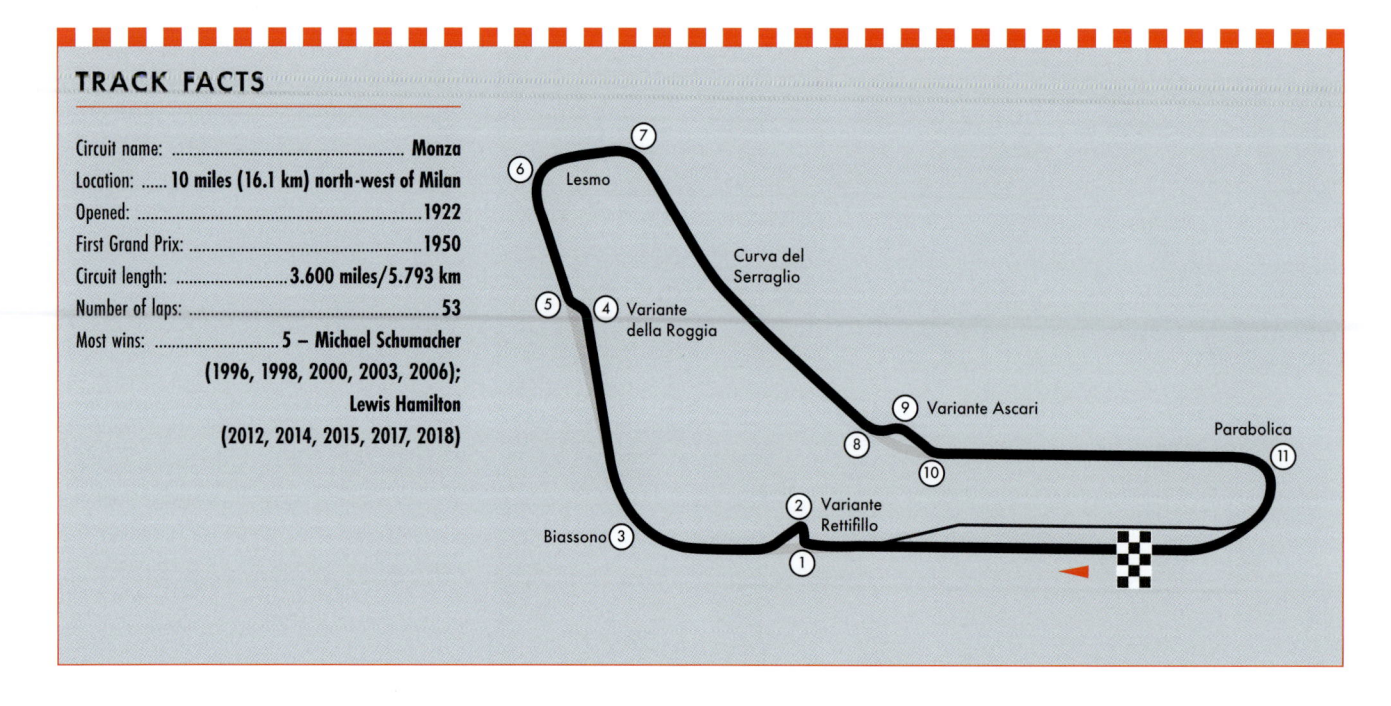

TRACK FACTS

Circuit name: .... Monza
Location: .... 10 miles (16.1 km) north-west of Milan
Opened: 1922
First Grand Prix: 1950
Circuit length: .... 3.600 miles/5.793 km
Number of laps: 53
Most wins: .... 5 – Michael Schumacher
(1996, 1998, 2000, 2003, 2006);
Lewis Hamilton
(2012, 2014, 2015, 2017, 2018)

ITALY

ITALY | 71

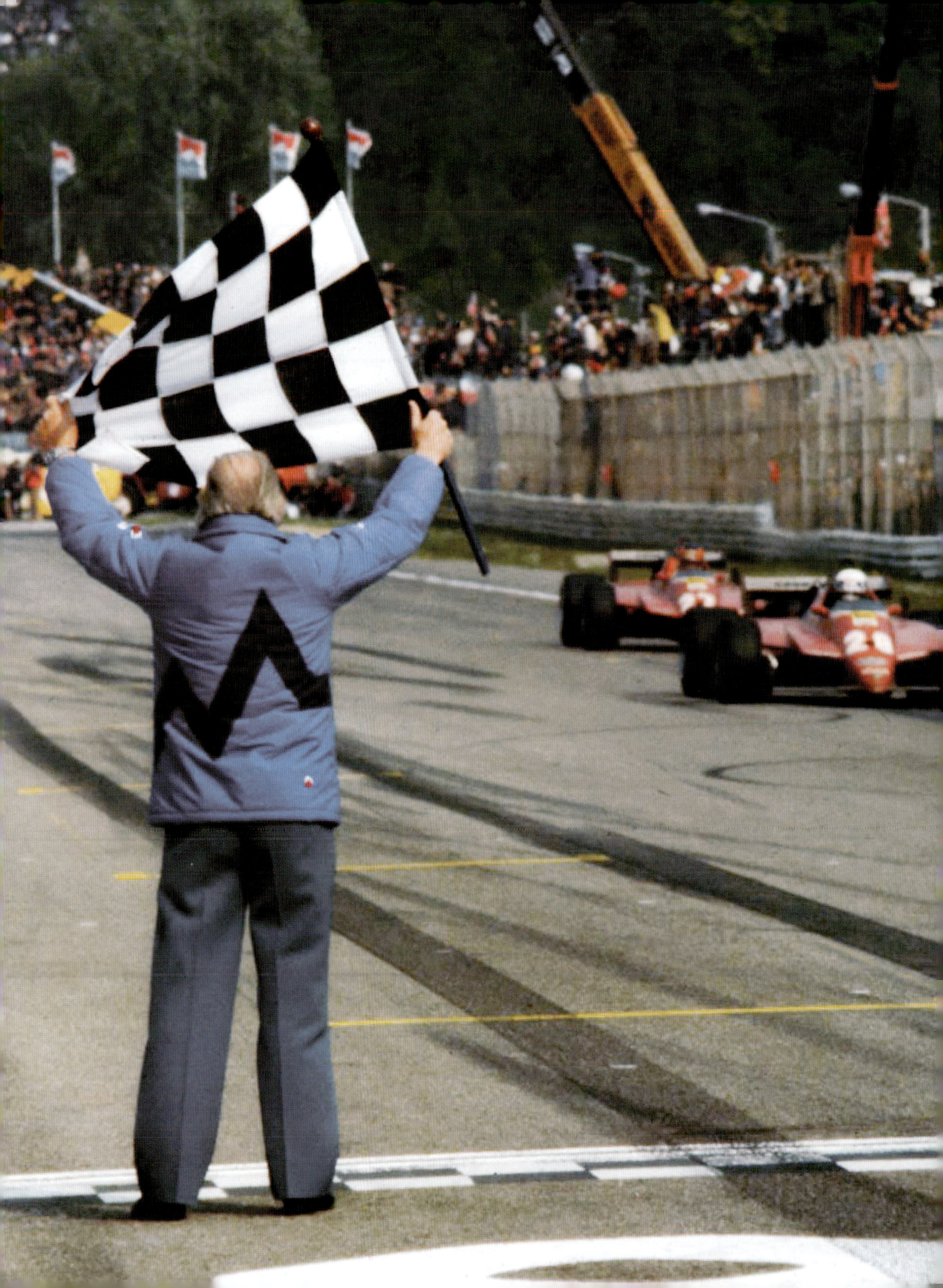

Imola

Built in 1952 in the town of Imola on the southern flank of the Lombardy Plains, this lovely circuit has been modified over the years but, like Monza, it remains true to the way it was created.

Hemmed in by a river running behind its narrow paddock and climbing slowly through orchards on its upper side, there has never been much space at Imola, but the use of the site's topography to create some fabulous rising and falling twists and turns along with a flat-out blast along the valley floor are what give Imola its character. The pick of the corners is Acque Minerale, a surprisingly high-speed right-hander out of a compression.

Its early races were mainly national events for single-seaters, sportscars and touring cars, but Imola hosted a non-championship race in 1963, with victory going to Jim Clark for Lotus.

With the safety of Monza called into question after Ronnie Peterson's fatal accident in the 1978 Italian GP, recently upgraded Imola was afforded the chance to host the race in 1980, with victory going to Brabham's Nelson Piquet. Because the event was run so successfully, the sport's governing body thought that it was worthy of a Grand Prix of its own and so created the title San Marino GP so that it could have one, even though Imola is 50 miles (80.5 km) from the tiny principality.

Despite there having been some brilliant Grands Prix here, Imola will always be remembered for the dreadful events of the 1994 San Marino GP, for a huge accident for Rubens Barrichello on the Friday, a fatal accident for Roland Ratzenberger on the Saturday and then Ayrton Senna being killed in the race.

Naturally, modifications were made after this, with a chicane being inserted before Tamburello and another on the approach to Tosa.

The COVID pandemic brought Imola back into the F1 fold in 2020 when extra venues in Europe were needed as travel, particularly in the Far East, was restricted, and this gave a new generation of fans a chance to witness its charms.

Left: Didier Pironi is just ahead of Gilles Villeneuve at the end of their controversial race at Imola in 1982.

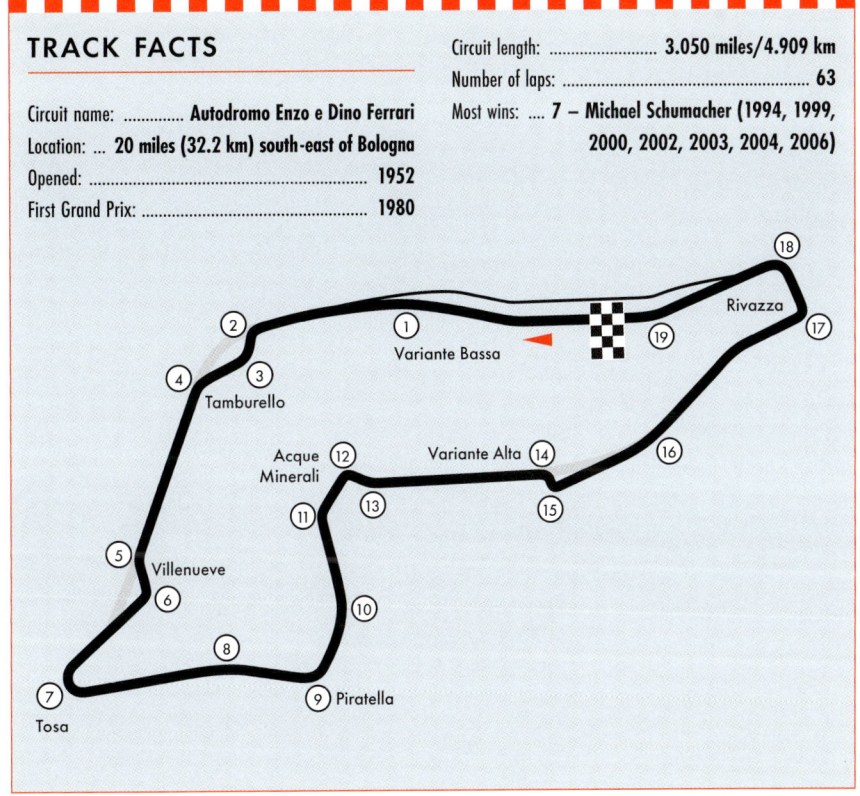

TRACK FACTS

Circuit name: **Autodromo Enzo e Dino Ferrari**
Location: **20 miles (32.2 km) south-east of Bologna**
Opened: **1952**
First Grand Prix: **1980**
Circuit length: **3.050 miles/4.909 km**
Number of laps: **63**
Most wins: **7 – Michael Schumacher (1994, 1999, 2000, 2002, 2003, 2004, 2006)**

ITALY

Mugello

For a motor-racing mad country, Italy is quite like Germany in that it has hosted its Grand Prix at only a handful of circuits. Naturally, Monza is the nation's number one, with Imola a distant number two and Pescara a one-off oddity in 1957. However, this circuit in Tuscany finally got its chance to join them in 2020 when the FIA was seeking circuits in Europe to fill gaps in its COVID-decimated World Championship calendar, giving it the honorary title of the Tuscan GP.

Fans of racing beyond F1, whether that is junior single-seater categories, touring cars, sportscars, GTs or motorbikes, knew the circuit well before then, but the rise and fall of its lap won it plenty of plaudits as Lewis Hamilton dominated for McLaren. A home win for Ferrari was always going to be a struggle in a year in which the tifosi's team was off form, but the fans enjoyed the experience.

There had been an event called the Circuito di Mugello in the 1920s, run around a 40-mile (64.4-km) loop of roads that included the Futa Pass. Then, in the 1950s, the Mille Miglia road race blasted past its gates. However, the current Mugello circuit opened for racing in 1974 with its location just 14 miles (22.5 km) to the north of Florence ensuring that its race meetings were well supported. Sadly, the fan base dwindled and so did Mugello's finances, leading to talk of its permanent closure in the 1980s. Fortunately, Ferrari elected to buy it, chiefly to be used as a test venue for its road and race cars, and so it survived.

The lap starts at the bottom of its shallow valley, rising immediately after the first corner before the cars turn to the right. Then it snakes across the face of the slope through a run of esses and dives into and then out of the valley to climb to the opposite side before a series of sweeping curves and a wonderful long left-hander bring the cars back onto the start-finish straight.

F1's visit is sure to be a one-off, but it was a real pleasure to see today's fastest cars being put through their paces in such a wonderful setting.

Right: The restrictions caused by COVID in 2020 meant that Mugello got to host a World Championship round and Ferrari celebrated its 1,000th start, but Sebastian Vettel couldn't conjure up a win.

Following pages: Daniel Ricciardo leads teammate Lando Norris through Monza's first chicane on the first lap in 2021, on a day that the Australian raced on to give McLaren its first win in nine years.

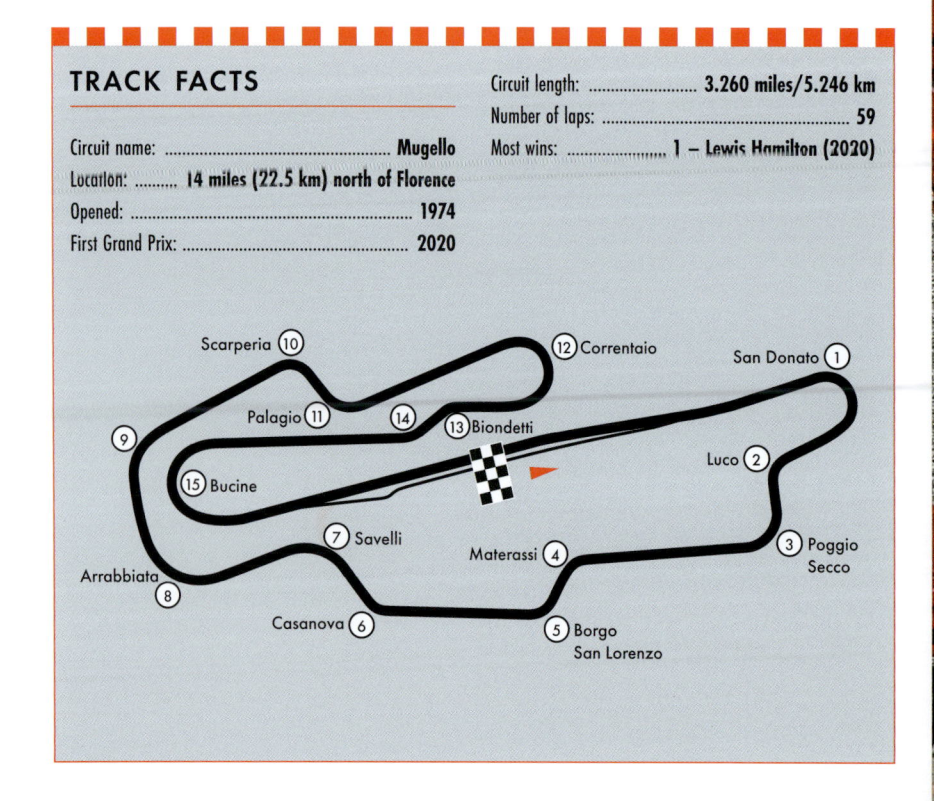

TRACK FACTS

Circuit name: Mugello
Location: 14 miles (22.5 km) north of Florence
Opened: 1974
First Grand Prix: 2020
Circuit length: 3.260 miles/5.246 km
Number of laps: 59
Most wins: 1 – Lewis Hamilton (2020)

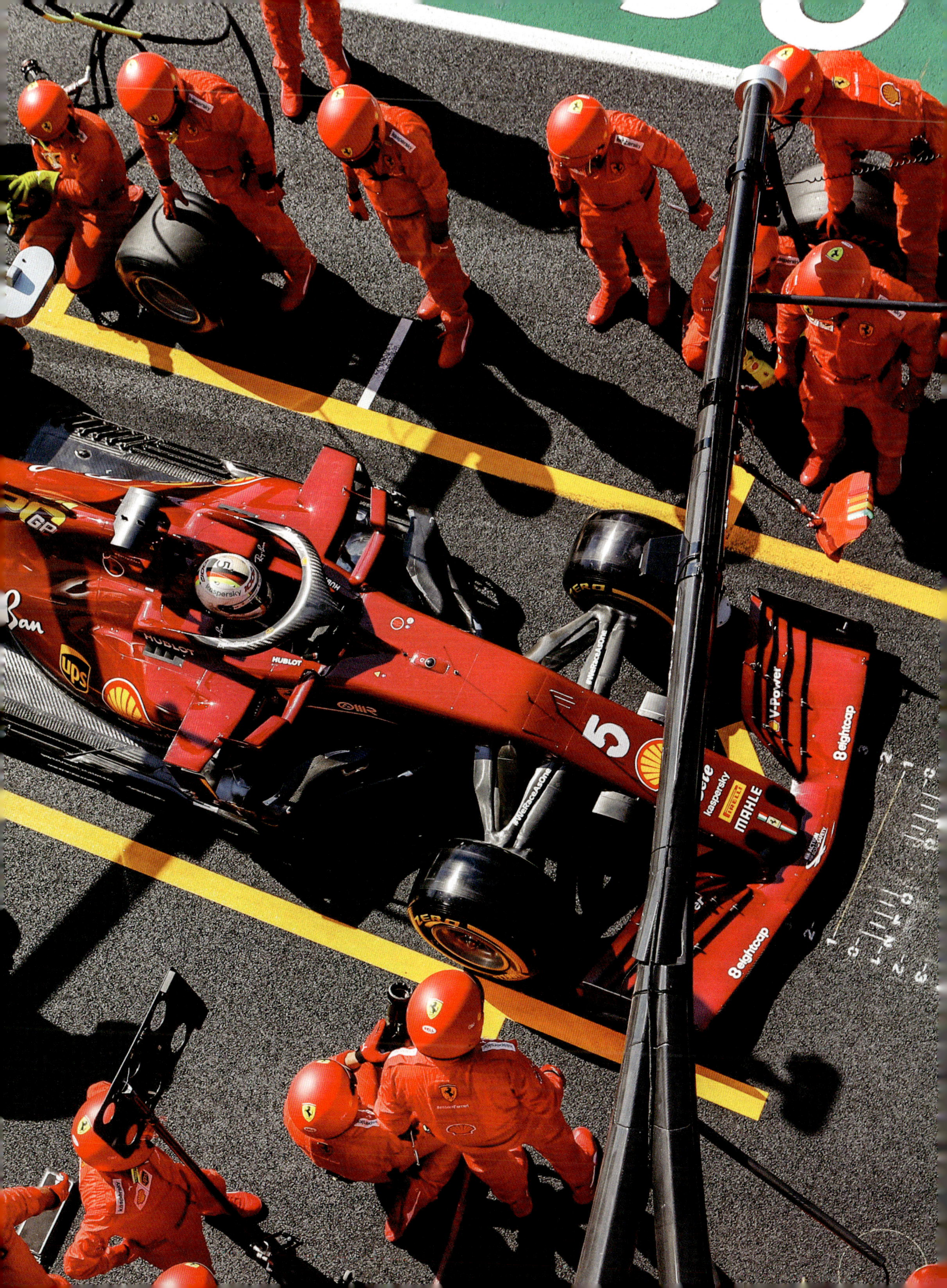

HUBLOT
ups
5
V-Power
8eightcap
kaspersky
MAHLE
8eightcap

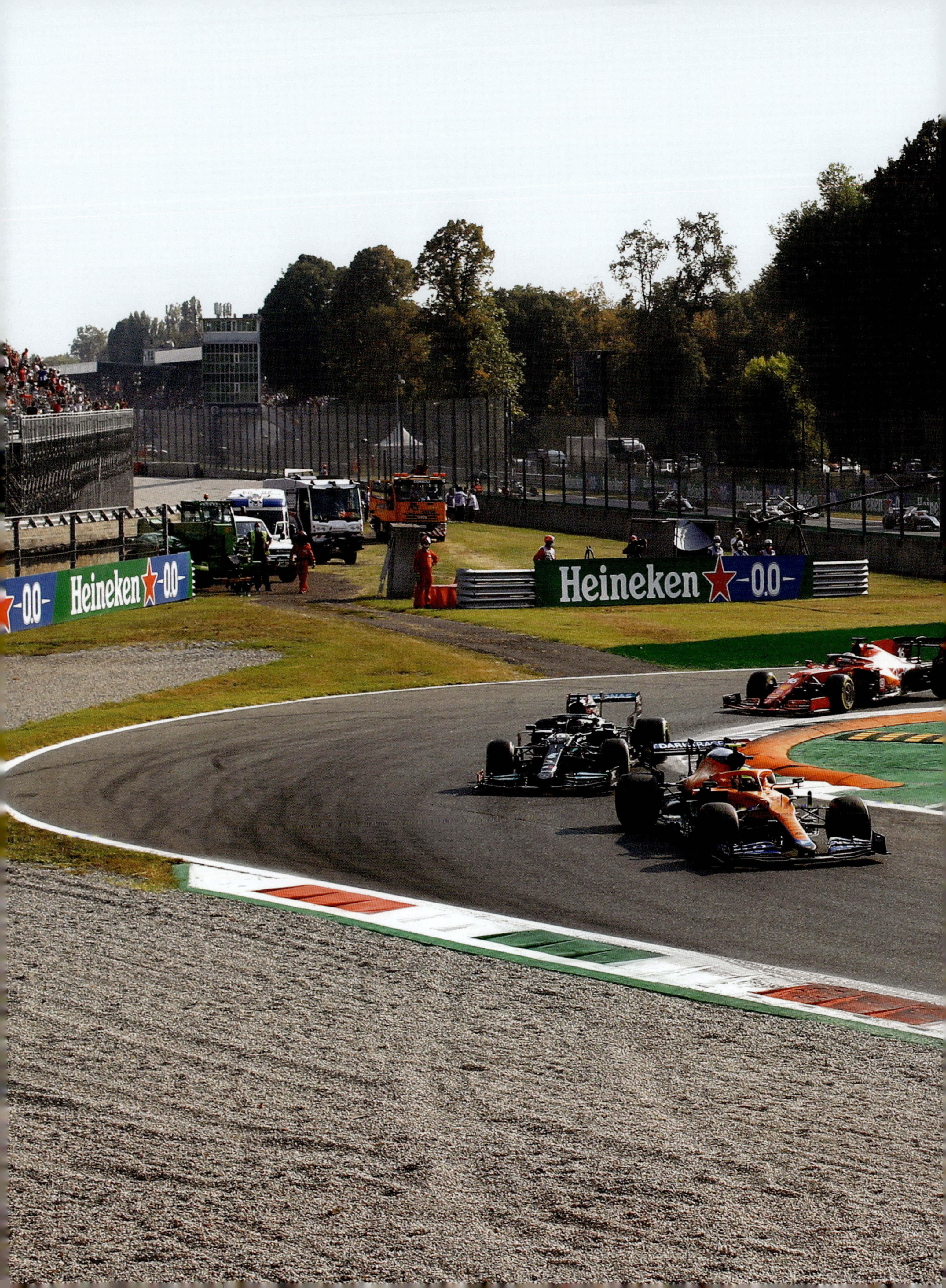
Heineken 0.0
Heineken 0.0

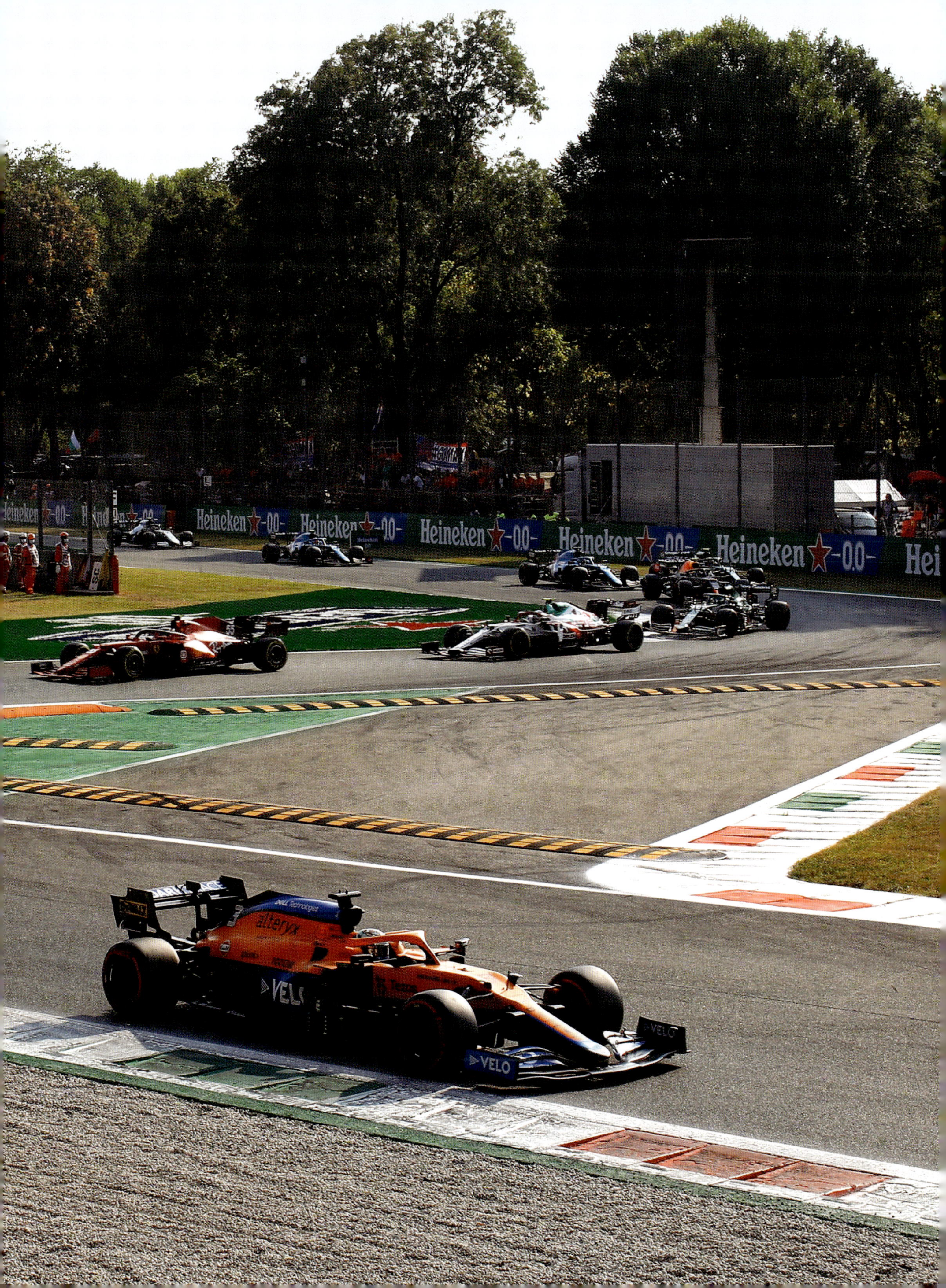
Heineken 0.0
alteryx
VELO

MOMENTS

Monza's layout is simply made for drama and it has provided some truly epic and memorable races over the decades.

Moss beats the heat

The cancellation of the Belgian and Dutch GPs led to Pescara being included in the 1957 World Championship. Enzo Ferrari had run on this 15.5-mile (25-km) circuit of public roads between the Adriatic coast and the Abruzzi mountains in 1924 and nothing had changed when F1 arrived. Juan Manuel Fangio put his Maserati on pole, with only Stirling Moss looking a likely challenger in his Vanwall as Ferrari had decided to boycott the race. It was extremely hot on race day and Moss soon led after passing fast-starting Luigi Musso. Then Musso's engine lost oil, but Fangio slid on it and buckled a wheel, leaving Moss so far ahead that he was able to pit for a cool drink and still win.

The ugliest of internecine squabbles

Ferrari teammates Didier Pironi and Gilles Villeneuve got on as well as any teammates can, but it turned nasty at the San Marino GP in 1982, a race already harmed by ten of the seventeen teams withdrawing after a disagreement with FISA. Although Renault filled the front row, Alain Prost retired early on, then René Arnoux pulled off at two-thirds distance. This put Ferrari in front and orders were given that Villeneuve would stay in front and that they would slow to save fuel. Except that Pironi sprinted clear. Villeneuve caught and passed him, then slowed again. With a lap to go, Pironi let Villeneuve back in front. Then, as they cruised home, Pironi dived past to win. Villeneuve never spoke to him again.

Five cars covered by just 0.61 second

The finish to the 1971 Italian GP remains the closest group finish ever. Clay Regazzoni's Ferrari and Ronnie Peterson's March set the early pace, with the lead changing constantly as the cars hunted in packs down the straights that were still uninterrupted by chicanes. Going into the final lap, Peterson led a five-car pack, but François Cevert's Tyrrell was in front as they entered the last corner, only for Peterson to outbrake him and slither wide. As Cevert tucked in, he found BRM's Peter Gethin diving up the inside and, as they accelerated to the line, it was Gethin who won, by just 0.01 seconds from Peterson, 0.09 seconds from Cevert, 0.18 seconds from Surtees' Mike Hailwood and 0.61 seconds from his BRM teammate Howden Ganley.

Opposite: Pierre Gasly has a private moment after taking a surprise breakthrough win at Monza in 2020.

Below: Peter Gethin (arm aloft) wins, just, for BRM in 1971's incredible five-way final lap sort-out.

Gasly strikes for the underdogs

Every now and then a surprise result occurs in F1 that makes everyone smile. This was one of those moments as Pierre Gasly won for little-fancied AlphaTauri, by working his way forward from tenth on the grid. He was helped when Mercedes' race leader Lewis Hamilton entered the pits just after they had been closed after Kevin Magnussen's Haas had broken down in the pit entry. Gasly had pitted just in time and was third when the pits reopened and this turned into the lead. For the rest of the race, Gasly defended from Carlos Sainz Jr and he held on to beat the McLaren driver by the slender margin of 0.4 seconds. The sight of Gasly sitting alone on the podium after the ceremony, soaking up the moment, was priceless.

LIECHTENSTEIN

This tiny country in the mountains between Austria and Switzerland has no circuits, yet it still managed to produce one F1 driver.

With no circuits within the mountainous confines of Liechtenstein, Rikky von Opel was forced to head abroad to develop his racing skills. He could certainly afford to do so, as he was a scion of the family that owned Opel. However, Rikky chose, as many rich kids did, to race under an alias, choosing the name 'Antonio Bronco' for his first year of racing in Formula Ford in 1970 to keep his family name out of the headlines should anything go wrong.

Having performed to his expectations, he stepped up to British F3 in 1971 then did well enough to win the secondary title with a works Ensign in 1972.

Then, displaying the power that comes with prodigious wealth, he simply commissioned Ensign to build an F1 car for 1973. Not surprisingly, as Mo Nunn's Ensign outfit was learning about F1 too, their results weren't spectacular, with thirteenth place at Silverstone his best showing. Moving across to Brabham after being disappointed with the new Ensign at the first race of 1974, Rikky was able to finish in ninth place twice, in the Swedish and Dutch GPs, in more competitive machinery. However, he then failed to qualify for the French GP at Dijon-Prenois and elected to end his time as a racing driver.

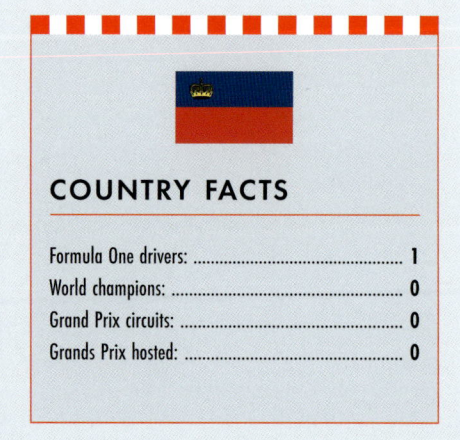

COUNTRY FACTS

Formula One drivers:	1
World champions:	0
Grand Prix circuits:	0
Grands Prix hosted:	0

Below: Rikky von Opel's brief time in F1 was not a success but he remains his country's only F1 driver.

MONACO

Monaco will always have a special place in F1. It may be an anachronism, but it's still the jewel in the World Championship crown.

Monaco offers F1 a wonderful anachronism with its old-fashioned but famous course.

The principality has been home for the majority of F1 drivers for the past forty years, partly because of its attractive climate, but principally for the tax breaks that it offers them. It also means that they get to be able to sleep in their own beds for their home Grand Prix, something that is becoming ever more of a treat as they race in twenty-four-plus Grands Prix per year.

Only four true Monegasque drivers have had a shot at F1 though, starting with Louis Chiron and the less well-known non-qualifier André Testut in the 1950s, followed by Olivier Beretta in the 1990s and, most recently, by far the best of the lot of them: Charles Leclerc.

The Grand Prix also offers an opportunity for other drivers to race on the world-famous street course, with F3 drivers traditionally competing in the main support race, although this is now for F2 drivers. A race for the Porsche Supercup has also long been on the agenda.

In the past decade, there has been a historic Grand Prix meeting every second year, with an array of races for cars that raced here over the years, not only in the Grand Prix but also in the support races. There have also been visits by the FIA Formula E Championship, albeit to race on a shortened loop of the circuit as the full climb up to Casino Square and then on around the full lap would have sapped too much power out of these electric-powered cars.

COUNTRY FACTS

Formula One drivers:	4

Selected F1 drivers:
- **Olivier Beretta**
- **Charles Leclerc**
- **Louis Chiron**
- **André Testut**

World champions:	0
Grand Prix circuits:	1

- **Monte Carlo**

Grands Prix hosted:	70

Below: Monaco is still F1's most famous venue.

DRIVERS

Charles Leclerc was brought up and educated in Monaco, so he had a special desire to try to become the first hometown winner around its streets.

Louis Chiron

Louis (pictured below) was a Grand Prix star in the late 1920s and the 1930s, with the Monegasque racer winning his home Grand Prix in a Bugatti in 1931. He would later win the French GP in 1937 and, after the Second World War, in 1947. He was fifty when the World Championship started in 1950, but still had enough speed to finish third on his home track for Maserati. In 1951, Louis reverted to driving a Lago-Talbot, but his days in a competitive F1 car were behind him, as a ride with OSCA yielded little in 1953. His final Monaco GP came in 1958, but he failed to qualify.

Olivier Beretta

There was a thirty-six-year gap between Louis Chiron and André Testut trying to qualify for their home Grand Prix in 1958 and the next Monegasque driver. This was Olivier, who had shone in F3 by finishing third in his home race and winning in Pau in 1990. He broke a wrist in the 1991 Monaco F3 GP. Stepping up to F3000 produced one win but generally spasmodic results across two seasons. However, Olivier broke into F1 with Larrousse in 1994 and came seventh in Germany before his funds ran out. He turned to GTs and was FIA champion with Karl Wendlinger in a Viper in 1999.

André Testut

The least illustrious of the quartet of Monegasque F1 drivers to date was André Testut who failed to qualify his patriotically liveried Maserati 250F in 1958 when running in Monaco's racing colours of white with red details. More of a sportscar specialist than a single-seater racer, André had a second attempt to qualify for his home race in 1959, but that ended in disappointment, although a relief for his rivals, as he was fourteen seconds off the pace. Later that year, he landed a works OSCA drive for the Le Mans 24 Hours (sharing with Jean Laroche), but was forced to retire from the race.

Charles Leclerc

Charles's father contested Monaco's F3 Grand Prix, so it was likely that he too would race. He was very good, too, ranking second in World and European karting when he was fifteen. This form continued through junior single-seater series before he won the GP3 and F2 titles in 2016 and 2017 respectively. Ferrari already had Charles under its wing and placed him with Sauber for 2018 as the Swiss team used Ferrari engines. Charles made everyone in F1 sit up with his pace in qualifying and this was enough to win him a seat with Ferrari for 2019. He very nearly won on his second outing, at Sakhir, and went on to take his first win at Spa-Francorchamps with a second victory coming, pleasingly, on Ferrari's home ground at Monza. Since then, Charles has been Ferrari's team leader, but first Mercedes' then Red Bull's form, plus Ferrari's tactical blunders, have kept him from the title. However his three wins in 2024, including glory in Monaco, show that he is back on track.

CIRCUIT

There have been nips and tucks across the years, but the very essence of this tight, twisting and narrow circuit remains today.

Monaco

It seemed like a brilliant idea when Anthony Nogues proposed a race around the streets in the 1920s to help boost Monaco's image, but the fact that F1 continues to have a Grand Prix here annually is harder to comprehend, as many circuits have been dropped for falling below the World Championship's criteria for circuit safety, paddock space and having all the requisite facilities. Yet, of course, Monaco will surely always be part of the show, as it's the one above all others that the sponsors love, for the glamour of the setting and the chance to impress their clients. For the teams, the working conditions, although improved, are still below standard.

The circuit has scarcely changed since that first Grand Prix in 1922, as it still runs alongside the harbour, climbs to Casino Square and snakes its way back again. There have been tweaks to at least give modern F1 cars more of a chance of carrying some speed, but the essence of the place remains. The desire to be seen on the grid before the race draws in celebrities like bees to a honey pot.

The start-finish straight is more of a curve, with a slight kink to the left before the drivers must drop to third gear and turn right. This takes them onto a climb up through a kink at Beau Rivage then a fast left at Massenet. The track has barriers right at the circuit's edge at this point, but the cars are released from this claustrophobic setting when they burst into Casino Square before dropping to Mirabeau. This tight right leads them downhill to the Grand Hotel hairpin before a pair of right-handers take them onto a long, curving run through a tunnel under the hotel.

The track then drops again down to the Nouvelle Chicane as it reaches the harbourside and drivers race past the giant motor yachts there, through a high-speed left at Tabac, before a left-right flick is followed by the reverse as the cars negotiate the Piscine section. La Rascasse comes next, a right-hand hairpin into a short climb and a flick through Virage Antony Nogues to complete the lap. Places to try to pass a rival on this narrow, twisting circuit are few and far between and, with contemporary F1 cars being so wide and long, it is all but impossible, with most place-changing coming when the cars pit.

In a way, the more outdated the circuit becomes, the more its charm and link with its illustrious past cements its place on the World Championship calendar. F1 wouldn't be the same without Monaco.

Opposite: Sergio Pérez leads for Red Bull Racing in 2022, followed by Ferrari's Carlos Sainz Jr.

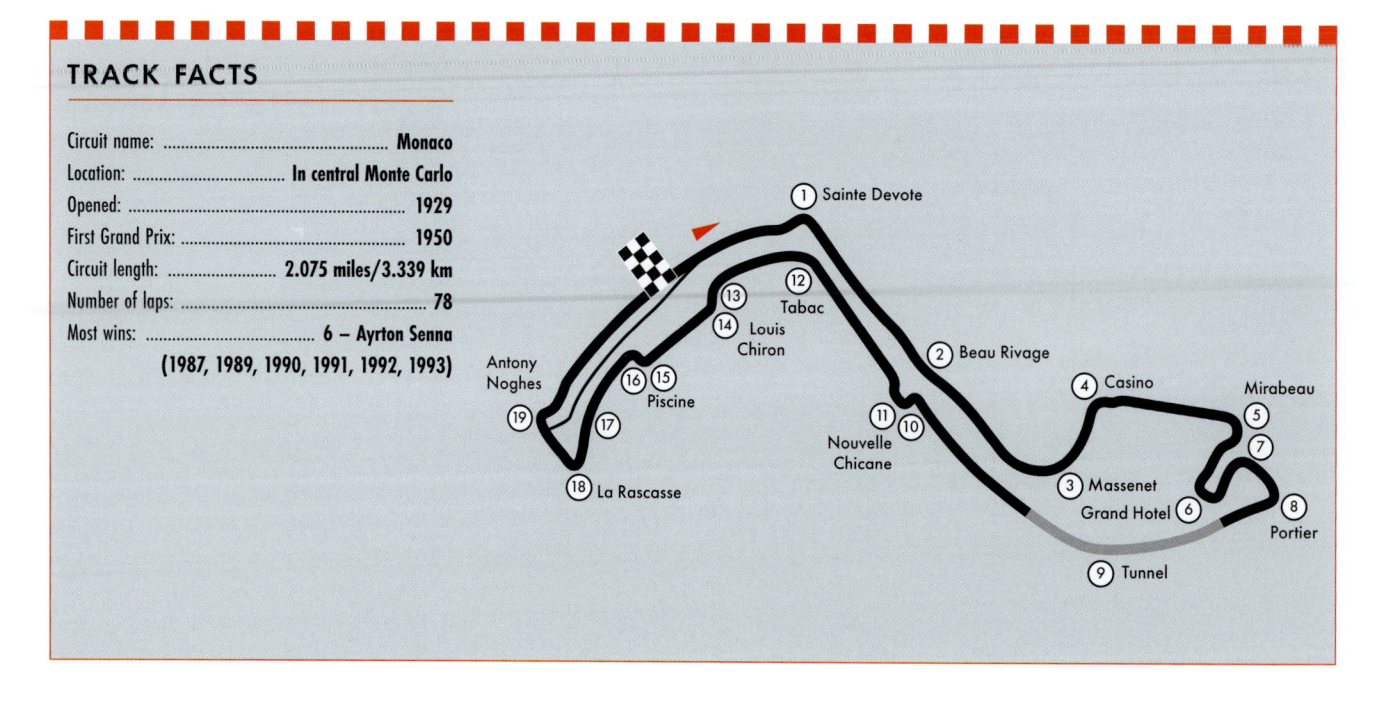

TRACK FACTS

Circuit name:	Monaco
Location:	In central Monte Carlo
Opened:	1929
First Grand Prix:	1950
Circuit length:	2.075 miles/3.339 km
Number of laps:	78
Most wins:	6 – Ayrton Senna (1987, 1989, 1990, 1991, 1992, 1993)

MONACO 85

MOMENTS

The lack of space is always a factor, while even great races have been shaped by a brush with the barriers.

Brains beat brawn

Stirling Moss produced some extraordinary drives, but his run to victory here in 1961 was one of his greatest as he took on and beat the Ferraris that would dominate the first year of a new set of technical regulations. Moss was driving a Rob Walker Racing Team Lotus 18 and stuck it on pole, but Richie Ginther used the extra 30bhp his Ferrari possessed to blast into the lead. Moss gave chase and took over after fourteen laps, then spent the next eighty-six being put under pressure from Ferrari's Phil Hill and Ginther. Yet Moss resisted all attacks, knowing that, with his power deficit, he couldn't afford to lose momentum when trying to find a way to lap backmarkers. He never cracked.

Brabham falls at the last

It had seemed that Jackie Stewart would win in 1970, but then his Tyrrell-run March hit engine troubles. This promoted veteran Jack Brabham into the lead, but the forty-four-year-old, already a winner of the opening round at Kyalami, was being hunted down by Jochen Rindt. The Austrian's pursuit was relentless, and his Lotus got ever closer to the Brabham, bringing the gap down from fourteen seconds to just one-and-a-half seconds going into the last lap. With just two corner to go, though, the normally unflappable Brabham was distracted by backmarkers, missed his braking point for the Gasworks Hairpin, slid into the barrier and Rindt dived through to win. Brabham reversed out and was still able to finish second ahead of Henri Pescarolo's Matra.

Does anybody want to win?

The closing laps of the 1982 Monaco GP was a lap charter's nightmare. It had been a race that looked to be heading to Renault, with first René Arnoux then Alain Prost leading. That was until lap seventy-four of seventy-six, but then Prost slid off on a track that was turning from greasy to wet. Riccardo Patrese took over for Brabham, but he too spun off at the start of the penultimate lap at the hairpin. This put Didier Pironi in front, and he led onto the final lap, but then his Ferrari's electrics failed, which should have put Andrea de Cesaris's Alfa Romeo into the lead, but it ran out of fuel and so a recovered Patrese came through to take it.

Opposite: Daniel Ricciardo turns in to Tabac corner on his way to victory for Red Bull Racing in 2018.

Below: Andrea de Cesaris might have triumphed for Alfa Romeo in 1982, but his car ran out of fuel.

Leclerc is Monaco's first hero

It took the end of Mercedes' years of domination then the sudden falling away of Red Bull Racing's competitive edge as the 2024 World Championship got into its swing for Charles Leclerc to think that he might have a chance of winning at home in his Ferrari. Ferrari was the first team to match up to Red Bull to put Max Verstappen under pressure. Carlos Sainz Jr had won the third round, in Saudi Arabia, but it was Charles who led the way in Monaco. He put his SF24 onto pole, something that is extra vital here, and his cause was helped by an early red flag, as this allowed the drivers to make a tyre change before the restart and, as they didn't need to change again, he was never challenged.

NETHERLANDS

Dutch motorsport has always been strong, but it had to wait for Max Verstappen for Zandvoort to host a champion of its own.

Zandvoort, opened in 1948, is the home of Dutch motorsport, a sporting venue tucked into the coastal dunes that is easily reached by train from Amsterdam. It was made on roads built there by the Germans in the Second World War, with linking sections suggested by John Hugenholtz, giving it a fast, flowing course up and over the dunes.

The challenge was an immediate attraction and, after a quartet of trial Grands Prix between 1948 and 1951, Zandvoort was selected to host a round of the World Championship in 1952. Alberto Ascari won it at a canter as he led home a Ferrari one-two-three. Thus, the Netherlands became a largely regular part of the championship for the next three decades. Despite only a trickle of Dutch drivers taking part, huge crowds flooded in, albeit never entirely sure whether they would be basking in sunshine, blasted with sand as winds gusted off the North Sea or drenched by a passing storm. Yet, they knew that they would be entertained, as there were some great vantage points and the Tarzan hairpin at the end of the main straight always provided overtaking and incident.

As F1 became more global, the Dutch GP was culled after 1985 to make way for more races beyond Europe and it took both modernisation and the rise of Max Verstappen for it to make its return.

Dutch fans have another circuit, Assen. However, this has always focused more on motorbike racing, and four-wheeled competition there is largely for national series.

Opposite: Race winner Max Verstappen waving to his fans during the Dutch GP in 2022.

Below: Mario Andretti and Ronnie Peterson make their escape for Lotus on lap 1 in 1978.

COUNTRY FACTS

Formula One drivers: 16
Selected F1 drivers:
- Christijan Albers
- Michael Bleekemolen
- Nyck de Vries
- Robert Doornbos
- Jan Flinterman
- Carel Godin de Beaufort
- Boy Hayje
- Jan Lammers
- Ben Pon
- Huub Rothengatter
- Giedo van der Garde
- Dries van der Lof
- Gijs van Lennep
- Jos Verstappen
- Max Verstappen
- Roelof Wunderink

World champions: .... 1 – Max Verstappen (2021, 2022, 2023, 2024)
Grand Prix circuits: 1
- Zandvoort

Grands Prix hosted: 34

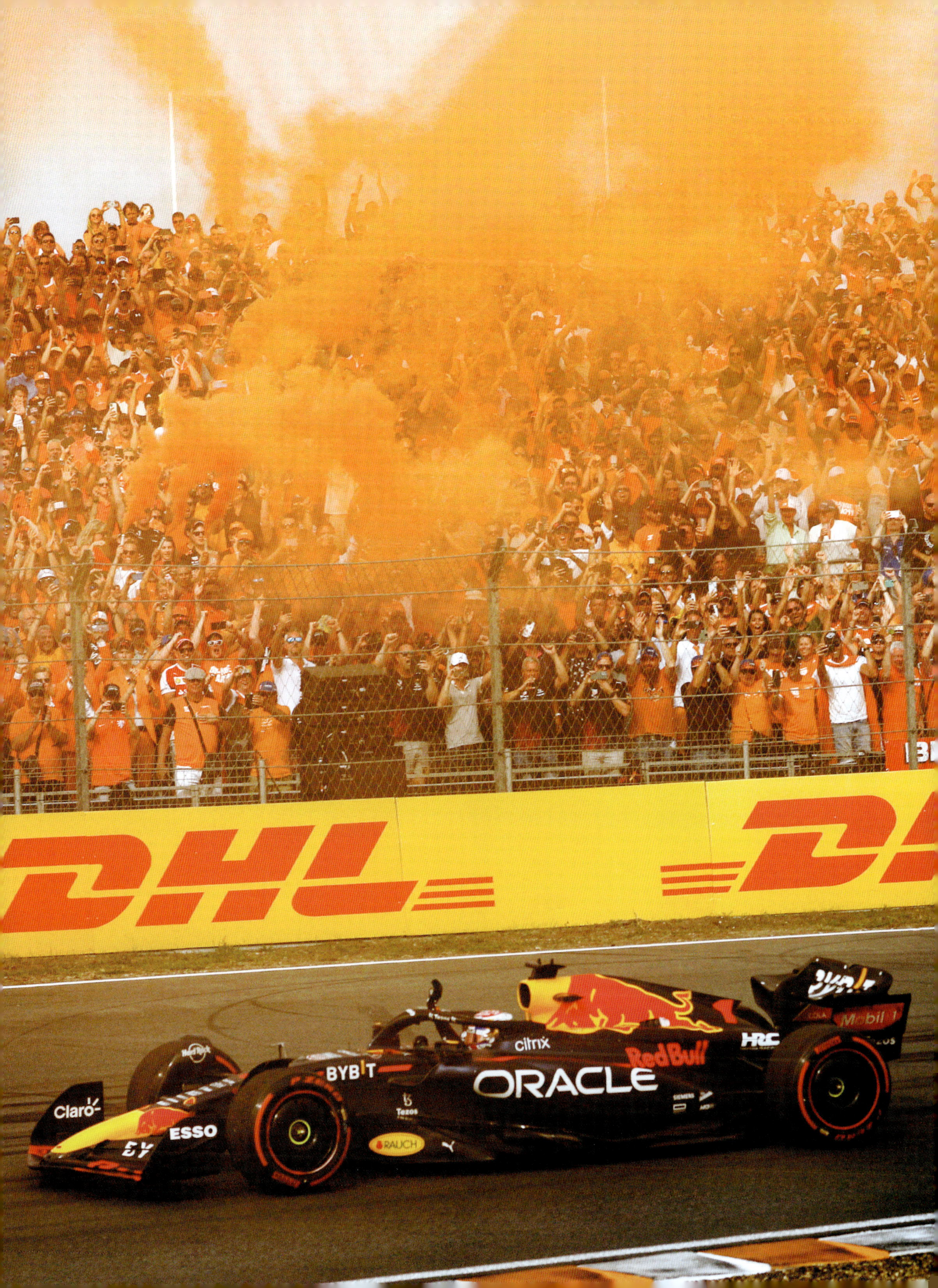
DHL
ORACLE
Red Bull
BYBIT
ESSO
citrix
Mobil 1
Claro
RAUCH

DRIVERS

Despite having produced only sixteen Grand Prix drivers, the Netherlands' one Grand Prix winner, Max Verstappen, is also a multiple world champion.

Carel Godin de Beaufort

Racing was very different when this Dutch aristocrat did Grands Prix for fun in the late 1950s. At first, this jovial giant campaigned in a Porsche sportscar against the F1 regulars, run as Ecurie Maarsbergen, which was named after his family seat. In 1960, though, Carel had a new approach, having bought an ex-Stirling Moss Cooper. For 1961, he opted for a Porsche, run in Dutch sporting orange. He kept this for the next three seasons, claiming points for four sixth-place finishes and three podium finishes in non-championship events. Sadly, Carel crashed fatally in practice for the 1964 German GP.

Huub Rothengatter

Huub's results were seldom sparkling in the junior categories, but he was dogged and kept chasing deals that would keep him in the game. He was never fast enough to be a future F1 champion as he worked through F3 and then F2, but he did win an F2 round at Zolder. That was in 1980 and it took until 1984 before he graduated to F1. This came with Spirit, and he raced to eighth at Monza. Then he moved to Osella and finished seventh in Adelaide, then took an eighth for Zakspeed in 1986. After that, he helped Jos Verstappen to reach F1.

Christijan Albers

His father may have been a rallycross driver, but Christijan preferred single-seaters. After success in Formula Ford, he won races in German F3 and then the title in 1999. Then came Formula 3000, but this wasn't a success, so he raced in DTM, first as a privateer then as a works driver, just losing out to Bernd Schneider in 2003. With Minardi looking for funds, Christijan got his F1 break in 2005 and was gifted fifth place at Indianapolis when the Michelin runners withdrew. Moving to Midland produced less and he was dropped midway through 2007 after forty-six starts.

Jos Verstappen

Jos set a template for Max to copy. After shining in karts, he went straight to Formula Opel Lotus and won the Benelux series. He then won the 1993 German F3 title before impressing enough in an end-of-season F1 test to become Benetton's test driver. With JJ Lehto still recovering from a neck injury, Jos stepped up to partner Michael Schumacher for the first two races and then again when the Finn lost form. After a pit fire at Hockenheim, Jos finished third in Hungary and Belgium, but lost his ride and raced on in F1 with Simtek, Arrows, Tyrrell, Stewart and Minardi, appearing in 106 Grands Prix.

Max Verstappen

Racing blood courses through Max's veins, as his father Jos drove in over 100 Grands Prix and his mother Sophie (Kumpen) was a top kart racer. Having been world kart champion in 2013, Max was immediately a race winner in European F3 and beat his father by going from karts to F1 in two years (rather than three) when Scuderia Toro Rosso signed him for 2015. Although just seventeen, Max was far from timid and claimed a pair of fourth places. Although he started a second campaign with Toro Rosso, he was promoted to Red Bull Racing after just four rounds and promptly won on his first outing, at Barcelona. Mercedes and Lewis Hamilton dominated the next few years, but Max became the heir apparent and grabbed a gift in Abu Dhabi to pip Hamilton to another title. In 2022, Max won a record fifteen rounds and waltzed to another title. He scorched to nineteen wins and a third title in 2023 but had to fight much harder for his fourth in 2024.

CIRCUIT

Flowing in its original form, the Zandvoort circuit has been chopped and changed, even being given a banked final corner for F1's return.

Zandvoort

Zandvoort in its original form was majestic, a circuit on which the cars could really be stretched through wide open corners. The lap began with a lightly banked right-hand hairpin, Tarzan, out of which the circuit doubled back behind the paddock.

Subtle undulations and a gentle esses through Gerlach Bocht brought the cars to one of the key corners, Hugenholtz Bocht. Named after the circuit director, it dropped into a compression, turned through 180 degrees and then fed the cars up a climb to Hunserug. Accelerating hard, the next few corners twisted right and left, all taken flat-out. Then came the trickiest bend of all: Scheivlak. This is all but blind on entry as it dives over a crest before plunging down to the right. The return from the circuit's furthest point of the pits was fast, with the final corner onto the main straight, Bosuit taken in top gear.

Then came problems in the 1980s as the loss of F1 after 1985 led to financial ruin. This led to Zandvoort being taken over by the town council and being chopped in length, having to turn right at Hunserug, with this cut-through removing almost half of its length to move it further away from a holiday camp to its east. The traditionalists were horrified, but Zandvoort survived.

In 1999, Zandvoort got back its best corner as the run to Scheivlak was restored, with a hard right not far beyond it feeding the cars into a sequence of twisting corners to reinstate a lap length similar to the original. Then, with investment from Prince Bernhard van Oranje, a Grand Prix dream was rekindled. Upgrades included the opening out and banking of Hugenholtz Bocht and the final corner, the Arie Luyendyk Bocht being banked to eighteen degrees to help cars slingshot onto the straight.

The long wait for Zandvoort's return to the F1 calendar was due to a have ended in 2020, but Dutch fans had to wait a further year as the world adjusted to the COVID pandemic. It's safe to say, though, with Max Verstappen rising towards the top in F1, the delay only whetted their appetite.

Opposite: Jan Lammers guides his Theodore through Hugenholtz Bocht in his home race in 1982.

Following pages: Hugenholtz Bocht was turned into a lightly banked corner for its F1 return in 2021.

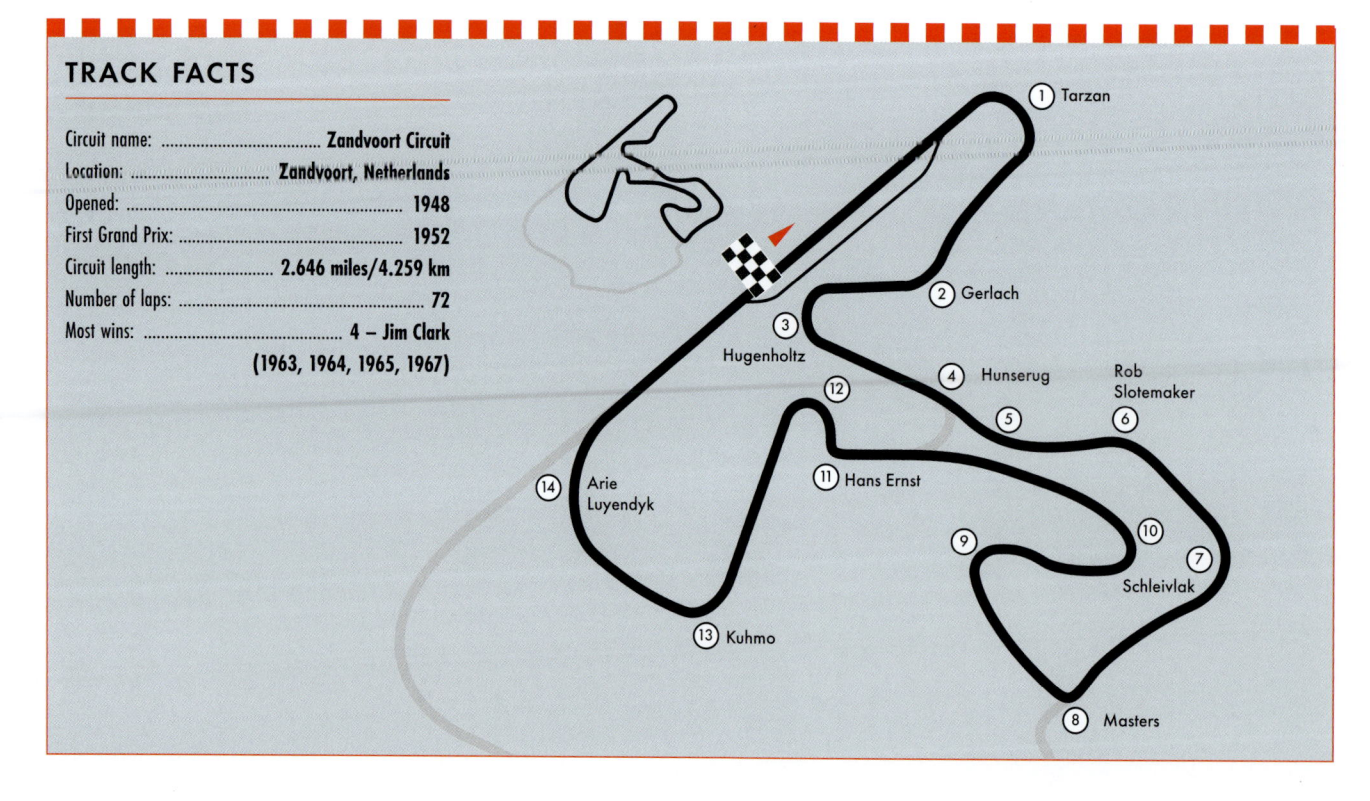

TRACK FACTS

Circuit name:	**Zandvoort Circuit**
Location:	**Zandvoort, Netherlands**
Opened:	1948
First Grand Prix:	1952
Circuit length:	2.646 miles/4.259 km
Number of laps:	72
Most wins:	4 – Jim Clark (1963, 1964, 1965, 1967)

1. Tarzan
2. Gerlach
3. Hugenholtz
4. Hunserug
5.
6. Rob Slotemaker
7. Schleivlak
8. Masters
9.
10.
11. Hans Ernst
12.
13. Kuhmo
14. Arie Luyendyk

NETHERLANDS

NETHERLANDS | 93

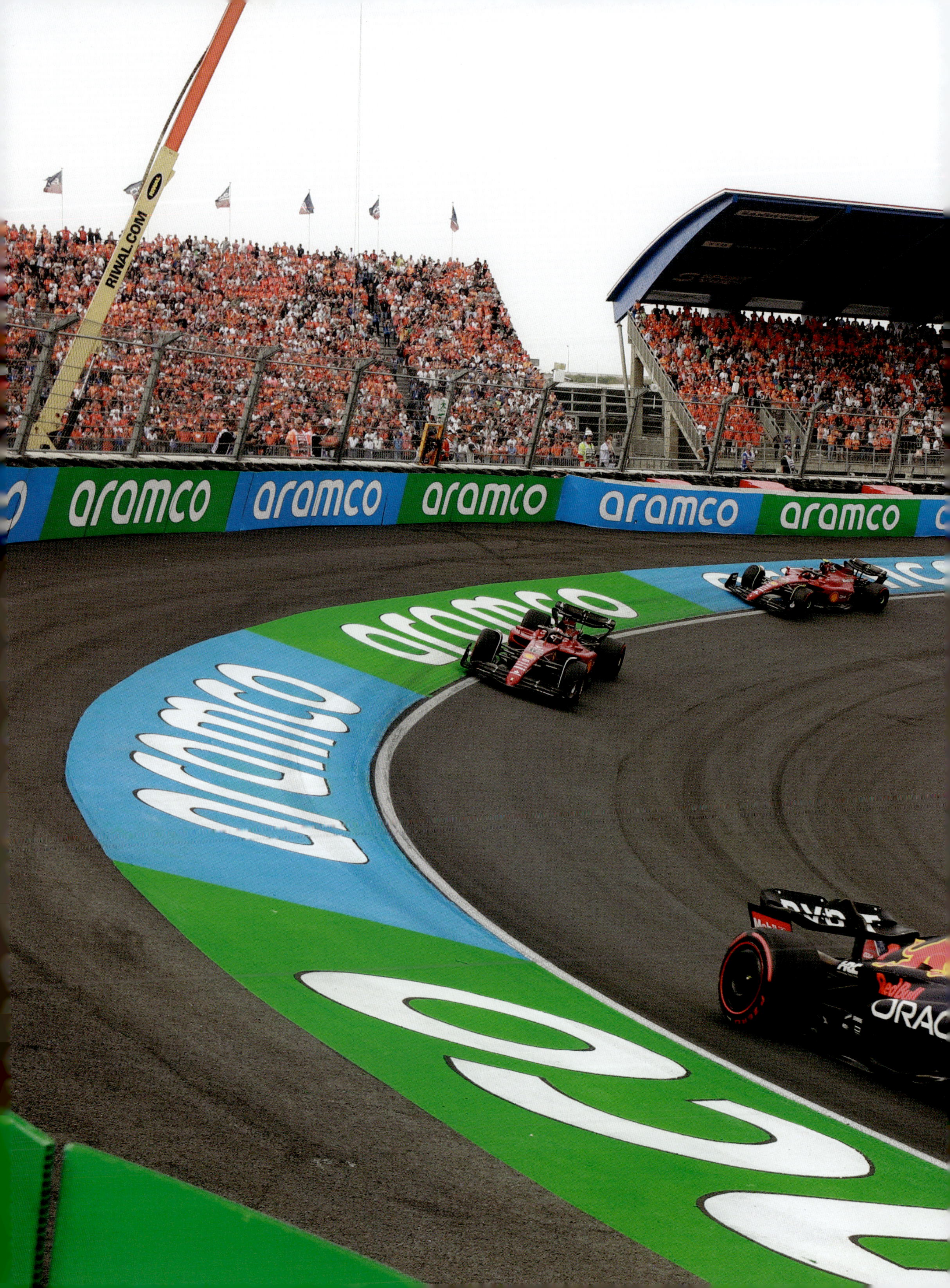
RIWAL.COM
aramco
aramco
aramco
aramco
aramco

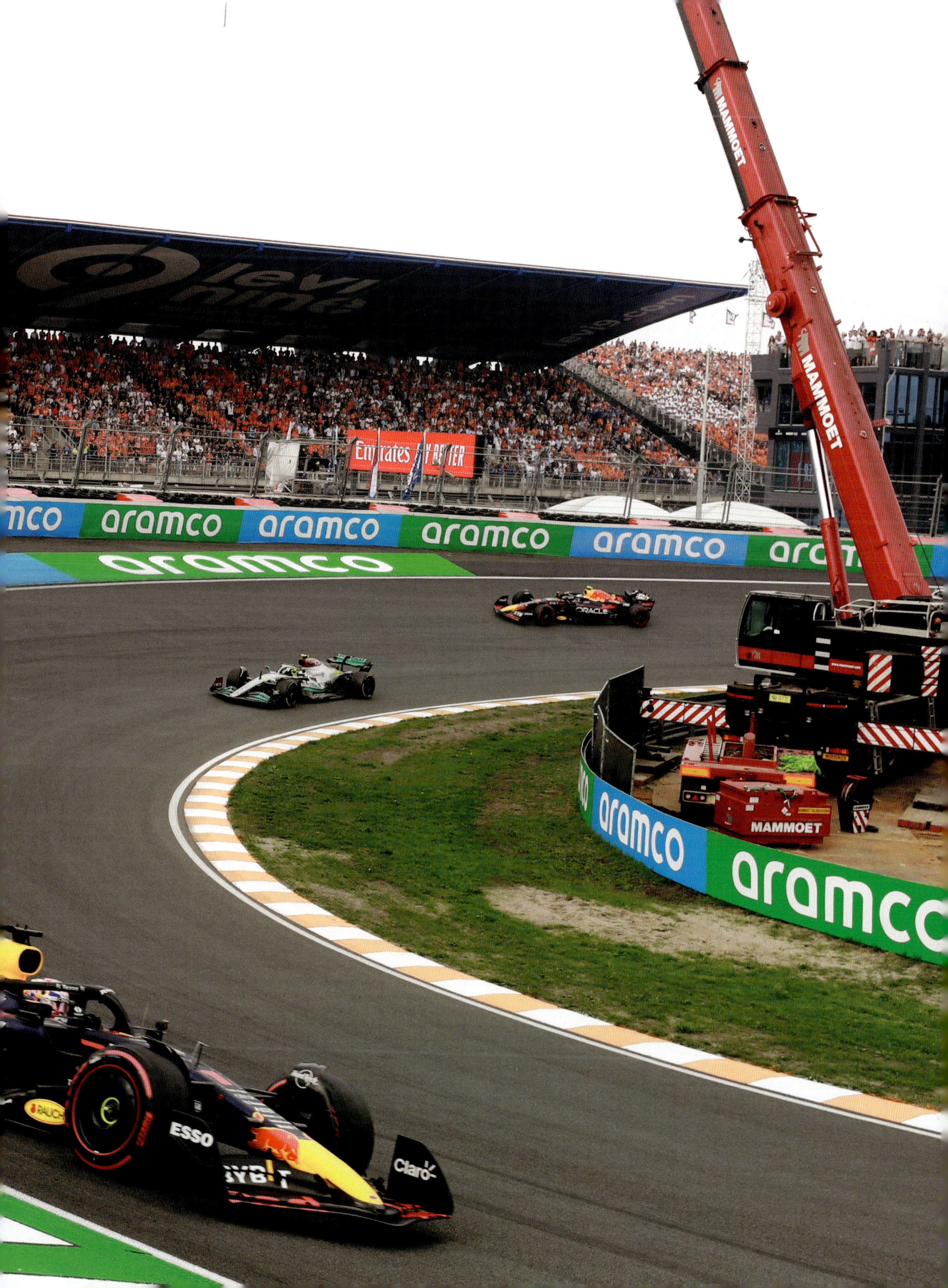
MAMMOET
aramco
ORACLE
ESSO
Claro

Clark finds the gears

What made the 1967 Dutch GP a historic event was the debut of an engine. Financed by Ford and built by Cosworth, the new DFV V8 not only secured a win first time out but would go on to become the backbone of F1 into the 1980s. Graham Hill had done most of the testing and claimed pole by half a second over Dan Gurney's Eagle, while Jim Clark could only finish eighth after suffering wheel bearing failures. Hill rocketed clear at the start and was passing tailenders by the eighth lap. It wasn't to be his day, though, as a camshaft drive broke and Clark passed Jack Brabham for the lead on lap sixteen and then went on to win with ease. The writing was on the wall.

MOMENTS

Zandvoort's history is peppered with great races, including surprise results like BRM's long-awaited first win, but this quartet stand out.

Lauda's last victory

Arriving in 1985 for what would be the last Dutch GP for decades, Niki Lauda had just five points after ten rounds after a run of retirements, whereas McLaren teammate Alain Prost shared the championship lead on fifty points with Ferrari's Michele Alboreto. Yet, the Austrian wanted to shine in his final F1 season, and it all came good at Zandvoort. Tenth on the grid didn't suggest it would be his day, but Niki had elected to pit early on this abrasive track, and it was just enough to get ahead when Prost stopped thirteen laps later. The French ace caught him with a few laps to go, but, despite trying everything, Niki held him off for one of his most satisfying victories.

Hunt's breakthrough

BRM stunned everyone when it scored a surprise maiden win here in 1959. Sixteen years later, another British team, Hesketh, did the same, although this came as less of a surprise as James Hunt had finished second in Argentina. It was an all-Ferrari front row of Niki Lauda and Clay Regazzoni, with Hunt and Jody Scheckter's Tyrrell sharing row two. The track was damp, and Hunt was the first to pit for slick tyres on the seventh lap as it dried. This proved key, as Lauda waited a further six laps before pitting. When the Austrian rejoined, Hunt was ahead and so was Shadow's Jean-Pierre Jarier, who held him off until lap forty-four. Lauda caught Hunt with twenty laps to go, but he had no tricks to defeat the British driver.

Verstappen delights at home

The 2021 season marked F1's return to Zandvoort after thirty-six years off the F1 calendar and it produced the result the fans had been waiting for as Max Verstappen raced to a home win. With the grandstands and dunes overflowing with orange-clad Max fans, he pipped Lewis Hamilton to claim pole. This was vital as, although it had been hoped that the new banked final corner would increase the amount of overtaking, this didn't appear to be as easy as thought. Max then made a break before the first corner, shaking Hamilton's Mercedes off his tail and thus removing the threat of a passing move using DRS. Hamilton even made a third pit stop to try to challenge, but it didn't work, and the crowd went wild.

Opposite: Jim Clark leads the field over the dunes in 1967 as he heads for a debut win for the Ford DFV.

Below: James Hunt keeps his Hesketh ahead of Niki Lauda's Ferrari on his way to his first F1 victory.

POLAND

Poland has a Grand Prix winner in Robert Kubica, but the country needs an international-standard circuit if it wants to boost its domestic scene.

COUNTRY FACTS

Formula One drivers:	1
World champions:	0
Grand Prix circuits:	0
Grands Prix hosted:	0

There was a circuit in the centre of the city of Lwów in the early 1930s, with top names Hans Stuck and Rudolf Caracciola winning the Polish GP for Auto Union and Mercedes respectively. The circuit was unpopular, though, as its narrow course was dotted with sharp corners. Then, with the arrival of communism after the Second World War, there was no further international motor racing.

Racing picked up again in the 1970s, with the best drivers racing rudimentary Formula Junior cars, competing on a circuit built near Poznań in 1977. However, once communism ended, all aspiring drivers knew that they would need to go beyond their borders to succeed.

One such driver who did this is Robert Kubica, who followed a stellar karting career in which Lewis Hamilton considered him his most talented rival. He advanced through junior single-seaters and, after taking the World Series by Renault title in 2005, earned his F1 break with BMW Sauber midway through 2006. Incredibly, a third-place finish on his third outing confirmed his talent and he went on to give the team its first win in Canada in 2008. Cruelly, an accident in a pre-season rally left him with an awful arm injury that wrecked his F1 career.

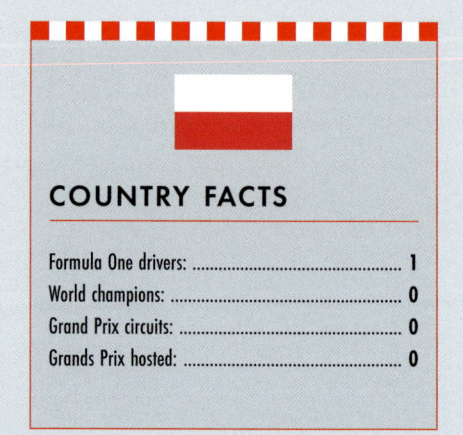

Below: Robert Kubica, shown here at the start of the 2007 season, remains Poland's only F1 driver.

PORTUGAL

Portugal has long lagged behind neighbouring Spain in the battle to be the predominant racing country on the Iberian Peninsula.

Racing in Portugal began in the 1930s when the Vila Real circuit near Porto hosted a street race. Its route in and out of town included a narrow bridge and even ran over a railway level-crossing. This was used for sportscar and touring-car races into the 1970s, but it had by then been superseded by a street circuit in the heart of Porto that hosted the first Portuguese GP, for sportscars, in 1951. As the World Championship expanded, Portugal got to join its ranks in 1958 with the first of two Grands Prix separated by a one-off in 1959 around the Monsanto Park circuit near to the country's capital, Lisbon. However, this circuit scared many of the drivers and F1 never returned, although the circuit continued to be used until 1971.

It took a further fourteen years until F1 returned, this time to Estoril, just inland from the Atlantic coast to the west of Lisbon, and it would hold the Grand Prix through until 1996 before being considered no longer safe enough for F1. The World Rally Championship used to use Estoril for a super stage through until 2001, drawing huge crowds in this rally-mad country.

Most of the racing in Portugal today is in championships for F3 and GT cars shared with their Spanish counterparts.

The Algarve International Circuit became the country's premier circuit after it opened in 2008 and it attracts top-level international championships like the European Le Mans Series and, due to COVID, a one-off Grand Prix in 2020.

COUNTRY FACTS

Formula One drivers: 4
Selected F1 drivers:
- Pedro Lamy
- Tiago Monteiro

World champions: 0
Grand Prix circuits: 4
- Algarve International Circuit
- Monsanto Park
- Porto
- Estoril

Grands Prix hosted: 16

Below: Lewis Hamilton's Mercedes returns to the pits after taking pole for the 2020 Portuguese GP..

DRIVERS

Pedro Lamy has been Portugal's standout F1 driver, but Portuguese-speaking Ayrton Senna landed the result that delighted the fans the most.

Pedro Lamy

Pedro was a fast-rising star in the junior single-seater series, winning the European GM Lotus in 1991 and the German F3 crown in 1992. He had a strong campaign in F3000 in 1993 and then made it to F1 with Lotus as a late-season replacement for Alex Zanardi. However, soon after scoring his best F1 finish, eighth place in the Pacific GP in 1994, Pedro had an incredible escape from an accident in testing at Silverstone when his Lotus had its rear wing break and he flipped over a fence and landed at the entrance of a pedestrian tunnel. This broke both of Pedro's knees and one of his wrists, but he recovered to be able to race again in 1995, joining tail-end Minardi for whom he raced for the next two years. Later, he became a successful GT driver, landing the FIA GT2 title in 1998 and winning the Nürburgring 24 Hours four times.

Tiago Monteiro

This second-generation racer was seen as good but not great. Yet he got his foot in the F1 door when Minardi signed him as a test driver in 2004. After a change of ownership, Jordan signed him for 2005 and Tiago's greatest result came in the United States GP when he finished third out of six starters, after the seven teams using Michelin rubber boycotted the race following a Michelin tyre failure. The team was renamed as Midland for 2006 and Tiago came ninth in Hungary, but his F1 days were soon over, and Tiago then spent over a decade in the World Touring Car series.

MOMENTS

Though only intermittently held throughout the history of F1, the Portuguese Grand Prix has provided ample classic moments.

An act of sporting behaviour

Stirling Moss could have been world champion in 1958 after adding to his points haul by winning at Porto, but he spoke up in support of rival Mike Hawthorn, whose Ferrari had suffered brake failure on the final lap and gone up an escape road. To rejoin, Hawthorn went in the opposite direction to the flow of the lap and was disqualified. Moss had noticed what had happened, yet defended his compatriot, saying that Hawthorn had only been going in the wrong direction in the escape road and so his second place was restored, and Hawthorn went on to beat Moss by one point to claim the title.

Senna sets the standard

Ayrton Senna put on one of the performances of the ages when he won the 1985 Portuguese GP. Having been set to open his Lotus account until retiring from third place in Brazil, he qualified on pole at Estoril and simply drove away from his rivals in extremely wet conditions. Senna did have one wild moment when he had all four wheels on a soaked grass verge, but he survived that and was able to motor on to give Lotus its first win since 1982, beating the only other driver on the same lap, Ferrari's Michele Alboreto, by just over a minute.

Villeneuve goes around the outside

The final Grand Prix held at Estoril came in 1996 and it is remembered for two things. One was for Jacques Villeneuve's phenomenal pass to overtake around the outside at the long final corner, and the other reason was that his victory meant that Williams teammate Damon Hill would have to head to the final round with his quest to become the sport's first second-generation world champion still unsecured. Villeneuve started badly and fell to fourth behind Michael Schumacher. When they caught a backmarker, Schumacher hesitated and Villeneuve passed, taking the long way around. He then closed on Hill and ran out the winner.

Below: Ayrton Senna produced one of F1's legendary performances when he won for Lotus in 1985.

CIRCUITS

Estoril has hosted the majority of Portuguese GPs, but Porto, Monsanto Park and the Algarve International Circuit have all had a go.

Estoril

Opened in 1972, Estoril proved itself by hosting an F2 meeting in 1975, but it had fallen into disrepair by the 1980s and required upgrades before the World Championship agreed to visit in 1984. Built on rocky, scrub-covered hillside, the circuit dips from the start line down to the first corner, a fast right-hander followed further down the slope by another. The track continues to drop from there to Turn 3 at which it doubles back up the slope to feed into a hairpin onto the infield straight. After a kink in its middle, the straight dips again down to a second hairpin, then enters a series of right-handers as it drops to the lowest point of the lap. A fast uphill right was replaced by a slow loop with a steep hairpin following an accident that left Alex Caffi's Footwork trapped in a dangerous position in 1990. After a slow left-hander, Estoril's final corner is a wonderful, wide, 180-degree turn around which Jacques Villeneuve pulled off an outstanding passing move in 1996. Estoril lost its World Championship slot after that year, as it was no longer deemed to be up to F1 safety standards due to its lack of run-off areas.

Porto

Porto had hosted the Portuguese GP four times before F1 came to town in 1958 and 1960, as the race was initially for sportscars. The track was marked by a near total lack of protection from kerbs and lamp posts, save for a few straw bales that largely just marked the course. Even running across a broad square just after the start, the cars had to traverse tramlines. The 4.6-mile (7.4-km) lap started with a pair of left-handers and then climbed the Avenida da Boavista followed by another ascending straight. From there, a twisting but flowing descent brought the cars back down to the pits.

Algarve International Circuit

If there was anything positive about the COVID pandemic when it hit in 2020, it was that the reshuffling of the World Championship calendar led to the inclusion of some brilliant circuits at which F1 would otherwise never have hosted a Grand Prix. This undulating circuit inland from Portimao was probably the prime example. Opened in 2008, it had become popular for sportscar, GT and motorbike racing, but its twists and its marked dips and climbs worked brilliantly to make F1 look more dynamic, with the drop from Turn 11 and then the steep climb up to Turn 12 providing the most notable challenge.

Opposite: Jacque Villeneuve keeps his Williams ahead of Michael Schumacher's Ferrari at Estoril in 1996 as he heads for the fourth win of his rookie season.

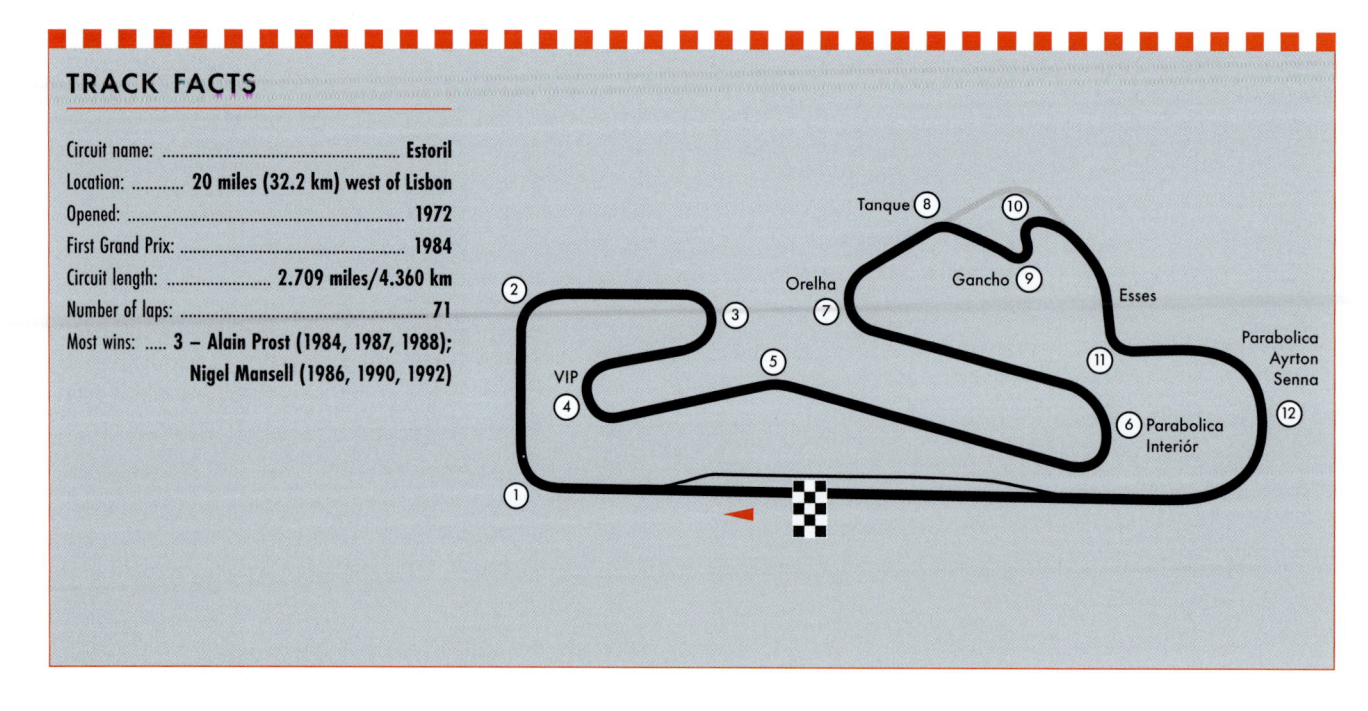

TRACK FACTS

Circuit name:	Estoril
Location:	20 miles (32.2 km) west of Lisbon
Opened:	1972
First Grand Prix:	1984
Circuit length:	2.709 miles/4.360 km
Number of laps:	71
Most wins:	3 – Alain Prost (1984, 1987, 1988); Nigel Mansell (1986, 1990, 1992)

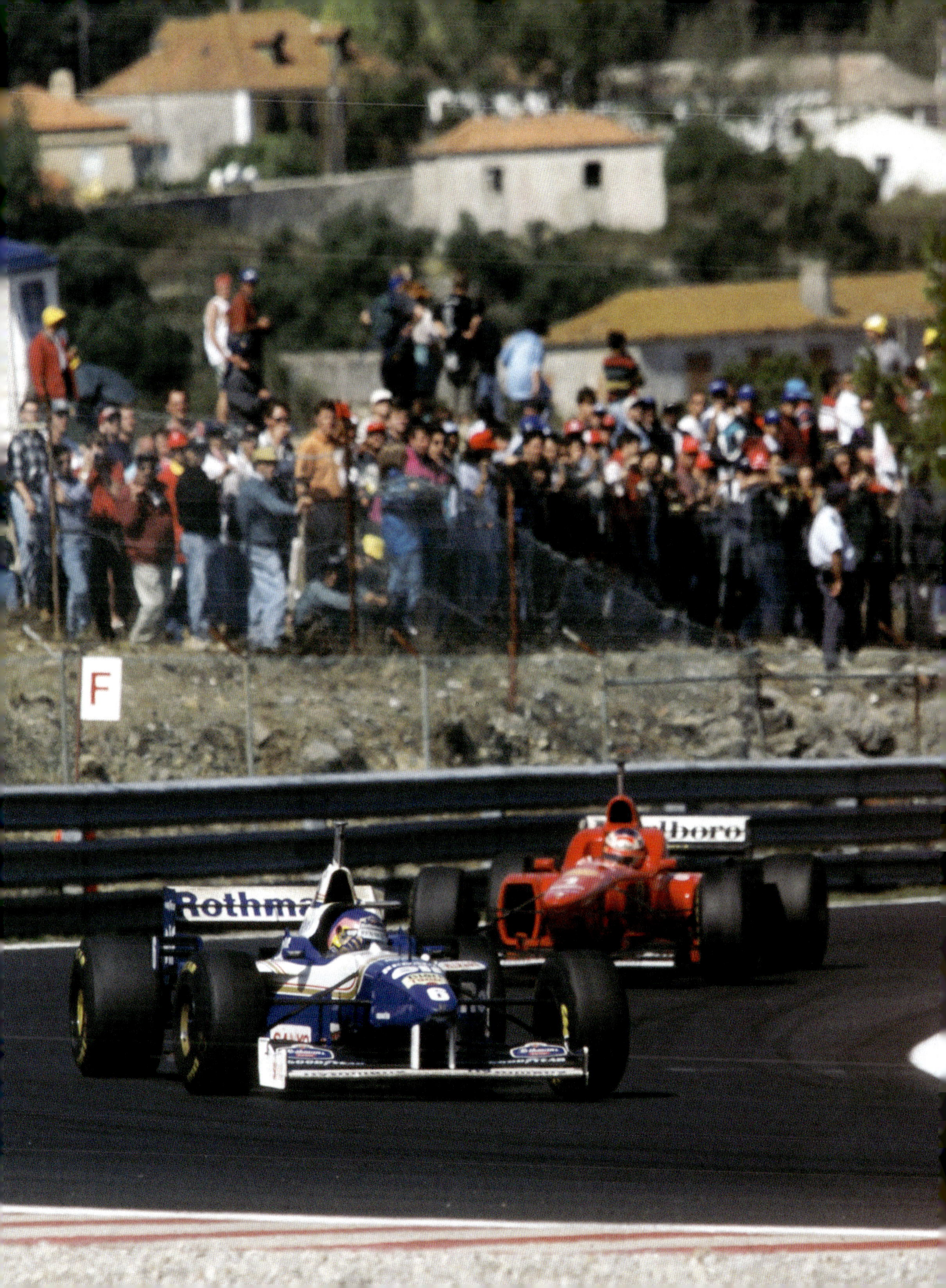
F
Rothma

RUSSIA

There had long been plans for a Russian GP, usually in or near Moscow, but the Black Sea resort of Sochi beat them to it.

There was no way that the World Championship was going to hold a race when the USSR was still in existence, although talk of a Russian GP soon surfaced when communism went into abatement. Yet it took far longer than many expected, especially considering how Hungary stole a march by hosting a Grand Prix from 1986. At this point, there was a domestic racing scene centred on Estonia using Formula Easter single-seaters, but little else.

F1 ringmaster Bernie Ecclestone was keen to take F1 to Russia and plans were mooted time and again for a Grand Prix to be held in or near Moscow or St Petersburg. The Moscow Raceway was built, but this was ignored as it was decided that a street circuit might be better.

While these plans were being considered and dropped, Vitaly Petrov led the way for Russian drivers in F1, joining the World Championship in 2010 with Renault.

Then President Putin took an interest and Russia got its Grand Prix after all, albeit not in its leading cities but in Sochi, a coastal resort on the Black Sea. He decided that it would work if F1 used some of the infrastructure that had been put up to host the Olympic Winter Games in 2014 and the first race was to get it ready in time.

Daniil Kvyat was next, stepping up to F1 in 2014, with Sergey Sirotkin and Nikita Mazepin also making the grade since then. However, the Russian GP was dropped from the calendar following Russia's invasion of Ukraine in 2022.

COUNTRY FACTS

Formula One drivers: 4
World champions: 0
Grand Prix circuits: 1
- **Sochi Autodrom**
Grands Prix hosted: 8

Opposite: Lando Norris might have taken his first F1 win here in 2021 but stayed on slicks after it rained.

Below: Russia's national colours on display on the gird in the pre-race ceremony at the 2014 Russian GP.

WHEN YOU DRIVE NEVER DRIN
НИ КАПЛИ АЛКОГОЛЯ ЗА РУЛЕ
ineken
ARKTRACE

Daniil Kvyat

With an eye to helping the most promising Russian driver when the first Russian GP was shaping up, Red Bull helped Daniil to advance, and he proved up to the challenge when he won the GP3 title in 2013. This opened a door for him at Scuderia Toro Rosso just in time for that first Russian GP and he did well enough to be promoted to Red Bull Racing for 2015 when he came second in Hungary. However, he was dropped back to Toro Rosso in 2016 when Max Verstappen replaced him. Daniil's final F1 season, in 2020, produced a fourth-place finish at Imola.

Sochi Autodrom

The first race for the Sochi Autodrom was to get it ready in time for its F1 debut in October 2014 as the builders were allowed in to modify some of the facilities that it shared with the Winter Olympic Games at the end of February. Yet, they did the job and F1 had somewhere new to go racing. The lap offered a good run to Turn 2, where most of the overtaking happens, particularly on lap one, and then an unusually long and broad arc to the left after that, but it's otherwise stop-start in nature apart from the curving return straight.

Above: The charge to the first corner on lap 1 of the 2017 Russian GP, a race won by Valtteri Bottas.

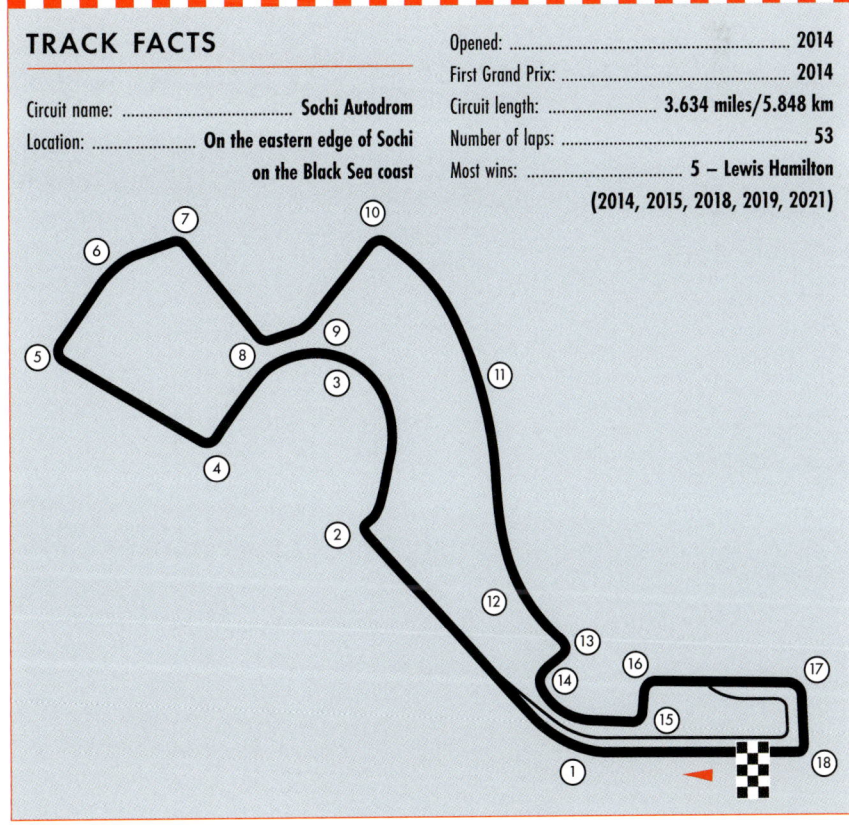

TRACK FACTS

Circuit name: Sochi Autodrom
Location: On the eastern edge of Sochi on the Black Sea coast
Opened: 2014
First Grand Prix: 2014
Circuit length: 3.634 miles/5.848 km
Number of laps: 53
Most wins: 5 – Lewis Hamilton (2014, 2015, 2018, 2019, 2021)

RUSSIA | 107

SPAIN

Part of the championship since 1951, Spain moved its Grand Prix around, but the fans preferred bikes, until Fernando Alonso arrived.

Spain took an unusual approach when its Grand Prix became part of the World Championship in 1951, as it took the race to the people by running it on a street circuit in the Pedralbes district of Barcelona rather than using Lasarte, an 11-mile (17.7-km) loop of public roads near San Sebastian that had hosted the Spanish GP in the 1930s.

Pedralbes held the Grand Prix again in 1954 before a thirteen-year gap, until the purpose-built Jarama circuit outside Madrid brought F1 back to Spain.

Designed by John Hugenholtz, the creator of the Zandvoort and Suzuka circuits, it held the race on and off until 1990. In that time, though, Barcelona welcomed F1 back four times between 1969 and 1975 on another street circuit. This one was in its hilltop Montjuich Park, on a track used in the 1930s, but it didn't return after four spectators were killed in 1975.

After four years off the calendar, Jerez landed the race in 1986 and kept it until 1990, but this circuit in south-west Spain fell out of favour following Martin Donnelly's near fatal accident in 1990, although it would later host the roving European GP twice.

Spain was still seeking a star of its own and took a stride towards this when the Barcelona-Catalunya circuit opened in 1991. It was modern and loved by the teams for then regular testing, but its layout counted against it producing memorable races. Despite a street race in Valencia hosting five European GPs, the Barcelona-Catalunya circuit remains the home of the Spanish GP.

Below: Jochen Mass triumphed in the shortened 1975 Spanish GP at Montjuich Park.

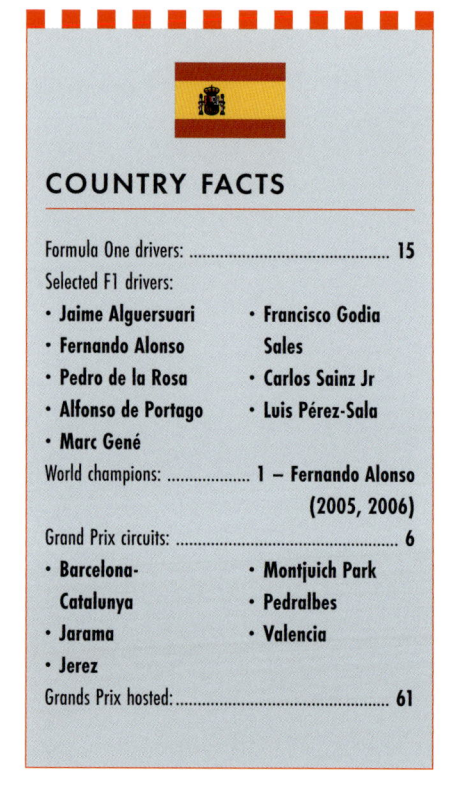

COUNTRY FACTS

Formula One drivers: 15
Selected F1 drivers:
- Jaime Alguersuari
- Fernando Alonso
- Pedro de la Rosa
- Alfonso de Portago
- Marc Gené
- Francisco Godia Sales
- Carlos Sainz Jr
- Luis Pérez-Sala

World champions: .... 1 – Fernando Alonso (2005, 2006)

Grand Prix circuits: 6
- Barcelona-Catalunya
- Jarama
- Jerez
- Montjuich Park
- Pedralbes
- Valencia

Grands Prix hosted: 61

Opposite: Carlos Sainz Jr races his Ferrari past his home fans as he heads towards fourth place in 2022.

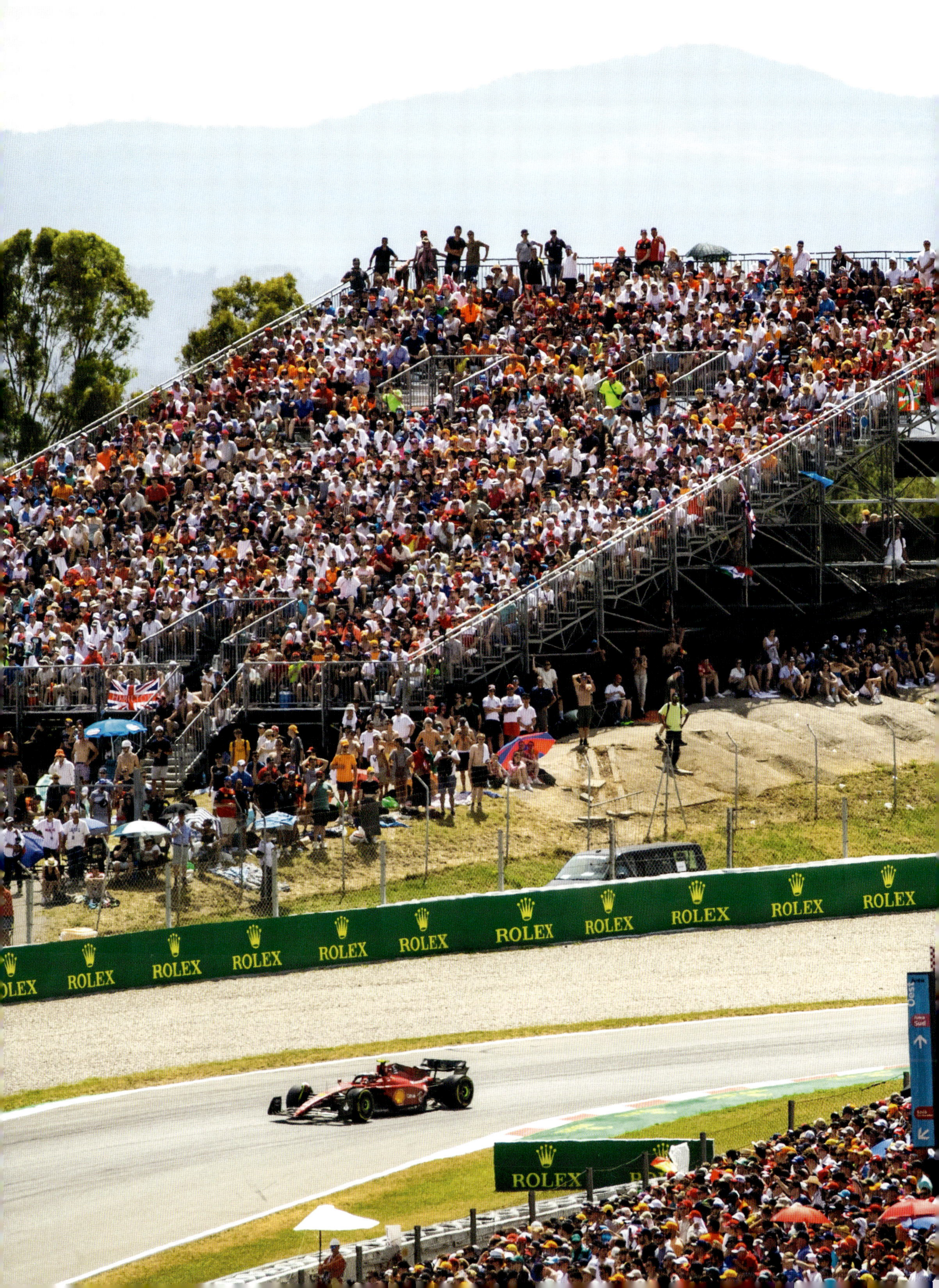
ROLEX

DRIVERS

Alfonso de Portago shone in the 1950s, but it took until Fernando Alonso's arrival for Spain to have its first F1 winner.

Fernando Alonso

One of F1's mysteries is how Fernando has claimed just two titles. Having become world kart champion at fifteen, he won the first single-seater series he contested and stepped straight up into F1's feeder formula. He scored a dominant win at Spa and that was enough to land him his F1 break with Minardi for his third year in cars. A more competitive ride with Benetton in 2003 helped him to his first win in Hungary. In 2005, with the team racing as Renault, Fernando took the first of two F1 titles in a row, ending the Schumacher-Ferrari period of dominance. Yet, after being pipped with McLaren in 2007, poor career choices hurt him as a return to Renault didn't work. So he joined Ferrari and won as he pleased, but not titles. His second spell at McLaren was a disaster, but a swansong at Aston Martin, twenty-two years after his F1 debut, showed that he is still among the best as he grabbed eight podium finishes to rank fourth in 2023.

Carlos Sainz Jr

A lot of sportspeople follow a successful sporting parent into their arena. Not so Carlos Sainz Jr, as he chose not to follow his World Rally champion namesake into rallying. After winning a Formula Renault title, he stepped up to GP3 and was on the verge of losing Red Bull backing, but he won the 2014 Formula Renault 3.5 series and this got him into F1 with Scuderia Toro Rosso and he was soon scoring points. He moved to Renault then McLaren, for whom he peaked with a second-place finish at Monza. However, it took a move to Ferrari for Carlos Jr to become a grand prix winner.

Alfonso de Portago

De Portago was a dashing aristocrat who shone in equestrian events, twice contesting the Grand National, and he was also an international-level swimmer, as well as being in the Spanish bobsleigh team. When he took up motor racing in 1954, he went straight in at the deep end, coming second in the Buenos Aires 1,000km sportscar race. After racing impressively for Ferrari in 1955, 'Fon' was given his World Championship F1 debut in 1956 and shared second place at Silverstone. All set for 1957, he was killed when a tyre is thought to have exploded near the end of the Mille Miglia road race.

Pedro de la Rosa

It wasn't until this racer from Barcelona hit F1 in 1999 that Spanish fans had much to be excited about. Points first time out for sixth place for Arrows in Melbourne promised much, but the car was usually fragile. A move to Jaguar in 2001 produced a fifth-place finish, but it wasn't until Pedro went to McLaren midway through 2006, when Juan Pablo Montoya quit after three years as its test driver, that he had a decent car and his reward was a career-best second place in Hungary. His second F1 return was in 2010 when he joined Sauber.

Jaime Alguersuari

The patronage of Red Bull helped a lot of up-and-coming drivers. However, although this scholarship scheme had a ruthless way of culling all but the best, Jaime was one who made it all the way to F1. In fact, he was the then youngest F1 starter, at nineteen years four months and three days when he was promoted midway through 2009 when he contested the 2009 Hungarian GP. Racing for Scuderia Toro Rosso, Jaime achieved a pair of seventh-place finishes in 2011, but he was then dropped for 2012 to make way for Daniel Ricciardo and quit F1 to be a DJ.

CIRCUITS

Shared by six circuits, the Spanish GP has long been firmly rooted at Barcelona-Catalunya, although talks of a Madrid street race are circulating.

Barcelona-Catalunya

It is hard for modern F1 fans to think of a time when Spain might not have had a front-running F1 driver, as Fernando Alonso has been at the top of the game for more than two decades. However, although the desire was always there, Spain simply wasn't producing the drivers for the first five decades of the World Championship. Conversely, world motorcycle racing titles were seemingly gathered for fun.

Often seen as a hindrance to national progress, the antagonism between capital city Madrid and Barcelona actually helped in Spanish motor racing circles, as it led to the money being found for the Catalunyan region to build a circuit of its own. A plot was chosen in rolling hills to the north of Barcelona and a modern circuit was laid out to use its terrain well. With a fast corner onto a long pit straight that led into a tight first corner, there was the overtaking opportunity that racing requires, although a bold move into Turn 1 would compromise their line into Turn 2. Campsa, Turn 9, was also a hallmark corner, entered over a blind brow and it was crucial as it led the cars onto an infield straight down to another possible passing place. The circuit uses its gradient changes well, as drivers have to position their cars just right for the uphill kink and near 180-degree uphill right-hander that follows to set themselves up for the homeward sweep to the finish.

Sadly, in the name of safety, a chicane was inserted between Turn 13 and the final corner in 2007 and this made the races more processional as it all but eliminated any opportunity for a driver trying to pass a rival into Turn 1. As a consequence, races at Barcelona-Catalunya tended to be less exciting than they needed to be. Fortunately, sense prevailed and the chicane was finally removed in time for the World Championship's visit in 2023.

With this tweak and other updates, aspiring Spanish racers have this and a growing number of Spanish circuits on which to cut their teeth, with Motorland Aragon, Navarra and Valencia's Ricardo Tormo circuits all now part of the mix.

The circuit continues to draw in the crowds, with Fernando Alonso and Carlos Sainz Jr both going well, but great scraps remain rare and it's the odd results, like Pastor Maldonado's win in 2012, that are remembered most.

Opposite: The scrap between Nigel Mansell's Williams and Ayrton Senna's McLaren was extraordinarily close and fraught on the circuit's debut in 1991.

TRACK FACTS

Circuit name: **Circuit de Barcelona-Catalunya**
Location: **15 miles (24.1 km) north of Barcelona at Montmeló**
Opened: **1991**
First Grand Prix: **1991**
Circuit length: **2.894 miles/4.657 km**
Number of laps: **66**
Most wins: **6 – Michael Schumacher (1995, 1996, 2001, 2002, 2003, 2004)**

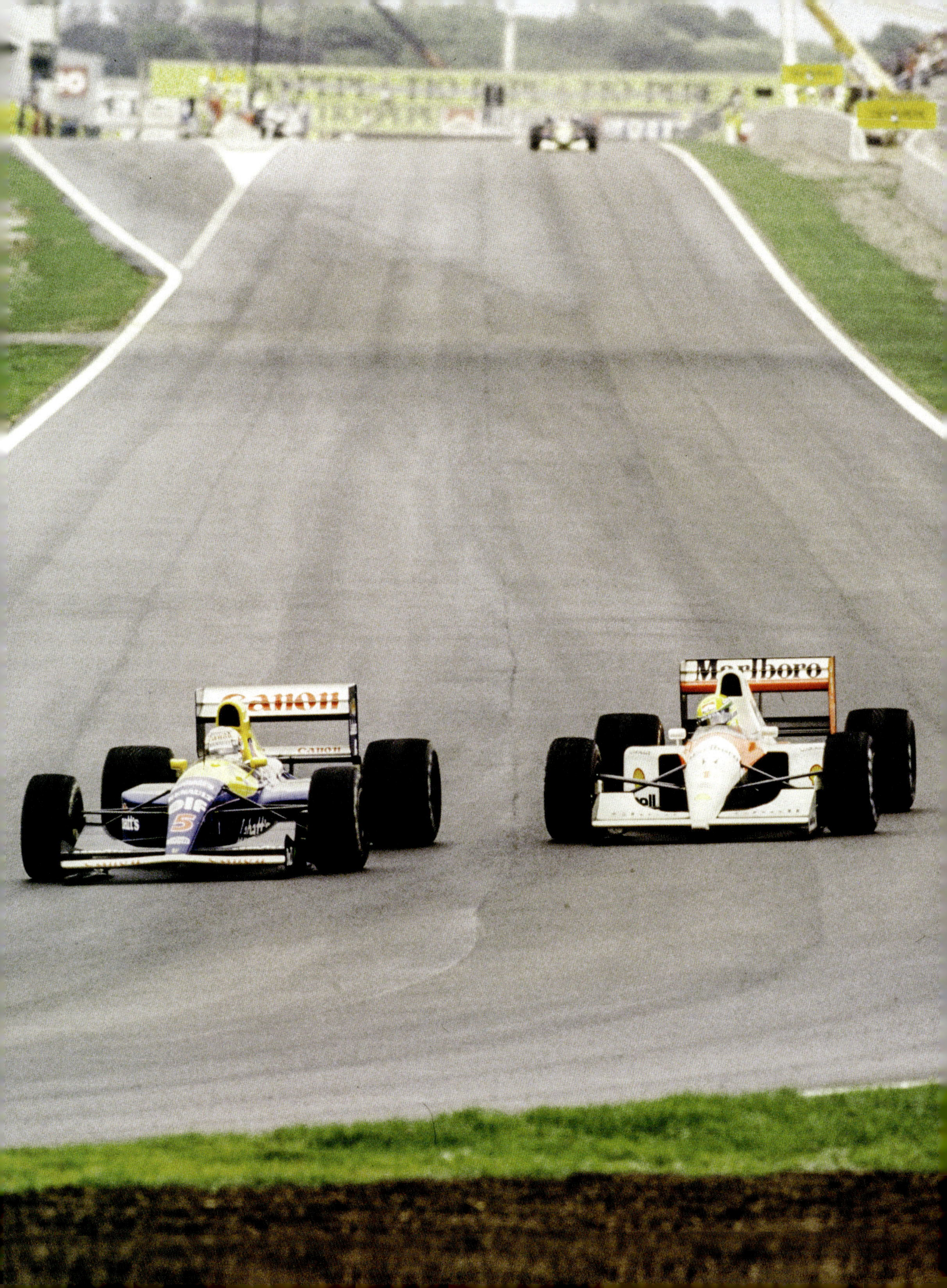
Canon
Marlboro

Marlboro
Marlboro
Marlboro Marlboro Marlboro Marlboro Marlboro
Marlboro Marlboro Marlboro Marlboro
LUBRI
MICHELIN
Leyland

Jarama

Despite its long main straight feeding into a tight first corner, in a style replicated three decades later by F1 circuit architect Hermann Tilke, Jarama was never considered a great circuit.

When it opened in 1967, though, it was thought to be modern alongside traditional circuits such as Spa-Francorchamps and the Nürburgring. However, track designer John Hugenholtz was angered by his plans having been altered, with a twisting infield section included instead of a straight leading through an open corner onto the start-finish straight. This meant that the nature of the track was low-speed and constricted.

The start of the lap offered a kinked entry to a long right-hander followed by a short straight intersected by the Varzi kink and then a pair of tight corners. Accelerating out of the second of these, Farina, the drivers would then power through an uphill kink and climb the Rampa Pegaso to a pair of rights that turned the cars downward through an esse to a lightly banked corner that would then turn them up to Monza, a tight right that would then feed them through the high-speed final corner, Tunel, onto the start-finish straight.

A decade after F1 left, the lap had a loop added to the top of the Rampa Pegaso, taking the track further up the slope.

After passing the test of holding a non-championship race in its first season, won by Jim Clark for Lotus, Jarama hosted the World Championship for the first time the following year and Lotus won again, this time with Graham Hill at the helm, just a month after Clark's death in an F2 race at Hockenheim.

The final Spanish GP to be run at Jarama was in 1981 and the way that Gilles Villeneuve's powerful but badly handling Ferrari was able to hold up a train of faster rivals proved that F1 had outgrown the place. The cars needed places where they could overtake and, for cars of F1 level of performance, there were none.

Left: Gilles Villeneuve held up a queue of cars with his Ferrari in 1981 but held on to take victory.

Following pages: Fernando Alonso punches the air with delight as he thrills the fans by scoring a home win with his Renault in 2006.

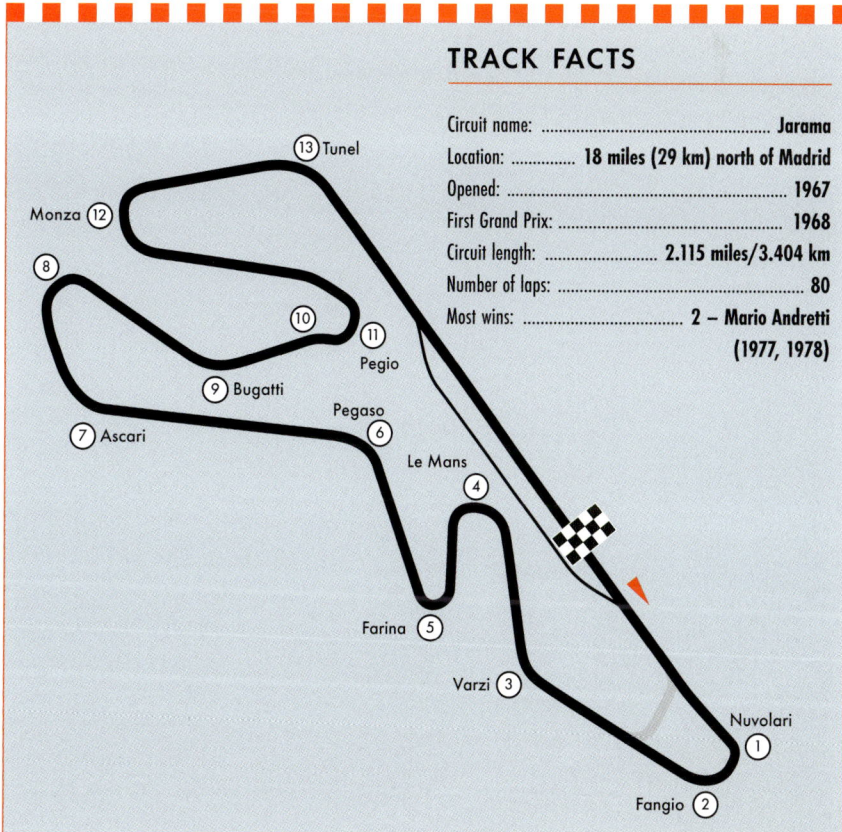

TRACK FACTS

Circuit name:	Jarama
Location:	18 miles (29 km) north of Madrid
Opened:	1967
First Grand Prix:	1968
Circuit length:	2.115 miles/3.404 km
Number of laps:	80
Most wins:	2 – Mario Andretti (1977, 1978)

SPAIN | 115

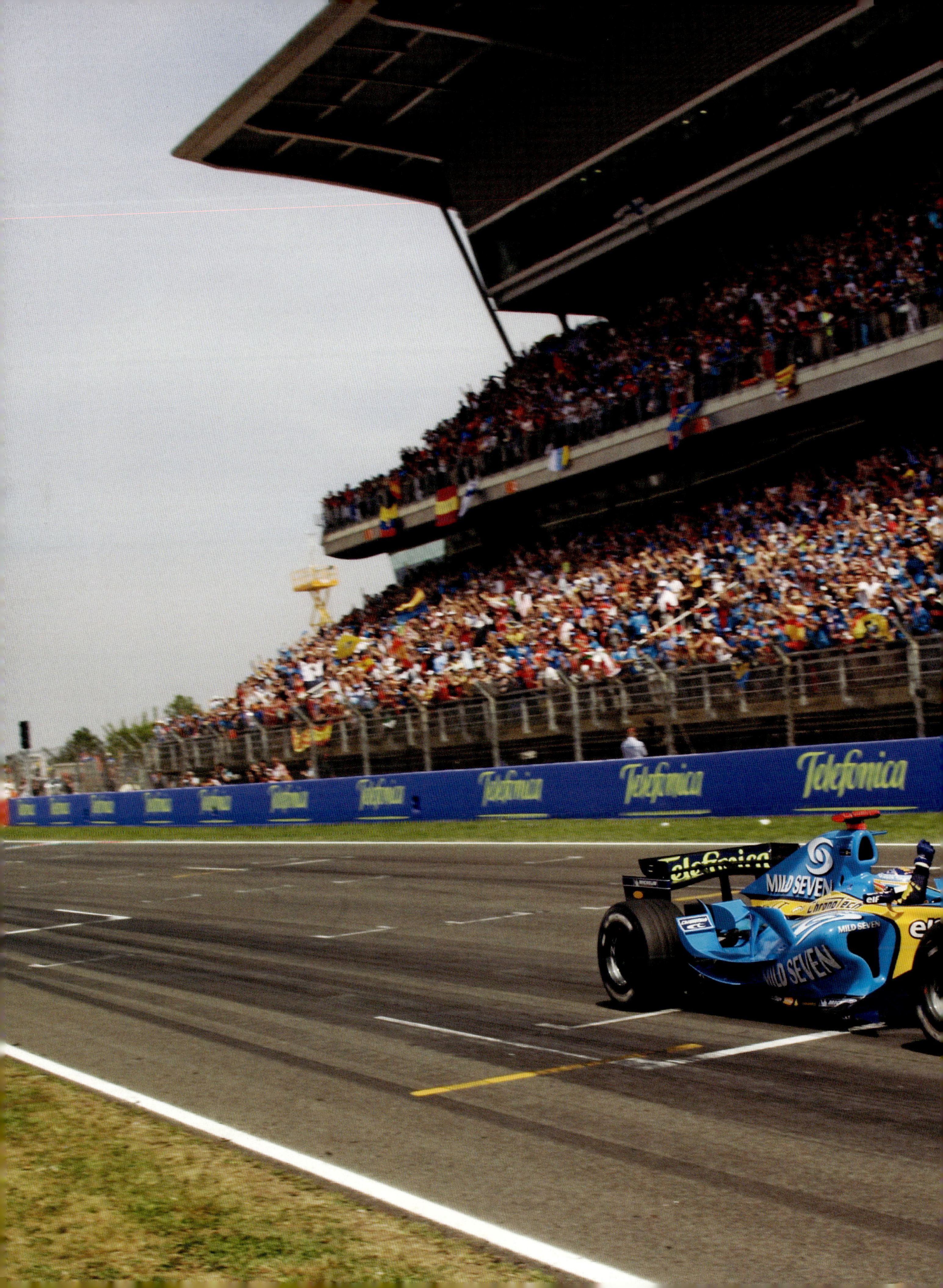
Telefonica
MILD SEVEN

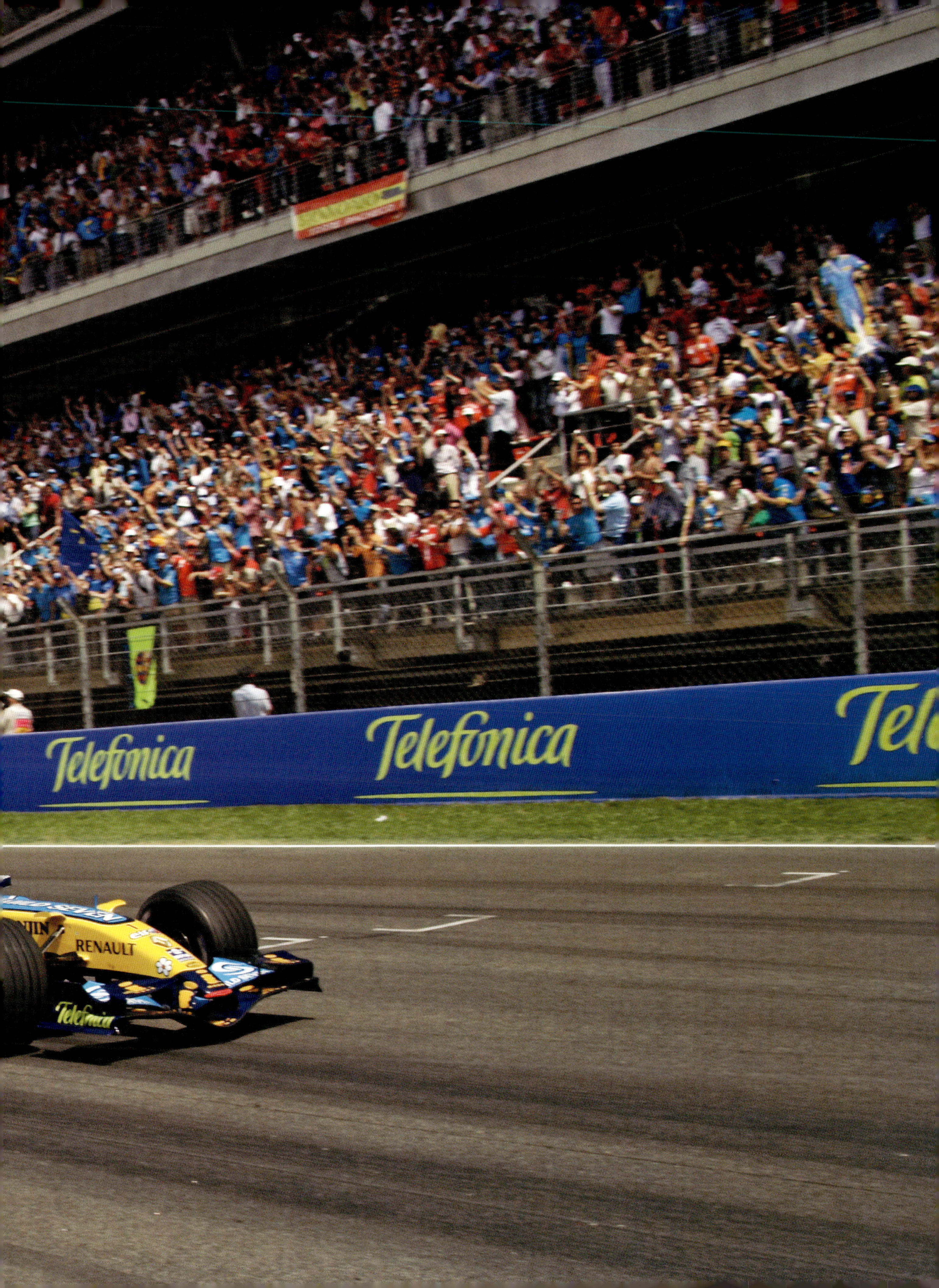
Telefonica
Telefonica
RENAULT
Telefonica

MOMENTS

Only the Jerez circuit used to regularly provide excitement, but the greatest races held in Spain occurred at four of its other F1 circuits.

Villeneuve delays a train of cars

There's an irony that the Grand Prix for which Jarama stands out in the minds of F1 fans is the one in which there was almost no overtaking. This was in 1981, when Ferrari's 126CK, which was all turbocharged power and no handling, had no answer to the pace of the Williams FW07Cs or the Brabham B49Cs. Yet, the Italian team came away with victory thanks to the sheer doggedness of Gilles Villeneuve who took the lead after qualifying seventh and then held up a train of cars for the rest of the race, with Jacques Laffite's Ligier, John Watson's McLaren, Carlos Reutemann's Williams and Elio de Angelis' Lotus simply unable to get past, with the first five covered by just 1.24 seconds.

Opposite: Fernando Alonso increased his tally of home wins by winning for Ferrari in Valencia in 2012 after advancing from eleventh on the grid.

Below: Michael Schumacher moved his Ferrari across on Jacques Villeneuve's Williams at Jerez in 1997 and ended up stuck in a gravel trap.

Mansell toughs it out with Senna

F1 has always been a visually strong sport and the 1991 Spanish GP produced one of the images of the decade when the Circuit de Catalunya as it was then known provided the stage for an epic tussle between two of the greats: Ayrton Senna and Nigel Mansell. The pair, in McLaren and Williams respectively, might only have been fighting over second place in the early laps, as Gerhard Berger led for McLaren, but Mansell was faster onto the main straight and pulled alongside. And there they sat at 180mph, just centimetres apart on a damp track. It was thrilling, but the Williams was faster and through went Mansell, with Senna later spinning and dropping to fifth while Mansell went on to win.

Schumacher gets physical, Häkkinen wins

When Jerez hosted the European GP for a second time in the final round of the 1997 season, there was the extraordinary outcome of the first three qualifiers setting identical times, down to 0.001 seconds. Michael Schumacher made the better start to get ahead of pole-starting title rival Jacques Villeneuve. Just after two-thirds distance, though, with Villeneuve shaping up to go ahead after their one planned pit stop, Schumacher moved his Ferrari across on him into the Dry Sack hairpin and came out worst off, his Ferrari stuck in a gravel trap, while Villeneuve was passed by the McLarens, with Mika Häkkinen taking his first win. However, third place was enough for Villeneuve to become champion.

Alonso wins on streets of Valencia

The start of the 2012 season was remarkable, as the first seven rounds were won by seven different drivers. Then, fittingly as it was on home soil, Fernando Alonso became the year's first double winner when he triumphed around the circuit laid out around Valencia's dock area. Driving for Ferrari, he qualified only eleventh, so would have had no thought of anything other than scoring as many points as he could. Alonso gained three places on the first lap as Sebastian Vettel pulled clear in his Red Bull. Yet, Alonso moved up to fourth after their pit stops and then to third when Lewis Hamilton had a slow pit stop before passing Romain Grosjean's Lotus for second. On that very same lap, Vettel retired and so the race was his.

SWEDEN

Sweden remains the only Scandinavian country to have hosted a World Championship event and produced a Grand Prix winner.

The first circuit used in Sweden was on a loop of public roads on the northern edge of Kristianstad in 1955. It hosted a sportscar race with good enough effect to be awarded World Sports Car Championship rounds in each of the next two years, with Phil Hill and Maurice Trintignant winning for Ferrari in 1956, then Stirling Moss and Jean Behra being first home for Maserati in 1957. These were the first Swedish GPs, but it took until 1973 for the next one.

Jo Bonnier was making pioneering forays in F1 at this stage and produced a shock result in the 1959 Dutch GP when he gave BRM its first win, and his exploits fired the interest of a nation, with circuits opening at Karlskoga (1955), Anderstorp (1968), Kinnekulle and Mantorp Park (1969) and Knutstorp (1970). These produced a flock of young racers seeking more and competitive national championships were established.

Ronnie Peterson and Reine Wisell led the way and a push from within led to Sweden's first F1 race, the 1973 Swedish GP, at Anderstorp. Denny Hulme won that race for McLaren, but the most famous win came in the final year that F1 came to town: 1978. This was the race that Niki Lauda won with the Brabham BT46B 'fan car', a machine that was adjudged to be outside the spirit of the rules and which never raced again, but the way that it was designed with a giant fan to suck the car down to the track was a stroke of genius.

Stefan Johansson reached F1 in the 1980s, just after Anderstorp lost its Grand Prix.

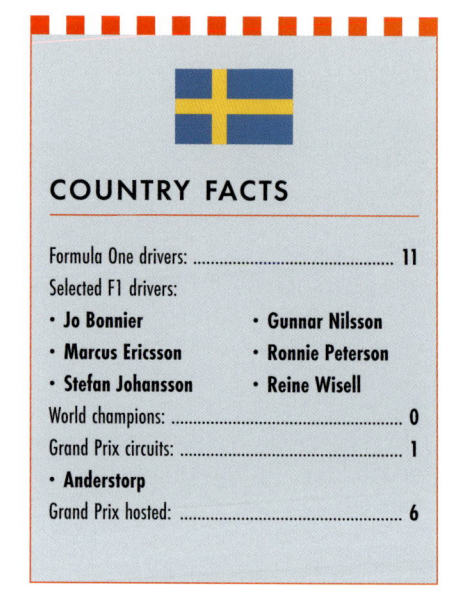

COUNTRY FACTS

Formula One drivers: 11
Selected F1 drivers:
- **Jo Bonnier**
- **Gunnar Nilsson**
- **Marcus Ericsson**
- **Ronnie Peterson**
- **Stefan Johansson**
- **Reine Wisell**

World champions: 0
Grand Prix circuits: 1
- **Anderstorp**

Grand Prix hosted: 6

Below: Niki Lauda takes the chequered flag after his win by more than thirty seconds over his closest rival in the controversial Brabham 'fan car' in 1978.

Ronnie Peterson

Big, blond Ronnie was a prolific winner in F3 as he and compatriot Reine Wisell rose through the ranks. March snapped him up and put him in both F1 and F2 in 1970. His progress was rapid and four second places left him as runner-up to Jackie Stewart in 1971. It took a move to Lotus in 1973 for his first win, at Paul Ricard, with Ronnie's sideways style making him the most popular driver. When Lotus lost form, he returned to March, but he was back with Lotus from 1977, winning again in 1978 before he was killed in an accident at Monza.

Anderstorp

This remains one of the strangest circuits to host the World Championship, as not only was it built on a marsh 100 miles from the closest city, but it also had its start line at one point of the lap and its finish line at another. It also had a few lightly banked corners and its back straight could be used as a runway. The 1978 season was cruel, as Sweden lost both of its F1 stars, with Peterson crashing at the Italian GP and Gunnar Nilsson succumbing to cancer, and F1 never returned, although touring car series visited in the 1980s and GTs at the turn of the millennium.

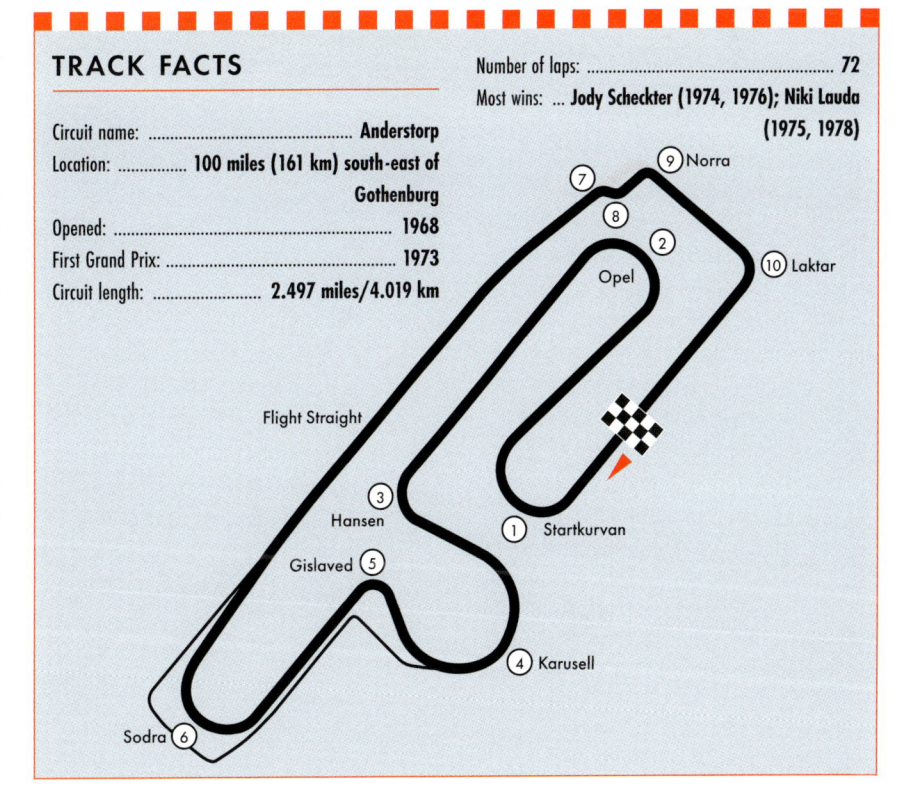

TRACK FACTS

Circuit name: Anderstorp
Location: 100 miles (161 km) south-east of Gothenburg
Opened: 1968
First Grand Prix: 1973
Circuit length: 2.497 miles/4.019 km
Number of laps: 72
Most wins: Jody Scheckter (1974, 1976); Niki Lauda (1975, 1978)

SWEDEN | 121

SWITZERLAND

Two Swiss racers became Grand Prix winners, but the banning of racing within the country's borders has certainly held back generations of drivers.

Switzerland was home to great hill-climb courses on which the top stars of the day competed in the 1930s. They were also able, from 1934, to compete in the Swiss GP on the Bremgarten circuit.

Following the Le Mans disaster in 1955, though, when more than eighty spectators were killed, Switzerland banned all motorsport within its borders.

Switzerland's leading F1 star in the 1960s was Jo Siffert, then, in the 1970s, it was Clay Regazzoni's turn.

There were two further Swiss GPs, the first a non-championship event at Dijon-Prenois in France, which was won by Ferrari's Swiss ace Clay Regazzoni, and the second a World Championship round in 1982. This was won by Keke Rosberg and represented the only victory in his title-winning year with Williams.

International motorsport finally made a return to Switzerland in 2018 following the creation of Formula E, the series for electric racing cars, appearing on temporary street circuits first in Zurich and then in the capital Bern.

Since then, Swiss interest in F1 has largely been focused on its one team: Sauber. Based at Hinwil in the canton of Zurich, and now racing as the Alfa Romeo team, it has been in F1 since 1993, with a high point of a one-two finish in the 2008 Canadian GP with Robert Kubica beating Nick Heidfeld.

Bremgarten

Fast, tricky and surrounded by trees is the best way to sum up Bremgarten, and that was before any rain had fallen, as the trees overhanging much of the high-speed lap made its surface slow to dry and many a driver skidded off as a result, often without a good outcome.

Bremgarten's lap, all four and a half miles of it, was most unusual and all the trickier for it, in that it didn't include a single straight. Instead, it was corner after corner, the majority of which were taken at full throttle.

The lap began with a blast from the grid past Weiermannhaus and up through the incredibly fast Carriere, Batlehen, Eicholz and Jorden sweepers before the drivers reached the first slower bend. This was the right-hander called Eymatt Corner. The return leg was faster still, running through Wohlenstrasse and Glasbrunnen before turning hard right at the Forsthaus hairpin for the final blast onto the curving start-finish straight.

COUNTRY FACTS

Formula One drivers: 24
Selected F1 drivers:
- Sébastien Buemi
- Emmanuel de Graffenried
- Rudi Fischer
- Clay Regazzoni
- Jo Siffert
- Mark Surer

World champions: 0
Grand Prix circuits: 1
- Bremgarten

Grand Prix hosted: 5

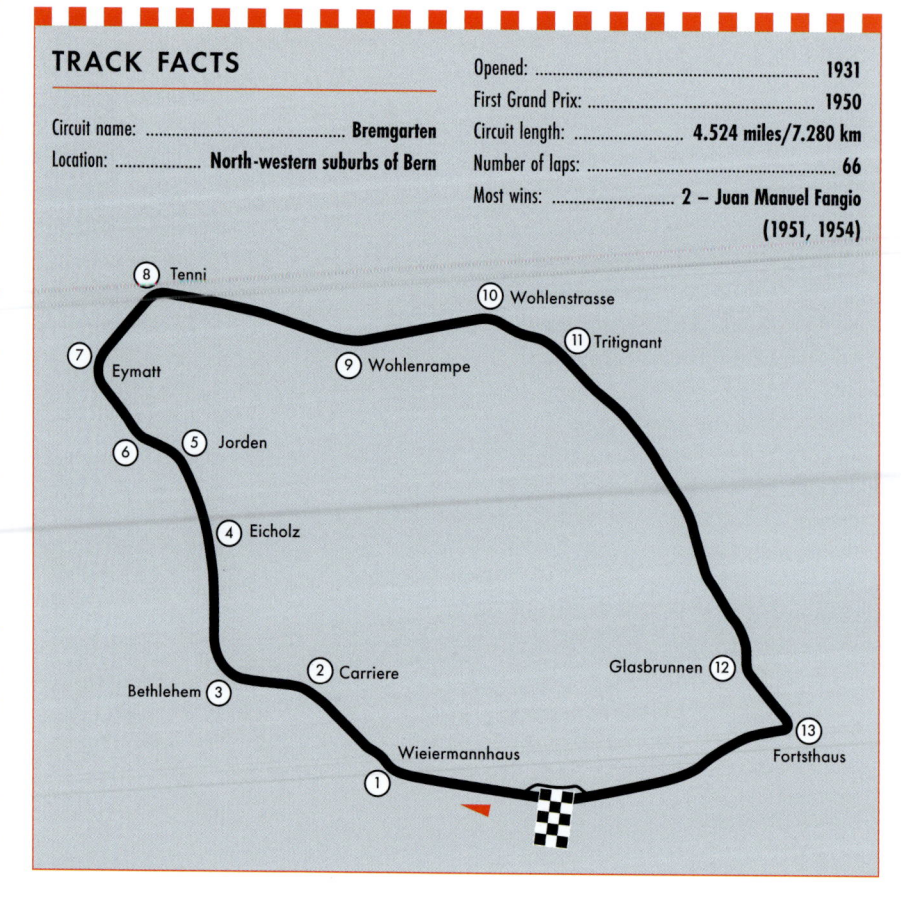

TRACK FACTS

Circuit name: Bremgarten
Location: North-western suburbs of Bern
Opened: 1931
First Grand Prix: 1950
Circuit length: 4.524 miles/7.280 km
Number of laps: 66
Most wins: 2 – Juan Manuel Fangio (1951, 1954)

TURKEY

One of the best new circuits in recent decades, Istanbul Park, was used eight times before it was brought back during the COVID pandemic.

Turkey's motorsport history was not lengthy when it started thinking about joining the World Championship. Indeed, its background was more in rallying and it had just started hosting a round of the World Rally Championship in 2003.

When the World Championship was looking to hold more Grands Prix each year outside Europe, it didn't stretch the envelope very far when it added the Turkish GP to the calendar in 2005.

The project was led by Mümtaz Tahincioğlu and he had a vested interest in his son, who raced as Jason Tahinci and was competing in Formula Renault at the time before advancing to GP2. The race ran from 2005 until 2012 but then was revived in 2020 as a result of the need to find F1 venues in countries not closed by travel restrictions during the COVID pandemic.

Turkish fans would love a top driver of their own to cheer on if the Turkish GP is ever to make a further return, and gamer-turned-racer Cem Bölükbaşi is best placed as he competed in F2 in 2022 and then in Japan's Super Formula in 2023.

Istanbul Park

The drivers loved this circuit when they first saw it in 2005 as its lap contained some wonderfully challenging sections.

The lap was designed to run in an anti-clockwise direction and it started quite like that other anti-clockwise circuit, Interlagos, by having its start-finish straight dip into the first corner, also a left-hander.

From here, the track arced to the right, then snaked through three corners and up an incline to Turn 7. This wide right-hander turns through 180 degrees before the track dips again as it reaches the toughest corner, Turn 8. This is an even longer, even more open left. A short straight then leads to a left-right chicane and then a rising, flat-out kinked straight that takes the cars to the Turn 12 hairpin, a key point for overtaking.

The first Turkish GP was won by Kimi Räikkönen for McLaren before Felipe Massa won three in a row for Ferrari. However, the race that stands out was the one featuring intra-team rivalry between Red Bull Racing's Sebastian Vettel and Mark Webber in 2010 when they clashed at Turn 11 and blew a one-two finish. Webber had been asked to turn his engine setting down and he assumed that this meant to hold station, so was surprised when Vettel went to pass him and refused to give way, handing the race to McLaren's Lewis Hamilton.

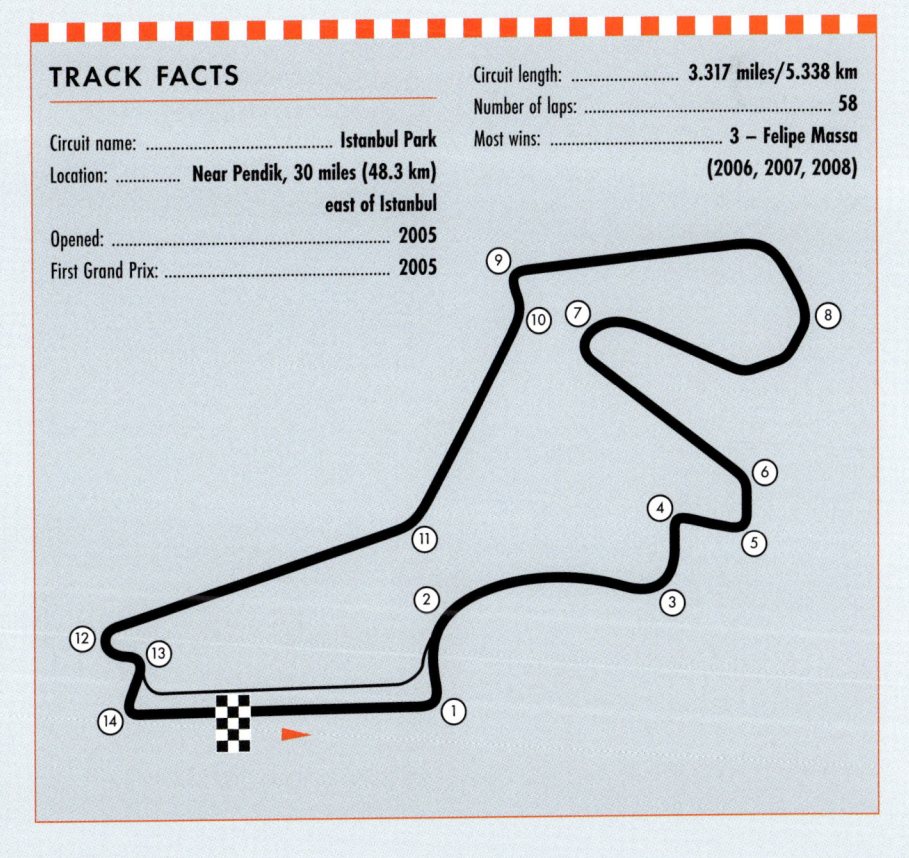

COUNTRY FACTS

Formula One drivers:	0
World champions:	0
Grand Prix circuits:	1
• Istanbul Park	
Grands Prix hosted:	9

TRACK FACTS

Circuit name:	Istanbul Park
Location:	Near Pendik, 30 miles (48.3 km) east of Istanbul
Opened:	2005
First Grand Prix:	2005
Circuit length:	3.317 miles/5.338 km
Number of laps:	58
Most wins:	3 – Felipe Massa (2006, 2007, 2008)

UNITED KINGDOM

France, Italy then Germany set the pace, but Britain hit the front in the 1960s through clever design and is still a pre-eminent force in F1.

Britain can boast the world's first purpose-built circuit, Brooklands, which was built in 1907, and this fired up the nation, with participation in motor racing expanding fast and the Tourist Trophy road races proving very popular, especially on the Ards loop in Northern Ireland.

However, a lack of investment from the motor manufacturers led to first the Italians and then the Germans stealing a march before the Second World War and thrashing the best British challengers in the Donington GP in 1937. After the war, though, often using now-defunct airfields, like Goodwood and Silverstone, the British racing scene was reignited.

Crystal Palace was recommissioned, Brands Hatch opened its doors, a circuit was built at Aintree, followed by purpose-built tracks like Oulton Park, Mallory Park and Castle Combe, plus converted airfields like Snetterton and Thruxton. This gave great variety to the club racer and soon the British Formula Ford and F3 series became the training ground for the world's young stars.

In 1977, Donington Park was brought back to life. Then, in 1986, Birmingham provided something very different when it created a street course for F3000 races.

The British GP, given the honour of hosting the first round of the first World Championship in 1950, set the ball rolling at Silverstone and it has remained the country's number-one circuit, but other tracks like Aintree in the 1950s and Brands Hatch from the mid-1960s to the 1980s, have also had turns hosting the race while Donington Park hosted a round under the courtesy title of the European GP in 1993. This longevity, plus British engineering genius in the 1960s, led to the majority of the F1 teams being based in the UK.

It is this solid motorsport base that keeps Britain at the forefront of the sport, as well as the expertise in running racing teams in sports-prototype, GT and touring car championships, and officiating at race meetings.

Opposite: Rain or shine, the British GP is always a sell-out, with fans packing every bank and grandstand.

Below: Ayrton Senna fell to fifth at Donington Park in 1993 but was so fast in the wet that he passed Alain Prost for the lead before the lap was complete.

COUNTRY FACTS

Formula One drivers: 165
Selected F1 drivers:
- Tony Brooks
- Jenson Button
- Jim Clark
- David Coulthard
- Lewis Hamilton
- Mike Hawthorn
- Damon Hill
- Graham Hill
- James Hunt
- Eddie Irvine
- Nigel Mansell
- Stirling Moss
- Jackie Stewart
- John Surtees
- John Watson

World champions: ... 10 – Mike Hawthorn (1958); Graham Hill (1962, 1968); Jim Clark (1963, 1965); John Surtees (1964); Jackie Stewart (1969, 1971, 1973); James Hunt (1976); Nigel Mansell (1992); Damon Hill (1996); Lewis Hamilton (2008, 2014, 2015, 2017, 2018, 2019, 2020); Jenson Button (2009)

Grand Prix circuits: 4
- Aintree
- Brands Hatch
- Donington Park
- Silverstone

Grands Prix hosted: 79

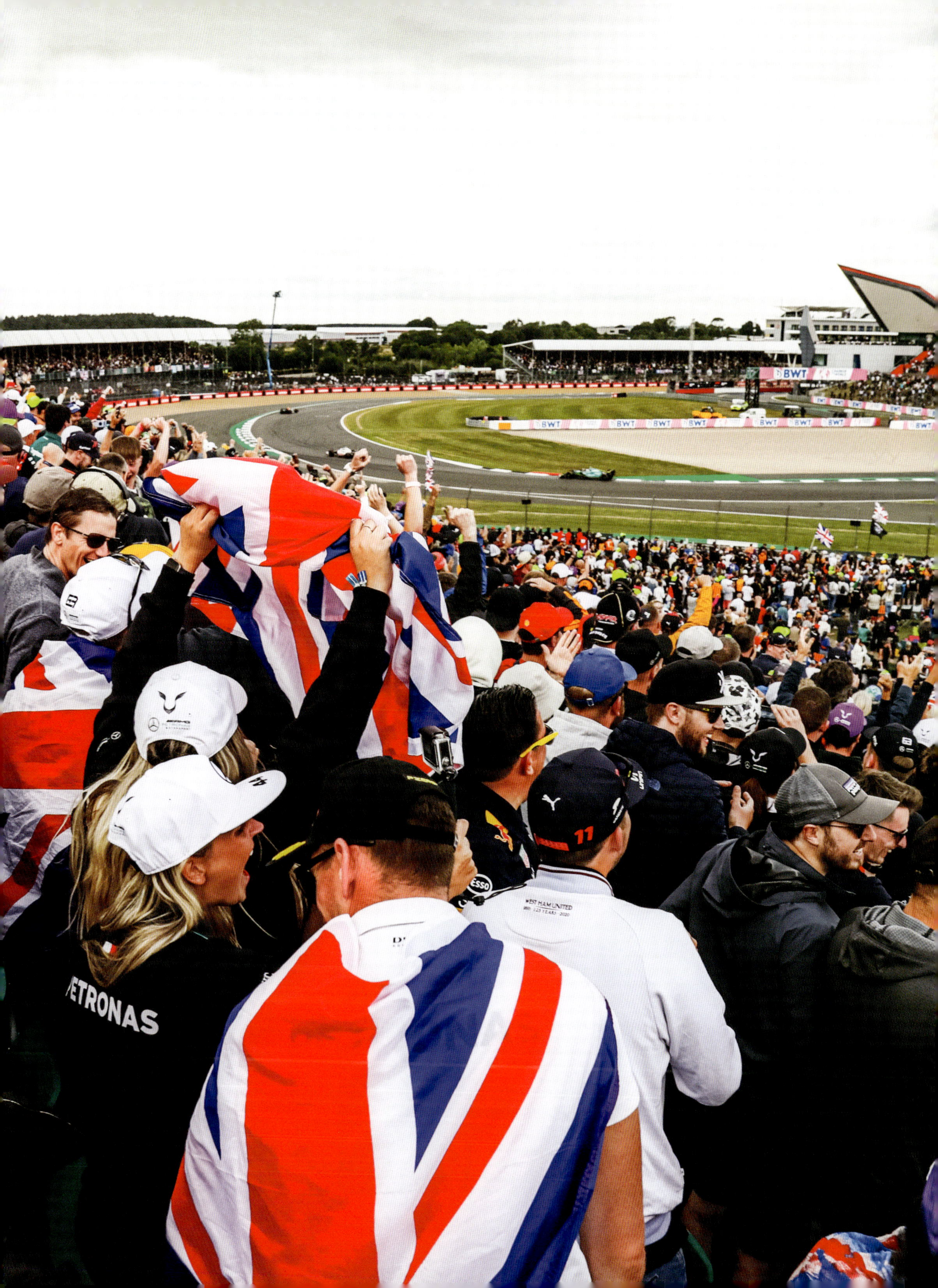
BWT
ETRONAS
11
WEST HAM UNITED

DRIVERS

British drivers have had a prodigious time in F1 and its list of ten world champions is testament to that.

Jackie Stewart

Jackie was ahead of his time and demanded safety be considered in a sport that was still killing drivers. Jackie was a skilled shot, but was drawn to racing by brother Jimmy. Jackie leapt from GTs in his first year to dominating British F3 in 1964 to F1 in 1965. He was even a winner in that first year with BRM as he ranked third as compatriot Jim Clark became champion. Ken Tyrrell signed him to lead Matra's attack in 1968 and he was runner-up again, then champion in 1969. Tyrrell then built his own cars and Jackie reigned supreme in 1971 and 1973 before retiring.

Jim Clark

Hailed as the best of his age, this unassuming Scot was able to do what others could not and make it look easy. He starred for Border Reivers in sportscars in 1959 and Lotus signed him for 1960 and he and Colin Chapman forged a bond. As Chapman's ideas flowed, so Lotus became more competitive and Jim was second to BRM's Graham Hill in 1962, then cleaned up in 1963, was pipped by John Surtees in 1964 and was champion again in 1965. When news came through that he had died in an F2 race in 1968, it was almost too much for his contemporaries to take in.

Graham Hill

Graham was the popular face of racing in the 1960s. He had to work as a mechanic before being given his racing break. After starting in F1 with Lotus in 1958, a move to BRM brought his first win, in the opening race of 1962, and he won three more to become Britain's second world champion. Runner-up in 1963, 1964 and 1965, he returned to Lotus in 1967, then, when Jim Clark was killed in 1968, did a remarkable job by winning the drivers' crown. He would later form his own team, Embassy Racing, but died in a light aircraft accident returning from a test.

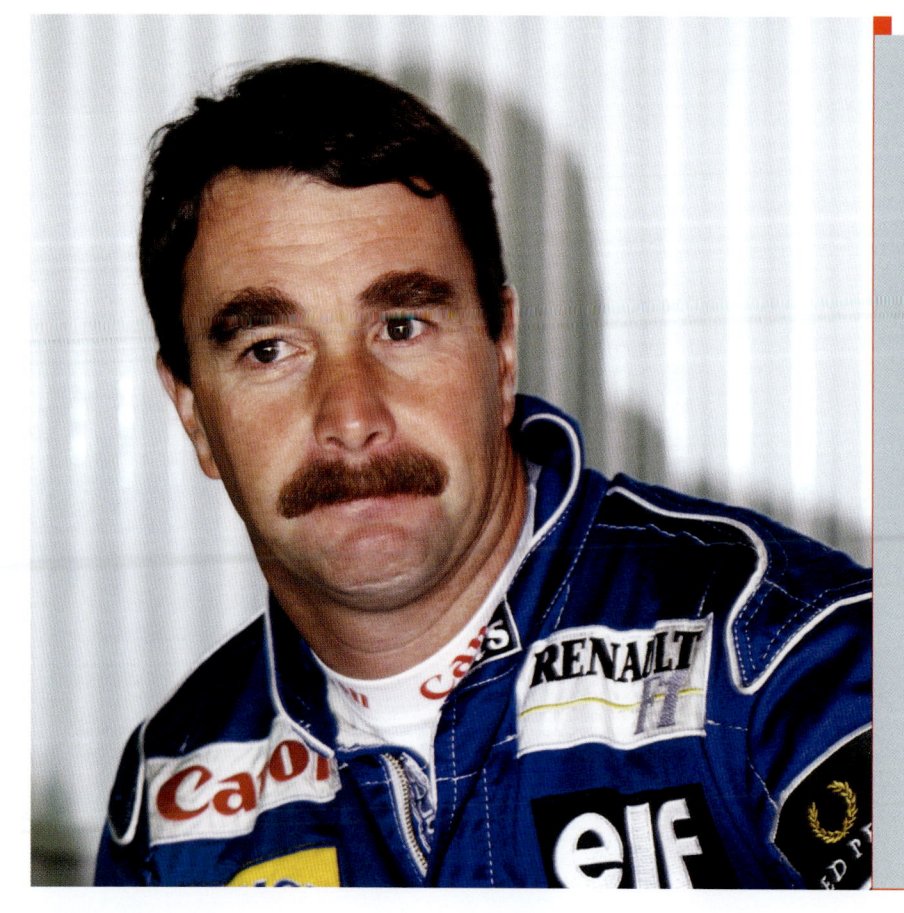

Nigel Mansell

Nigel was often his own worst enemy in his early days, always finding reasons to complain but, through dogged self-belief, he made it to F1 and finally earned adulation for his never-say-die approach. Lotus gave him his break in 1980 and a first win was lost when he crashed while leading at Monaco in 1984, but he got it with Williams in 1985. Then there was the heartbreak of a blow-out in the final race of 1986 denying him a title. A move to Ferrari added to his fan base, but his second spell with Williams delivered when he dominated in the FW14B in 1992.

UNITED KINGDOM

Lewis Hamilton

Lewis made the passage from child karting prodigy to world champion look so easy, and his record tallies of Grand Prix wins and pole positions, 103 apiece, plus his seven world titles is testament to that ability. Already with interest and some financial assistance from McLaren after he approached them at an awards evening, Lewis became a champion in Formula Renault, Formula 3 and GP2 before the team gave him his F1 break in 2007 when he was a winner by his sixth Grand Prix and only missed winning the title by one point as Ferrari's Kimi Räikkönen took the crown. He made amends in 2008 before McLaren's form gradually faded. It took a move to Mercedes in 2013 for him to challenge again and he gathered poles, fastest laps, wins and titles by the handful, adding six more F1 crowns by 2020, missing out only in 2016 when his teammate Nico Rosberg pipped him and then in 2021 when he was edged out by Max Verstappen in Abu Dhabi.

CIRCUITS

Silverstone is Britain's pre-eminent circuit, but Grands Prix have also been held at Brands Hatch, Aintree and Donington Park.

Silverstone

Like many an airfield that was left without a purpose after the end of the Second World War, in 1948 the Royal Automobile Club identified Silverstone as a place where cars could be raced and a circuit was created out of sections of the runways and access roads. It was ready to host the first British GP.

By 1949, the circuit was modified as sections were added and the runways dropped. By 1950, when Silverstone opened the inaugural World Championship, the circuit's shape was defined, with the start line moved to between Woodcote and Copse.

One of the reasons that Silverstone has stood the test of time is that it kept on tweaking its format to stay relevant as F1 cars became ever faster. The high-speed run from Copse, through Maggotts and Becketts then onto the straight to Stowe, Club, Abbey and the last corner, Woodcote, remained, but the multi-car accident triggered by Jody Scheckter in 1973 led to a chicane being in place there by the time the British GP returned in 1975. In 1987, the run from Abbey to Woodcote was then broken by the insertion of the Luffield chicane.

Four years later, there was a major facelift. The first modification inserted an esse at Becketts, making one of the best corners in F1. The second was making Stowe tighter and adding a drop into Vale then a chicane at Club. The change was completed by the straight before Luffield being cut short by the entry to a loop into the infield, taking in new corners Priory and Brooklands. In 1994, a chicane was added to reduce speeds at Abbey. So many changes, but it was still very much Silverstone.

Then came the big change when a new pit complex was built between Club and Abbey and a whole new foray into the infield undertaken. Instead of kinking to the left, Abbey now went right, fed into a kink at Farm and then forced drivers to hit the brakes hard for Village. From there, the tight Loop took them left and then left again through Aintree onto a new infield straight that ran all the way down to Brooklands.

Silverstone is more than just the home of the British GP, as it is used year-round to host everything from international-standard sportscar races to regular club racing. Its facilities were augmented by a special circuit for its racing school on the infield alongside the Hangar Straight and there is now even a technical university and a museum on site.

Opposite: David Coulthard takes the applause from his mechanics as he leads home a McLaren one-two result ahead of teammate Mika Häkkinen in 2000.

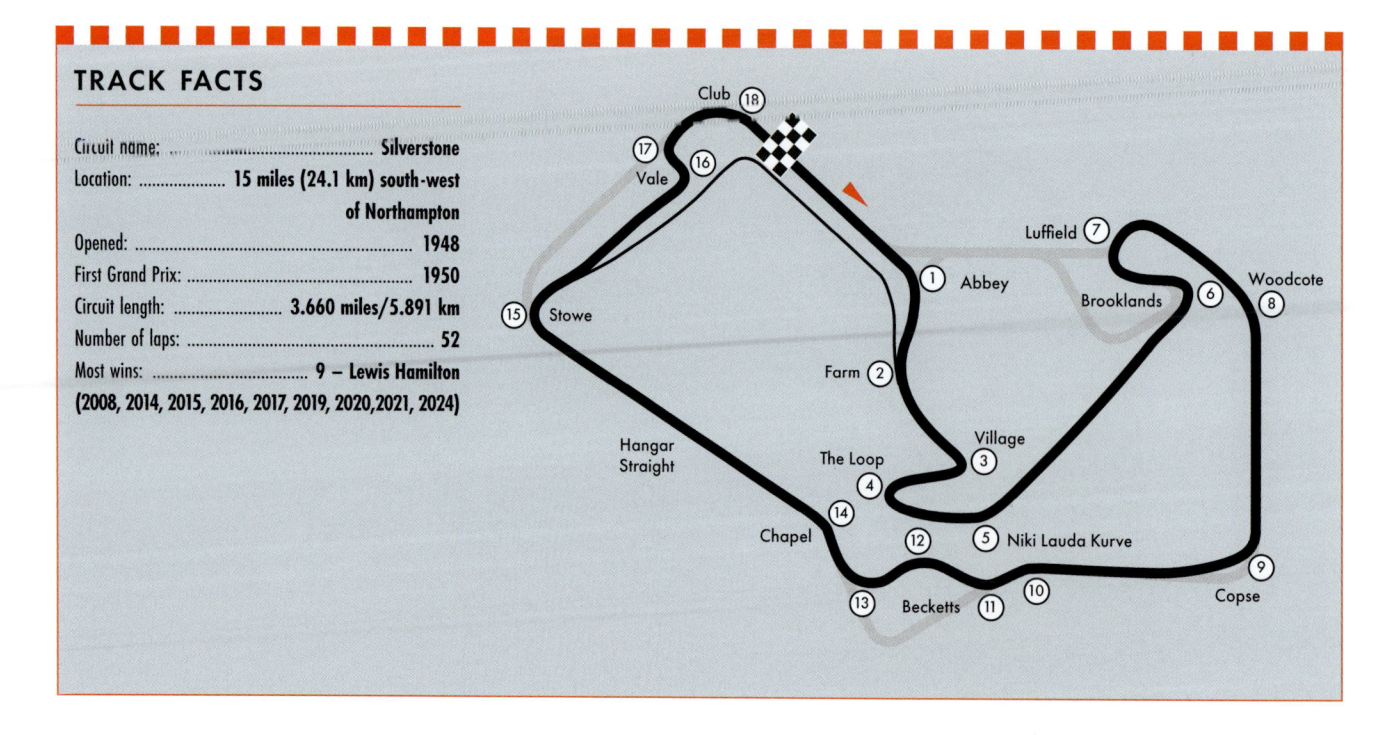

TRACK FACTS

Circuit name:	Silverstone
Location:	15 miles (24.1 km) south-west of Northampton
Opened:	1948
First Grand Prix:	1950
Circuit length:	3.660 miles/5.891 km
Number of laps:	52
Most wins:	9 – Lewis Hamilton (2008, 2014, 2015, 2016, 2017, 2019, 2020, 2021, 2024)

128 | UNITED KINGDOM

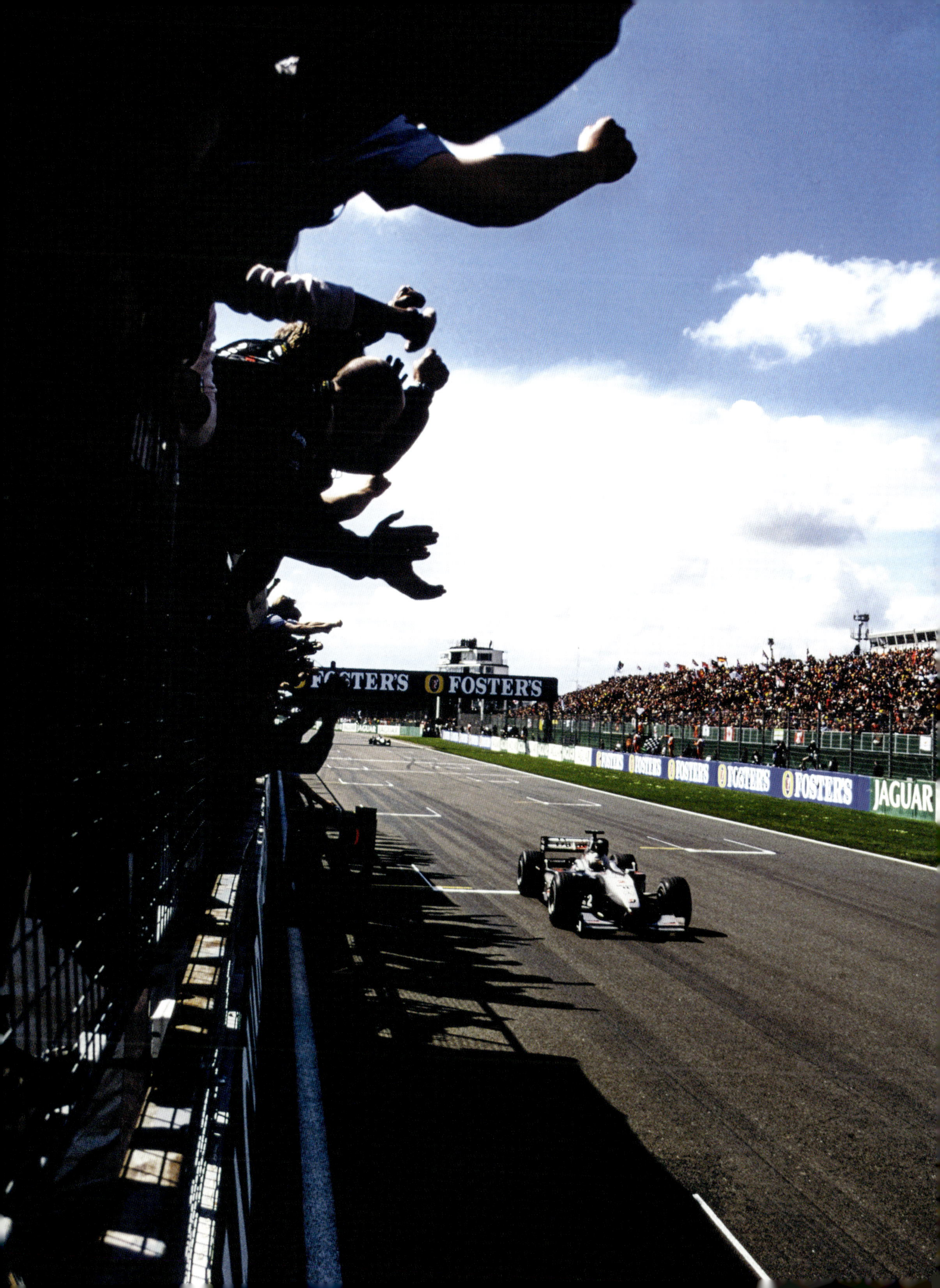
FOSTER'S
FOSTER'S
FOSTER'S
FOSTER'S
FOSTER'S
FOSTER'S
JAGUAR

Lucas
Lucas
Lucas
Lucas
PLACE
1ST.
2ND.
3RD.
4TH.
5TH.
EVENT
3
LAPS
76
Shell
SUPER
MULTI-
GRADE
Shell
SUPER
MULTI-
GRADE
Grand Prix
Marlboro
11

Brands Hatch

This circuit began its life as a bicycle-racing venue. That was in 1926 and motorbikes soon followed, racing on a kidney-shaped track in the undulating countryside. It was inevitable, especially being so close to London, that car racing would follow, and it did, in 1950.

As its popularity grew, so did the desire for a longer lap and it was boosted from 1 mile (1.6 km) to 1.24 (2 km) miles by the addition of a run up the hill to a hairpin called Druids. The other change came when the direction of flow was changed to clockwise. Pit buildings and a grandstand followed, with a racing school bringing on aspiring talent, including Graham Hill.

The biggest change came in 1960 when the track more than doubled in length so that it could hold international meetings. The western end of the old kidney shape was given an uphill left-hander, and this was the start of the Grand Prix loop. This was followed by a kinked straight over a brow and into a dip before rising for the first of three fast right-handers, Hawthorn Bend, dipping Westfield and Dingle Dell Corner and then a left at Stirling's. The lap was completed by emerging from the woods to rejoin the original circuit for high-speed Clark Curve, through which drivers would try to carry as much speed as possible to help them on the run to the lap's trickiest corner, Paddock Hill Bend, which plunged sharply from entry to exit.

The British GP had ended its alternation between Silverstone and Aintree and so Brands Hatch took Aintree's slot in 1964 and hosted some epic races through until 1986. Since F1's departure, other modifications have included a chicane slowing progress through Dingle Dell Corner and a tightening of Graham Hill Bend, the first corner after Druids, to slow the car along Cooper Straight, but the nature of the place remains. The Grand Prix circuit isn't always used, with lower-level meetings using just the Indy Circuit, the layout that was first used in 1953 but had its name changed after a visit by the Indycar series in 1978.

Left: There was mayhem just after the start of the 1976 British GP when Clay Regazzoni spun at Paddock Hill Bend and James Hunt's McLaren was tipped into the air, forcing the race to be restarted.

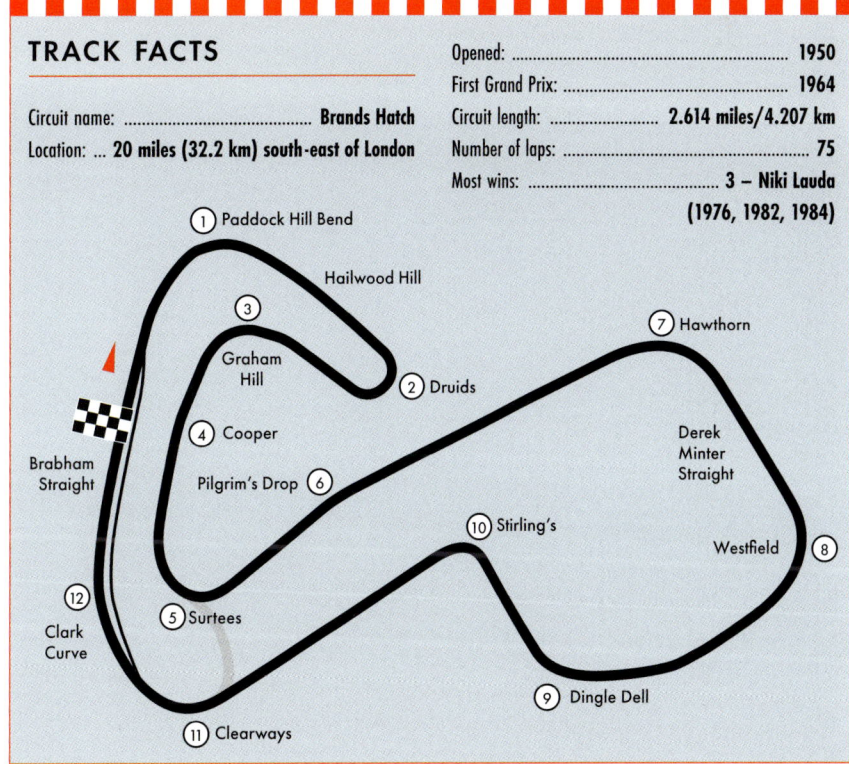

TRACK FACTS

Circuit name:	Brands Hatch
Location:	20 miles (32.2 km) south-east of London
Opened:	1950
First Grand Prix:	1964
Circuit length:	2.614 miles/4.207 km
Number of laps:	75
Most wins:	3 – Niki Lauda (1976, 1982, 1984)

1. Paddock Hill Bend
2. Druids
3. Hailwood Hill
4. Cooper
5. Surtees
6. Pilgrim's Drop
7. Hawthorn
8. Westfield
9. Dingle Dell
10. Stirling's
11. Clearways
12. Clark Curve

Graham Hill
Derek Minter Straight
Brabham Straight

UNITED KINGDOM | 131

Aintree

The Grand National steeplechase is one of the best-known horse races in the world and it has attracted huge crowds to Aintree since 1839. Aintree's owners had invested heavily in huge grandstands and, looking at the growth of motorsport in the 1950s, decided to add a car-racing circuit to their facility on the northern flank of Liverpool.

The lap started with a straight past the main grandstand feeding into a right-hander and a short straight alongside a canal. A low-speed loop interrupted the basically triangular shape of the track, before a short straight to the open right-hander, Canal Curve, that led the cars onto the longest straight, with an esse and then the unsettling Melling Crossing just before the braking point for the final corner of the lap, Tatts Corner, a long right-hander back onto the start-finish straight.

The circuit opened in 1954 and was awarded the opportunity to host the British GP the following year. The decision was vindicated as this, too, attracted enormous crowds. Better still, it got a British winner, as Stirling Moss moved past Mercedes team leader Juan Manuel Fangio to take his first World Championship win. Two years later, Moss took over Tony Brooks' car mid-race, as he was recovering from injuries suffered at Le Mans, to give Vanwall its first win.

British teams were becoming ever more competitive as they led the way in mounting the engine behind the driver and, fittingly, it was Cooper that won on the next visit in 1959, courtesy of Jack Brabham. In 1961, with Ferrari best prepared for F1's new rules, Wolfgang von Trips took victory.

Then came 1962 when the Lotus 25 was the car to have, as it was F1's first monocoque and offered supreme chassis rigidity. Combine this with the nascent ability of Jim Clark and the rest could only watch as he blasted off into the lead from pole. John Surtees tried to give chase in his Bowmaker Racing Team Lola, but Clark led every lap.

F1 moved on after that and only the shorter club layout was used after 1964 until closing its doors in the early 1980s.

Right: Jim Clark's Lotus begins to pull away from John Surtees, Dan Gurney and Bruce McLaren at the start at Aintree in 1962.

Following pages: Max Verstappen pulls away in front of The Wing into a short-lived lead in 2021.

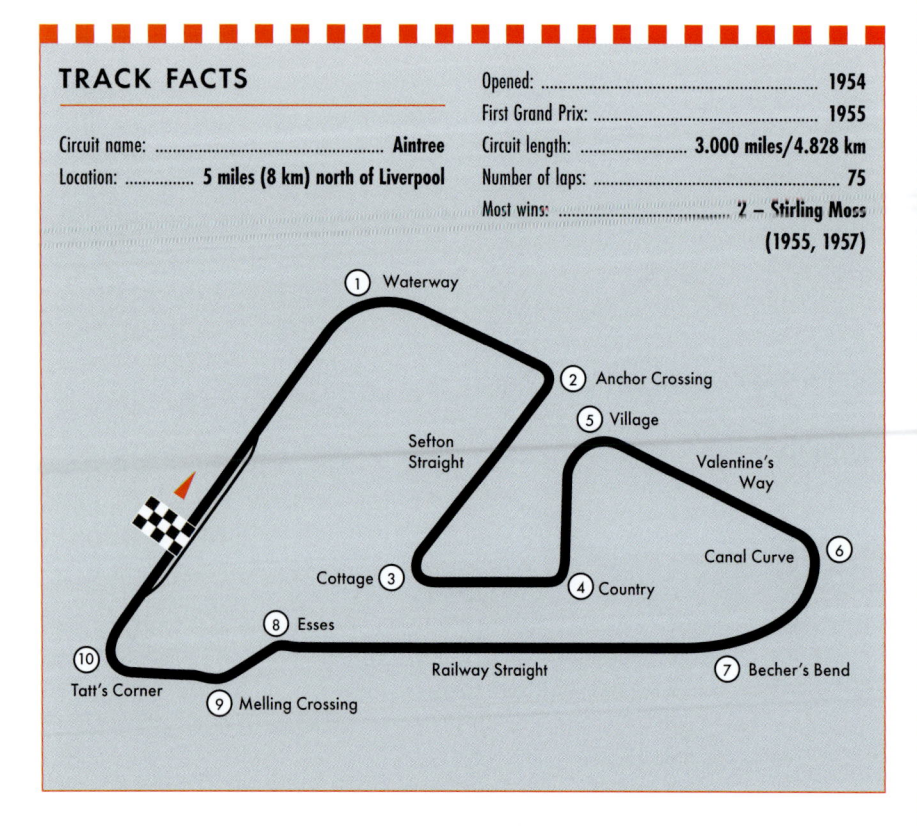

TRACK FACTS

Circuit name:	Aintree
Location:	5 miles (8 km) north of Liverpool
Opened:	1954
First Grand Prix:	1955
Circuit length:	3.000 miles/4.828 km
Number of laps:	75
Most wins:	2 – Stirling Moss (1955, 1957)

1. Waterway
2. Anchor Crossing
3. Cottage
4. Country
5. Village
6. Canal Curve
7. Becher's Bend
8. Esses
9. Melling Crossing
10. Tatt's Corner

Sefton Straight
Valentine's Way
Railway Straight

UNITED KINGDOM

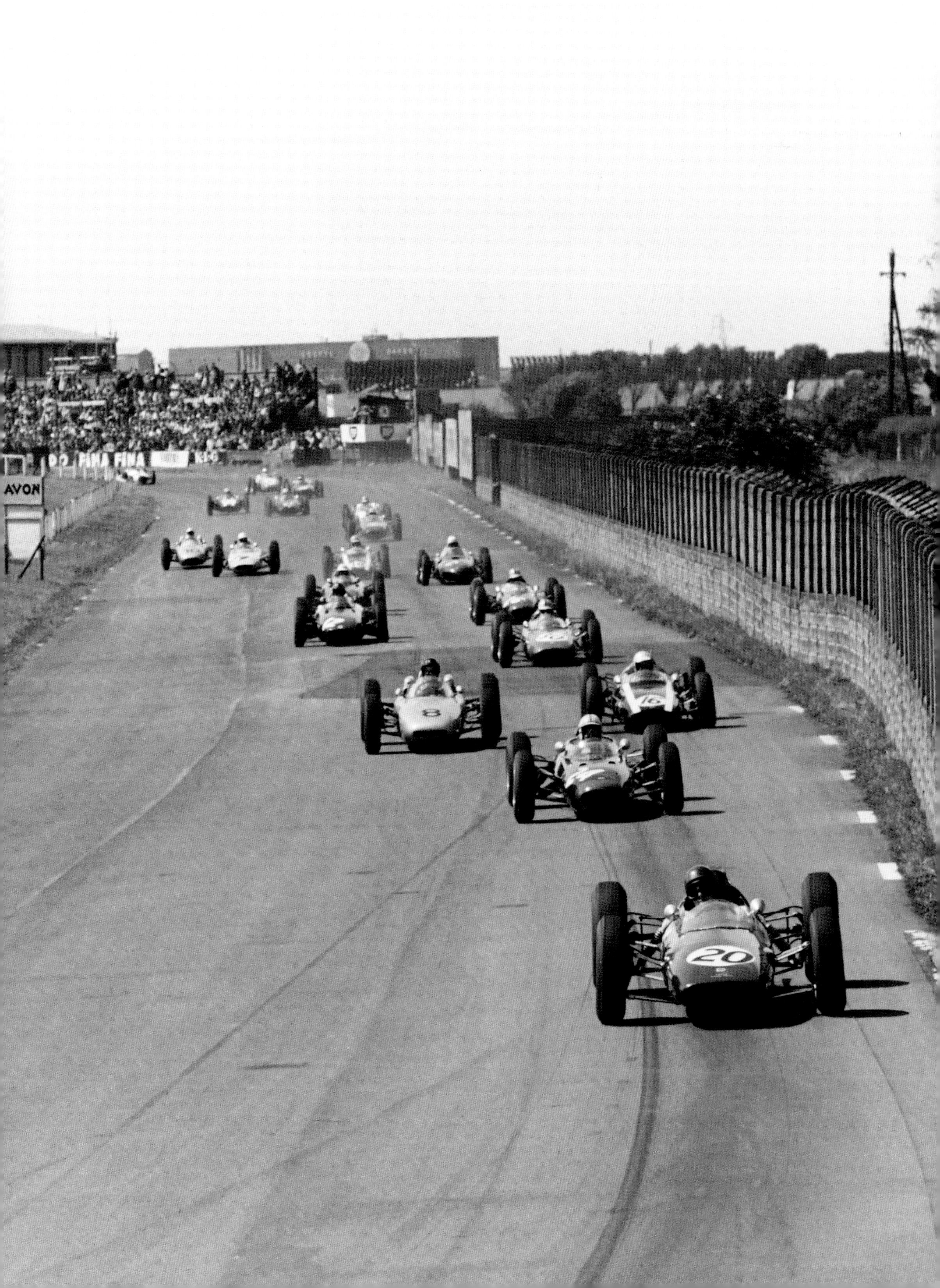
AVON
FINA FINA
8
20

DHL
DHL
DHL
DHL
DHL
DHL
PIRELLI
PIRELLI
PIRELLI
PIRELLI
PIRELLI
PIRELLI
PIRELLI

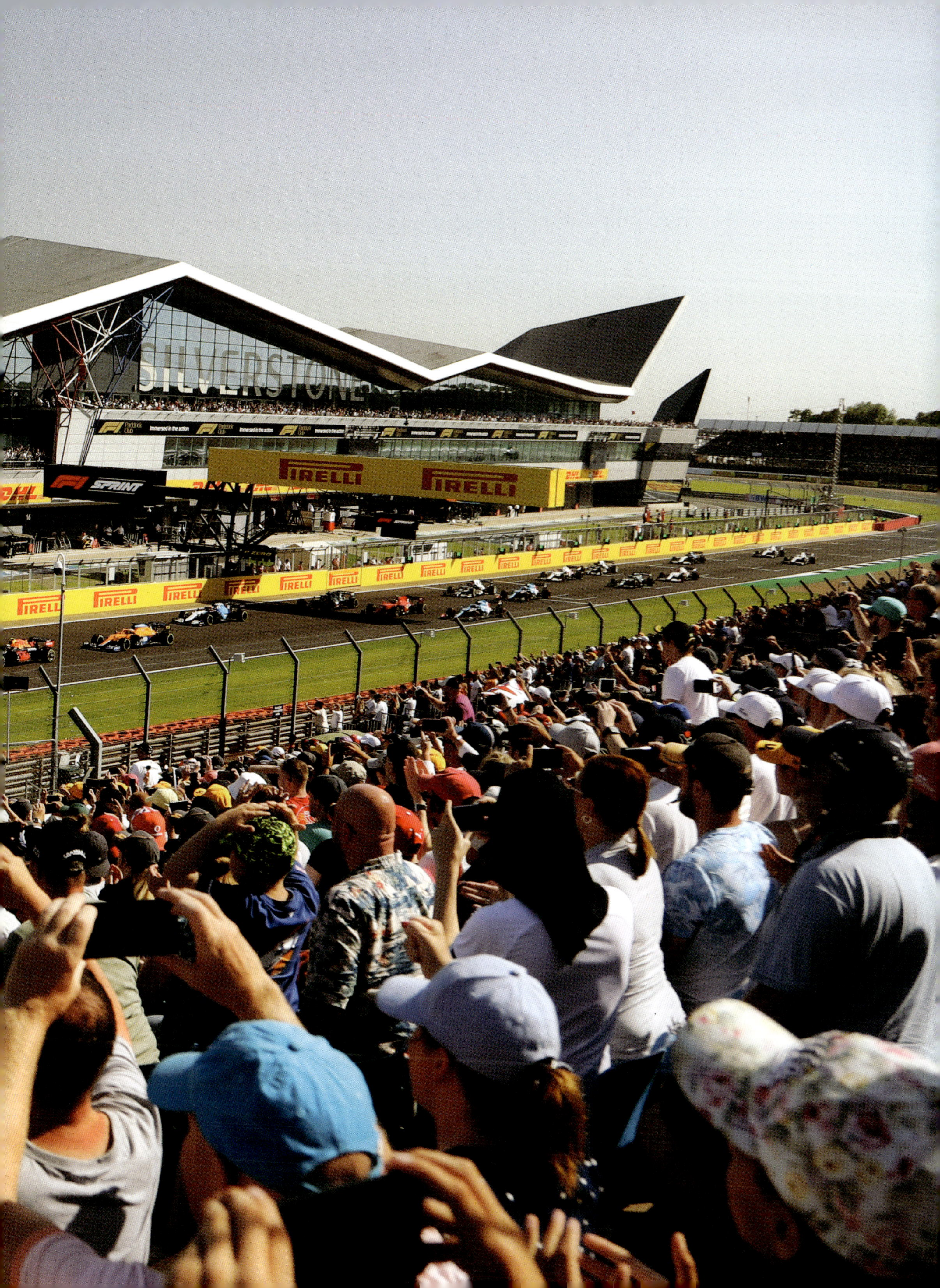
SILVERSTONE
PIRELLI
PIRELLI
F1 SPRINT
DHL

MOMENTS

The huge crowds attending British GPs over the decades have been spoiled with some outstanding races at a variety of circuits.

Brands Hatch crowd goes wild

The 1976 Hunt versus Lauda soap opera was at full tilt when the teams arrived at Brands Hatch for the British GP. Lauda started from pole, with Hunt second, but Clay Regazzoni slid the second Ferrari into Lauda at Paddock Hill Bend and spun, pitching Hunt's McLaren into the air. The crowd went crazy when it was suggested that Hunt may not be allowed to take the restart. Lauda duly led away, but Hunt got faster and faster, passed him for the lead after forty-four laps and went to win, only to be stripped of victory as the sport's governing body agreed with Ferrari that Hunt's car had been out of the race before the red flag had been shown.

Jackie Stewart versus Jochen Rindt

Across a career that earned him three F1 drivers' titles, Jackie Stewart loved the Matra MS80 most as it was the car that took him to his first title in 1969. In that season of six wins, it was his victory at Silverstone that people remember the most. The reason for this is that it came after a tremendous scrap with Lotus team leader Jochen Rindt, the pair operating on another level to their rivals. Rindt led early on, but it was nip and tuck, sometimes side-by-side, and stayed like that for sixty-two enthralling laps, both drivers trusting each other implicitly. Then Rindt limped into the pits, a wing endplate having come loose and Stewart went on to finish a lap clear of all others.

Senna stuns at Donington Park

Very few Grands Prix are celebrated for the opening lap alone, but when Donington Park hosted the European GP in 1993, Ayrton Senna put on a masterclass. He had qualified his McLaren fourth, with Alain Prost's Williams on pole. Torrential rain was the order of the day and much of what happened on lap one was obscured by spray. Prost led away from teammate Damon Hill, but Michael Schumacher disrupted Senna's progress and Sauber's Karl Wendlinger dived past him. But Senna fought straight back and demoted Schumacher's Benetton coming out of the first corner, passed Wendlinger through the Craner Curves, went around Hill by McLeans and dived by Prost into the Melbourne hairpin.

Opposite: Lewis Hamilton produced one of his first great F1 drives when he mastered changing conditions to win for McLaren in 2008.

Below: Jackie Stewart balances his Matra as he keeps Jochen Rindt's Lotus behind him in 1969.

Hamilton's wet-weather masterclass

Lewis Hamilton had wowed F1 in his rookie season in 2007. In 2008, he was better still, but it was his drive in wet but changeable conditions at Silverstone that was his best of the year. He arrived with the media on his back for not scoring in the previous two races and then added a little pressure by running wide on the lap that would have earned him pole. Starting his McLaren from fourth on a wet track, he moved directly to second behind teammate Heikki Kovalainen. On lap five, he took the lead. Then Kovalainen spun and Kimi Räikkönen closed on Hamilton as the track dried. They pitted together, but fresh intermediates were key and Hamilton stormed clear.

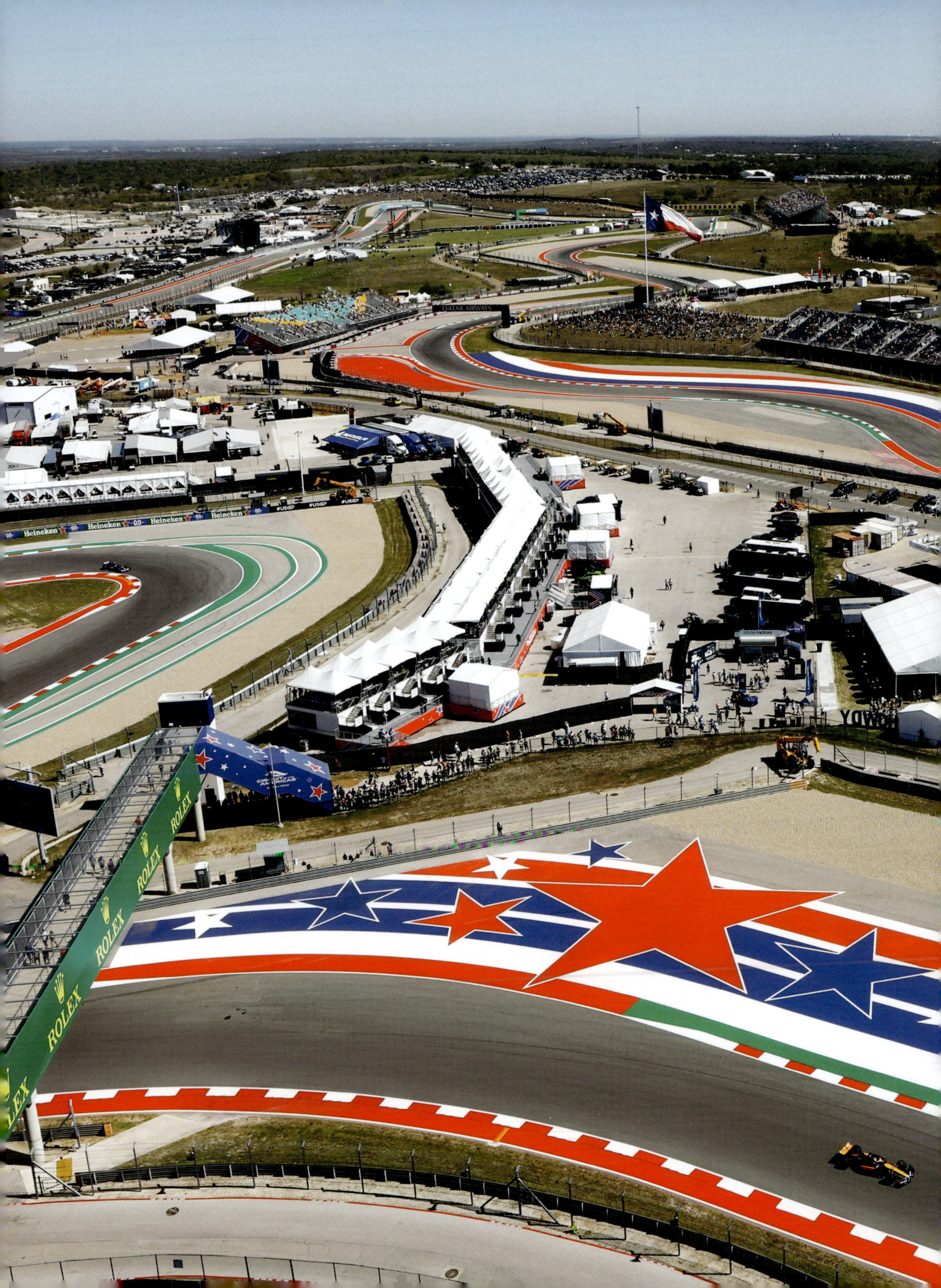
QATAR AIRWAYS
Heineken
#USGP
ROLEX

AMERICAS

As in many sports, the United States has always been happy with its own competition, being strong on sportscar racing on road circuits plus Indycar and NASCAR racing on ovals. Yet, in the 1950s, a few of the young drivers began to look to a more international diet. This led to the first United States GP held at Sebring in 1959. Since then, the race has moved around the country and, just as it seems that the Circuit of the Americas has become its home, the championship organisers have added two more races, at Miami and Las Vegas, to the calendar.

Argentina and Brazil have been more steadfast in their support of F1, with Argentina leading the way in an attack spearheaded by the dominant star of the 1950s, Juan Manuel Fangio. Into the 1970s, Brazil assumed South American dominance as Emerson Fittipaldi became the first of a string of Brazilian world champions. Each of these nations is blessed with national series at several circuits. Mexico has followed a similar pattern and, like Argentina, has been on and off the F1 calendar due to the country's ability or otherwise to afford to host a Grand Prix. They are racing-mad nations with a long history in the sport so should, in the opinion of the author, always be part of the show.

Canada has made a success of its Grand Prix in Montreal, while Chile, Colombia, Uruguay and Venezuela have all provided F1 drivers but are never likely to host a Grand Prix.

ARGENTINA

Juan Manuel Fangio dominated F1's first decade and Argentina's Grand Prix was one of the first flyaways, but it has long been dropped.

By the end of the 1957 season, after the first eight World Championships had been completed, five had been won by one man, Argentina's greatest: Juan Manuel Fangio. He might not fit the modern image of a Grand Prix driver, as he was forty-six by the time he claimed the last of these, but he was the absolute gold standard through the 1950s, shining in a type of racing that could not have been more different if it had tried, to the long-distance road races that formed the first part of his career.

With President Peron anxious that Fangio would boost Argentina's reputation abroad, there was government assistance for the best of Argentina's racers to travel to Europe to take on the best there, with José Froilán González also becoming a Grand Prix winner.

Peron wanted Argentina to have a top-ranking circuit of its own too, so one was built to the south of capital city Buenos Aires. This immediately superseded an array of street circuits around the country that had hosted races for Grand Prix cars immediately after the Second World War and it was welcomed into the World Championship to take F1 beyond Europe for the first time in 1953.

After a break between 1960 and 1972, the Argentinian GP returned just in time to showcase Argentina's next F1 great, Carlos Reutemann, with a third spell from 1995 to 1998. The national racing scene is strong, chiefly its touring-car series, but Argentina had to wait until 2024 for its newest F1 driver, Franco Colapinto.

Opposite: Michael Schumacher took on and beat the McLarens in Buenos Aires in 1998.

Below: Stirling Moss made the tyres on his Cooper last in searing heat to win in 1958.

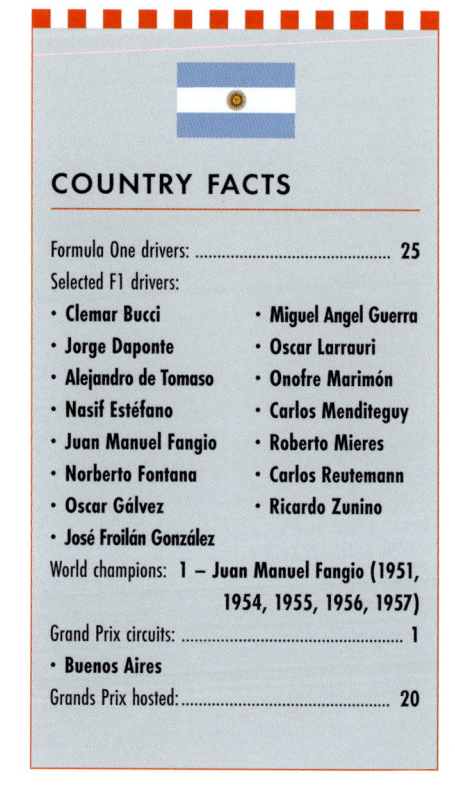

COUNTRY FACTS

Formula One drivers: 25
Selected F1 drivers:
- Clemar Bucci
- Jorge Daponte
- Alejandro de Tomaso
- Nasif Estéfano
- Juan Manuel Fangio
- Norberto Fontana
- Oscar Gálvez
- José Froilán González
- Miguel Angel Guerra
- Oscar Larrauri
- Onofre Marimón
- Carlos Menditeguy
- Roberto Mieres
- Carlos Reutemann
- Ricardo Zunino

World champions: 1 – Juan Manuel Fangio (1951, 1954, 1955, 1956, 1957)
Grand Prix circuits: 1
- Buenos Aires

Grands Prix hosted: 20

FORMULA 1
WORLD
GOODYEAR
Marlboro
Asprey
Marlboro
OMP
M. Schumacher

DRIVERS

All-time great Juan Manuel Fangio is Argentina's stand-out star, but a couple of other Argentinian drivers have won Grands Prix.

José Froilán González

To win for Ferrari is an accolade of which most drivers can only dream. Yet, to become the driver who gave the Italian team its first win in a World Championship Grand Prix is something to which only José Froilán González can lay claim. He started racing in Europe in 1950 and did well enough to land a works ride for 1951 when he achieved this famous feat after beating the otherwise-dominant Alfa Romeos in the 1951 British GP. Large of physique, indeed he was known as 'The Pampas Bull', José's last top result came when he finished second in his home Grand Prix in 1957.

Onofre Marimón

After Fangio, Reutemann and Gonzalez, Onofre was in the next rank of Argentinian F1 drivers to step onto a World Championship podium. This was after he finished third in the Belgian GP in 1953 in a works Maserati. Urged to try single-seaters by family friend Fangio, Onofre had a brief run in the 1951 French GP, then got his break with Maserati in 1953, starting with that third place at Spa-Francorchamps. He came third at Silverstone in 1954 too, but was then killed in the next race when he crashed in practice for the German GP at the Nürburgring.

Carlos Menditeguy

Carlos was the other Argentinian to step onto a World Championship podium after completing a Maserati one-two-three at his home Grand Prix in 1957. Impressive form in sportscars landed 'Charly' his single-seater break and he finished fifth in his first World Championship event outside Argentina at Monza in 1955. Cruel fortune followed in his home Grand Prix in 1956 when Carlos led but missed a gear, broke a halfshaft and slid into a fence. The 1957 season promised more, as he raced for Maserati in the Monaco, French and British GPs, but he quit after Maserati thought he was too hard on his machinery.

Carlos Reutemann

Argentina had to wait until the 1970s for its next talent to emerge. This was Carlos Reutemann, a driver who shone in F2 after taking on the best Europeans in 1968 when they headed south for the Temporada series through the European winter months, then impressing in his second state-financed season in Europe in 1971. In 1972, he hit F1, landing a ride with Brabham and progressing as the team became more competitive in 1974 to take his first wins. He moved on to Ferrari then Lotus then Williams with whom he blew his 1981 title shot at Las Vegas when he out-psyched himself.

Juan Manuel Fangio

F1's first true great started his competition career in Argentina's gruelling long-distance road races, driving a Chevrolet that supporters from his town of Balcarce had helped him to buy. His first big win came in the Gran Premio del Norte, all 5,900 miles (9,495 km) of it, in 1940. By the end of the decade when international visitors came to compete in a series of Formula Libre races in 1948, Juan Manuel Fangio got to show that he could drive single-seaters too. In 1949, he had a full campaign in Europe, winning six non-championship races and earning a ride with Alfa Romeo for the inaugural World Championship in 1950. In 1951, he stepped up from runner-up to world champion and, after missing 1952 through injury, he came back to add the 1954 and 1955 titles with Mercedes, the 1956 crown for Ferrari and his last one, again with Maserati, in 1957.

CIRCUIT

Argentina has a large number of circuits, but only one has hosted a Grand Prix: the one built in its capital, Buenos Aires, in 1952.

Buenos Aires

Long-distance road races for saloon cars were the staple of Argentinian racing from the 1930s, but then street races became all the rage after the end of the Second World War, with tracks laid out in Buenos Aires, Mar del Plata, Mendoza and Rosario attracting entries from Europe through Europe's winter months. Then, following Buenos Aires' example of building a purpose-built circuit in 1952, other cities around Argentina, such as Córdoba and Mendoza, followed suit in the 1960s. Many European racers got to try these too as Argentinian circuits hosted the Temporada series for F2 cars from 1964 to 1968.

Yet, only Buenos Aires' circuit – named the Autódromo Oscar Alfredo Gálvez after a local star racing driver, having initially been called the Autódromo 17 de Octubre in deference to the date President Peron became president in the 1950s (up to the point that he was sent into exile in 1955) – has ever been seen as being of F1 standard.

Built on land that was too waterlogged to farm on the southern edge of Buenos Aires, the circuit opened in 1952 and was ahead of its time in offering numerous circuit configurations, with enough cut-throughs for a dozen different track layouts. The one that was used for the Grand Prix in the 1950s was relatively twisty No. 2, before the 1972 and 1973 Argentinian GPs ran on a circuit with a shorter run to and from the final corner. From 1974, though, the full-fat No. 15 layout was used, with an extension of two long straights and two fairly fast corners around a reservoir adding 1.6 miles to the lap length. For F1's return in 1995, however, the high-speed loop was dropped and a far twistier section added as more than a mile was lopped off the lap length.

The venue's greatest days came in the 1950s, when Fangio gave the home support plenty to cheer by winning four years in a row, for Maserati in 1954 and 1957, Mercedes in 1955 and Ferrari in 1956.

Argentina's economic woes, with inflation its constant enemy, even today, led to the Buenos Aires circuit being dropped from the World Championship.

Opposite: Jody Scheckter leads Carlos Reutemann in 1977, when he gave the Wolf team a dream start and won on its debut outing.

Following pages: A packed pit lane before the cars were sent out onto the track in 1957.

TRACK FACTS

Circuit name:	Buenos Aires
Location:	20 miles (32.2 km) south of central Buenos Aires
Opened:	1952
First Grand Prix:	1953
Circuit length:	2.645 miles/4.257 km
Number of laps:	72
Most wins:	4 – Juan Manuel Fangio (1954, 1955, 1956, 1957)

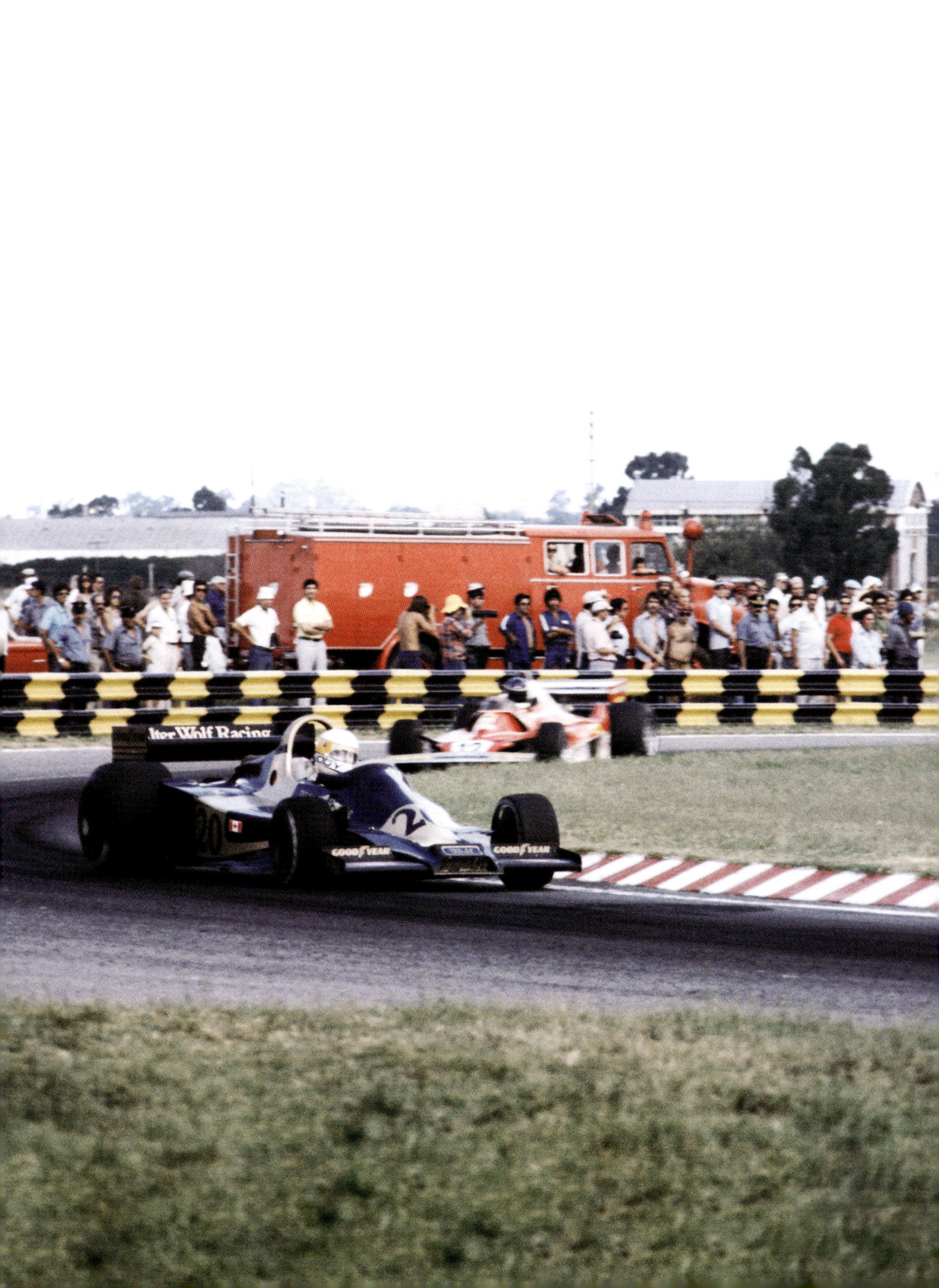
lter Wolf Racing
GOODYEAR
GOODYEAR

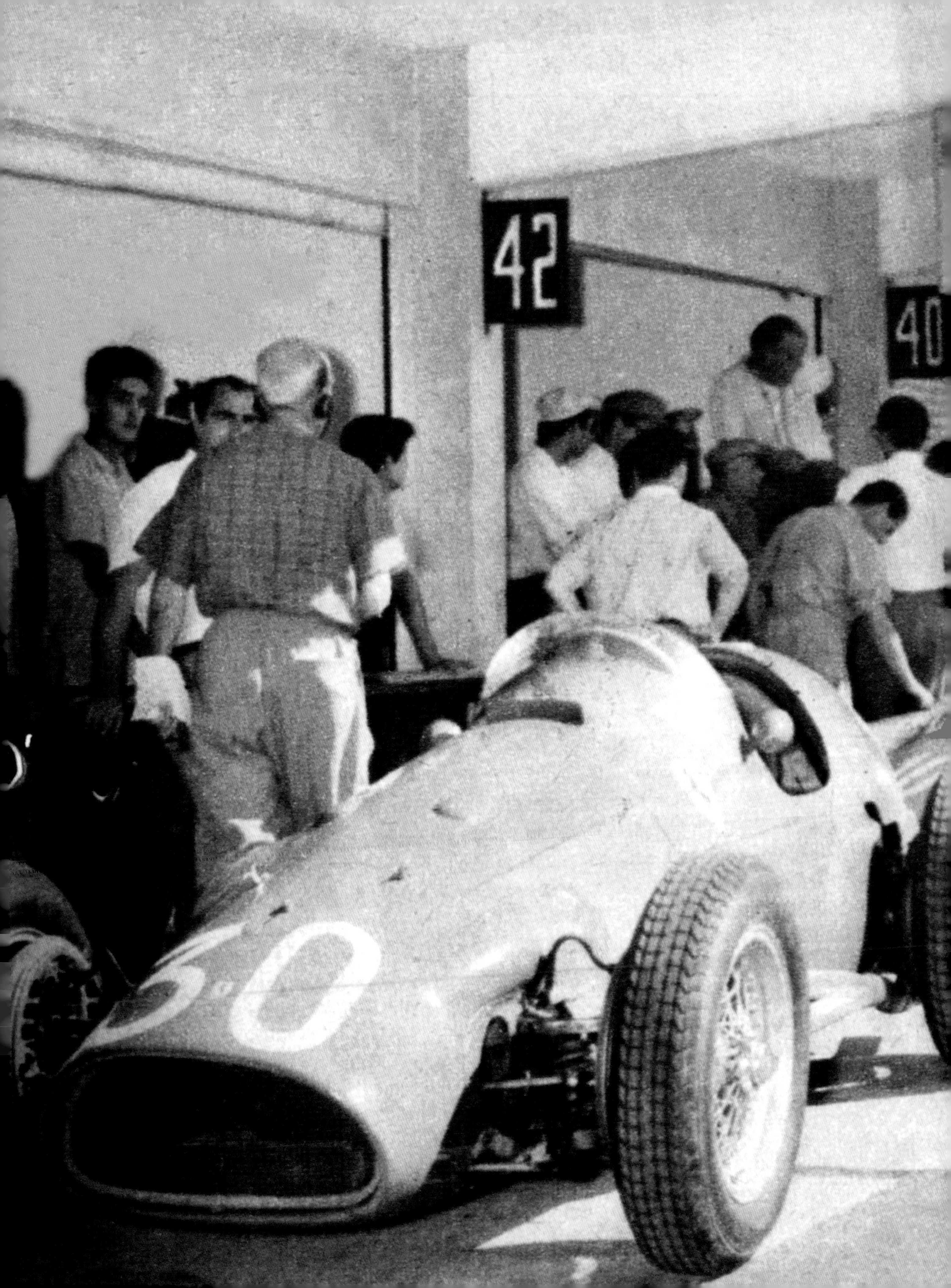
42
40

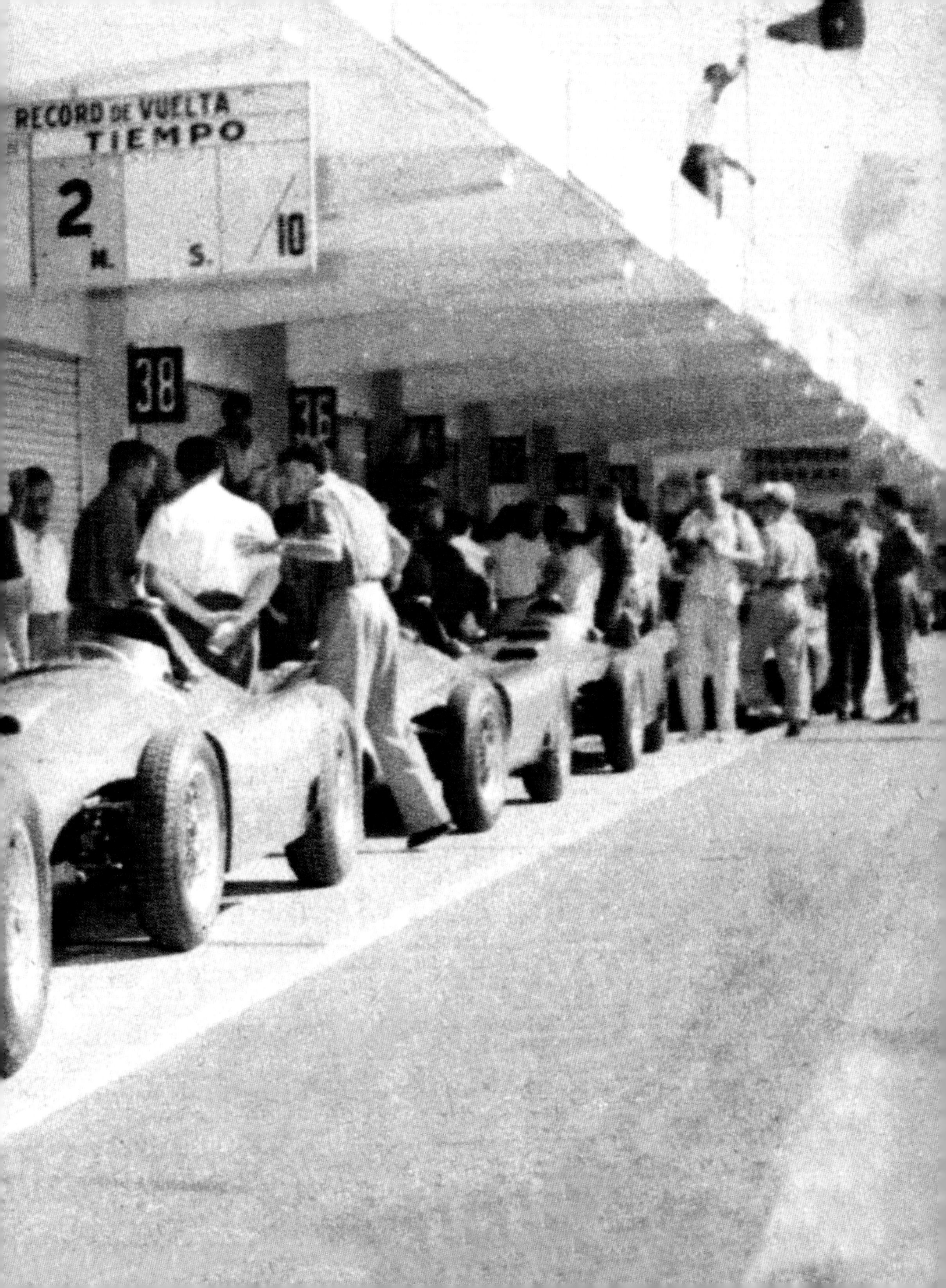
RECORD DE VUELTA
TIEMPO
2
M.
S.
10
38

MOMENTS

Soaring temperatures and spikes of action were features of the Argentinian GP and it was also the scene of history being made in 1958.

Moss scores first rear-engined win

Stirling Moss had no expectations of winning the 1958 season opener, but win he did and history was made, as this was the first World Championship win by a car which had the engine positioned behind the driver. Juan Manuel Fangio set the pace in his Maserati, with Moss's Rob Walker Racing Cooper seventh on a ten-car grid, with teams like BRM and Vanwall not making the trip due to confusion about a change to 'Avgas' aviation fuel. Knowing that he was 100bhp down on the Maseratis and Ferraris, the tactic chosen was to run the race on one set of tyres, and this put him into the lead on the thirty-fifth lap of eighty. Ferrari's Luigi Musso began closing, still expecting Moss to pit, then realised too late what Moss was trying to do.

Reutemann denied on home ground

Starting his third year in F1 with Brabham, Carlos Reutemann began 1974 with high hopes. Helped by a first-corner melee that delayed Mike Hailwood, Clay Regazzoni and the Shadows of Peter Revson and Jean-Pierre Jarier, with John Watson and Jody Scheckter having to pit. James Hunt usurped poleman Ronnie Peterson, then lost his clutch and this let Peterson back ahead, with Reutemann climbing from sixth to second by the end of the first lap. Two laps later, Reutemann took the lead and he managed to stetch this to thirty seconds over McLaren's Denny Hulme before his BT44's airbox began to fall apart. A misfire set in and Hulme went past with a lap and a half to go. A lap later, Reutemann parked up, his car, embarrassingly, having run out of fuel.

Michael Schumacher beats the McLarens

McLaren began 1998 by waltzing to one-two finishes for Mika Häkkinen ahead of David Coulthard at both Melbourne and Interlagos. Then came Buenos Aires and Michael Schumacher cheered Ferrari fans by toppling them. Coulthard led away from pole, with Häkkinen moving past Schumacher into second. Early on the second lap, Schumacher was back in second and set off after the Scot. He took the first possible opportunity to pass Coulthard, diving up the inside into the first corner in a move that the kindest might call 'robust'. Coulthard was tipped into a spin and fell to sixth, but Schumacher's Ferrari was unscathed. Now in a straight battle with Häkkinen, Schumacher's one-stop choice worked better than the Finn's two-stopper and he won with ease.

Opposite: Juan Manuel Fangio acknowledges his home crowd as he blasts his Mercedes across the finish line to victory in 1955.

Below: Carlos Reutemann steers his Brabham through the penultimate corner in the 1974 Argentinian GP when he led but ran out of fuel.

Juan Manuel Fangio takes a home win

Searing temperatures were often a factor in Buenos Aires and 1955 was one of F1's hottest visits. Juan Manuel Fangio arrived in good spirits with Mercedes, but was outqualified as compatriot José Froilán González put his Ferrari on pole, with Lancia's Alberto Ascari next up and then Fangio. In the race, though, Fangio took the lead on the first lap, but it was so competitive that both Ascari and González took turns in front before Ascari crashed out. González, chunky of frame, had to call at the pits to be refreshed and allow teammate Nino Farina to take over as his own car had already gone out. Fangio, though, stopped once to pour water over himself but then raced on to win by ninety seconds.

BRAZIL

Brazilian fans have had plenty to cheer about, with Emerson Fittipaldi, Nelson Piquet and Ayrton Senna all becoming world champion.

The Brazilians have always loved motor racing and there was a lively national scene packed with street races in the 1930s, chiefly in São Paulo. Wanting to match the leading European racing nations in having permanent circuits that they would be able to use more frequently, Interlagos was built in 1940 on a hillside on the outer edge of the city.

With racing blossoming at Interlagos in the 1950s, the national scene grew. Minor circuits held races, but it was only really in the 1970s that the standard really rose and other leading Brazilian cities got in on the act. Brasilia struck first and built a circuit to the north-east of the national capital, even attracting the non-championship Presidenta Medici GP that Emerson Fittipaldi won for McLaren. He had already had adulation at home, though, as he won Brazil's first-ever World Championship race at Interlagos the year before for Lotus and had just repeated the feat, this time for McLaren.

Rio de Janeiro watched on with envy and elected to build a circuit of its own, Jacarepaguá, getting the job completed in 1977. Suddenly, Brazil had three world-class circuits and the national scene really took off, turning the trickle of young talent that it sent to further their careers in Europe to a torrent.

Jacarepaguá held the Brazilian GP in 1978, when Carlos Reutemann won for Ferrari, then took the race over from Interlagos from 1981 until 1989, after which it returned to Interlagos where it has remained ever since.

Opposite: George Russell leads teammate Lewis Hamilton into Interlagos's first corner to win the penultimate round of 2022.

Below: Carlos Pace won once in F1, doing so for Brabham in round two in 1975 at Interlagos.

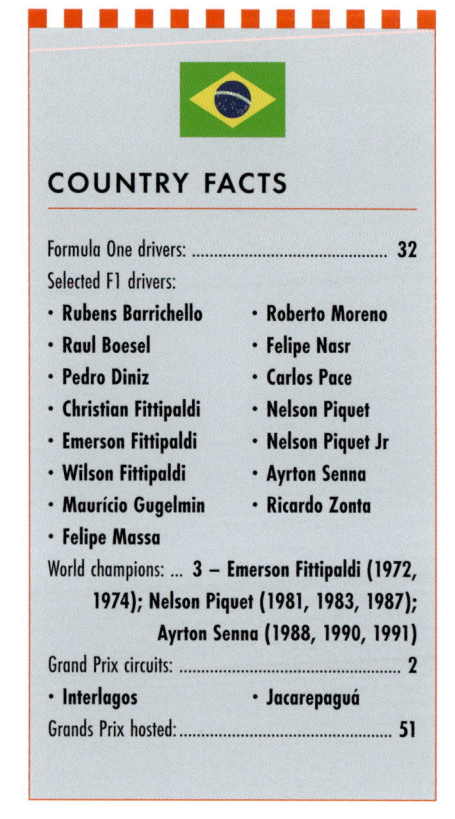

COUNTRY FACTS

Formula One drivers: 32
Selected F1 drivers:
- Rubens Barrichello
- Raul Boesel
- Pedro Diniz
- Christian Fittipaldi
- Emerson Fittipaldi
- Wilson Fittipaldi
- Maurício Gugelmin
- Felipe Massa
- Roberto Moreno
- Felipe Nasr
- Carlos Pace
- Nelson Piquet
- Nelson Piquet Jr
- Ayrton Senna
- Ricardo Zonta

World champions: ... 3 – Emerson Fittipaldi (1972, 1974); Nelson Piquet (1981, 1983, 1987); Ayrton Senna (1988, 1990, 1991)
Grand Prix circuits: 2
- Interlagos
- Jacarepaguá

Grands Prix hosted: 51

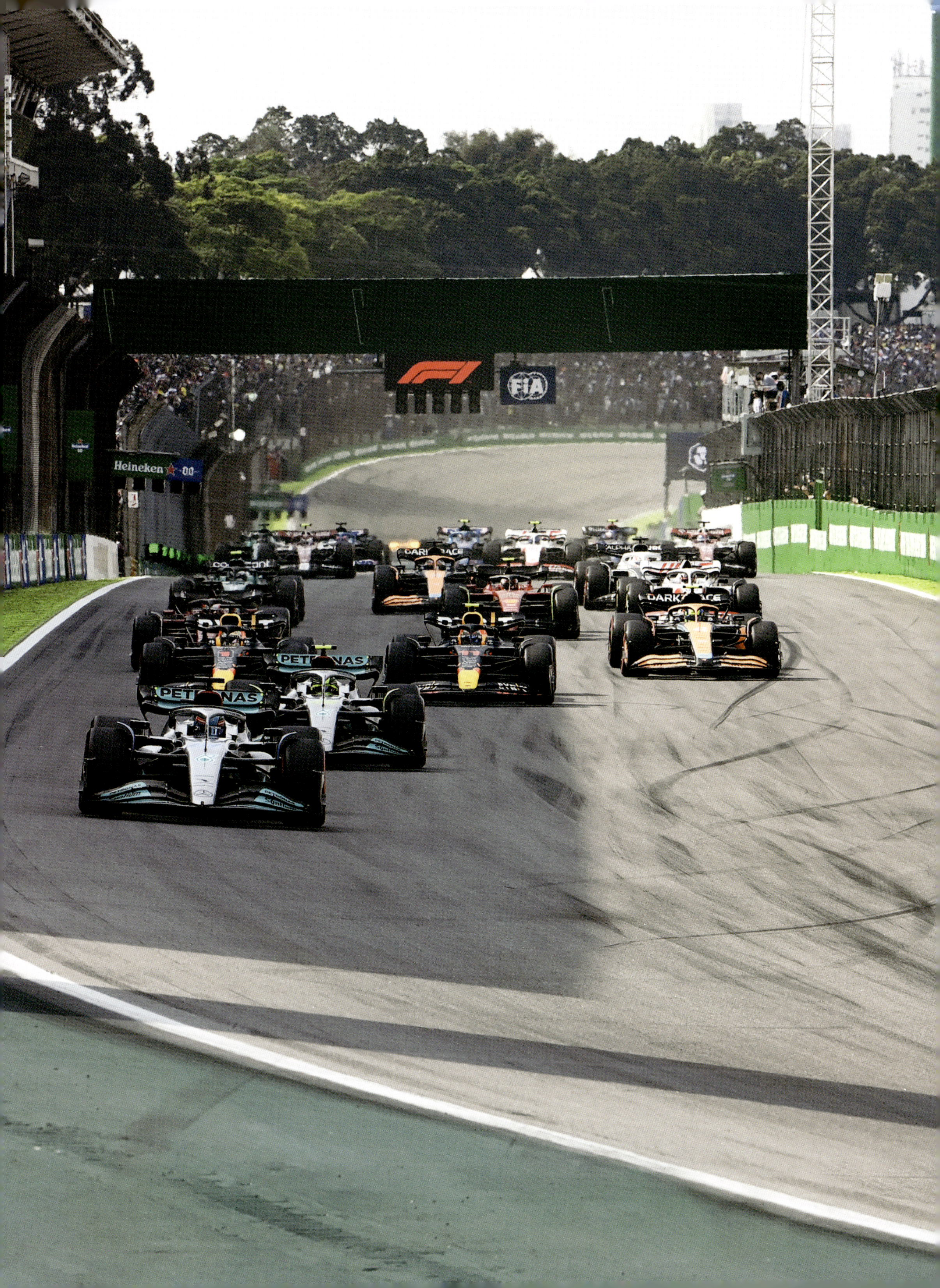
Heineken
FIA

DRIVERS

Brazil has been blessed with some of F1's greatest talents, claiming three multiple world champions with Ayrton Senna being the best of the lot.

Ayrton Senna

Incredibly fast and able to operate on a level above his rivals in terms of focus and intensity, Ayrton was also uncompromising. He was among the world's top kart racers before he went to race Formula Ford in England and although he found it tough living away from home, he won titles. After a classic scrap with Martin Brundle for the 1983 British F3 crown, Ayrton stepped up to F1 in 1984. Toleman wasn't a top team, but he took second at Monaco. Then Lotus got him, and Ayrton won second time out at Estoril. It took a move to McLaren in 1988 for the wins to really flow and he beat teammate Alain Prost to the title, winning another in 1990 once Prost had joined Ferrari and then a third in 1991. With Williams in the ascendancy, he joined them for 1994 and found a challenger in Benetton's Michael Schumacher, but he died at the third race at Imola.

Emerson Fittipaldi

Here was a driver who was a trendsetter, and not just because of his sideburns. Emerson was the first Brazilian to succeed in Europe. Older brother Wilson had tried this three years earlier but came home, while Emerson went up in 1969 and sped through Formula Ford and F3 with Lotus, then tried F2 in 1970, stepped up to F1 at midseason and was a winner before the year was out. Emerson became world champion in 1972, moved to McLaren in 1974 and was champion again. A move to his brother's team proved unwise, however, and he retired at the end of 1980.

Rubens Barrichello

Winning the GM Lotus Euroseries and British F3 titles in his first two years in Europe and then ranking third in F3000 earned Rubens his F1 break with Jordan in 1993. A third place in 1994 was followed by second in Canada in 1995. Stewart GP signed Rubens for 1997 and he took second at Monaco, but it took a move to Ferrari in 2000 for that first win at Hockenheim. Although number two to Michael Schumacher, he added eight more wins before joining Honda. His final wins came in 2009 when the team became Brawn, but Rubens raced on until the end of 2011.

Felipe Massa

This is the Brazilian who was world champion for thirty seconds. This was in the 2008 Brazilian GP, just before Lewis Hamilton gained a place on the final lap. Felipe's pedigree was clear when he was picked up by Sauber. A little wild in 2002, he stepped down in 2003 before returning and maturing enough for Ferrari to sign him for 2006. Turkey became his happy hunting ground, as he won there three times before having a lucky escape when hit on the helmet by a spring in Hungary in 2009, and although he raced on in F1 until 2017 he was never a winner again.

Nelson Piquet

Emerson Fittipaldi blazed a trail for Brazilians and Nelson was one of the next young pretenders to go to Europe. He went straight to F3 and impressed but stayed for a second year when he, fellow Brazilian Chico Serra and Derek Warwick fought over the title. Before the year was out, Nelson had his first taste of F1, for Ensign. For 1979, though, he was a Brabham driver, and this was to be his team for seven seasons, with his first win coming in 1980, his first title in 1981, his second in 1983 before a move to Williams brought his third in 1987.

CIRCUITS

The circuits that have hosted the Brazilian GP, São Paulo's Interlagos and Rio de Janeiro's Jacarepaguá, could not be more different.

Interlagos

Opened in 1940 on the southern outskirts of São Paulo, Interlagos, meaning 'between the lakes', took its name from its site, a hillside that is dotted with lakes. The circuit was just short of five miles long and its original course can still be seen when F1 visits, with the old banked first corner being built into the hillside at the feet of the grandstands just beyond the point at which the current first corner dives to the left at the end of the pitwall. This lengthy circuit was used all the way until 1989, when a shorter circuit was introduced, using much of the original circuit but cutting out several loops down to the bottom of the slope. The new lap was just 2.677 miles (4.309 km) long.

With neighbour Argentina having had a competitive racing scene after the Second World War and a World Championship round since 1953, Brazil was desperate to get in on the act and so it hosted a series of F2 races in 1971 and 1972. Known as the Torneio races, Emerson Fittipaldi won the first pair and one of the three the following year, with fellow Brazilian Carlos Pace also winning. These were followed by a non-championship F1 race in 1972 and this was enough for Brazil to host a round of the World Championship in 1973.

Whereas the original circuit went up and down the hillside ten times and was more high-speed in format, the second iteration goes up and down the slope just six times. The first curve is a steep esse and the track continues to descend to Descida do Lago before coming back up to start a snaking passage from behind one end of the paddock, hitting high points at Ferradura and Cotovelo and rejoining the old sweeping run up the slope to the finish line just after Junção, sweeping through flat-out Arquibandas and on through the final kink where the track sits low between the pitwall and the front of the grandstands.

The atmosphere at Interlagos remains the most febrile of the lot, making every Grand Prix feel like a party and every Grand Prix with a Brazilian driver in the reckoning like a festival.

Opposite: Ferrari's Felipe Massa wins in 2008 but the title would go to Lewis Hamilton.

TRACK FACTS

Circuit name:	Interlagos
Location:	9 miles (14.5 km) south of central São Paulo
Opened:	1940
First Grand Prix:	1973
Circuit length:	2.677 miles/4.309 km
Number of laps:	71
Most wins:	4 – Michael Schumacher (1994, 1995, 2000, 2002)

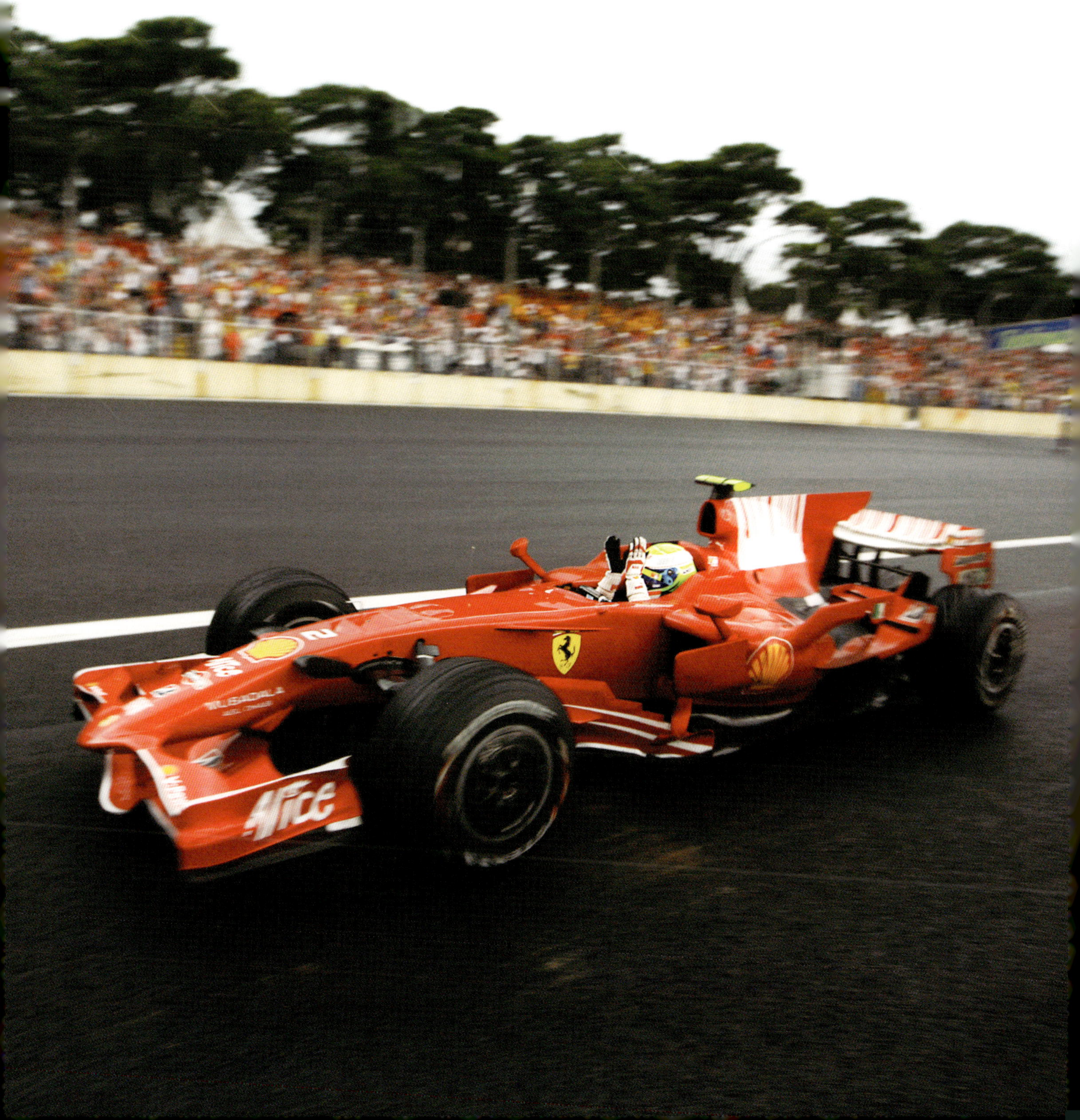

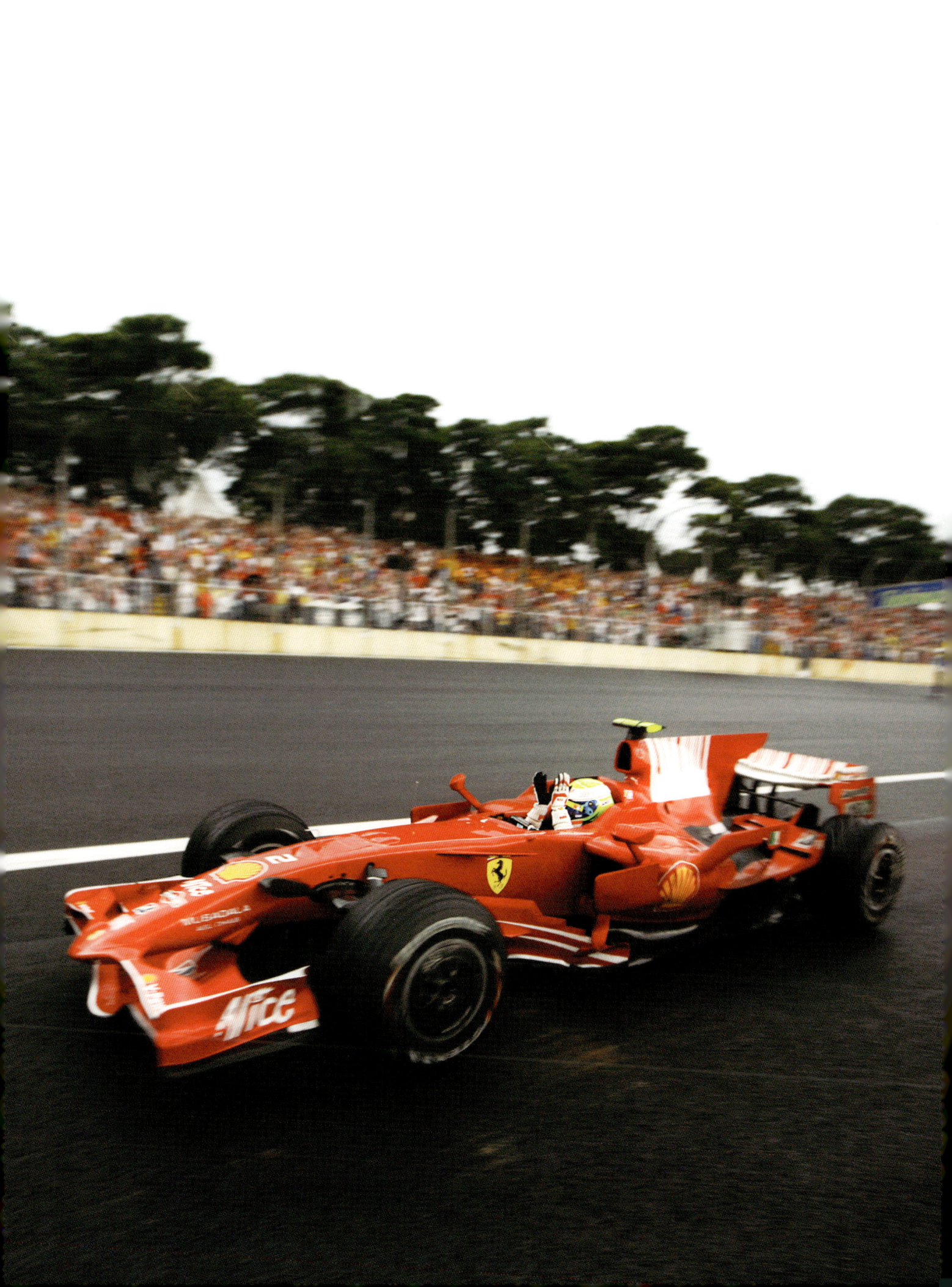

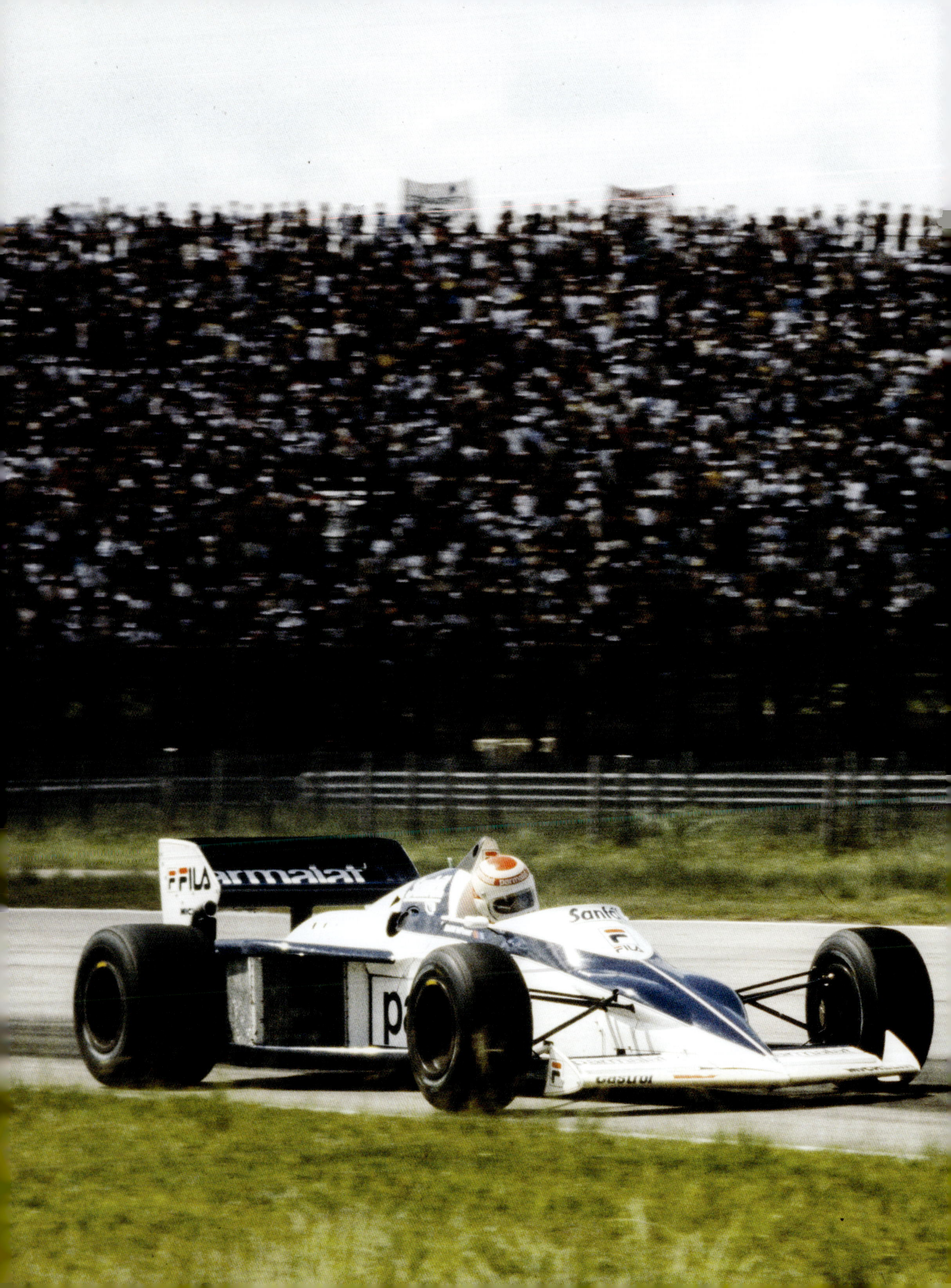
FILA

Jacarepaguá

Opened for racing on a flat piece of marshy land outside Rio de Janeiro in 1977, Jacarepaguá had some nobbly hills in the background, but it was never going to be as attractive as Interlagos which nestled into a rolling hillside. Furthermore, its lap simply didn't provide the same level of challenge.

The lap began with a long, open right-hander, a sharper turn to the left and then a broad hairpin. From here, a kink then an open corner and a tighter one brought the cars to its main straight. There was a wide, open left-hander at the end of the straight, followed by a swerve to the right and another to the left before arriving at Lagoa, a tight left. The very quick Box corner caught the attention before drivers had to brake heavily for the tight final turn, Vitória, onto the short start-finish straight.

The World Championship was welcomed for the first time in 1978 and victory was taken by Carlos Reutemann for Ferrari. It seemed, though, that Jacarepaguá might be a one-hit wonder, a waste of money, as the Brazilian GP returned to Interlagos the following year.

However, F1's embrace of ground-effects technology meant that the cars struggled to work over Interlagos's notoriously bumpy surface and so F1 returned to Jacarepaguá in 1980 and stayed there for nine years. It took until 1983 for a home winner, when Nelson Piquet won for Brabham to make up for having his win there in 1982 taken away for being underweight. Piquet then won here again in 1986, this time for Williams, and he had the circuit named after him when he won the third of his F1 titles in 1987.

After losing the Brazilian GP after 1989, Jacarepaguá kept its name up in lights by hosting an Indycar round from 1996 to 2000 on an alternative oval circuit. This was something that world champion and later Indycar champion Emerson Fittipaldi arranged because the Indycar grid had become packed with Brazilians, including André Ribeiro who won the first of these races.

Left: Nelson Piquet began 1983 with a home win and went on to his second title.

Following pages: Rubens Barrichello leads the pack at Interlagos in 2009 in his Brawn.

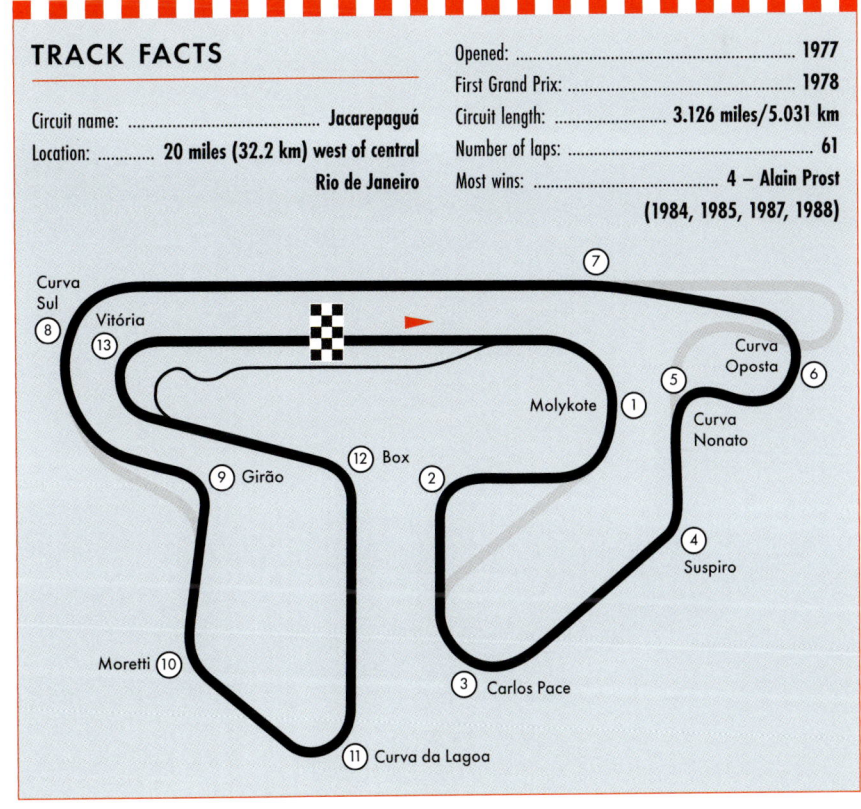

TRACK FACTS

Circuit name: Jacarepaguá
Location: 20 miles (32.2 km) west of central Rio de Janeiro
Opened: 1977
First Grand Prix: 1978
Circuit length: 3.126 miles/5.031 km
Number of laps: 61
Most wins: 4 – Alain Prost (1984, 1985, 1987, 1988)

BRAZIL 157

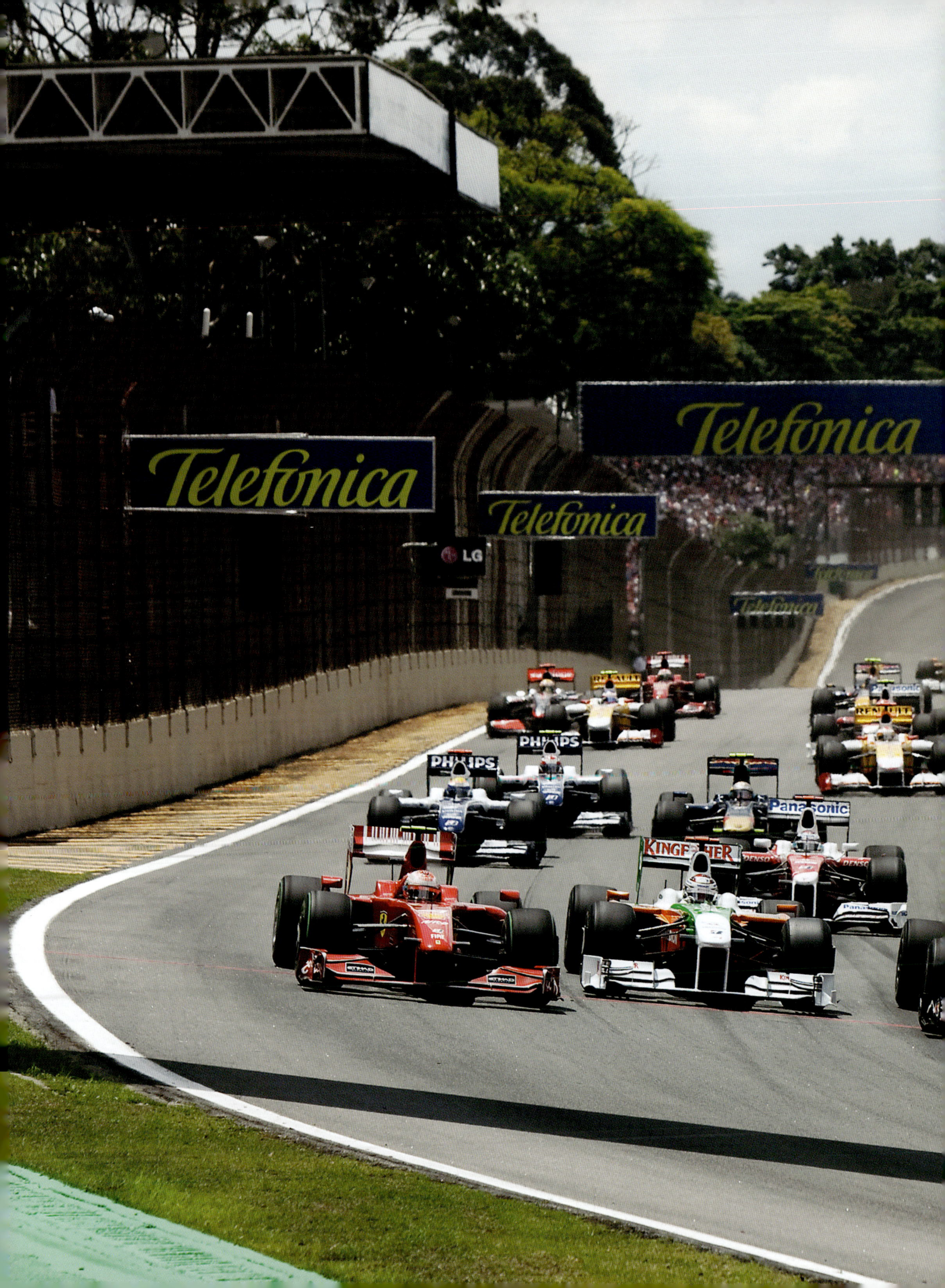
Telefonica
Telefonica
Telefonica
LG

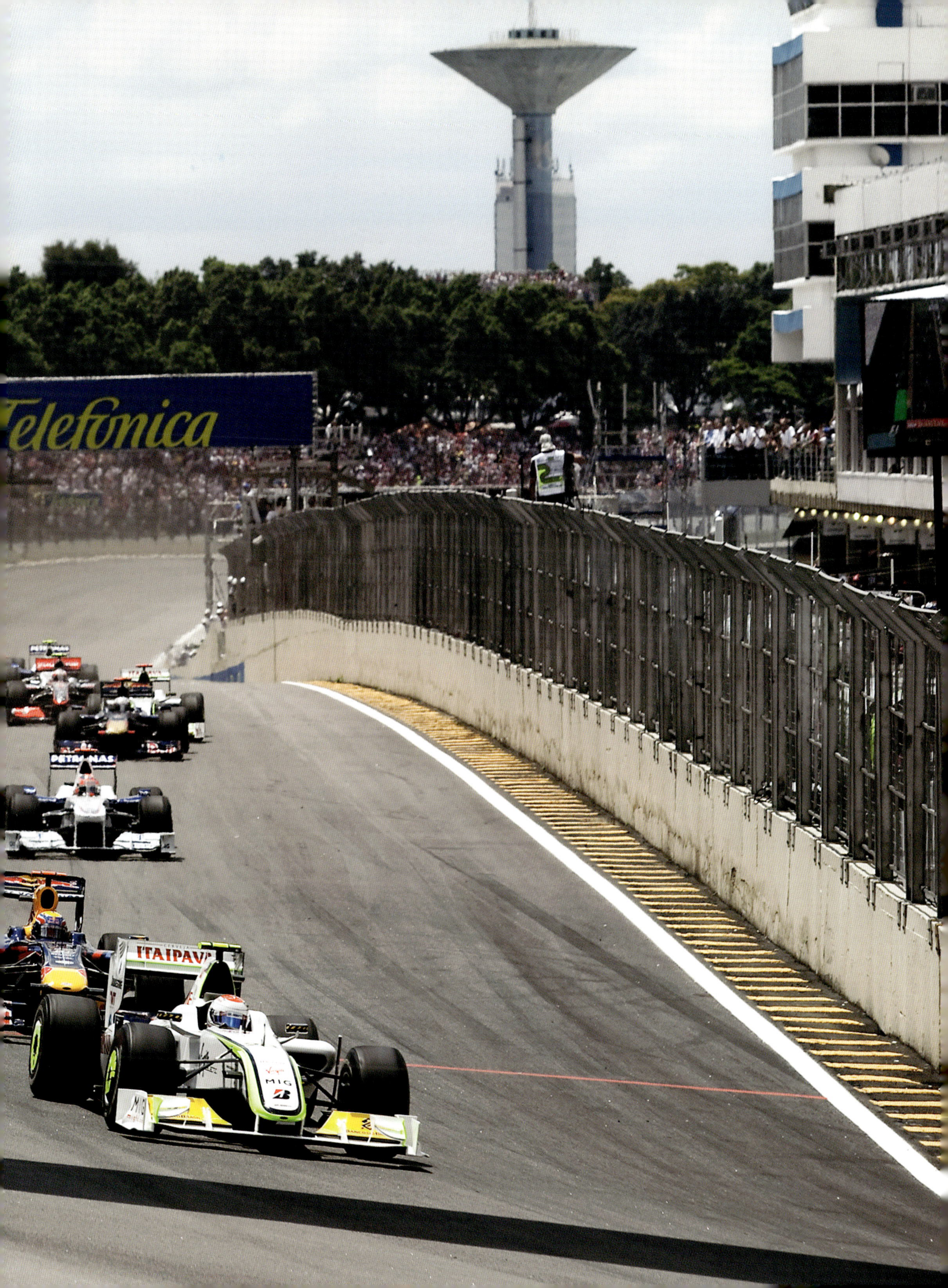
Telefonica
ITAIPAVA
PETRONAS

MOMENTS

Races at Jacarepaguá were seldom exciting, whereas the ones at Interlagos inevitably are and this quartet are among the best.

Hamilton sneaks his first crown

For a few moments after Felipe Massa had won his home Grand Prix in 2008, he thought he had become world champion. Cruelly, he hadn't, as Lewis Hamilton would go on to take the crown. Massa had led from pole, knowing that he had to win, while Hamilton knew that he only had to finish fifth. The track was wet but soon dried and McLaren left Hamilton out a lap too long and he fell back to seventh. With seven laps to go, rain sent drivers in for rain tyres and Hamilton emerged fifth, which was enough, before he fell to sixth, which wasn't. Ferrari's Massa raced to victory, and his crew erupted but, aghast, they saw that Hamilton had passed Timo Glock in the final few corners to be crowned champion instead.

Verstappen splashes to victory

The sport's historians will be forever divided on just how great Max Verstappen's victory was at a very wet Interlagos in 2024. His performance in streaming conditions was remarkable as he overcame starting seventeenth because of a red flag scuppering his best lap, plus a further five-place penalty. Yet, there is a factor that led to this turnaround. This is that the race was red flagged just after the frontrunners had pitted for fresh tyres and those that hadn't thus rose to the front of the queue and then were allowed to change them without losing their place in the race order before the race restarted. The Alpines also benefitted and early race leader George Russell had to follow them home in fourth.

Senna wins at home at last

Ayrton Senna had twenty-eight Grand Prix wins and two drivers' titles to his name when he arrived at Interlagos in 1991, and he had good momentum after winning the season's opening round at Phoenix. What he wanted above all else was a win on home turf and so sticking his McLaren on pole was a good start, but he was hounded by Nigel Mansell's Williams until its gearbox failed with twelve laps to go. Then Ayrton realised that his was failing too, with gears coming and going. Eventually, he stuck it in sixth gear for the final lap, not ideal on slicks in the rain, and prayed. Riccardo Patrese was closing fast in the second Williams, but Ayrton had done just enough and the crowd went wild.

Opposite: Emerson Fittipaldi takes the chequered flag for Lotus at Interlagos in 1973.

Below: Ayrton Senna finally landed a home win in 1991, despite his McLaren missing third and fifth gears towards the end of the race.

Fittipaldi entertains his home crowd

Emerson Fittipaldi won the first Brazilian GP in 1973 with Lotus, but then returned to Interlagos in 1974 and did it again, this time for McLaren. Teammate Denny Hulme had won the season opener in Argentina, but Fittipaldi put his M23 on pole here. He was beaten away at the start by Carlos Reutemann from the outside of the front row in his Brabham, and then Ronnie Peterson led for a few laps for Lotus, but Emmo took over on the sixteenth lap. When Peterson had to pit because of a puncture, the pressure was off. Emmo was now in total control and was given a helping hand when a sudden downpour brought the race to a premature end, not that the happy home crowd minded.

BRAZIL | 161

CANADA

The Canadian racing scene is only competitive up to a point, and all its drivers who reached F1 headed overseas to make their mark.

Compared to the United States, the Canadian racing scene is nowhere near as rich in depth or history. Its long winters and late springs might have something to do with that, but it took decades to create facilities at which the country's aspiring drivers could learn. Indeed, its most talented driver to date, Gilles Villeneuve, spent his youth and early twenties racing snowmobiles instead.

Mosport Park opened in 1961 and this provided a venue for the first Canadian GP, a race for sportscars that was won by Pete Ryan in a Lotus 19. It would remain a sportscar race for a further four years.

The greatest days of racing in Canada came from the mid-1960s when the Can Am series and its powerful sportscars rumbled into town. Most of the rounds were held in the USA, but St Jovite and Mosport Park were in from the start, with a race in Edmonton following.

Racing was exploding in Canada and its Grand Prix became a World Championship round in 1967, with Jack Brabham triumphant at Mosport Park. Then, in a pattern of alternation, St Jovite held the race in 1968, won by McLaren's Denny Hulme. However, St Jovite was thought too narrow and bumpy, so Mosport Park held the Canadian GP from 1971 until 1977.

Then a new circuit arrived and took the race over, as Mosport Park had become considered dangerous. The new circuit was on an island on the other side of the St Lawrence River from Montreal and it has been there ever since.

Below: Max Verstappen leads away for Red Bull at the start of the 2022 Canadian GP.

Opposite: Jacky Ickx blasts his Ferrari past the autumn colours in 1970.

COUNTRY FACTS

Formula One drivers: 15
Selected F1 drivers:
- George Eaton
- Lance Stroll
- Nicholas Latifi
- Gilles Villeneuve
- Al Pease
- Jacques Villeneuve
- Peter Ryan

World champions: 1 – Jacques Villeneuve (1997)
Grand Prix circuits: 3
- Montreal
- St Jovite
- Mosport Park

Grands Prix hosted: 53

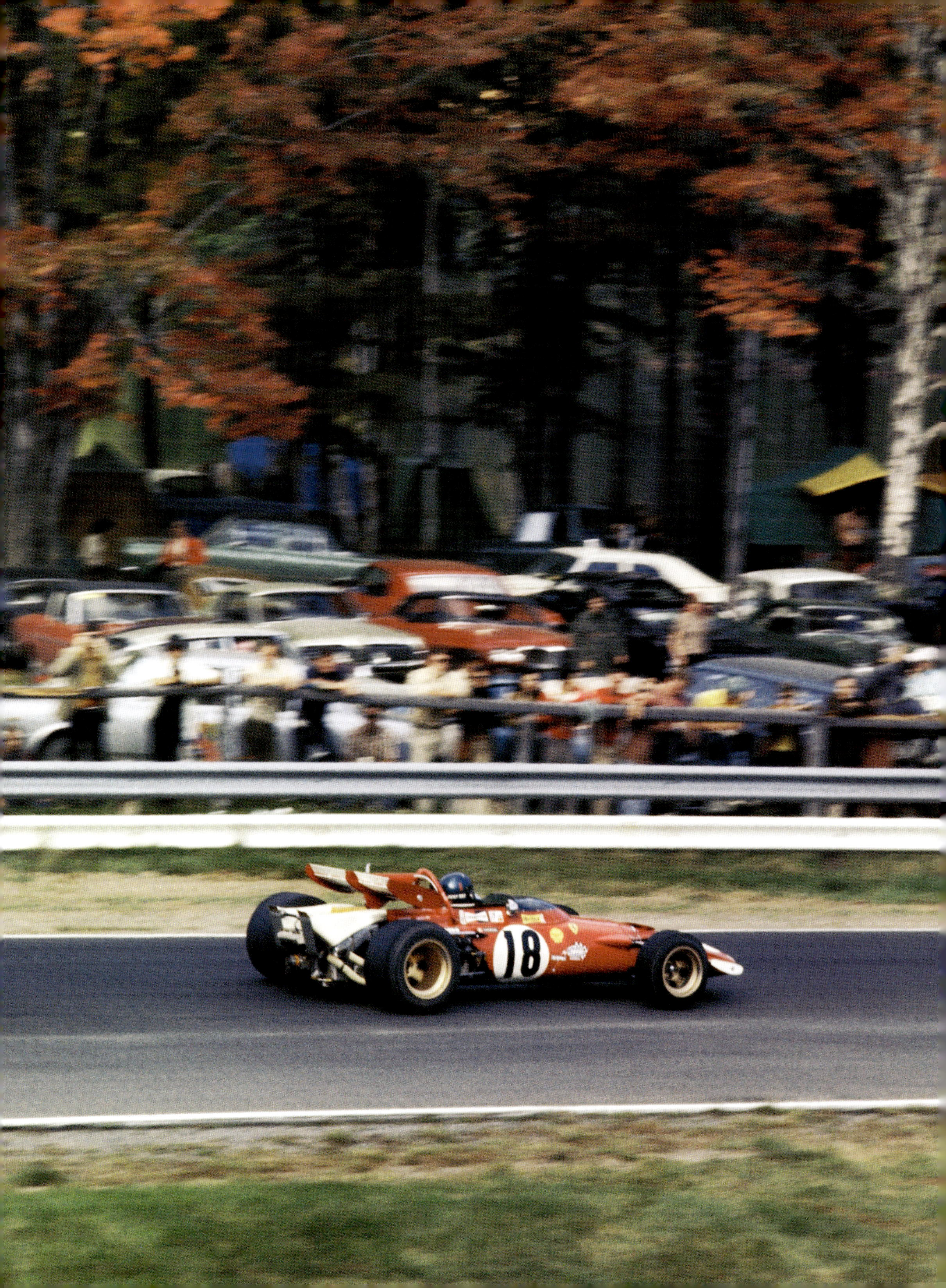
18

DRIVERS

Gilles won Grands Prix, son Jacques won the world title and the rest, thus far, have only played a supporting role to the Villeneuves.

Lance Stroll

Propelled into racing by his father Lawrence, who not only raced Ferraris and owns the St Jovite circuit but also now runs Aston Martin, Lance was a quick learner, winning the Italian F4 title before he turned sixteen. After winning the Toyota Racing Series title in New Zealand, Lance won the European F3 crown at his second attempt. With money no object, he jumped straight into F1 in 2017. Two seasons at Williams removed his rough edges and resulted in a third-place finish in Baku, a result he equalled twice in 2020 for Racing Point before the team became Aston Martin.

Nicholas Latifi

Canadian fans waited years to get a driver in F1 after Jacques Villeneuve's retirement then two came along together, with Nicholas following Lance Stroll. Although he didn't have a karting pedigree, Nicholas went straight to F3, so it was little surprise that he found it tough in his first two years. Family wealth meant that he could afford to race what he wanted, but he didn't impress in Formula Renault 3.5 and it took him four years to shine in GP2/F2, finishing as runner-up in 2019. With Williams needing a driver with a budget, Nicholas got his F1 break in 2020, but he quit after three seasons.

George Eaton

Being a scion of a family who owned the country's largest department stores helped George to afford to go racing, first with an AC Cobra and then in a McLaren sportscar. After going well in Can Am, he tried single-seaters, racing in Formula A in 1969. The year was marked by BRM inviting him to contest two end-of-year F1 races and George landed a full-season contract for 1970. His pace was nothing to write home about, though. Until he came to the Canadian GP, when knowledge of St Jovite helped him to qualify in the top half of the grid and come home tenth.

Gilles Villeneuve

Gilles was happy to perform on the edge. Famously, on his F1 debut at the 1977 British GP, he spun his McLaren time and again in practice, explaining to the team that you have to find the limit to know where it is. Fortunately, he was quick too. Ferrari snapped him up for 1978 and, famously and fittingly, he won the final race of the year, in Canada. In 1979, Ferrari was at the front, and he added three wins as he became runner-up behind teammate Jody Scheckter, but all this panache ended at Zolder in 1982 when he crashed in qualifying.

Jacques Villeneuve

Canada's only world champion grew up at circuits as he followed his father around until Gilles was killed when Jacques was eleven. So it came as a surprise when he too started racing, first in the Italian F3 series and then in Japan. Racing in Formula Atlantic came next, and this led to Indycars in 1994. Jacques finished second in the Indy 500. In 1995, he put that right and became Indycar's youngest champion. The door to F1 soon opened and he almost won first time out for Williams, ranking second to teammate Damon Hill. In 1997, Jacques won seven Grands Prix to land the title. He took an odd move in 1999 to join BAR, an all-new team and eleven retirements in the first eleven races set the tone. Two podiums in 2001 marked progress, but his last win was behind him and since his F1 career dwindled, Jacques has raced where and what he fancies.

CIRCUITS

Mosport Park and Mont-Tremblant hosted Grands Prix in Canada before F1 found its more permanent home there in Montreal, at a circuit which had a magic about it as it produced a home winner at its first attempt.

Montreal

The World Championship, and Canada in particular, knew that running its Grands Prix miles from major cities was not the best way to boost its crowds. Street races could do that, but they came with a huge amount of disruption that had to be repeated each year. So, when a new home for the Canadian GP was being considered in the late 1970s, Montreal came up with the great idea of placing its race right next to but not in the city. Its chosen site was the Île Notre-Dame, an island just across the St Lawrence River that was easily accessible by the metro.

The island had been used when Montreal hosted the EXPO trade show in 1967 and again when the rowing lake was built there for the 1976 Olympic Games. There was limited space into which to squeeze an F1 circuit, pits, paddock and grandstands, but they managed.

The lap is necessarily long and thin, defined by the shape of the island and, having moved the pits from their initial location on the run from the hairpin to the where they are now in 1988, begins with a swerve to the right before the first real corner turns the cars to the left. The next corner follows almost immediately and turns the cars through 180 degrees and, after a short burst of acceleration they enter a series of esses. These tighten up at Turn 6 before the drivers get a proper blast all the way to the hairpin save for chicanes at Turns 8 and 9. The hairpin, L'Épingle, is one of the best places to overtake, or drivers can try to slipstream up the straight and make a move into the final corner, a right-left chicane onto the start-finish straight.

Canadian hero Gilles Villeneuve gave the circuit a dream debut by winning here in 1978, but it is also known for accidents, notably drivers hitting the wall out of the final chicane, for Jean Alesi's tears of joy when he took his first win, for Daniel Ricciardo beaming after hunting down Nico Rosberg in 2014 and for the torrential downpour that delayed play in 2011.

With so many of the circuits that were built specifically to host a Grand Prix in the following four decades being designed by Herrmann Tilke, this one remains distinctive and all the better for that.

Opposite: Jacques Villeneuve ran hard for Williams in 1996, but had to settle for second.

TRACK FACTS

Circuit name: .... **Circuit Gilles Villeneuve**
Location: .... **On Île Notre-Dame,**
                              opposite Montreal
Opened: **1978**
First Grand Prix: **1978**
Circuit length: .... **2.710 miles/4.361 km**
Number of laps: **70**
Most wins: .... **7 – Michael Schumacher**
(1994, 1997, 1998, 2000, 2002, 2003, 2004);
Lewis Hamilton
(2007, 2010, 2012, 2015, 2016, 2017, 2019)

CANADA

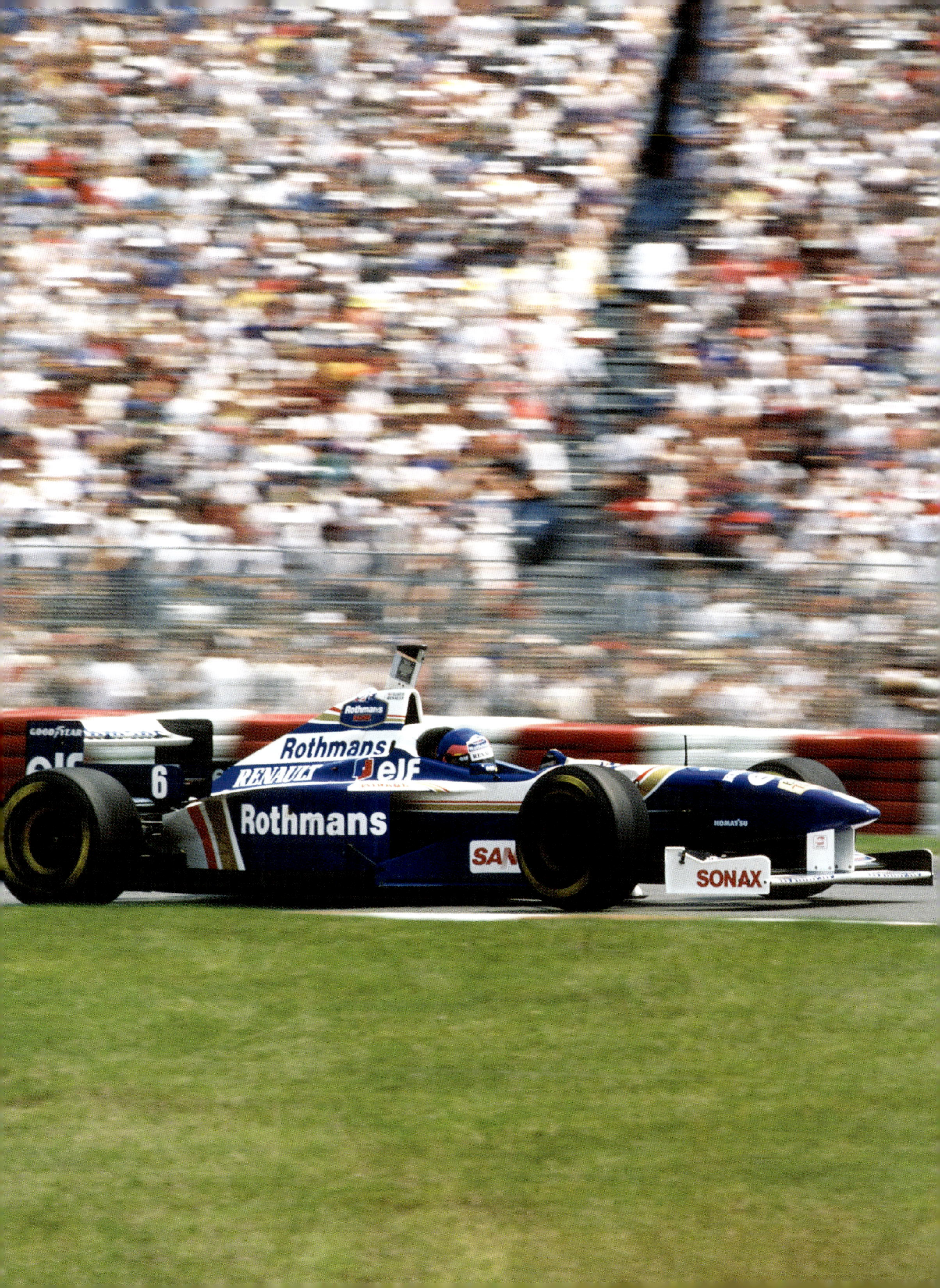
Rothmans
RENAULT
elf
6
Rothmans
SONAX

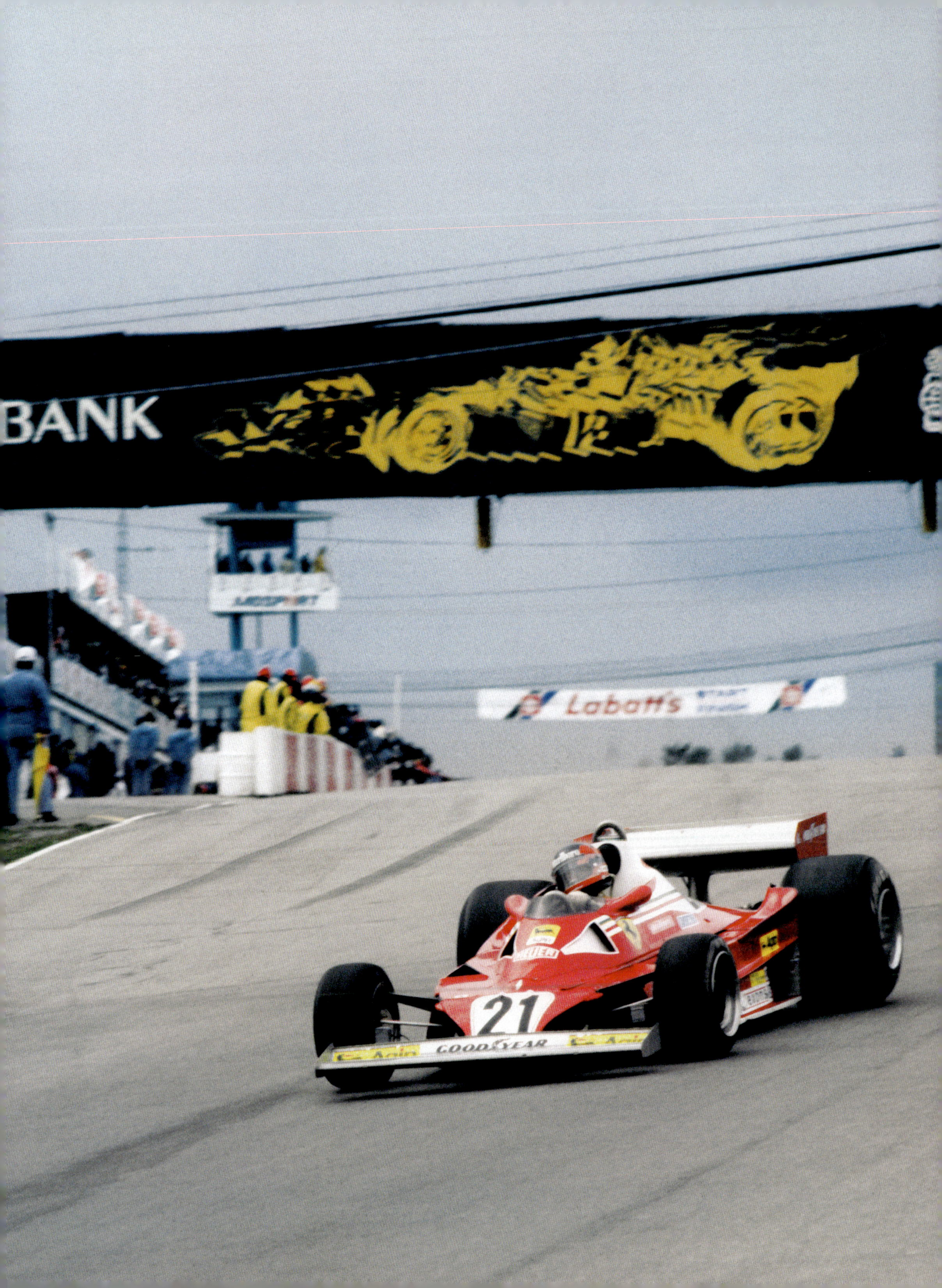
BANK
Labatt's
21
GOODYEAR

Mosport Park

The Mosport Park circuit had been built in 1961 and ran an annual sportscar race, but Canada was celebrating its centenary in 1967 and so sought a World Championship round as part of its celebrations to put Canada on the F1 map.

Mosport Park looks a picture in autumn, its hilly setting surrounded by trees changing from green to gold. The teams would have been impressed by its setting when the World Championship visited for the first time, if only they had been able to see much as the event was hit by heavy rain.

The lap starts with a fast right into an uphill straight and then a fast left. Turn 3 was tighter and Turn 5, Moss Corner, probably came as a relief as the cars slowed down here. Then came the return leg, a fearfully fast curving run over a crest before the esses and a tight right onto the short pit straight.

The drivers described it as a real challenge, but, unfortunately, there were accidents, most famously when John Surtees saw his suspension break in a sportscar race in 1965 and his Lola flipped. A dozen years later, Ian Ashley got airborne in his Hesketh and hit a scaffolding TV tower.

The 1973 Canadian GP was another race hit by rain and this led to F1's first use of a safety car. It came out so that a clash between François Cevert and Jody Scheckter could be cleared up, but the race was thrown into confusion as the track was drying fast and everyone had pitted to change tyres, leading to the safety car coming out in front of the wrong car. This delayed actual leader Emerson Fittipaldi enough for victory to go to a confused Peter Revson for McLaren.

After F1 quit here after the 1977 Canadian GP because of the lack of run-off, Mosport Park knew that its time running international-standard races was coming to an end when Manfred Winkelhock was killed there in a World Sports Car Championship race in 1985.

Left: Gilles Villeneuve presses on in his debut race for Ferrari at Mosport Park in 1977.

Following pages: Aston Martin racer Lance Stroll rounds Montreal's hairpin in 2022.

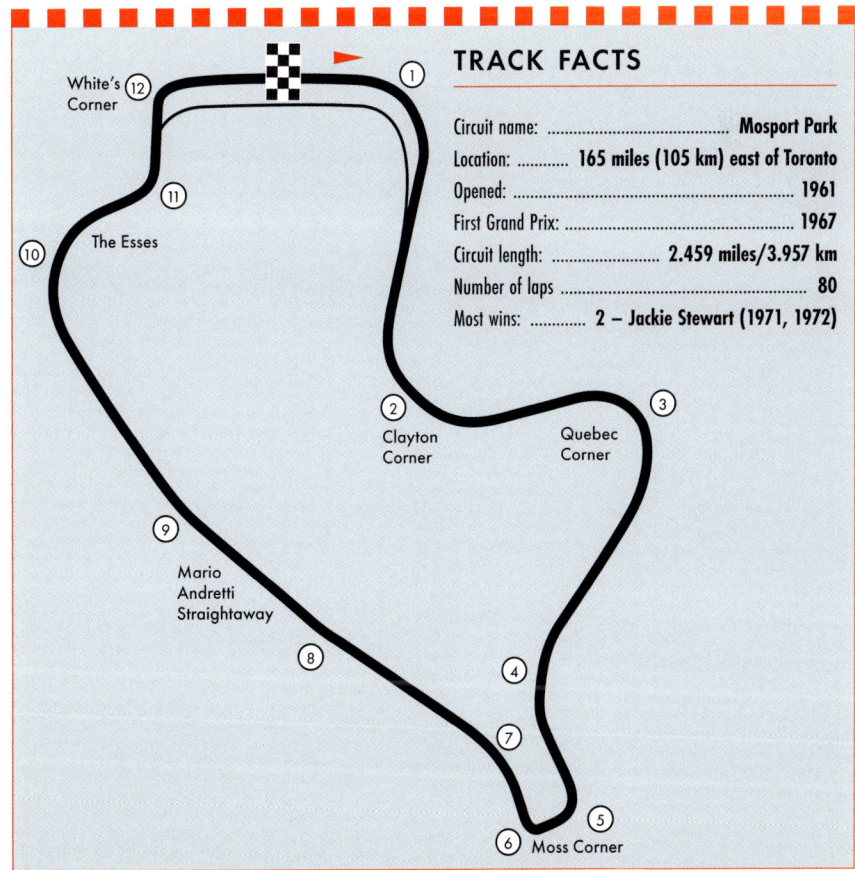

TRACK FACTS

Circuit name:	Mosport Park
Location:	165 miles (105 km) east of Toronto
Opened:	1961
First Grand Prix:	1967
Circuit length:	2.459 miles/3.957 km
Number of laps:	80
Most wins:	2 – Jackie Stewart (1971, 1972)

CANADA

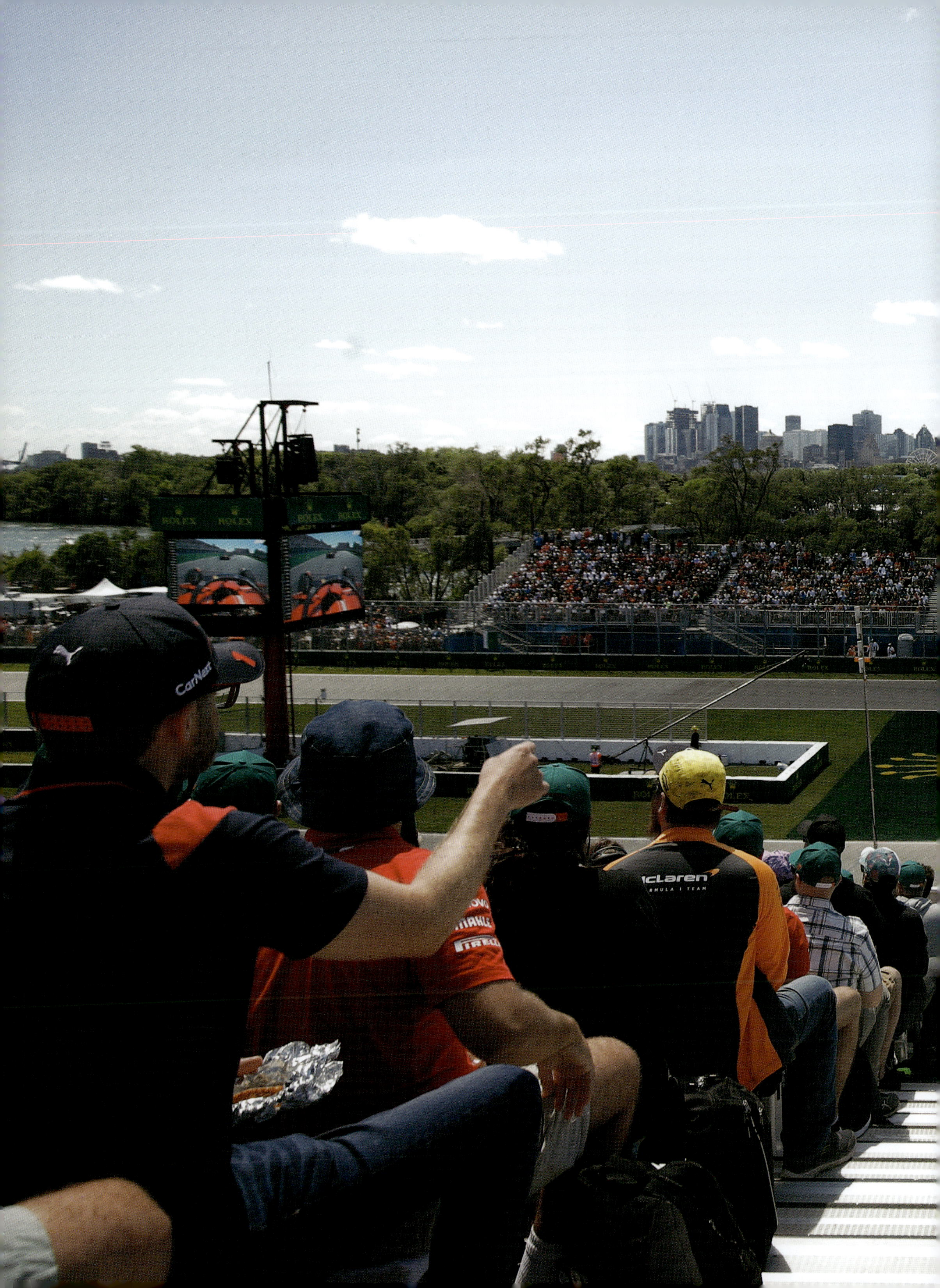
ROLEX
CarNext

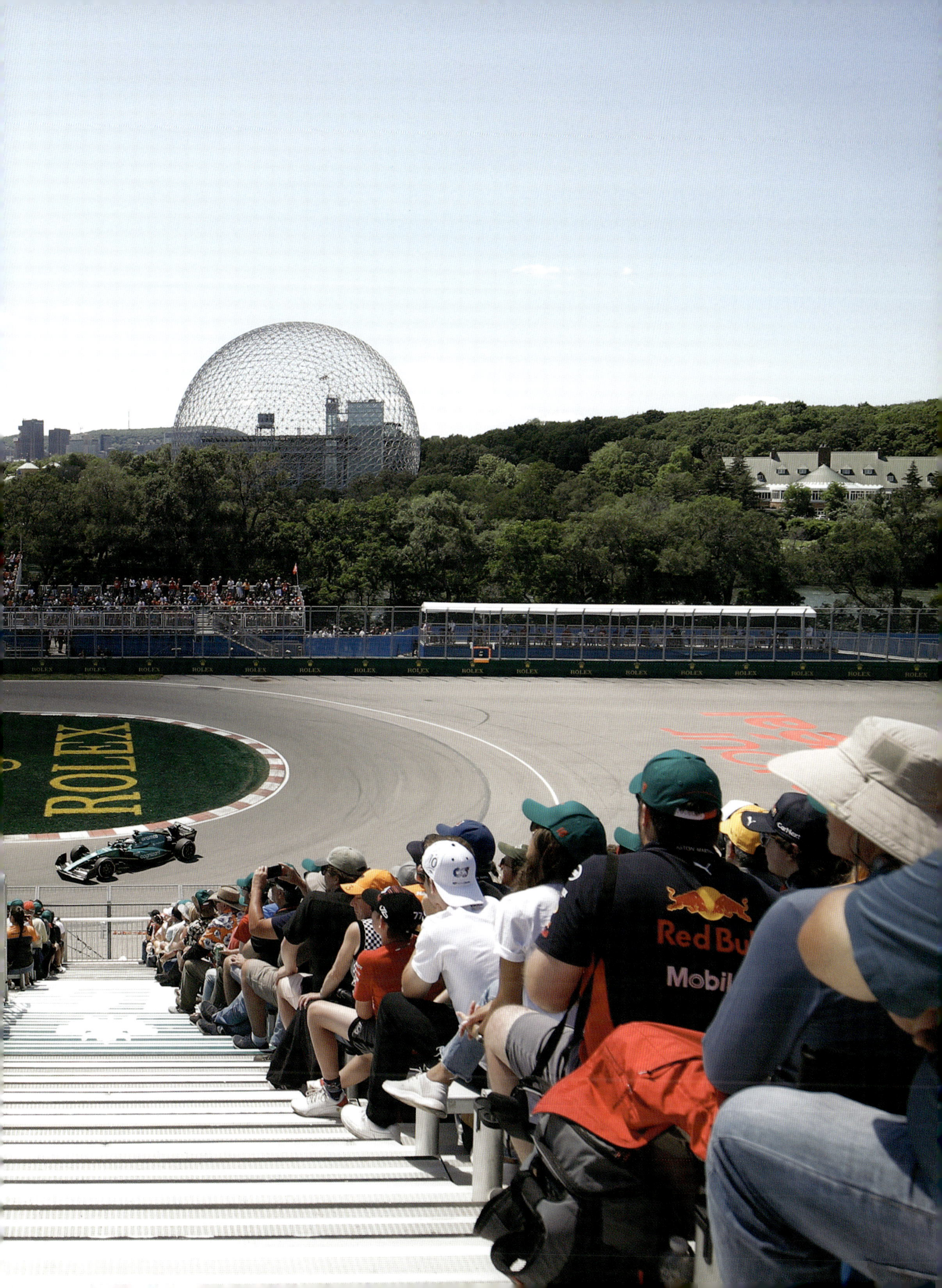
ROLEX

MOMENTS

There have been many extremely dramatic Grands Prix in Canada, shaped frequently by rain and, sometimes in Montreal, by the barriers.

Villeneuve sends the crowd wild

The 1978 Canadian GP was the first to be held in Montreal and Gilles Villeneuve produced a performance that would have been a scriptwriter's dream. It was the final round of his first full season, prior to which he had a best result of third place to his name. Putting his Ferrari third on the grid was a good start, but he immediately lost a place and Lotus stand-in Jean-Pierre Jarier shot off into the lead. Bit by bit, Gilles moved forward. Then, at two-thirds distance, Jarier suffered an oil leak and retired, and Gilles took over. The crowd went wild as he completed the final laps to take his first F1 victory. No wonder they then gave the circuit his name.

Opposite: Jenson Button produced one of his great drives to win for McLaren in 2011.

Below: Robert Kubica was a surprise winner for the BMW Sauber team in 2008.

Ickx triumphs at St Jovite

The St Jovite circuit, now owned by Lawrence Stroll, hosted the Canadian GP in 1968 and 1970. The second of these visits was the more competitive of the pair after Denny Hulme had won the earlier race by a lap. The 1970 race was the round after Jochen Rindt had been killed at Monza, but he still held the points lead. Jacky Ickx knew that he had to win the last three races to overhaul the late Lotus driver's points tally and he qualified on the outside of the front row. Jackie Stewart led away from pole in his Tyrrell, but he had a stub axle break at one-third distance and Ickx assumed a lead that he was never in danger of forfeiting.

Kubica leads a Sauber one-two

Taking a team's first win is special, but Sauber had the rare experience of claiming first and second in Canada in 2008, a feat previously achieved by Jordan in Belgium in 1998. The team made its F1 debut in 1993, but only became competitive with the arrival of BMW backing in 2006. When Robert Kubica qualified second in Montreal a podium result looked likely, but not a win as Lewis Hamilton was easily fastest for McLaren. However, there was a safety car deployment and he failed to see the red light at the pit exit and crashed into Kimi Räikkönen's Ferrari. Kubica had had a faster stop and was sitting in front of the pair, but escaped unscathed and that was enough for his first win.

Button stars in the wet

Jenson Button qualified only seventh for the 2011 Canadian GP, with Sebastian Vettel on pole for Red Bull ahead of Ferrari's Fernando Alonso. The race began behind a safety car because of standing water on the track. Button survived a clash with his McLaren teammate Lewis Hamilton and then got hit with a drive-through penalty for going too fast behind the safety car, dropping to fourteenth. Then the race was stopped for two hours to allow conditions to improve, and Button clipped Alonso just after the restart. Then, getting more than his rivals out of dry-weather tyres, he caught Vettel for the lead on the final lap, pressured him into a mistake at Turn 6 and the win was his.

CHILE

With most of the racing in South America centred on Brazil and Argentina, Chile has had to play a supporting role.

Chile's first permanent circuit, the Autódromo Las Vizcachas, was built in the Puente Alto district of capital city Santiago in 1965. Although not long, at just 1.86 miles (3 km), it was a spectacular venue, as spectators could sit on a hillside with the Andes soaring behind them as they looked across most of the circuit.

Although seven people were killed following a collision in 1975, racing continued from 1977 and it attracted the top regional series, Codasur F2. Sadly, the circuit was shortened when land was sold for housing and the Codegua circuit opened in 2014 to become Chile's new racing base.

The only Chilean driver to reach F1 thus far is Eliseo Salazar, who did so in 1981, racing for March then Ensign after arriving in Britain to race F3 just two years earlier. For 1980, he moved up to the Aurora British F1 series and impressed by winning three rounds to be runner-up. And so, with good financial backing, he made it to the World Championship. Things went better when he joined ATS in 1982 and came fifth at Imola, but he soon turned to racing sportscars.

More recently, the Formula E series visited Chile with street races at a couple of venues in Santiago.

COUNTRY FACTS

Formula One drivers:	1
World champions:	0
Grand Prix circuits:	0
Grands Prix hosted:	0

COLOMBIA

Colombia has a racing scene of its own, but no circuit of international standing, which is why its two F1 drivers headed overseas.

Racing has taken place in Bogotá since the 1950s, first on a street circuit and later a purpose-built circuit, the Autódromo Ricardo Mejia. With an eye to attracting F1, this opened with a flourish in 1971 with international stars headed by Graham Hill being invited down for a pair of F2 races. Two years after it shut in 1980, the Autódromo de Tocancipá opened to save the Colombian racing scene. As well as national championships, it hosts the Bogotá 6 Hours sportscar race that, unusually, runs in reverse direction around the track.

Colombia's rising stars knew, though, that if they wanted to be the best they would need to head abroad in pursuit of greater competition. Roberto Guerrero shone in British F3 then F2. Ensign gave him his F1 break in 1982, but the car was uncompetitive, as was the Theodore he raced in 1983, so he moved on to star in Indycars. Juan Pablo Montoya went first to the USA then to Europe and when no F1 seat materialised, he returned to the USA and won the Indycar title as a rookie. Then Williams signed him for 2001 and he won at Monza. More wins followed as he ranked third in 2002 and 2003, then fourth for McLaren in 2005.

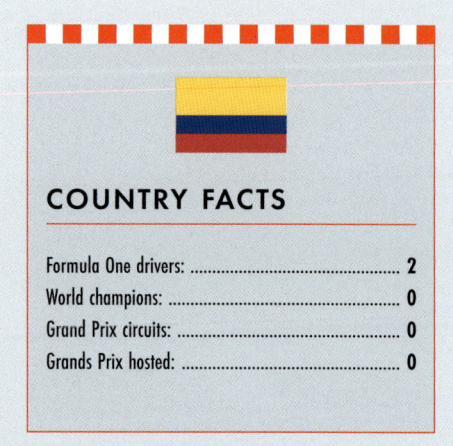

COUNTRY FACTS

Formula One drivers:	2
World champions:	0
Grand Prix circuits:	0
Grands Prix hosted:	0

Below: Juan Pablo Montoya starred for Williams in 2001 and later for McLaren.

MEXICO

There is a huge passion for racing in Mexico, with the Carrera Panamericana being replaced by three stints of the Mexican GP.

Road racing was the big draw in Mexico in the 1950s with the Carrera Panamericana drawing most of the world's top sportscar racers through the 1950s. However, it was the Rodríguez bothers, Pedro and the younger, faster, more volatile Ricardo, who got motor sport into the newspapers in Mexico at the end of the decade. A non-championship Grand Prix was held at the end of 1962, and it drew in the fans in droves. Sadly, Ricardo crashed fatally, but Mexico was part of the World Championship from the following year. Crowd control was almost non-existent back then, with fans overflowing onto the grass banking surrounding the circuit and some even crossing the track during the 1970 Mexican GP. This prompted the World Championship to move on, but Mexico got its race back for 1986 and kept it for another six years, during which time the World Sports-Prototype Championship visited too. Mexico City's third stint on the F1 calendar began in 2015.

A strong national F2/F3 series took aspiring Mexican racers, plus an array of drivers from overseas, to an assortment of tracks dotted around Mexico in the 1990s.

After F1's departure, and with an increasing number of Mexican racers competing in Indycars, the North American series began visiting Mexico City, followed by NASCAR in 2005. Since then, the inter-country A1GP series held races at Fundidora Park in Monterrey then Mexico City before Formula E brought its electric-racing show to the very middle of the capital before holding a subsequent race at Puebla.

COUNTRY FACTS

Formula One drivers:	6

Selected F1 drivers:
- Esteban Gutiérrez
- Pedro Rodríguez
- Sergio Pérez
- Ricardo Rodríguez
- Héctor Rebaque

World champions:	0
Grand Prix circuits:	1

- Mexico City

Grands Prix hosted:	24

Below: Max Verstappen leads the way through the baseball stadium section in 2022.

DRIVERS

Two Mexicans have won in F1, Pedro Rodríguez in 1967 and 1970 then Sergio Pérez in the 2020s, but none have won the country's home Grand Prix.

Sergio Pérez

Sergio headed to the United States to race single-seaters when he was fourteen, before a shift to Germany for two years. After two years in British F3, Sergio stepped up to GP2 in 2009 and performed better than people expected in 2010 to rank second. Two second places in his second year of F1 for Sauber earned him a ride at McLaren, but he wasn't kept on, so moved to Force India and stayed for seven years, during which time the team changed its name to Racing Point. At the end of his seventh campaign, it looked as though Sergio's F1 days were about to end when he kept himself in the game by scoring a timely win at the 2020 Sakhir GP. This was enough to land a ride with Red Bull Racing for 2021, with three more wins following in the next three years as he played a supporting role to Max Verstappen.

Pedro Rodríguez

Pedro started racing sportscars when he was fifteen. He and brother Ricardo won the Paris 1,000kms in a NART-entered Ferrari and shone at Le Mans, but Ricardo was killed in the non-championship 1962 Mexican GP. Pedro continued racing and made his World Championship debut for Lotus in 1963. Offered a one-off outing by Cooper in the 1967 South African GP, Pedro won and earned a full-season ride. BRM signed him for 1968 and he took his second win in Belgium in 1970. However, Pedro's main success came in sportscars, winning at Le Mans in 1968 then taking three wins for Porsche in 1971 before crashing fatally at the Norisring.

MOMENTS

The Mexican GP has offered some brilliant races since its debut in 1963. Here are a trio of the very best, including the extraordinary 1964 title battle.

Ninth place is enough for Hamilton

Lewis Hamilton had a tidy points advantage when he arrived for the 2017 Mexican GP and had hopes that he might land the title with two rounds still to run. However, the Mercedes driver was tipped into a spin by Sebastian Vettel's Ferrari in the first-corner complex on the opening lap and was left trailing after he had limped back to the pits for repairs. Max Verstappen had already got into the lead and would never be challenged as he raced to his third win, but with Vettel only finishing fourth, ninth place was enough for Hamilton to land his fourth F1 crown.

Title sorted on the final lap

There was a three-way shoot-out between British drivers for the World Championship crown in 1964. Graham Hill held the lead for BRM, with John Surtees five points down for Ferrari and Jim Clark having to win the race for Lotus to have a chance. A poor start dropped Hill to tenth, while Surtees fell to thirteenth with a misfire and Clark led away. Hill rose to third, which was all he needed to be champion, but then he was spun by Surtees's teammate Bandini and Clark looked set to win, only for his engine to fail on the final lap. Bandini then let Surtees past to take second and the title.

Senna's flat gives Ferrari a one-two

The 1990 Mexican GP should have been won by Ayrton Senna who led the first sixty laps, but his McLaren was hit by a slow puncture. This let Alain Prost's Ferrari through to win, while McLaren misunderstood Senna's radio message and advised him to stay out. With five laps to go, his right rear blew and the time it took him to do almost a full lap back to the pits meant that there was no point in continuing. The final lap was notable for Nigel Mansell making a move around the outside of Gerhard Berger's McLaren at the Peraltada to secure a Ferrari one-two.

Below: John Surtees leads Lorenzo Bandini in 1964 when Ferrari raced in the white and blue of the North American Racing Team.

CIRCUITS

Mexico's Grand Prix circuit is a noisy place when F1 comes to town and the fans' raw passion makes it a special place to be.

Mexico City

Opened in 1962, at the height of Rodríguez mania when the brothers looked set to challenge the world, the circuit was built in a park in the sprawling city's eastern suburbs and offered a lap with some spectacular high-speed sections combined with some more technical turns.

The broad main straight runs down an avenue of trees and leads to a right-left-right complex where initially there was just a right-hander. Then, after another straight, there's a sharp left followed by an equally sharp right. This points the cars towards the Turn 6 hairpin in front of a large grandstand that turns the cars around to start their homeward leg. What follows next is considered by the drivers to be one of the best sections of the lap, with a five-corner, sixth-gear esse that is made tougher still by rising over a slight crest before dropping on the other side. Originally, this led to a straight then a broad, bumpy, lightly banked final corner, the Peraltada, that was taken almost flat-out, or as fast as drivers dared over the much-feared bumps there, their cars not always fully attached to the track. Now, the track feeds to the right on the approach to the old corner and it enters a most unusual area, the heart of a baseball stadium. The cars arrive in front of the steeply stacked grandstand, go through a hairpin to the left and then a kink to the right before running through a gap in the grandstand and then entering the Peraltada halfway around. Although they immediately accelerate hard to get the best exit possible onto the start-finish straight, their entry speed is considerably slower than it used to be. Unfortunately, although the fans get to see the cars twist and turn, they seldom get to see much passing there. The thought of the current F1 cars powering through the full Peraltada and then running in slipstreaming groups down the main straight is a beguiling one. It would certainly boost the likelihood of overtaking moves into the first-corner complex, but it's unlikely ever to be reinstated.

One factor that all teams must consider is Mexico City's altitude of more than 6,000 feet (1,829 m), making the air thin and the cars, and drivers too, struggle that little bit more to get the oxygen that they need.

The memory of the late Rodríguez brothers lives on, as the circuit was renamed the Autódromo Hermanos Rodríguez after them.

Opposite: A home win continues to elude Sergio Pérez, shown here at speed in 2022.

TRACK FACTS

Circuit name: **Autódromo Hermanos Rodríguez**
Location: **Eastern suburbs of Mexico City**
Opened: **1962**
First Grand Prix: **1963**
Circuit length: **2.674 miles/4.303 km**
Number of laps: **71**
Most wins: **4 – Max Verstappen (2017, 2018, 2021, 2022)**

ORACLE
Mobil 1
Mobil
BYB!T
citrix
ORACLE
Red Bull
Tezos
telcel

UNITED STATES OF AMERICA

Formula One has fought a long battle to impress American racing fans, moving its Grand Prix around. Now, though, it has three.

The United States specialises in having its own sports and, as a result, took an age to embrace soccer, as it had its own football and ice hockey instead. Likewise, in racing, Indycar and NASCAR racing have been the bedrock for American fans, with F1 always seen as something foreign. Yet, since it hosted its first Grand Prix in 1959, interest has grown, bit by bit, but it had to move around before it found a foothold. It started at Sebring in Florida, then moved to Riverside in California in 1960. F1's third stop was Watkins Glen in upstate New York, where it stayed until 1980.

To keep fans on the West Coast happy, the United States landed a second Grand Prix, on the streets of Long Beach from 1976. Once Watkins Glen was no longer considered safe, it was reckoned that taking a race to Las Vegas would find new fans, but the idea didn't work in 1981 or 1982 and it took until 2023 before it tried again. Also in 1982, a race on a street circuit in Detroit was introduced and this proved popular, unlike one in Dallas in 1984 that was so hot that the track crumbled.

A street circuit in Phoenix held the Grand Prix from 1989 to 1991, but it wasn't a hit, so it was decided to take the race to the Indianapolis Motor Speedway, using one of the banked corners and otherwise snaking around the infield. After endless failed attempts to hold a street race in New York, Miami landed one from 2022.

Opposite: Ayrton Senna celebrates as he takes the chequered flag at Phoenix to open his 1991 campaign with a win for McLaren.

Below: Red Bull's Max Verstappen leads the field up the hill into COTA's Turn 1 in 2022 after getting the jump on Ferrari's Carlos Sainz Jr.

COUNTRY FACTS

Formula One drivers: 52
Selected F1 drivers:
- Mario Andretti
- Michael Andretti
- Ronnie Bucknum
- Eddie Cheever
- Mark Donohue
- George Follmer
- Richie Ginther
- Masten Gregory
- Dan Gurney
- Jim Hall
- Phil Hill
- Roger Penske
- Peter Revson
- Harry Schell
- Danny Sullivan

World champions: .... 2 – Phil Hill (1961); Mario Andretti (1978)
Grand Prix circuits: 12
- Caesars Palace
- Circuit of the Americas
- Detroit
- Fair Park
- Indianapolis
- Las Vegas
- Long Beach
- Miami
- Phoenix
- Riverside
- Sebring
- Watkins Glen

Grands Prix hosted: 69

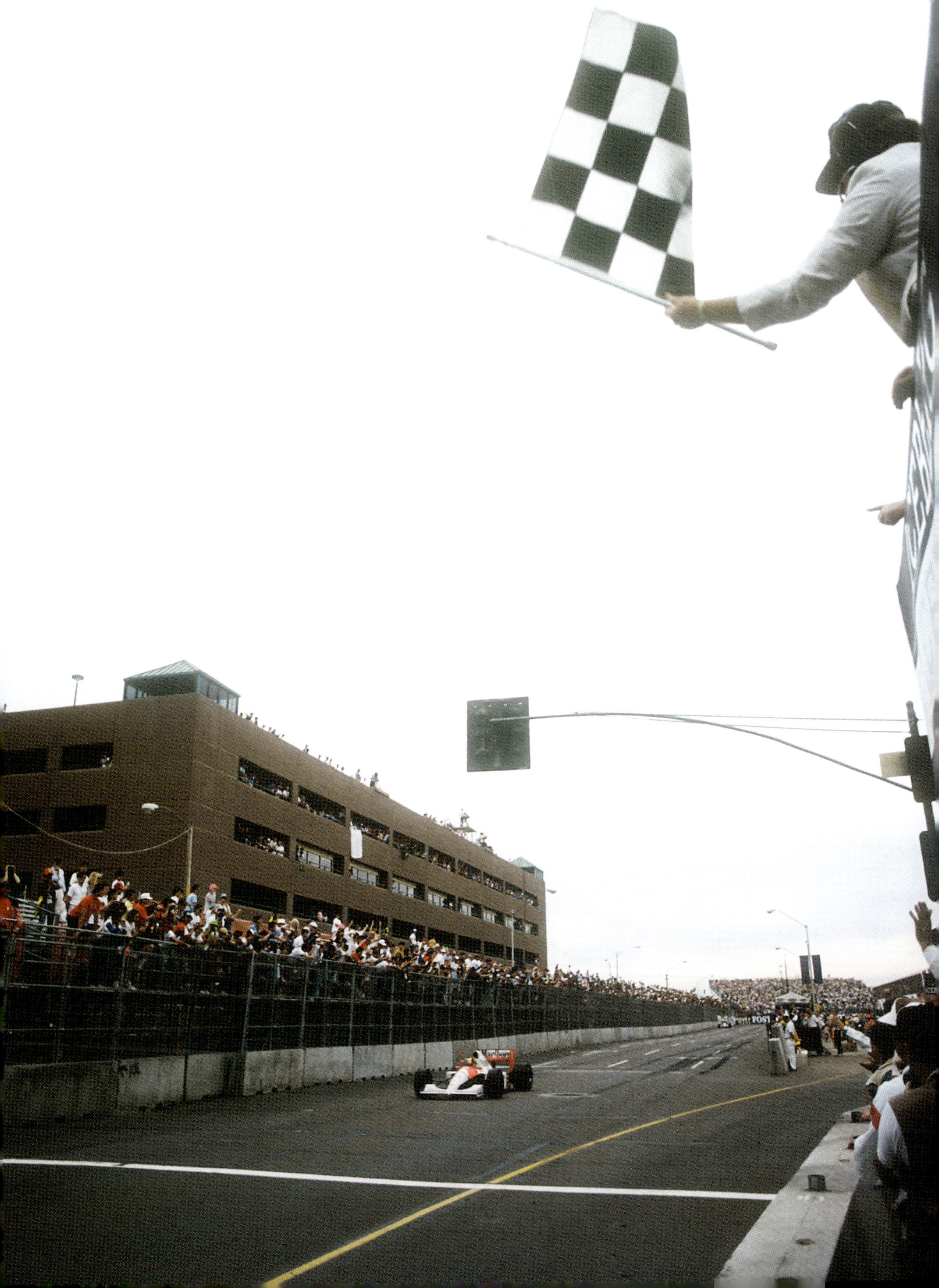

Mario Andretti

Born in Italy and inspired by watching races at Monza before the family emigrated to the United States, Mario went racing as soon as he could afford to, starting in sprint cars and midgets. With obvious ability, he advanced to Indycars by 1964 and won the first of his four Indycar titles in 1965. Mario then entered a double life as he dabbled with F1 from 1968 alongside his Indycar programme, even putting his Lotus on pole in his second F1 outing. Yet, although he scored his first F1 win in 1971, for Ferrari, it took until 1975 for his first full F1 programme, with Parnelli. Lotus was not competitive when he joined in 1976, but its ground effect 78 chassis put that right and he then stormed to the title in 1978 in its successor. His son Michael is also an Indycar champion and there's now a third generation of racing Andrettis, with grandson Marco driving in the Indy Racing League.

DRIVERS

Two world champions in seventy-four years represents slim pickings for American drivers, but interest is growing and more will surely follow.

Phil Hill

The United States' first F1 world champion raced sportscars with enough success to be signed by Ferrari. While his desire was to try F1, which he did in four Grands Prix in 1958, his string of sportscar wins, including the first of three wins in the Le Mans 24 Hours, was what made his name. Phil's first full year of F1 came in 1959 before he took his first F1 win in 1960, at Monza. Then came Phil's year of years in 1961 when the Ferrari was the car to have, and he took the title after teammate Wolfgang von Trips crashed fatally at the Italian GP.

Richie Ginther

Although Richie had a reputation as a good number-two driver throughout his career, he was good enough to win a Grand Prix. Like Phil Hill, he made his name in sportscars and came to the attention of Enzo Ferrari. He too wanted to try F1 for Ferrari and came second at Monza in 1960. Richie's engineering prowess developed the Ferrari 'sharknose' in which he came second in Monaco in 1961. Richie then moved to BRM, but was overshadowed by Graham Hill, then went better to rank second in 1963, but it took a move to Honda to land his only F1 win, which came in Mexico in 1965.

Mark Donohue

Mark raced sportscars with Walt Hansgen before Roger Penske took him under his wing. This was the start of a special relationship, as he raced to two United States Road Racing Championship titles in 1967 and 1968, also winning the first of three Trans Am titles in 1968. Second in the 1970 Indy 500 suggested a talent for single-seaters and third place on his F1 debut in the 1971 Canadian GP reiterated that. After storming to the Can Am title in a Penske Porsche in 1973, Penske ran Mark in F1 in 1975 until a deflating tyre triggered a fatal accident in Austria.

Dan Gurney

This is a driver who could do anything. Although never a world champion – the tall Californian was third in 1961 – Dan gave both Porsche, Brabham, and his own Eagle team their first F1 wins, he won sportscar classics including the Le Mans 24 Hours, Sebring 12 Hours and Nürburgring 1,000kms, seven Indycar races, also coming second twice in the Indy 500, as well as showing diverse skills by taking five NASCAR victories. Dan's Eagles won the Indy 500 three times and his All-American Racers concern then enjoyed considerable success in the IMSA sportscar series, helping Toyota to win the title in 1992 and 1993.

UNITED STATES OF AMERICA

CIRCUITS

Of the dozen circuits that have hosted Grands Prix in the United States, there are a few circuits that stand out as markers of F1's prominence in the country over the years.

Watkins Glen

This circuit was the first American circuit to grab hold of the United States GP and keep it for a repeat performance. This was in 1962 when F1 came back for more and Jim Clark followed fellow Scot Innes Ireland in winning for Lotus.

The first racing at Watkins Glen was on a 6.6-mile (10.6-km) circuit on public roads running from the middle of town. This was in 1948 but, after two fatal accidents, it was decided that it would be safer to have a purpose-built circuit, and this opened for business in 1956. The circuit was positioned on a wooded hilltop and used the gradient change to its advantage. The lap started low, turned through a 90-degree right-hander and then ascended the slope with a fabulous esse before running across the slope to a broad right-hander that fell from entry to exit before a straight, an open left and a tighter right at the bottom of the slope that fed the cars back onto the start-finish straight. The lap was only 2.35 miles (3.78 km) long, but this changed in 1971 when a loop known as 'The Anvil' was added on the return leg, adding a long, downhill left, Turn 6, then a tighter right onto a short straight and two uphill corners to rejoin the original circuit, making it far more of a challenge as it boosted the lap length to 3.377 miles (5.435 km).

The race was traditionally held in autumn when the leaves were turning. However, rain often blew through, turning the infield camping area into a swamp where rowdy fans once set fire to a coach. However, two fatalities in two years made people think that the performance of the cars had outgrown the circuit, as François Cevert crashed fatally in 1973 and then Helmuth Koinigg did the same in 1974. Although the US GP continued here, it moved on after Alan Jones' win here for Williams in 1980, with the Americans aware that a new image was needed to boost F1's appeal.

After F1 quit, Watkins Glen hosted three Indycar races, but before long had the unusual offering of NASCAR stock cars visiting for a rare race that did not take place on an oval.

To this day, Watkins Glen is a reminder of the wonderful undulating circuits in rural settings that were such popular venues from the 1960s to 1980s before they started to be dropped as they were no longer considered safe enough to contain the F1 cars should anything go wrong. That the upstate New York circuit was still hosting the IMSA Sportscar series with its 200mph sports-prototypes in 2023 suggests that perhaps F1 jumped too soon.

Opposite: Alan Jones's winning Williams runs ahead of Gilles Villeneuve's Ferrari in 1980.

TRACK FACTS

Circuit name:	Watkins Glen
Location:	80 miles (128.7 km) south-west of Syracuse in upstate New York
Opened:	1956
First Grand Prix:	1961
Circuit length:	3.377 miles/5.435 km
Number of laps:	59
Most wins:	3 – Graham Hill (1963, 1964, 1965)

184 UNITED STATES OF AMERICA

UNITED STATES OF AMERICA | 185

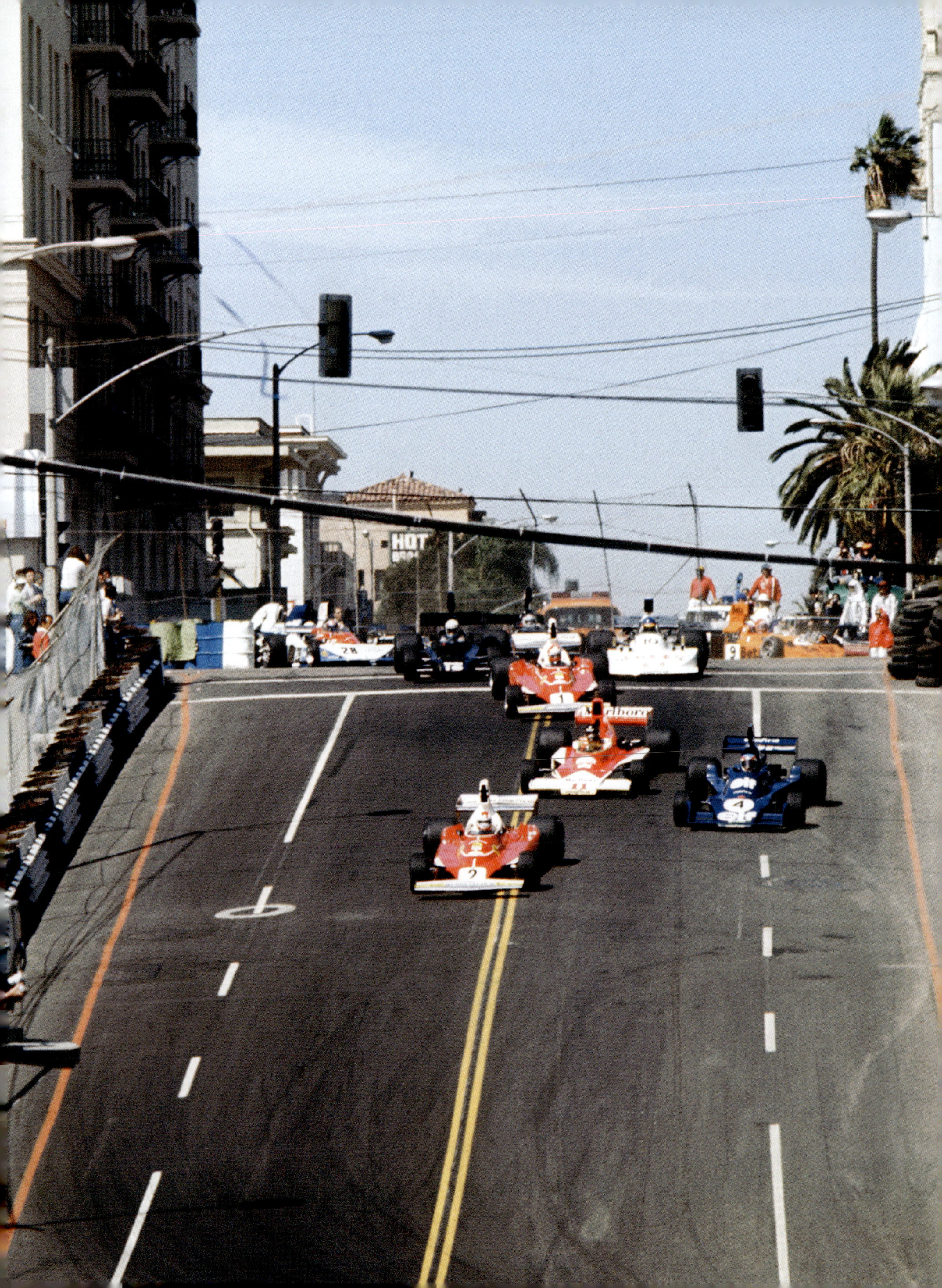

Long Beach

Other than the Monaco GP, it took more than two decades for the World Championship to offer fans another opportunity to see F1 cars race at a street venue. Although there had been several non-championship street races through the 1950s and 1960s, at circuits including Pau in France and Syracuse in Sicily, this Californian seaport became the second F1 street venue in 1976 with the organisers hoping that F1's cosmopolitan image would give their city a boost.

The circuit had been used by Formula 5000 single-seaters in 1975 and F1 liked what promoter Chris Pook had put on and so the United States Grand Prix West was born, with Clay Regazzoni winning for Ferrari on F1's first visit in 1976. This continued for another seven years before F1 moved on again and the event was taken on by the Indycar series.

What made the Long Beach circuit such a hit was its use of gradient as it climbed from sea-level Shoreline Drive to the loftiest point of its lap, Ocean Boulevard. Starting on the long, long arc of Shoreline Drive, the drivers had a curving run down to the first real corner, West Hairpin. Then the track snaked and climbed its way to the double rights of Pine Avenue and so onto Ocean Boulevard. Slowing things down, the next two corners were 90-degree bends, with the track dropping to Linden Avenue then running through a couple of tight corners before a short blast to East Hairpin. Often seen as a passing point, but more often the scene of failed moves, this led the cars onto Shoreline Drive along which they would attempt to line up a tow from a rival to enable them to try a passing move into West Hairpin. Overtaking was not easy.

Struggling to survive financially initially, the race was boosted in 1977 when Mario Andretti got the home fans cheering when he won for Lotus on F1's second visit. Sadly, Regazzoni had his Ensign's brake pedal snap and he ploughed into a wall at West Hairpin in 1980. From 1982, Shoreline Drive was interrupted with a three-corner complex, and its end truncated.

Left: Clay Regazzoni, Patrick Depailler and James Hunt dive over the Turn 1 drop in 1976.

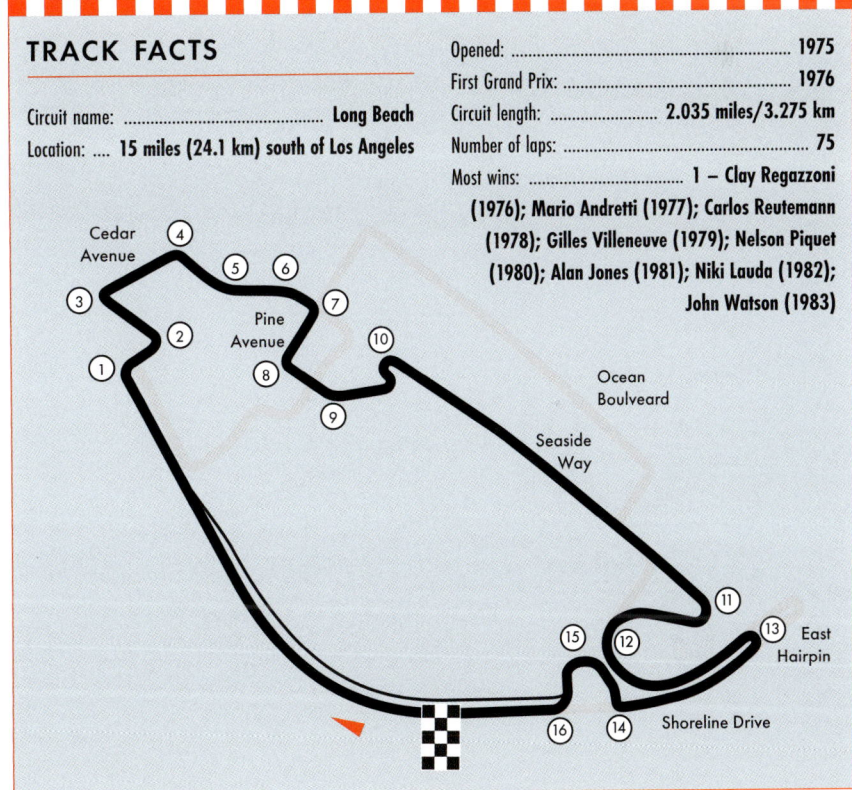

TRACK FACTS

Circuit name: .... **Long Beach**
Location: .... **15 miles (24.1 km) south of Los Angeles**
Opened: **1975**
First Grand Prix: **1976**
Circuit length: .... **2.035 miles/3.275 km**
Number of laps: **75**
Most wins: .... **1 – Clay Regazzoni (1976); Mario Andretti (1977); Carlos Reutemann (1978); Gilles Villeneuve (1979); Nelson Piquet (1980); Alan Jones (1981); Niki Lauda (1982); John Watson (1983)**

UNITED STATES OF AMERICA

Circuit of the Americas

Watkins Glen hosted the United States GP from 1961 to 1980, the Indianapolis Motor Speedway had the next lengthy run from 2000 to 2007, then the Circuit of the Americas was created with the intention of becoming the event's third long-term custodian.

The project was headed by former racer Tavo Hellmund, whose father has redeveloped Mexico City's Autódromo Hermanos Rodríguez in the 1970s. F1 circuit architect Hermann Tilke was commissioned to produce a circuit that used its rolling site near Texan state capital Austin. Another part of his brief was to try to incorporate some of the characteristics of the world's most testing corners. Despite occasional financial hiccoughs, work went ahead and was completed in time for this circuit to host the race from 2012 and the drivers adored it, from the 40-metre gain from the start line to the apex of the first corner hairpin all the way to the last of its twenty turns.

The plunge from this lofty hairpin was precipitous and drivers needed to get their car into place, often while still tussling for position on the opening lap, for the four-corner esse that followed. This was designed to echo Suzuka's uphill esse. The lap then opens out a bit before a kinked straight to its furthest point from the pits, the hairpin at Turn 11.

The nature of the lap then changes as the cars fire onto the lap's longest straight to a definite overtaking point into the tight left at Turn 12. Then it tightens up again with a series of sharp corners and a lengthy right over a slight rise around the foot of the vast observation tower. Getting a rapid exit out of Turn 20 onto the start-finish straight is a must if drivers want to have a shot at the chief overtaking spot into Turn 1.

Lewis Hamilton seemed to have a natural affinity to COTA, following his victory in its inaugural Grand Prix for McLaren by winning four of the next five visits for Mercedes. There has almost always been spectacle aplenty, almost invariably on the first corner of lap one, while having three passing points has kept the drivers on their toes.

Right: Lewis Hamilton became the centre of attention in 2012 by winning the first Grand Prix held at COTA, where he has since won four more times.

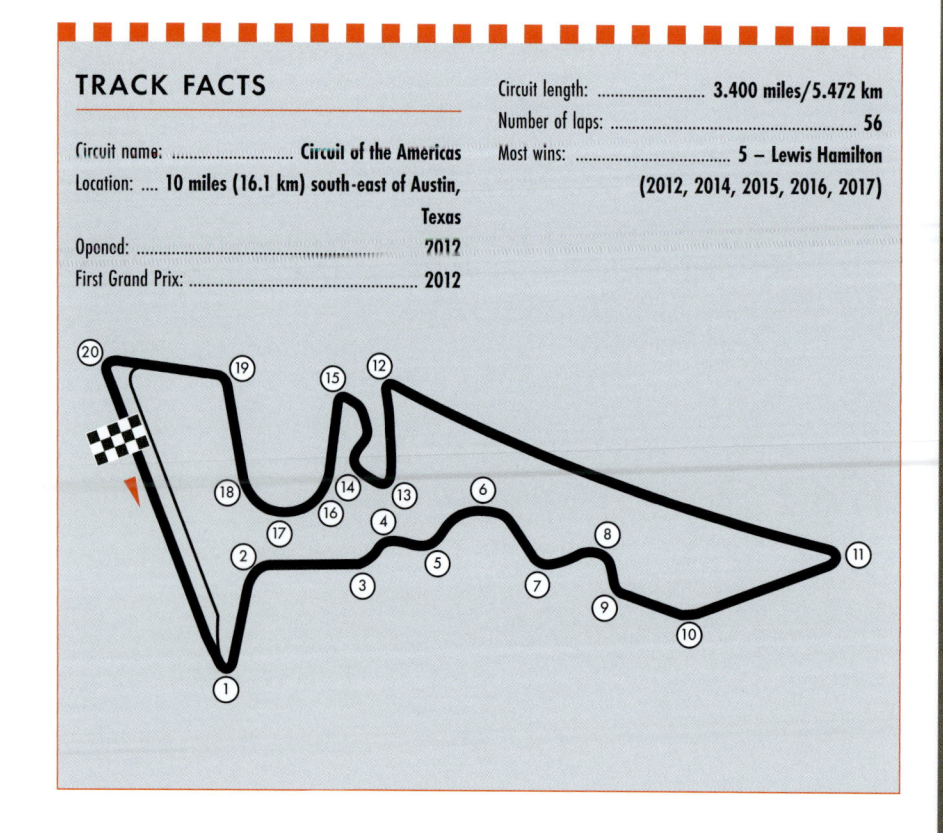

TRACK FACTS

Circuit name: .... Circuit of the Americas
Location: .... 10 miles (16.1 km) south-east of Austin, Texas
Opened: 2012
First Grand Prix: 2012
Circuit length: .... 3.400 miles/5.472 km
Number of laps: 56
Most wins: .... 5 – Lewis Hamilton
(2012, 2014, 2015, 2016, 2017)

UNITED STATES OF AMERICA

PIRELLI
verizon
Verizon
ercedes-Benz
Mobil 1
BOSS
UGO BOSS
JOHNNIE WALKER
Lucozade
Santander
MUMM
G.H.MUMM
CHAMPAGNE

Las Vegas

Although the two Grands Prix held in Las Vegas in 1981 and 1982 were disasters as the track was of little merit and the races failed to draw in the fans, there had long been efforts to take F1 back to the casino city.

A few years after Liberty Media bought Formula One, it invested £560m to prepare the stage for F1's return to Nevada at the end of 2023. This was not going to be the sort of temporary venue that could be overlooked like the Caesars Palace track was in the 1980s. No, this was made to be as loud and proud as possible, with its main straight running along Las Vegas's main strip, putting F1 in front of the most famous hotels and casinos rather than tucked away behind them.

Racing at night made the backdrop even more spectacular, and the racing proved to be great. However, there were logistical problems and the small matter of a drain cover that wasn't properly secured taking most of the floor off Carlos Sainz Jr's Ferrari. If these can be sorted, then the race will be a long-runner.

TRACK FACTS

Circuit name: Las Vegas Strip Circuit
Location: In central Las Vegas
Opened: 2023
First Grand Prix: 2023
Circuit length: 3.853 miles/6.201 km
Number of laps: 50
Most wins: 1 – George Russell (2024); Max Verstappen (2023)

Below: Pierre Gasly has little time to admire the backdrop as he races past the MSG Sphere in 2023.

Opposite: Red Bull's Max Verstappen becomes the first driver to win a Miami GP.

190 | UNITED STATES OF AMERICA

TRACK FACTS

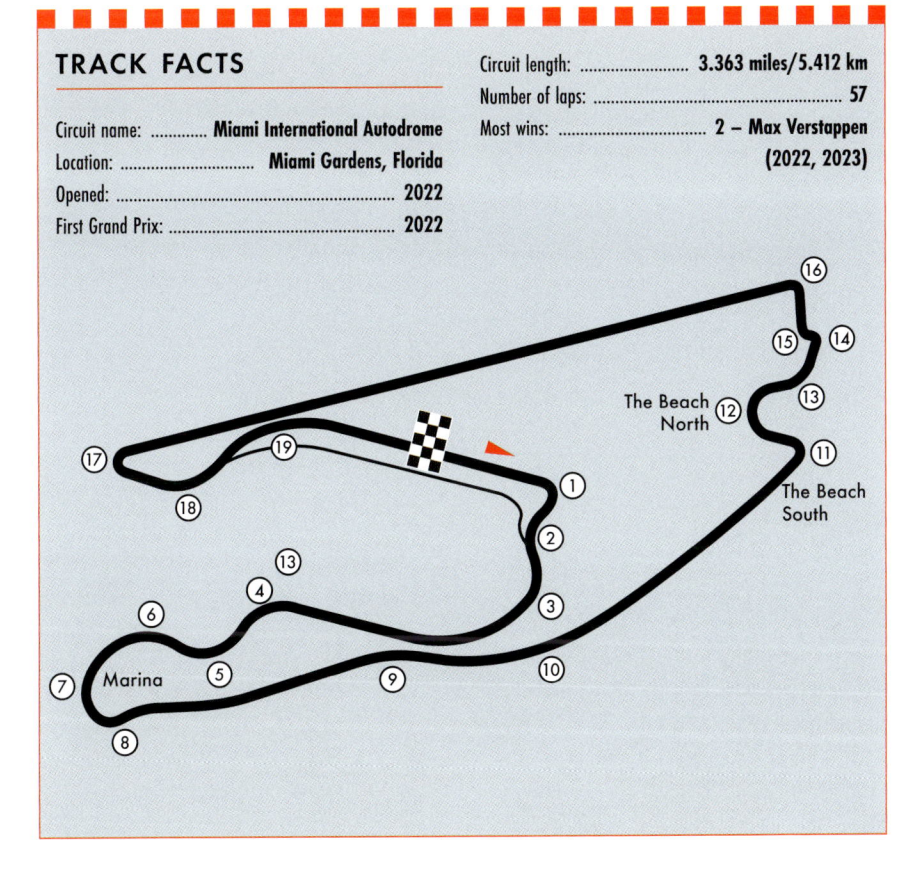

Circuit name: **Miami International Autodrome**
Location: **Miami Gardens, Florida**
Opened: **2022**
First Grand Prix: **2022**
Circuit length: **3.363 miles/5.412 km**
Number of laps: **57**
Most wins: **2 – Max Verstappen (2022, 2023)**

Miami

Numerous attempts to get F1 to hold a Grand Prix in Miami were tabled over the decades when the United States GP was floundering elsewhere. However, it took until 2022 for it to happen.

There had long been plans to use a temporary circuit downtown, where IMSA Sportscar series races were held from the 1980s, but the hassle of setting it up and tearing it down every year was considered too great. This is why creating the circuit in the car park of a sporting arena on the outskirts of the city seemed a more sensible option.

The arena in question is the Miami Hard Rock Stadium, home of the Miami Dolphins NFL team and a car park large enough to accommodate a 3.362 mile (5.411 km) circuit made up of nineteen turns.

The lap is sinuous early on, then it opens out from Turn 8 for a snaking blast to Turn 11 where it tightens up through a six corner sequence that leads to its longest straight.

UNITED STATES OF AMERICA | 191

MOMENTS

American F1 fans have been treated to some hugely exciting races across the decades, with this quartet the pick of the bunch.

Alan Jones triumphs at Watkins Glen

With the drivers' title already in the bag after taking his fourth win of 1980 in the Canadian GP, Alan Jones arrived at Watkins Glen in a relaxed frame of mind. This wasn't to mean that the combative Australian didn't want to give it his all. However, there was a new challenger as Bruno Giacomelli made the most of Alfa Romeo's new-found form to grab pole, with Jones fifth. Come the race, though, Giacomelli hared off into the lead while Jones locked up into the first corner and lost seven places. Poor Giacomelli was twelve seconds clear when his electrics failed mid-race, by which time Jones had passed rival after rival and was up to second, before going on to take a champion's win.

Ferrari aims at dead heat at Indianapolis

Ferrari had everything under control on the occasion of F1's third visit to the Indianapolis Motor Speedway for the penultimate race of 2002. Or so it seemed. Michael Schumacher had been crowned champion five rounds earlier, and Rubens Barrichello had been allowed to beat him in the Italian GP. There were no such plans here, but they had sufficient performance to outpace David Coulthard's McLaren. Then, having led pretty much all the way, Michael took it upon himself to slow coming out of the final corner to let Barrichello move alongside. But his attempts of orchestrating a dead heat went wrong and Barrichello won by about the width of one of the bricks that mark the finish line.

John Watson charges from the back

The final win of John Watson's F1 career came in a most extraordinary race at Long Beach in 1983. This was the last time that this street track held a Grand Prix and the Ulsterman marked it by mounting a charge from twenty-second on the grid. The McLarens had struggled for grip on their Michelin tyres and teammate Niki Lauda started one place further towards the back. On race day, though, all changed and suddenly their French rubber was way more suitable than the Goodyear tyres. A helping hand came when Keke Rosberg took Patrick Tambay out of the lead but, with their MP4/1Cs' lack of turbo power negated by considerable grip, they kept on rising for McLaren's first one-two since 1968.

Opposite: Ayrton Senna led every single lap to beat his McLaren teammate Alain Prost by more than half a minute in Detroit in 1988.

Below: John Watson produced a remarkable drive to rise from twenty-second to victory in 1983.

Ayrton Senna wins in Detroit

The Grand Prix on the streets of America's Motor City, Detroit, was invariably packed with incident, yet the seventh and final running of this Grand Prix in 1988 gave Ayrton Senna his third win there in succession. Having won twice on the bounce in Detroit for Lotus, he had joined McLaren and did the best thing you could do in qualifying for a race in which overtaking spots are limited: he put his car on pole. More than that, he did so by fully 0.8 seconds over Gerhard Berger's Ferrari. In the race, he edged even further clear and won from teammate Alain Prost, whose car developed a gearbox problem, by almost forty seconds in a performance of mesmeric precision and pace.

UNITED STATES OF AMERICA

URUGUAY

Uruguay has always been in the shadow of neighbours Argentina and Brazil, but it has hosted some non-championship F1 races.

COUNTRY FACTS

Formula One drivers:	4
World champions:	0
Grand Prix circuits:	0
Grands Prix hosted:	0

In the late 1940s, there was a street circuit laid out in the Playa Ramirez suburb of capital city Montevideo. A second street circuit, called Piriapolis, came next, with Juan Manuel Fangio crossing the border from Argentina to bag a couple of scalps in 1952. These were great days in South American racing, with many of their best, led by Fangio, heading to Europe in a quest for further glory.

The leading Uruguayan driver to take that passage was Eitel Cantoni who went in 1952 to race an Escuderia Bandeirantes Maserati. He had shone in pre-Second World War road events across South America, but his age, forty-six, counted against him. Alberto Uria went across the River Plate to contest the Argentinian GP in 1955, then did so again in 1956, sharing his Maserati with fellow Uruguayan Óscar González.

The chic Punta del Este coastal resort has long set up a street circuit for F3 and touring-car races, used more recently by Formula E, and there are now purpose-built circuits at El Pinar and Mercedes.

Uruguay's great racing hope in the 1990s, Gonzalo Rodríguez, failed to reach F1 after shining in F3000, so he headed to Indycars but was killed at Laguna Seca in 1999.

Below: Eitel Cantoni (left) dices with Ken Wharton's Cooper in the 1952 Italian GP.

VENEZUELA

Venezuela's time as a motor racing venue of note has passed, but it was certainly a destination for the stars in the 1950s.

Capital Caracas used to attract the top sportscar stars to its street race in the 1950s, with a stunning list of winners. Juan Manuel Fangio and Stirling Moss won in Maseratis, then Peter Collins shared the winning Ferrari with Phil Hill when it was upgraded into a Sports Car World Championship round in 1957. However, concerns over the circuit's safety led to its decline. The layout was basically up and down a major street, with a triangular turnaround at one end, a chicane in both directions down the street and a more open, bottle-shaped loop at the far end.

Ettore Chimeri was the first Venezuelan to reach F1 in 1960, only to be killed in a sportscar race a fortnight later. Next up was Johnny Cecotto, after he switched to four wheels following his 350cc world motorcycle title in the 1970s. After a debut F1 season with Theodore in 1983, he became Ayrton Senna's teammate at Toleman, but his career was cut short by a crash in practice for the British GP.

Pastor Maldonado was fast but wild, yet he won a GP2 race at Monaco then landed an F1 ride with Williams. His finest moment came when he drove without any of his all-too-usual mistakes to take a shock win in the 2012 Spanish GP.

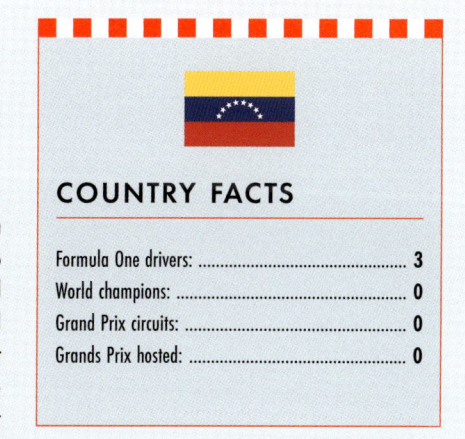

COUNTRY FACTS

Formula One drivers:	3
World champions:	0
Grand Prix circuits:	0
Grands Prix hosted:	0

Below: Johnny Cecotto races to his only point, for sixth place at Long Beach in 1983.

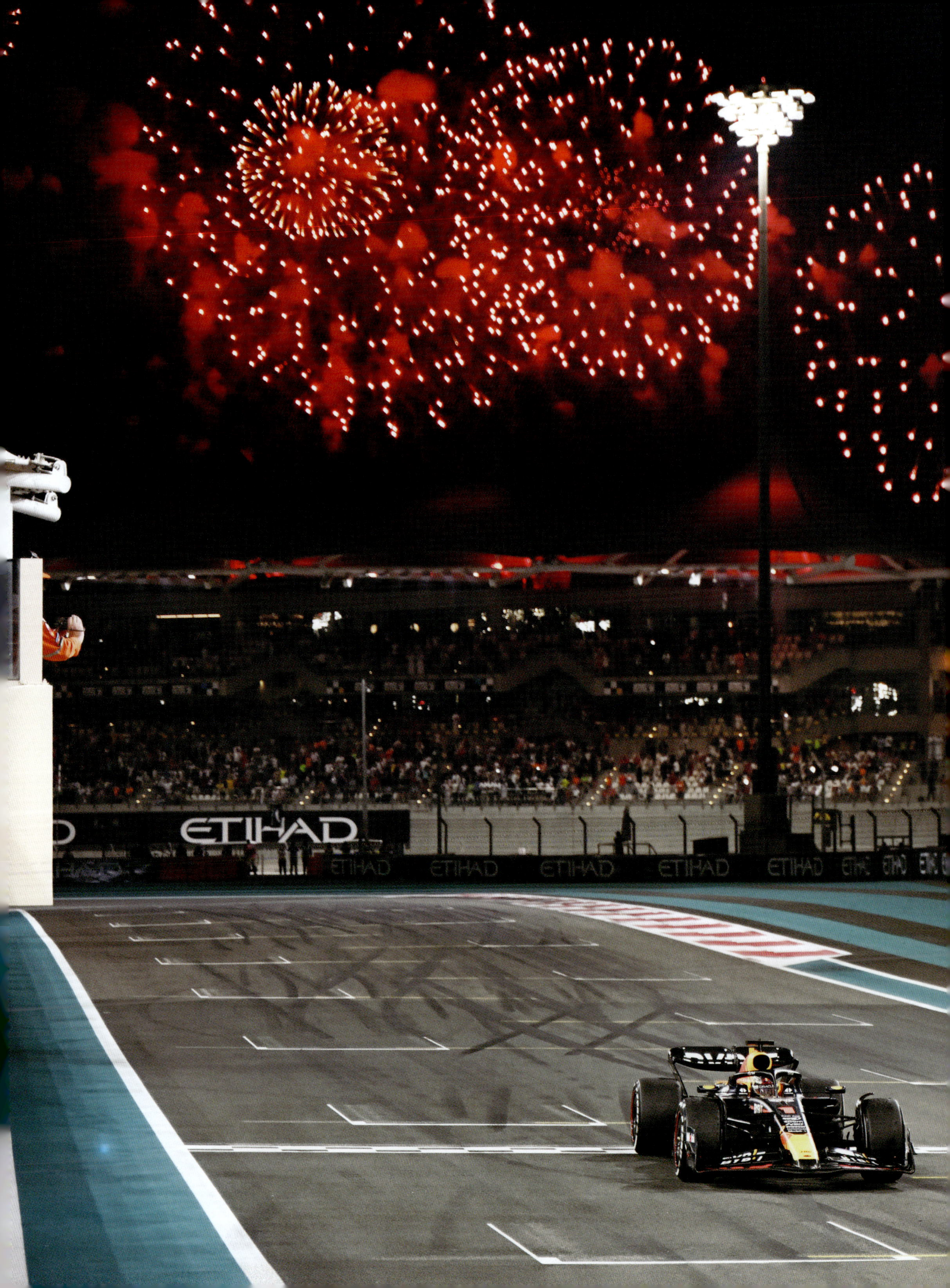
ETIHAD

ASIA AND THE MIDDLE EAST

The early Asian racing scene was centred on temporary street circuits in Singapore and the then Portuguese enclave of Macau before Japan began opening circuits in the early 1960s. It then developed incredibly strong national series for single-seaters and GTs with the fabulous Suzuka and Fuji Speedway as the pick of their circuits. Decades later, as F1 looked to exploit the burgeoning Chinese market, the teams got to see circuit architect Hermann Tilke's most monumental work, the Shanghai International Circuit. Since then, there has been an explosion of racing in China, albeit knocked back by travel restrictions during the COVID pandemic, with circuits being built throughout the eastern part of the country.

However, since then, the continent's real push has been in becoming a key part of the F1 calendar by putting the finances in place to host rounds of the World Championship, with most of this push coming from the oil-rich Middle East, creating circuits for Bahrain, Abu Dhabi, Saudia Arabia and Qatar.

Grands Prix in Malaysia, India and South Korea came and went, while one planned for Vietnam didn't even get to the start line, while Azerbaijan popped up and is still part of the show, with its temporary circuit around the streets of capital Baku proving to be a popular and markedly different venue.

Thailand and Indonesia have both produced F1 drivers but have yet to host Grands Prix, with the former at least being visited by regional series since the construction of the Chang International Circuit at Buriram.

AZERBAIJAN

The World Championship stepped beyond its normal bounds in 2016 when it took F1 to Baku, but it has stayed ever since.

The World Championship began its programme of trying to find countries beyond Europe in which to host Grands Prix in the 1990s. Leading commercial hubs around the world were attractive to the championship organisers, as were countries with a strong sporting history.

Then a third ingredient was added, as shown by the rise of races held in the Middle East: money. Azerbaijan had this, through its oil wealth, but it surprised even the sport's insiders when it announced that it would be joining the World Championship calendar in 2016, getting in ahead of numerous more global locations like New York and Moscow to land a Grand Prix of its own, as it had never featured on motor racing's radar before except for a couple of rounds of the FIA GT Series which were held on a different street layout in 2012 and 2013.

With no motor-racing history, there was no racing circuit at which to host its Grand Prix, so a street circuit was proposed which would be laid out around the capital, Baku. The design was good as it has produced some notable races since, with the seafront and the citadel providing some spectacular shots. In many ways, it was the first new Grand Prix for years to offer a circuit that had a backdrop that looked like nowhere else.

The most notable Grands Prix held on this unusual circuit came in 2017, when Sebastian Vettel drove into Lewis Hamilton behind the safety car, and then in 2021, when there were numerous high-speed blow-outs.

Baku City Circuit

The Baku City Circuit is a street circuit like few others in that it offers a layout with long enough straights to top 200 mph (321.87 kph). The Valencia street circuit used by F1 from 2008 to 2012 is the only other one that offered that degree of flow, until the Jeddah Corniche Circuit came along.

With the temporary pits being erected alongside a boulevard next to a park on the seafront of the Caspian Sea, the lap starts with a run of four right-angled corners past modern buildings. A chicane and then a tight right-hander bring the drivers to a short straight before the track turns left and uphill, with the wall of the citadel hemming the cars in as they start climbing. Reaching a plateau, the track flattens out as it bursts through a park from Turn 9 to Turn 12.

Finally, as the corners open out, the drivers can pick up speed along the broad streets past the city's grandest buildings, kinking left constantly until the next sharp corner is reached. This is Turn 16 and its notable challenge is the way that the track drops away sharply from the apex, with the drivers accelerating hard downhill through the gears and high-speed kinks onto the start-finish straight, hitting 210 mph (337.96 kph) past the pits before having to brake again for Turn 1.

COUNTRY FACTS

Formula One drivers: 0
World champions: 0
Grand Prix circuits: 1
• Baku City Circuit
Grands Prix hosted: 8

Opposite: Daniel Ricciardo guides his Red Bull through Baku's citadel section in 2017.

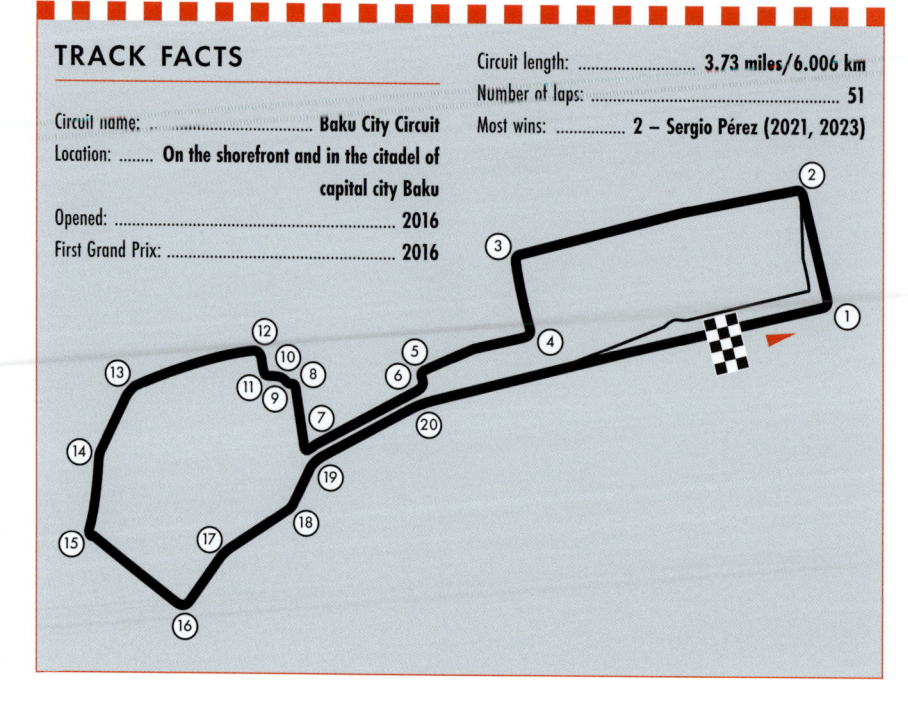

TRACK FACTS

Circuit name: .... Baku City Circuit
Location: .... On the shorefront and in the citadel of capital city Baku
Opened: 2016
First Grand Prix: 2016
Circuit length: .... 3.73 miles/6.006 km
Number of laps: 51
Most wins: .... 2 – Sergio Pérez (2021, 2023)

AZERBAIJAN

BAHRAIN

The first of the Middle Eastern nations to host a round of the World Championship, Bahrain set the tone with its purpose-built circuit.

Bahrain was increasingly aware at the start of the millennium that the nearby United Arab Emirates, specifically Dubai, was marketing itself as the go-to venue in the Arabian Gulf, both for business and sport, using the latter as a lure to boost tourism. Having considered this, Bahrain's Crown Prince Shaikh Salman bin Hamad Al Khalifa backed a project to attract Formula One.

Bahrain had no permanent circuit and its desert terrain was better suited to rally races, but the money was found to make it happen and the Bahrain International Circuit was built about 20 miles (32.2 km) south of capital city, Manama. The job of designing it went to F1's circuit architect Hermann Tilke and his remit was an unusual one, as he was asked not just to design a lap that offered variety and scope for overtaking, but also one that fell into unusually distinctive parts. In this case, the area around the pits and paddock would be the oasis area, with grassy verges, while the area beyond would represent the rocky desert on which it was built. Along with the distinctive ten-storey tower, with Arabic-style canopies overshadowing the pit exit and a smaller one housing race control at the entry to the pit lane, it was certainly not a location that could be mistaken for anywhere else, which was excellent.

Bahrain International Circuit

The Bahrain International Circuit has stood the test of time well. The combination of the first and second corners is enthralling on the opening lap as the first corner doubles back to the right, bunching the cars. Then, almost immediately, the drivers are into Turn 2, jockeying not only to defend their position but also to get their power down as early as they can for the kinked run out onto the desert section all the way up to the hairpin at Turn 4.

What comes next is one of the best stretches of track used by F1, up there with the esses at Silverstone, Suzuka and the Circuit of the Americas. Unusually, these turns are taken on a downhill run and drivers must get their exit under control so that they can position themselves for the Turn 8 hairpin.

From here, there's a short straight into a fast left-hander and then a tighter one. Running behind the paddock, there's a straight down to a possible passing place into Turn 11 before the track starts climbing the slope again. Once they have reached Turn 13, there's a downhill blast to the final two rights onto the pit straight.

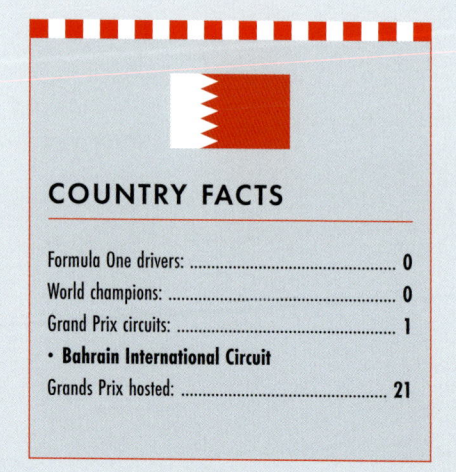

COUNTRY FACTS

Formula One drivers:	0
World champions:	0
Grand Prix circuits:	1

- Bahrain International Circuit

Grands Prix hosted:	21

Opposite: Charles Leclerc keeps his Ferrari ahead of Sergio Pérez's Red Bull in 2022 on his way to head home a Ferrari one-two finish.

TRACK FACTS

Circuit name:	Bahrain International Circuit
Location:	5 miles (8 km) south of capital city Manama at Sakhir
Opened:	2004
First Grand Prix:	2004
Circuit length:	3.363 miles/5.412 km
Number of laps:	57
Most wins:	5 – Lewis Hamilton (2014, 2015, 2019, 2020, 2021)

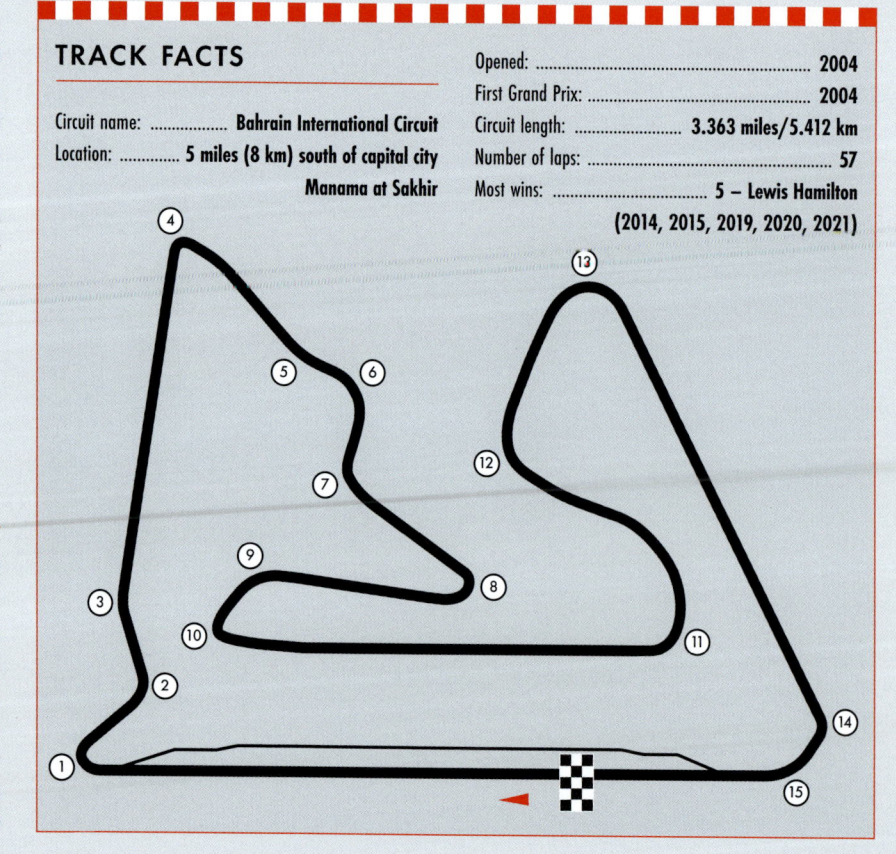

BAHRAIN

CHINA

There is an explosion of interest in China, but most fans have only seen its F1 venue, the Shanghai International Circuit.

Because of the Chinese governing party considering motor racing to be a capitalist pursuit, almost the only racing in China during the last century took place in the Portuguese enclave of Macau, with its annual races for single-seaters and sportscars or GT3 taking place on its streets from 1954. A permanent circuit was built at Zhuhai in 1996 after a GT race had been held in this coastal town 35 miles (56.3 km) west of Hong Kong in the previous years.

In 1998, Zhuhai was nominated as the reserve date on the World Championship calendar, but that came to nothing, and subsequent investment was pulled, especially when it was announced that Shanghai had won the right to welcome the World Championship in 2004.

Zhuhai had a visit from the A1GP single-seater series in 2007, as did a peculiar track laid out around an industrial estate in Beijing and a purpose-built circuit in earthquake-hit Chengdu. Since then, tracks have been opening at an extraordinary rate. Another circuit was built at Orodos in Inner Mongolia to host a round of the short-lived Superleague Formula in 2010 and, more recently, Chinese fans have been entertained by visits from the Formula E championship to street circuits in Beijing and the resort island of Sanya.

The national racing scene is developing at a considerable rate, particularly in the GT class, but the COVID pandemic led to three years of isolation.

COUNTRY FACTS

Formula One drivers:	1
World champions:	0
Grand Prix circuits:	1
• Shanghai International Circuit	
Grands Prix hosted:	17

Below: Lewis Hamilton and Mercedes teammate Valtteri Bottas lead the Ferrari's into Turn 3 on the opening lap of the 2013 Chinese GP.

Zhou Guanyu

With China having hosted a round of the World Championship since 2004, it took years longer than expected for the country to produce its first F1 driver. Zhou headed straight to Europe to race in F4 when he was only fifteen. With an eye to the Chinese market, Ferrari made him one of its academy drivers and Zhou spent the next three years racing in European F3 winning two races and ranking eighth in 2018 when his Prema Racing teammate Mick Schumacher won eight times as he raced to the title. Sponsorship rather than results brought his promotion to F2 in 2019 and this too turned into a three-year project with five podiums in the first year, followed by a win in Sochi in 2020 and then four wins helping him to rank third overall as Oscar Piastri won the title in 2021. Then, in 2022, he stepped up to F1 with Alfa Romeo and placed a career-high eighth in Canada, before matching that in Qatar in 2024..

Shanghai International Circuit

The long wait for a Chinese GP was over when the teams turned up at the Shanghai International Circuit for the first time in 2004 and they were staggered, firstly by the fact that the circuit had been built on marshland and that the site had been stabilised by sinking gigantic polystyrene blocks into the ground and, secondly, by the enormity of the pit buildings and grandstands. The track starts with a curling, uphill and then downhill four-corner sequence, has a snaking run behind the paddock and then a long straight down to a hairpin, which is the best place to try to pass.

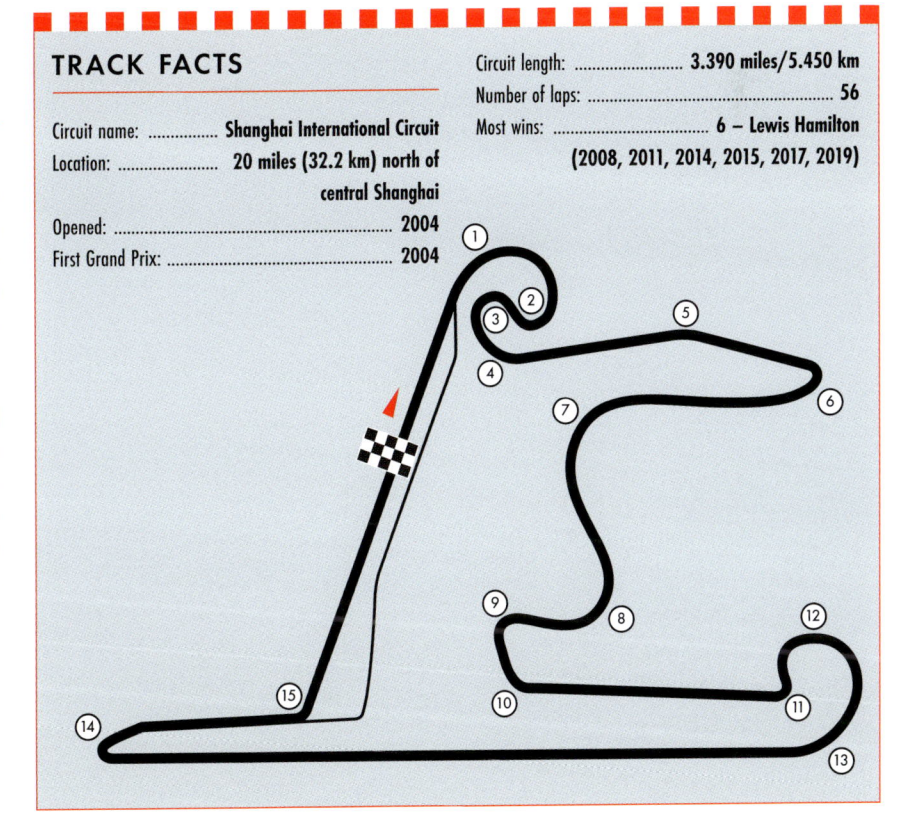

TRACK FACTS

Circuit name: Shanghai International Circuit
Location: 20 miles (32.2 km) north of central Shanghai
Opened: 2004
First Grand Prix: 2004
Circuit length: 3.390 miles/5.450 km
Number of laps: 56
Most wins: 6 – Lewis Hamilton (2008, 2011, 2014, 2015, 2017, 2019)

CHINA 203

INDIA

The Bangalore and Madras GPs were long in the past when India finally welcomed the World Championship in 2011.

There was racing in India before the country gained its independence from Great Britain in 1950, using temporary circuits. In the 1980s, though, the Indian GP for machinery of assorted vintage and assorted formulae was held on the Shovalaram airfield near Madras, now Chennai, with regular competitors including Karun Chandhok's father Vicky and former team owner Vijay Mallya.

Then, in the late 1980s, India gained its first purpose-built circuit, Irungattukotai, and this helped to develop Indian talent, although the best drivers needed to enter pan-Asian single-seater series if they wanted to advance further. As the Indian economy powered into the twenty-first century, there was a desire to bring F1 to India and so the Buddh International Circuit was built on a major sports complex near New Delhi after earlier plans for a Grand Prix in Kolkata and Hyderabad had come to nothing.

This was a great facility that was an instant hit with the drivers, but the paperwork for both getting into and out of India was a nightmare for the teams, with delays causing some severe logistical headaches. Subsequent financial problems stemming from a disputed tax bill owed to the state of Uttar Pradesh, meant that F1 made just three visits, which was a shame in terms of establishing F1 in a country that has a real love for motorsport.

Since then, India's MRF Challenge, held over the northern hemisphere winter, has attracted global talent in the early stages of their careers, while Formula E made its first visit to India recently, using a street circuit in Hyderabad.

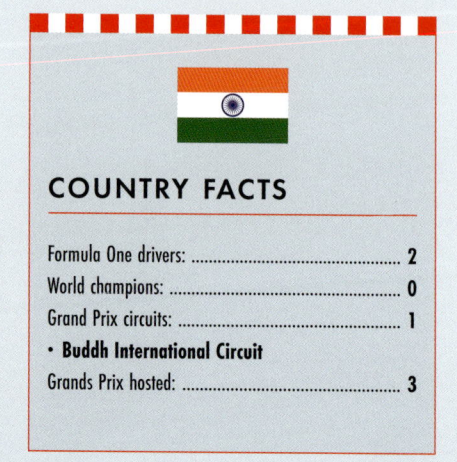

COUNTRY FACTS

Formula One drivers: 2
World champions: 0
Grand Prix circuits: 1
- **Buddh International Circuit**
Grands Prix hosted: 3

Below: Sebastian Vettel loved Buddh's sweepers and wrapped up his 2013 title there.

Narain Karthikeyan

After a season with Jordan in 2005, in which he finished fourth at Indianapolis in a race of just six starters, Narain raced for his national team in A1GP and had to wait until 2011 for his second shot. When it came, he only managed a season and a half with the tail-end HRT team, but he did manage two home appearances at the Indian GP. Narain then raced in Auto GP in 2013 and then the Japanese Super Formula series from 2014 to 2018 before moving from single-seaters to GTs in Japan, keeping his twenty-nine-year racing career going by crossing over to sports-prototypes to race in the Asian Le Mans Series in 2021.

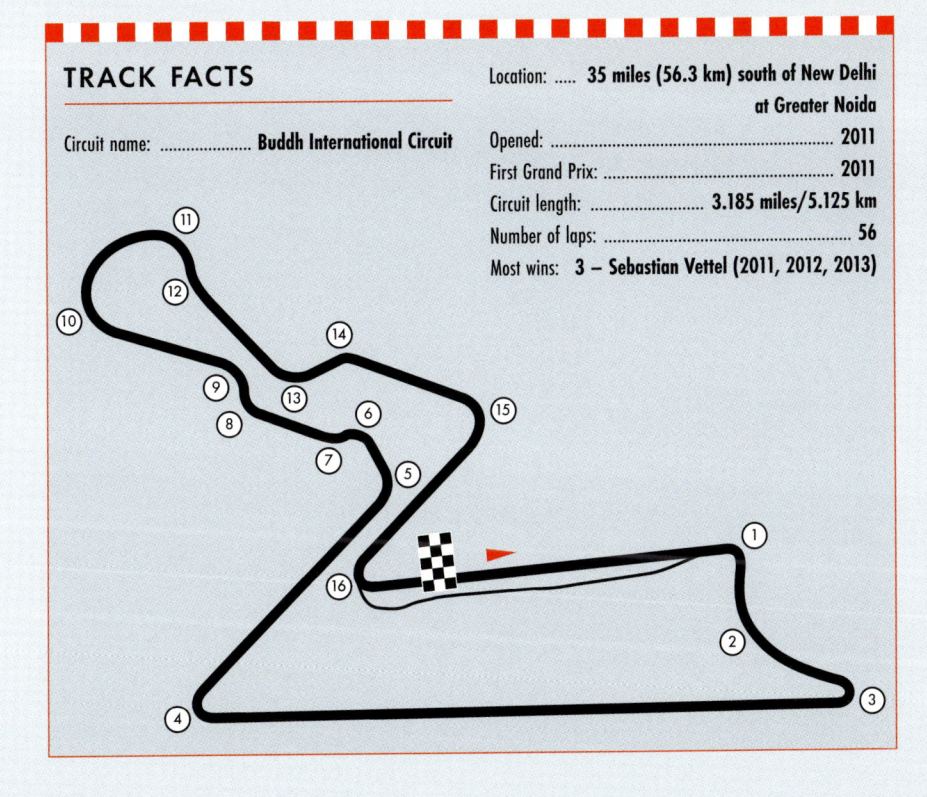

TRACK FACTS

Circuit name: .... Buddh International Circuit
Location: ..... 35 miles (56.3 km) south of New Delhi at Greater Noida
Opened: 2011
First Grand Prix: 2011
Circuit length: .... 3.185 miles/5.125 km
Number of laps: 56
Most wins: 3 – Sebastian Vettel (2011, 2012, 2013)

Buddh International Circuit

The loss of the Indian GP has been a shame for the sport, as it was one of the better modern facilities, offering a challenge to the drivers and some spectacular racing. The lap starts with a right into an uphill sweep to a hairpin at Turn 3. A real feature was the 0.7 mile (1.2 km) straight to Turn 4, this kicking up on entry to the tight right. The track dropped to Turn 5 then twisted its way up to the loop through Turns 10 and 11, dropped again before taking a crest at Turn 15, then diving down again to the final corner.

INDIA 205

INDONESIA

There is passion for motorsport in Indonesia, but its lone circuit, Sentul, has helped produce just one F1 driver to date.

Indonesia's first international-standard circuit was Sentul, which was opened at Bogor to the south of capital city Jakarta in 1993 and attracted both international-level two-wheeled and four-wheeled sport, with its highlight being the visits by the A1 GP Series in 2006.

The track had a long, thin profile, kinked in the middle, with a ninety-degree first corner being followed by a more open second corner leading down a straight to two tight corners before returning along another kinked straight into a chicane, then a short run behind the paddock before another right-left combination and a final pair of tight right-handers to bring the cars back onto the start-finish straight.

Thanks to plentiful backing, Rio Haryanto became Indonesia's only F1 driver to date when he competed for Manor Racing in the 2016 World Championship as the peak of a career that included winning the Formula BMW Pacific series title eight years earlier when it included races at Sentul among its rounds. His time in F1 lasted just half a season before he was replaced by Esteban Ocon.

Formula E came to race in Indonesia twice, first on a street circuit at Putrajaya then in Jakarta. In 2021, a second international-standard circuit opened at Mandalika on the island of Lombok.

COUNTRY FACTS

Formula One drivers:	1
World champions:	0
Grand Prix circuits:	0
Grands Prix hosted:	0

Below: Rio Haryanto ran two-thirds of the 2016 season for Manor then was dropped.

JAPAN

Japan has always had a strong racing scene of its own, but it has been a welcome part of the World Championship since 1976.

Japan spent decades racing largely on its own, with strong domestic championships for sportscars, single-seaters and touring cars. Car manufacturer Honda had Suzuka built in 1962 as the country's first permanent circuit, with a view to it being used as a test venue as much as a racing circuit. Toyota followed suit three years later with Fuji Speedway, which beat Suzuka to welcome F1 in 1976 but lost the deal after just two years.

In 1987, Japan was back, with Suzuka hosting a Grand Prix for the first time and its classic circuit became a firm favourite, with the Japanese fans earning respect for their intense but respectful loyalty to their heroes.

In the same way that Italy held a second Grand Prix for decades, so Japan got a second in 1994 and 1995 when the title of Pacific GP was awarded to the TI Circuit near Okayama. This came a couple of years after the Autopolis circuit made an abortive attempt to land an extra race. A few years later, with Honda engines being a key part of the Indycar package, the manufacturer helped finance the Twin-Ring Motegi circuit to host an Indycar race in Japan. This is a speed oval with a road course twisting in and out of it. The oval has been closed because of subsidence, but the road circuit lives on.

Japan has still not had a world champion or even a Grand Prix winner, with Takuma Sato – ranked eighth in 2004 – their best to date, but that time will surely come. If Red Bull sees fit to promote Yuki Tsunoda from its junior team to Red Bull Racing in the future, that might all change.

COUNTRY FACTS

Formula One drivers: 21
Selected F1 drivers:
- Kazuyoshi Hoshino
- Yuji Ide
- Taki Inoue
- Ukyo Katayama
- Kamui Kobayashi
- Kazuki Nakajima
- Satoru Nakajima
- Shinji Nakano
- Hideki Noda
- Takuma Sato
- Aguri Suzuki
- Toshio Suzuki
- Toranosuke Takagi
- Noritake Takahara
- Yuki Tsunoda

World champions: 0
Grand Prix circuits: 3
- Fuji Speedway
- Suzuka
- TI Circuit

Grands Prix hosted: 40

Below: Yuki Tsunoda's AlphaTauri lines up in front of the famous Ferris Wheel in 2022.

DRIVERS

The first Japanese drivers to hit F1 were insular, but the younger ones are far more cosmopolitan after developing their racing careers overseas first.

Takuma Sato

Takuma headed directly to Europe and did well enough to get to F3 for his third year, winning the British title in his fourth. Although he spent 2001 testing for BAR, he got his F1 break with Jordan in 2002, rounding out his year with a fifth-place finish at his home race at Suzuka. Jordan then lost Honda engines and Takuma went back to testing for BAR before getting a race seat for 2004. This peaked with third at Indianapolis, but that was as good as it got and, after racing for Super Aguri, Takuma moved to Indycars and went on to become a two-time Indy 500 winner.

Kazuki Nakajima

While his father Satoru got to F1 thanks to patronage from Honda, Kazuki got Toyota to back him and this landed him a test-driving role for Williams in 2007, as they ran Toyota engines. He spent the year racing in GP2, but was handed his F1 debut in Brazil at the end of the season and did enough to be awarded a full-season seat for 2008. Sixth place in the opening round was his best finish all year. After F1, Kazuki won the Formula Nippon title in 2012, then won the Le Mans 24 Hours in 2018, 2019 and 2020 plus the World Endurance title in 2018/2019.

Yuki Tsunoda

Japan's latest F1 hope gathered karting titles for fun and was just pipped to a world title in 2012, aged twelve. Yuki then concentrated on schoolwork for four years before winning Japan's F4 title in 2018. Red Bull then made this diminutive racer part of its scholarship programme and he spent 2019 learning Europe's circuits and immediately looked rapid when he graduated to F2 in 2020. He won three races to rank third and this opened the door for Yuki to step up to F1 with AlphaTauri in 2021. Fourth in the final round, he has not hit such heights since, as he waits for a Red Bull Racing seat.

Aguri Suzuki

Aguri's father ran the Japanese karting scene, so he was soon racing, landing his first title in the 1986 touring car series for Nissan and his second two years later when he won the All-Japan F3000 crown. Breaking into F1 with Zakspeed in 1989 because they ran Yamaha engines was a bad move and he failed to qualify. So, Larrousse felt far better in 1990 and Aguri's day of days came at Suzuka when he rose from tenth on the grid in his Larrousse to finish third. After further seasons with Larrousse, Footwork and Pacific, Aguri concentrated on running his own team, ARTA, in Japan.

Satoru Nakajima

Satoru was the man to beat in Japan in the 1980s, winning its F2 championship five times in six years between 1981 and 1986, so he was the obvious person to receive Honda backing as it ramped up its involvement in F1. This landed him a seat at Lotus for 1987, with no less a driver than Ayrton Senna as his teammate. Finishing fifth in his third race at Spa-Francorchamps was a good start and Satoru then came fourth at Silverstone and fourth again at the end of 1989 in Adelaide. After two years with Tyrrell failed to deliver a great deal and then Honda withdrawing from F1 at the end of 1992, Satoru realised that he might have more luck back home and has not only run a hugely successful single-seater team ever since but has also doubled up by running another team in Japan's fiercely competitive Super GT series, using Honda NSXs of course.

CIRCUIT

The challenge of Suzuka is every bit as tough now as it was when F1 made its first visit back in 1987.

Suzuka

Honda hired John Hugenholtz to design the Suzuka circuit for them as they liked how he had shaped Zandvoort and Jarama. Located inland from the city of Nagoya, the circuit opened its doors in 1962 and held the first Japanese GP, a race for sportscars, the following year.

Suzuka was created as a test venue for Honda's automotive range, although it was obviously to be used for racing too. What is unusual, though, is that the circuit is just part of an amusement complex with a huge Ferris wheel, a Suzuka landmark that towers over the outside of the final corner.

The circuit makes wonderful use of the site's gradient. The start-finish straight dips down to a medium-speed right to the first corner which leads to a tighter right at which the track starts to head back up the slope. The incline steepens as the cars reach the S-Curves and this is one of the trickiest stretches of track used by F1 anywhere. Flattening out at the Dunlop Curve, the drivers then have to negotiate two Degner corners with the tighter second one leading the cars under a bridge carrying the return leg of the circuit. A lefthand hairpin comes next and then a long, arcing run to the right that turns into a left at the highest point of the lap before dropping onto the start of the long run for home, with the homeward straight offering the 130R kink in its middle and a tight right-left chicane at its end. Passing is possible here, but far from guaranteed. Then there's one last corner onto the top end of the start-finish straight to complete a lap of this circuit that has changed little since it was given its World Championship debut in 1987.

For many years, Suzuka held the final round of the World Championship and so there were some tense shoot-outs, notably between Ayrton Senna and Alain Prost, Michael Schumacher and Damon Hill, then Schumacher and Mika Häkkinen. Having its race date shunted forward by around six rounds as the F1 calendar has expanded considerably has cost it that edge. For 2024, the change is more radical, with the Japanese GP being moved forward to become the fourth round of the championship, paired with the Chinese GP as the organisers try to make a more logical pattern to the teams' travel.

However, the drivers still love the old-school challenge that it offers.

Opposite: Valtteri Bottas blasts out of the pits on his way to victory for Mercedes in 2019.

Following pages: Robert Kubica leads Fernando Alonso in the 2008 Japanese GP at Fuji.

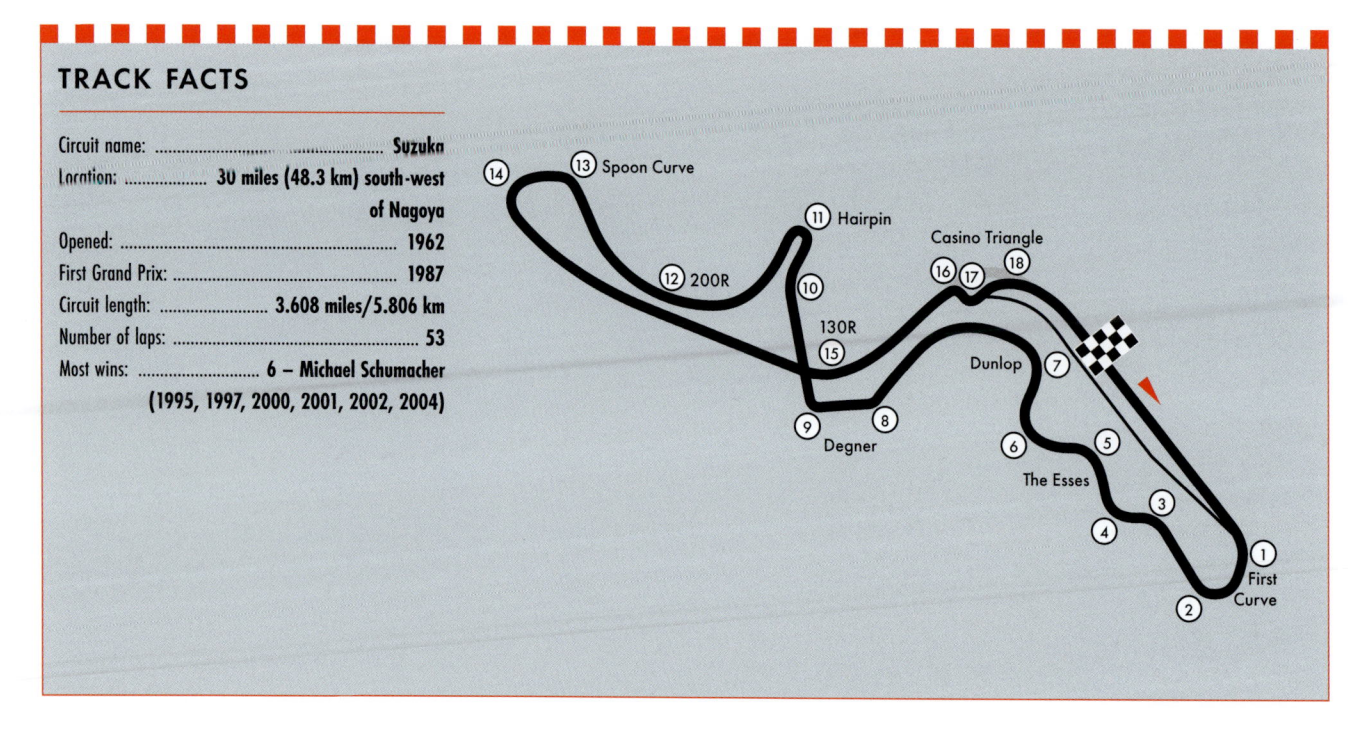

TRACK FACTS

Circuit name:	Suzuka
Location:	30 miles (48.3 km) south-west of Nagoya
Opened:	1962
First Grand Prix:	1987
Circuit length:	3.608 miles/5.806 km
Number of laps:	53
Most wins:	6 – Michael Schumacher (1995, 1997, 2000, 2001, 2002, 2004)

210 | JAPAN

JAPAN

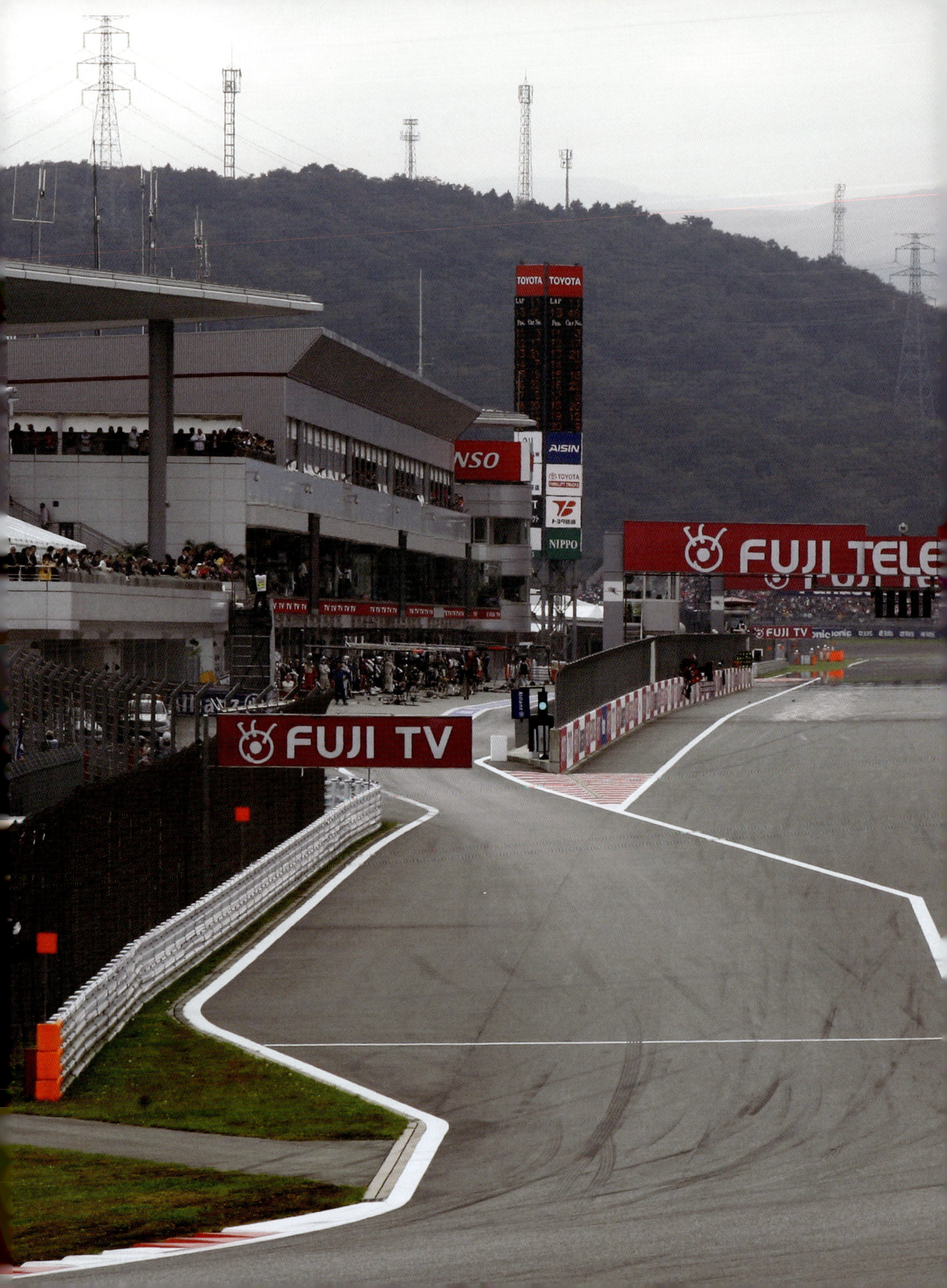
TOYOTA
TOYOTA
AISIN
NIPPO
FUJI TELE
FUJI TV
FUJI TV

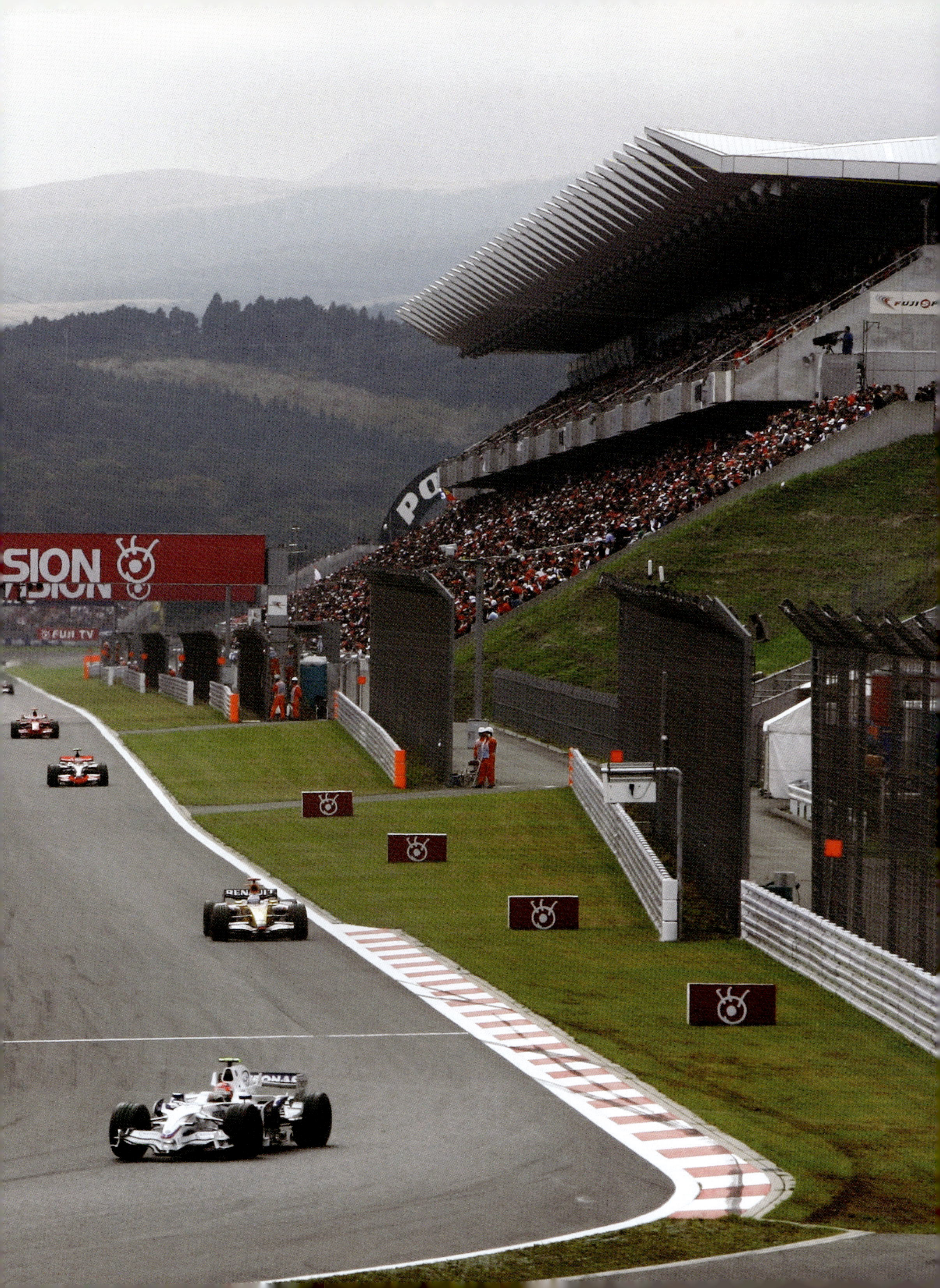
SION
FUJI TV
RENAULT

Prost and Senna get rough

After dominating F1 in their first year together at McLaren in 1988, Ayrton Senna and Alain Prost were scarcely speaking by the time they arrived at Suzuka for 1989's penultimate race. Senna needed to win to stay in the title hunt, but was jumped at the start by his teammate who then resolutely defended that advantage. With just six laps to go, Senna made a move into the chicane, but they clashed. Prost was out on the spot, but Senna had his car push-started and was first to the chequered flag. After an FIA hearing, Senna was disqualified as his car had been moved to a place of safety before being push-started and so Benetton's Alessandro Nannini was promoted to be winner.

MOMENTS

The arrival of rain often shakes up F1's visits to Japan, but holding late-season races has also meant title battles add tension.

Damon Hill's wet-weather masterclass

Michael Schumacher and Damon Hill had a terse contest over the 1994 World Championship. It was coming to a boil when they reached Suzuka and it was here that Hill produced his very best drive in conditions that were, as they can be here, awful. In fact, the race had to be red-flagged. Benetton then gambled on the second part of the race being stopped early and so only part-fuelled Schumacher's car. When the race kept going, he had to pit an extra time and then attack to cut his fourteen-second deficit. On a streaming wet track, he gave chase, but Hill didn't put a wheel wrong and his win reduced Schumacher's lead to just one point as they headed to Adelaide.

Mario Andretti wins, Hunt crowned

The 1976 season was all about Niki Lauda against James Hunt. F1's first visit to Fuji Speedway was the final round, with Lauda holding a three-point lead. Hunt led away on a waterlogged track. Two laps in, though, Lauda reckoned it was too unsafe to continue, meaning that Hunt had to be third to become champion. Twelve laps from the end, after the track had dried, he was still leading, but his tyres were chunking and Lotus' Mario Andretti went past. McLaren were signalling Hunt to come in, but he didn't see and continued until his front left popped. This dropped him to fifth and he thought he was only fourth at the finish, but he had made it back to third, so the title was his.

Schumacher takes win and title

The second visit to the TI Circuit for the Pacific GP came in 1995, but this time it was near to the end of the season so that it could be paired with the Japanese GP. Michael Schumacher knew that he could clinch his second title in a row with two rounds still to run. Looking to prevent this, Williams filled the front row and David Coulthard led the first half of the race while Schumacher made up ground. The Scot had established such a good lead that he changed to a two-stop strategy. However, he would later regret that as Schumacher took a lead he wouldn't lose when Coulthard came in for his second stop and raced on to the win and the title.

Opposite: McLaren teammates Ayrton Senna and Alain Prost famously become entangled at Suzuka's Casino Triangle in 1989.

Below: Eventual winner Mario Andretti makes a good start on a wet track to power his Lotus ahead of James Hunt's McLaren in 1976.

MALAYSIA

Malaysia became the first Asian country outside Japan to host a World Championship race in 1999.

Races were held on a street circuit at Johor Bahru in the 1950s and 1960s, but Malaysia long sought a permanent circuit of its own. One was built in 1968 not far from capital city Kuala Lumpur at Shah Alam, right beneath the Selangor royal palace. Unfortunately, it was forced to close after six children were hit and killed in 1977. Once modernised and made safer, the circuit reopened and hosted a round of the World Sports Car Championship in 1985, won by Porsche's Jacky Ickx and Jochen Mass, but the series never visited again, and the Selangor circuit dropped back to hosting national series events.

It took until the opening of Sepang in 1999 for Malaysia to return to the international roster. This was something on a far higher level and it offered F1 something very different in a part of the globe in which the World Championship was woefully underrepresented. As well as hosting a Grand Prix through until 2017, it also provided a hub for the South-east Asian series, with GT races and one-make series for Porsches and Lamborghinis the most popular, along with an annual twelve-hours race with an entry that is growing year on year, despite the soaring heat and humidity. Importantly, now there are also more cost-effective single-seater series to enable Malaysia's next generation of drivers onto the first step of the racing ladder.

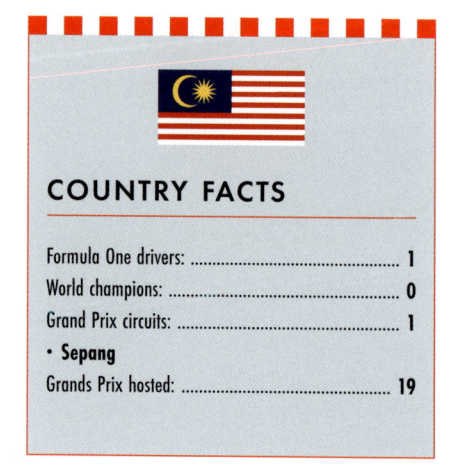

COUNTRY FACTS

Formula One drivers: 1
World champions: 0
Grand Prix circuits: 1
- Sepang
Grands Prix hosted: 19

Below: Max Verstappen passed Lewis Hamilton for the lead in 2017, then pulled clear to win for Red Bull Racing on F1's most recent visit to Sepang.

Sepang

This was the first circuit on which architect Hermann Tilke showed his trademark concept. He started with a tight corner at the end of the start-finish straight. This was followed immediately by a second corner, to give the drivers overtaking options. The site slopes from here through a long right-hander into a tight right, with the track kicking upwards on entry. Then comes a sweeping section, tightening at Turn 8. A hairpin at Turn 9 feeds the cars up through an arcing right and then down again. A tight right at Turn 14 feeds the cars onto the back straight to a final hairpin. Although it last hosted a Grand Prix in 2017, when Max Verstappen won for Red Bull Racing, and Malaysia's economy has dipped since, the circuit remains an important regional racing hub for junior single-seater categories and GTs.

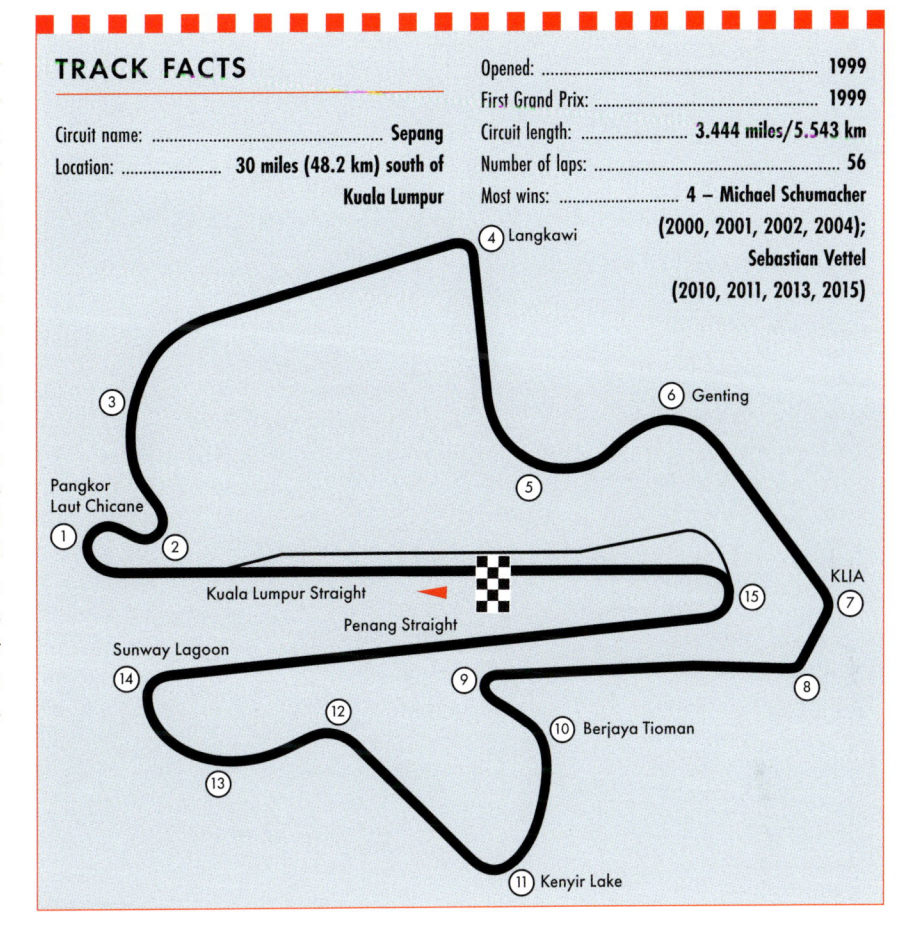

TRACK FACTS

Circuit name: Sepang
Location: 30 miles (48.2 km) south of Kuala Lumpur
Opened: 1999
First Grand Prix: 1999
Circuit length: 3.444 miles/5.543 km
Number of laps: 56
Most wins: 4 – Michael Schumacher (2000, 2001, 2002, 2004); Sebastian Vettel (2010, 2011, 2013, 2015)

Alex Yoong

Alex is Malaysia's only F1 driver. His early single-seater results weren't sensational, but the Malaysian government was keen to have a driver of its own having done the deal to host a Grand Prix from 1999 and so they financed his rides in F3000. At the end of 2001, with money running short, Minardi signed Alex for the final three rounds, for which he qualified last on all occasions. A full season followed in 2002 and he started with a career-best seventh in Australia, albeit three laps down. His best performances came after F1, when he was a winner in A1GP for Team Malaysia. This former water-skiing champion raced on in GTs across Southeast Asia through until 2018, winning the Audi R8 LMS Cup title each year from 2014 to 2016, and now spends his time trying to propel his son Alister up the single-seater ladder.

MALAYSIA | 217

QATAR

A Qatar GP was a surprise inclusion in the 2021 World Championship, brought in as a reserve, but it plans to stay on.

Qatar is a broad peninsula jutting into the Arabian Gulf that gained independence from being a British protectorate in 1971. Although only 125 miles (201 km) from north to south, its incredibly rich gas reserves give it a global reach.

It dipped its toe into the motor-racing pond as long ago as 2004 when it opened its first permanent racing facility at Losail just to the north of capital city Doha, and its first international visitor was the Moto GP motorcycle series. Four-wheeled motor sport was attracted there too, initially the Grand Prix Masters series for former F1 drivers in 2006.

To run after dark when temperatures are cooler, the entire circuit was floodlit in 2007. This gave Moto GP its first night race early the following year and the first car race to experience the power of these lights were those contesting the GP2 Asia series in 2009.

The World Touring Car Championship became a regular visitor between 2015 and 2019 before the COVID pandemic gave Lusail its big break as travel limitations meant that F1 could not visit the Far East, so Qatar stepped in and hosted a round of the World Championship in 2021, with Lewis Hamilton taking victory for Mercedes. Then, with China still out of bounds in 2023, a second visit followed.

F1 aside, the event that put little-known Qatar on the map, was of course the Football World Cup in 2022.

Lusail International Circuit

It started life in 2004, but Lusail has changed its name recently to the Lusail International Circuit, although little has changed about the track since it opened, save for the addition of more grandstand seats and a new pit complex ahead of the first Qatar GP in 2021.

The lap begins with a run down to a 140-degree right-hander and a matching left-hander before a short straight to Turns 4 and 5, a pair of ninety-degree rights. Next up is a hairpin, another tight corner at Turn 7, before the lap opens out a little, slowing again for Turn 10 but then entering a sweep to the left and a run of three high-speed right-handers. The end of the lap is quick all the way down to the final corner onto the start-finish straight. There is scope to overtake into Turn 16, but drivers know that a better bet is to make a clean exit from here, catch a tow from a rival down the kilometre-long straight and shape up for a passing move into Turn 1.

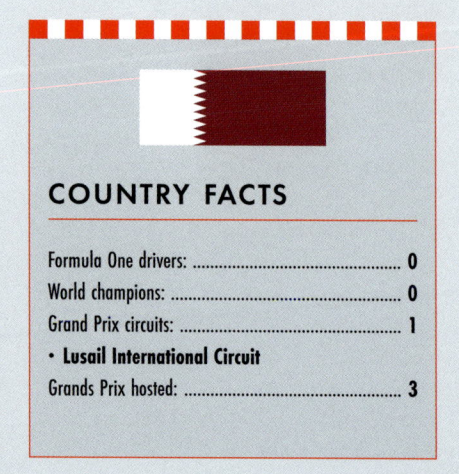

COUNTRY FACTS

Formula One drivers: 0
World champions: 0
Grand Prix circuits: 1
• Lusail International Circuit
Grands Prix hosted: 3

Opposite: Blasting off under the lights, Lewis Hamilton leads away from Pierre Gasly's AlphaTauri on his way to winning the 2021 Qatar GP.

TRACK FACTS

Circuit name: .... Lusail International Circuit
Location: .... 10 miles (16 km) north of Doha
Opened: 2004
First Grand Prix: 2021
Circuit length: .... 3.343 miles/5.380 km
Number of laps: 57
Most wins: .... 2 – Max Verstappen (2023, 2024)

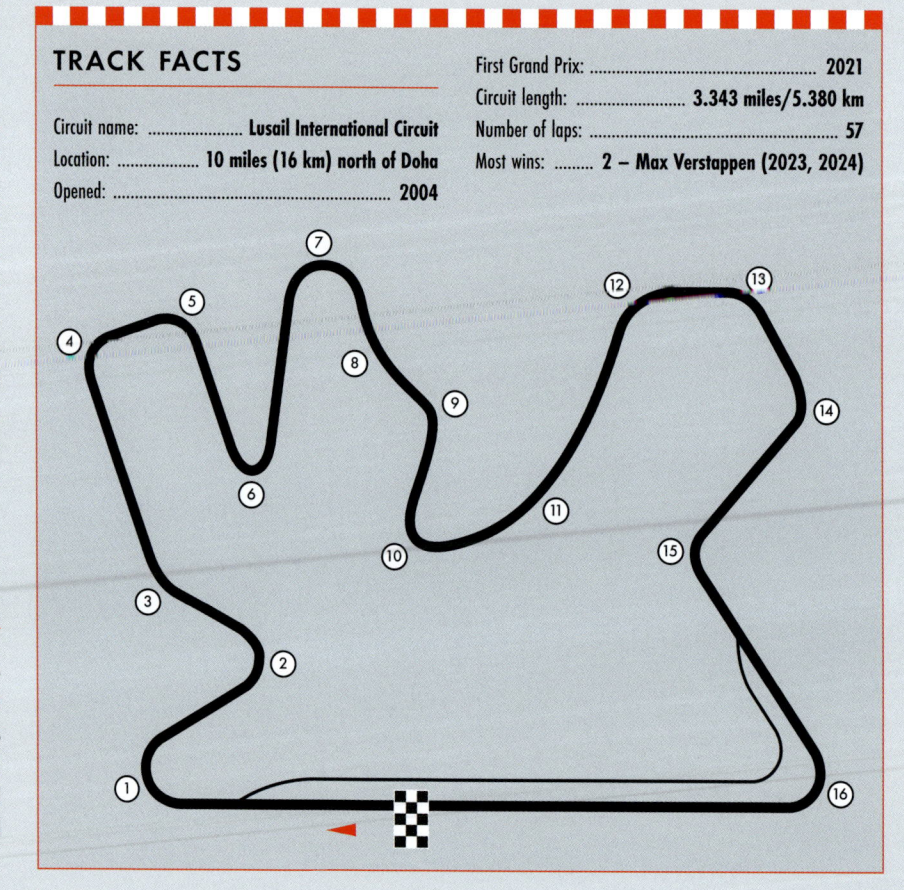

QATAR | 219

SAUDI ARABIA

This giant of the Middle East is a late starter in motor racing, but it is making huge strides to become a major player.

There had been talk for years of Saudi Arabia creating a venue to entice the World Championship to its shores, but, even as plans changed, nothing happened. So, it was left to Formula E to dip its toe in the waters, making a promising debut on the Diriyah street circuit near Riyadh at the end of 2019.

F1 did follow, however, when the ambitious Jeddah Corniche Circuit made its debut as the penultimate race of the 2021 season, showing that it is possible to build a street circuit that isn't stop-start in nature, with this one having two points on its lap where the cars can top 200 mph (321.9 kph).

Despite the expenditure and disruption of setting up this temporary venue and its facilities and then dismantling it immediately afterwards, the Jeddah Corniche Circuit is merely a stopgap that will be used until a permanent facility can be built at Qiddiya on the outskirts of the capital, Riyadh. You can be sure that this will be built to an exceptional standard, somewhere that will put down a new marker in a way that only circuits in oil-rich countries looking to boost their image can do.

Spurred on by having their own Grand Prix at last, young Saudi drivers will soon begin to climb the racing ladder after taking their early steps in regional single-seater series. As it stands, though, the highest-ranked Saudi driver is Reema Juffali who competes in the GT World Challenge. Compatriot Bandar Alesayi has been impressing in a regional Porsche series, but he is unlikely to head for F1 as he will turn forty-eight in 2024.

Jeddah Corniche Circuit

The construction of this circuit was achieved in a short time frame, and the result was impressive.

The lap is all about flow, which might seem strange as it fits twenty-seven corners into its 3.836-mile (6.174-km) course, but almost all these corners are high-speed swerves rather than the ninety-degree bends that littered early street circuits. In part, the site available, on a corniche overlooking a lagoon north of the centre of Jeddah, is so narrow that it is a case of what fits best. The other reason is that former Le Mans racer turned government minister Abdulaziz bin Turki Al Faisal wanted the F1 cars to be shown at their best, thus at speed. He got his desire, as the fastest laps average over 150 mph (241.4 kph).

After an initial left-right chicane, the tone of the lap is revealed by the time the cars reach Turn 4, as this is the start of a nine-corner esse that's taken in sixth and seventh gears, the corners coming at the drivers thick and fast. A short straight follows into a hairpin at Turn 13. Then, now on the lagoon side of the circuit, the drivers do it all over again all the way through even faster sweepers down to Turn 24 before opening out for an arcing left up to the turnaround point of the final corner, Turn 27.

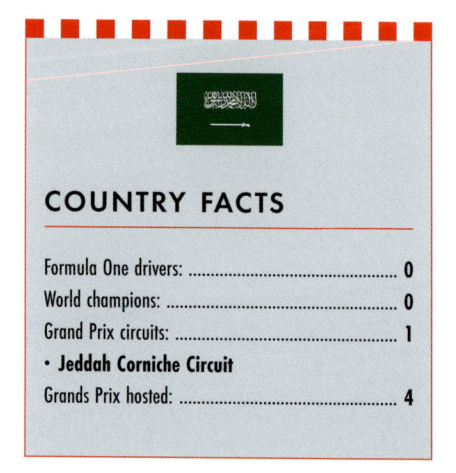

COUNTRY FACTS

Formula One drivers:	0
World champions:	0
Grand Prix circuits:	1
• Jeddah Corniche Circuit	
Grands Prix hosted:	4

Opposite: Victory in the 2021 Saudi Arabian GP kept Lewis Hamilton in the title hunt.

TRACK FACTS

Circuit name:	Jeddah Corniche Circuit
Location:	8 miles (12.9 km) to the north of Jeddah
Opened:	2021
First Grand Prix:	2021
Circuit length:	3.836 miles/6.174 km
Number of laps:	50
Most wins:	2 – Max Verstappen (2022, 2024)

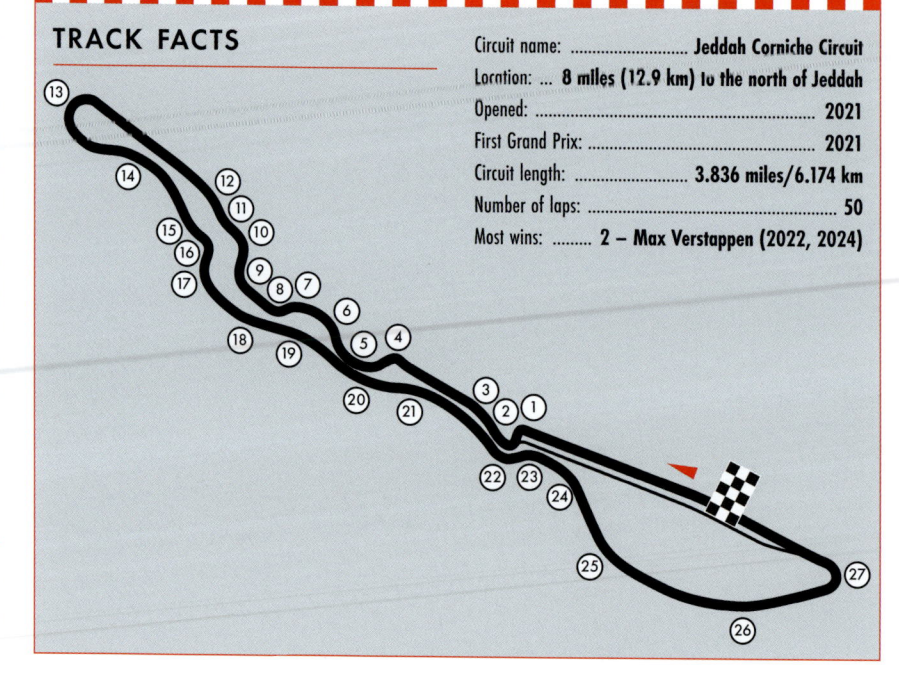

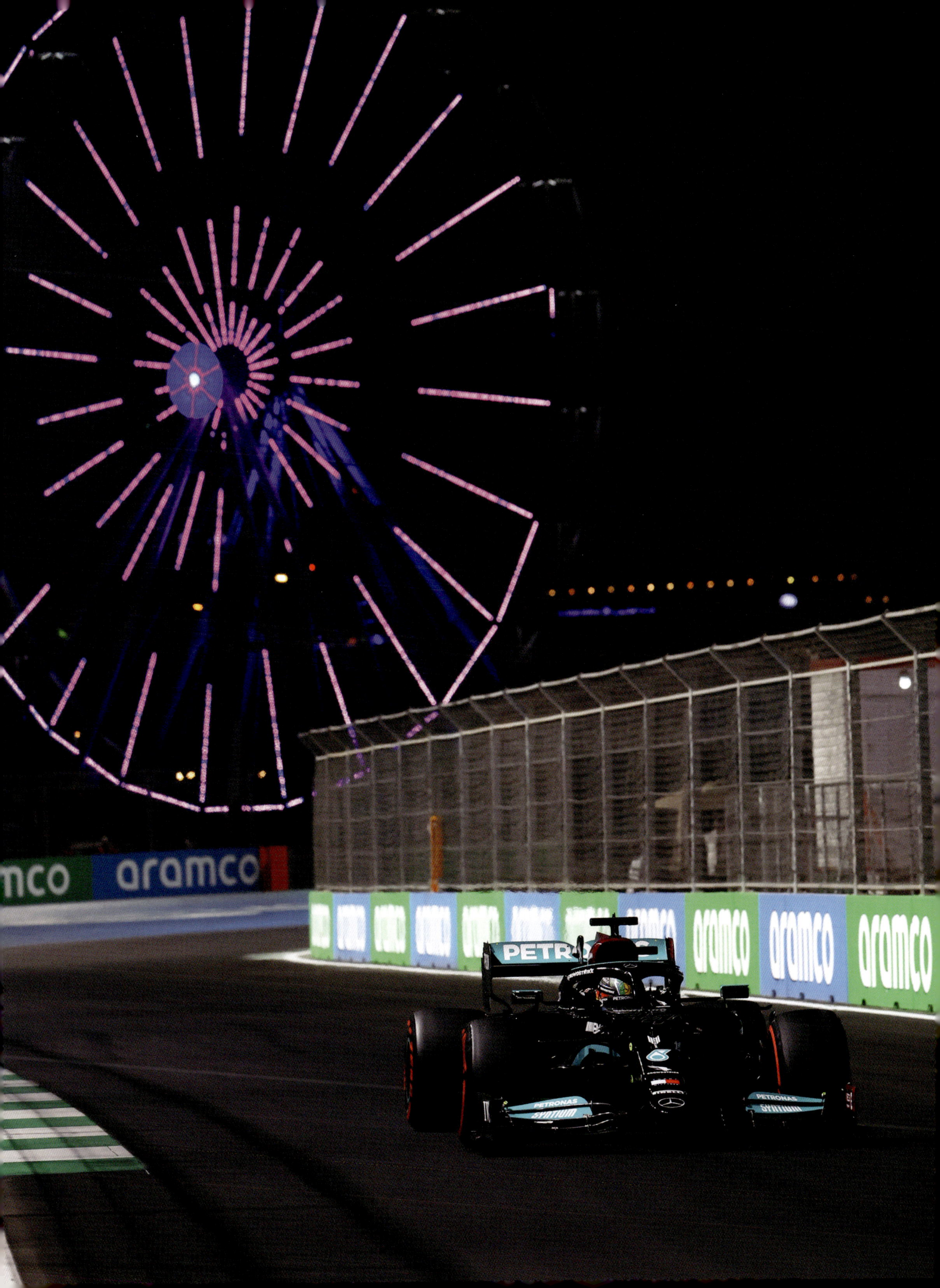
mco
aramco
aramco
aramco
aramco
PETRONAS
SYNTIUM

SINGAPORE

Hosting a Grand Prix in the heart of Singapore was always going to be spectacular, but making it a night race made it doubly so.

Singapore was long considered to be the perfect location for a Grand Prix, given it was in the optimum time zone to cater for both the European and South-east Asian and Australasian markets. There had been street races there in the 1960s and 1970s, but it took until 2008 before plans for F1's first visit came to fruition on a temporary site right in the heart of the city, between its central business district, its colonial quarter, and the new Marina Bay complex. It was certainly quite a hurry to get the facilities in place, as work started only twelve months before its first race date. Singaporean efficiency, however, got the job done, helped by the Singaporean government financing 60 per cent of the project.

That the facilities were spot-on at the first attempt, with no loose ends, added to Singapore's image of being a country that gets things done.

Apart from the impressive facilities, the drivers were also hit by the soaring temperatures and cloying humidity, so they were relieved that the race would be held after nightfall, when both factors would be in retreat. Another advantage for the European-based teams was that they tended to pretend that they were still in European time zones and would rise late in the [Singaporean] day and continue at the track as the sessions ran into the night, this way also nullifying some of the inevitable jet lag. From the first corner of the first visit, the drivers knew that they had a new challenge.

Marina Bay Circuit

The Marina Bay Circuit is that unusual thing: a street circuit on which the drivers not only don't feel as though they are constantly negotiating right-angled bends but are also able to power along straights long enough for them to catch a tow to enable them to try to line up a passing move into the next corner.

The lap starts with a sharp left into a more open right and this has often been the scene of contact on the opening lap. Then, from a lefthand hairpin, the track opens out a little. Once clear of Turn 5, there's a kinked straight past Singapore's tallest office blocks down to a hard stop for Turn 7.

The lap then starts its middle leg that takes the track past the city's grandest parks and most prestigious sportsgrounds as well as the Raffles Hotel then the Anderson Bridge.

Turning hard left at the foot of the landmark Marina Bay Hotel, the drivers then have a long blast past the Esplanade Theatre to enter a homeward leg that has them running past a Ferris Wheel. Then, a sequence of two more high-speed lefts feeds them back onto the start-finish straight.

COUNTRY FACTS

Formula One drivers: 0
World champions: 0
Grand Prix circuits: 1
• Marina Bay Circuit
Grands Prix hosted: 15

Opposite: This high-up shot shows Charles Leclerc chasing after Max Verstappen out of Turn 3 at the start of the 2022 Singapore GP.

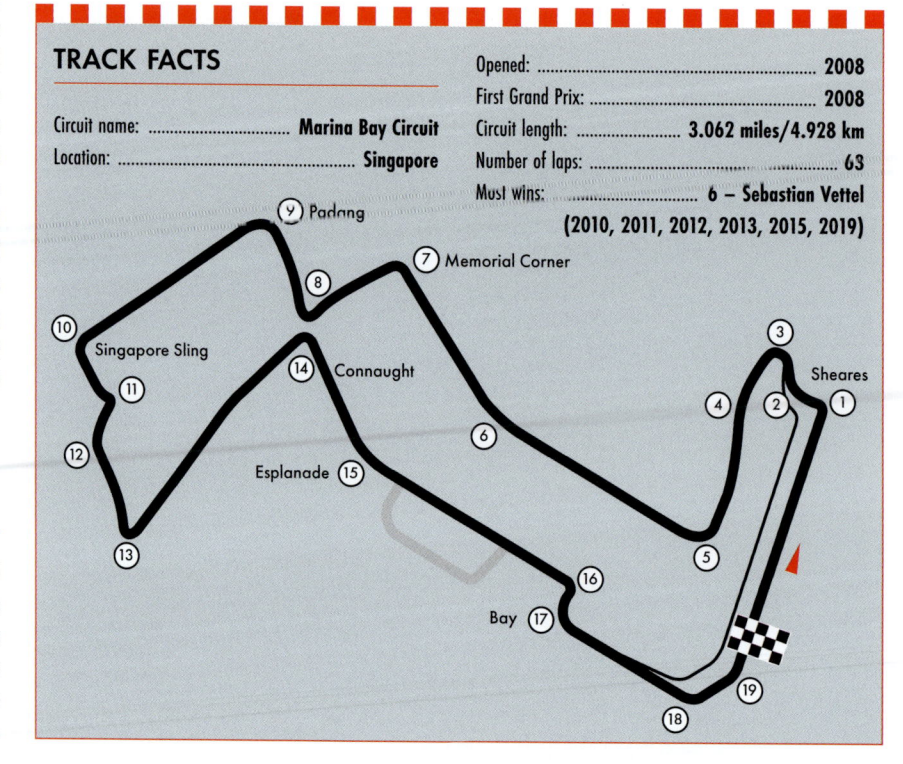

TRACK FACTS

Circuit name: Marina Bay Circuit
Location: Singapore
Opened: 2008
First Grand Prix: 2008
Circuit length: 3.062 miles/4.928 km
Number of laps: 63
Most wins: 6 – Sebastian Vettel (2010, 2011, 2012, 2013, 2015, 2019)

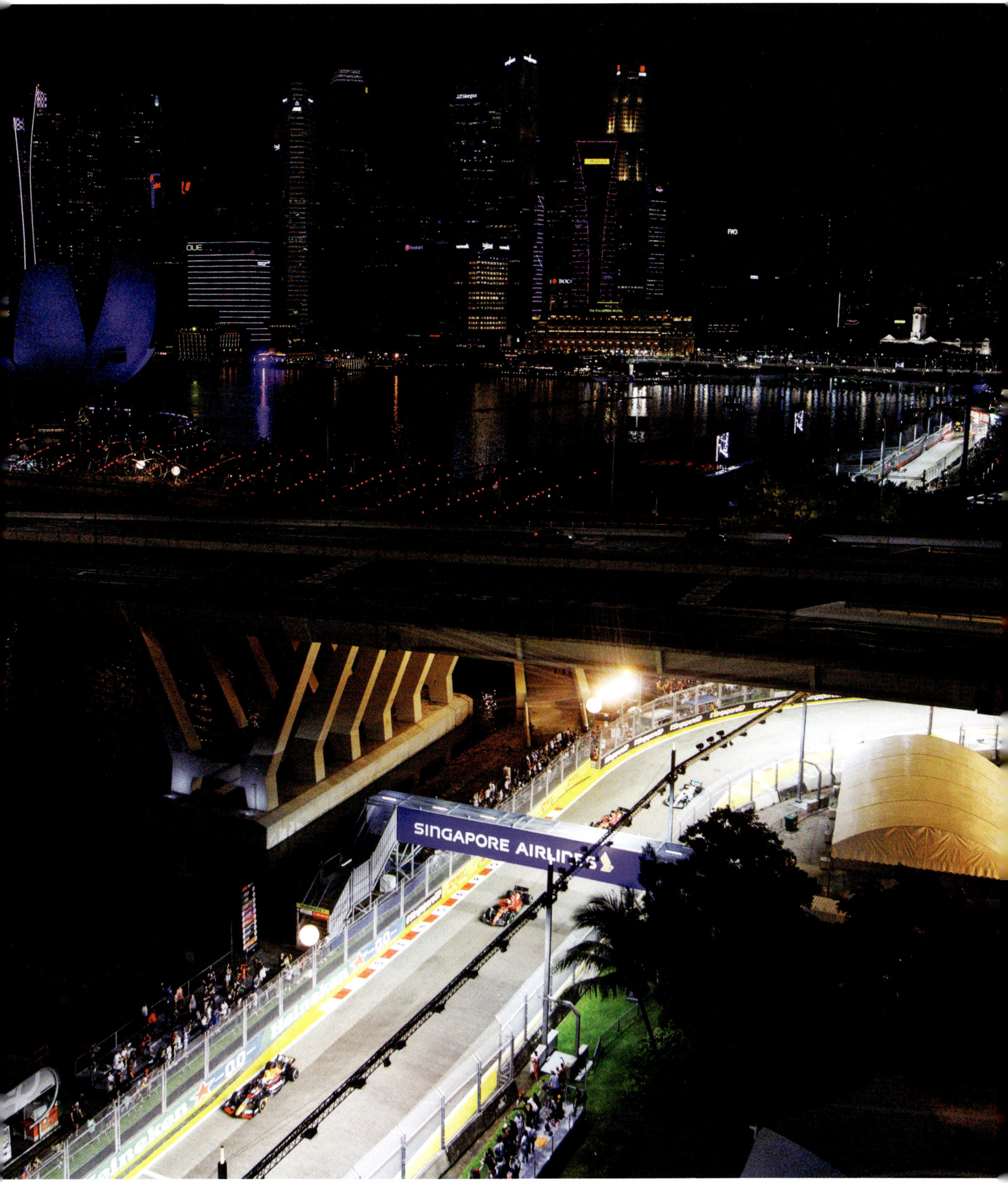
SINGAPORE AIRLINES
OUE
Heineken
0.0

SOUTH KOREA

South Korea has had a fast-expanding automotive industry for three decades, so it was no surprise when it welcomed F1.

South Korea had been angling to land a Grand Prix for years, being anxious to show the world how it was a thriving country with some world-leading industries. However, patience was required as it sought a place at motor racing's top table.

First there were plans for a circuit close to Kunsan City and later a suggestion that the city of Chinhae would create a temporary street circuit. Neither of these plans came to fruition, although a temporary circuit in Changwon hosted international F3 races between 1999 and 2003 contested by Jenson Button and Lewis Hamilton.

Instead, KAVO (Korea Auto Valley Operation) stole their thunder with its creation of the grandiose-sounding Korea International Circuit near Mokpo on the country's south coast. This opened for business in 2010, with the paint literally drying as the teams turned up. It really was a close-run thing. Although the distant location, a three-and-a-half-hour train ride from capital Seoul, was questioned when the circuit was proposed, the facility turned out to be remarkably impressive and the teams liked it. The downside was access and a lack of quality hotels to accommodate the cast of thousands from the teams, let alone the fans as well.

More recently, Formula E visited Korea and ran on a street circuit in Seoul and Korean racing fans know that the second home for their Grand Prix, should South Korea get a second World Championship chance, absolutely must be somewhere in or near the capital.

COUNTRY FACTS

Formula One drivers:	0
World champions:	0
Grand Prix circuits:	1
• Korea International Circuit	
Grands Prix hosted:	4

Korea International Circuit

The Korea International Circuit was built on reclaimed land and the idea was that the circuit would be part permanent and part temporary, with the section from Turn 3 to Turn 13 being the permanent part and the rest used only for international races.

A lap of the circuit starts with a blast down to a lefthand hairpin, somewhere into which ambitious drivers had to temper ambition with caution on the opening lap. Indeed, their best chance of overtaking came at the end of what was then F1's longest straight up to Turn 3 where a generous amount of track width gave them plenty of options into the right-hander.

A second straight followed down to a hairpin at Turn 4, with a few tight twists to follow before the drivers could accelerate hard and hang on through a series of sweeping turns all the way to the 100-degree right at Turn 10. Another run of five corners took them to the lap's signature finish which was a broad, near semi-circular right-hander that really put a load onto the drivers' necks.

Sadly, after hosting just four Grands Prix from 2010 to 2013, South Korea lost its place on the calendar and the circuit has been little used since then.

Left: Sebastian Vettel, shown here in 2013, won three of Korea's four Grands Prix.

TRACK FACTS

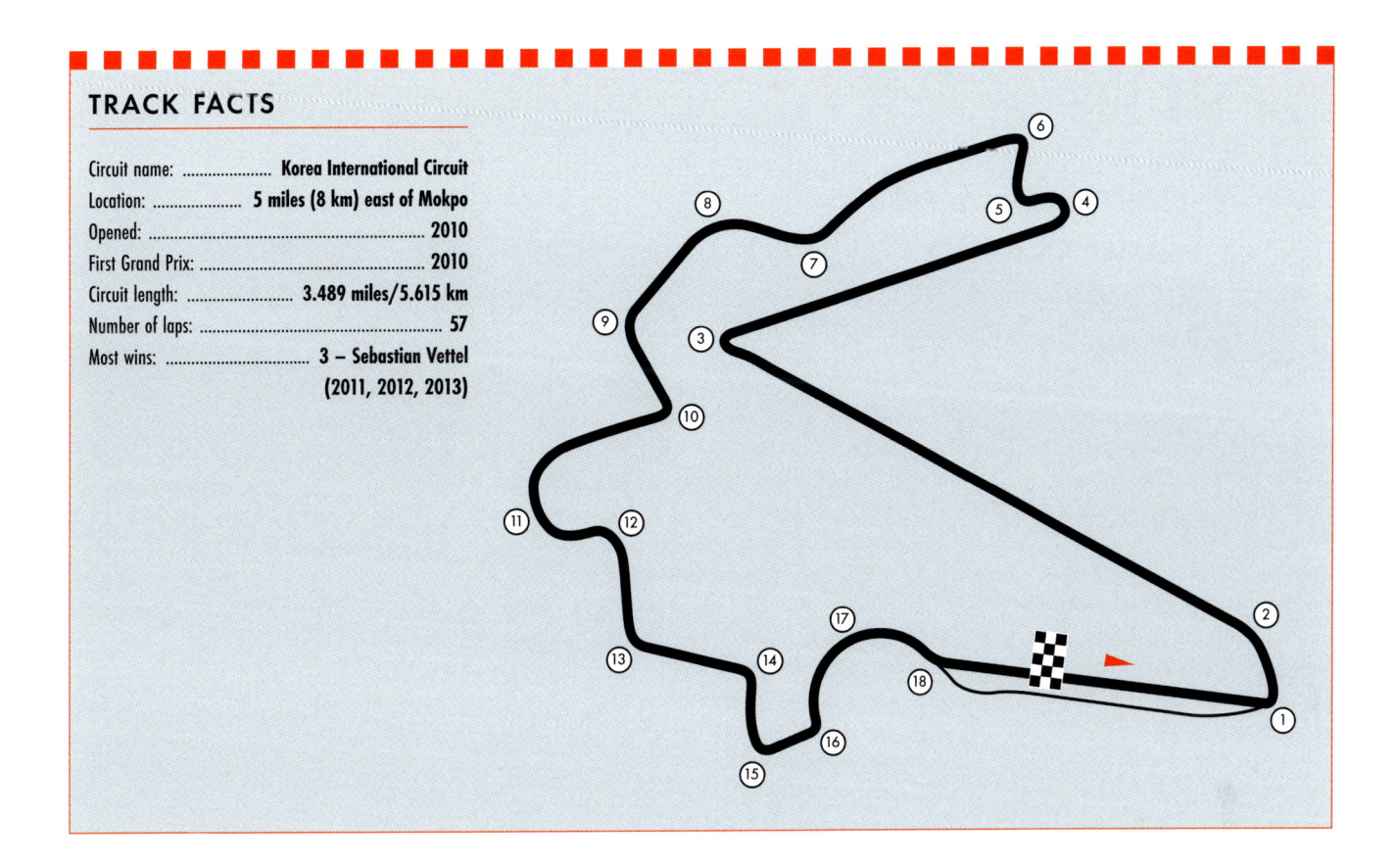

Circuit name:	Korea International Circuit
Location:	5 miles (8 km) east of Mokpo
Opened:	2010
First Grand Prix:	2010
Circuit length:	3.489 miles/5.615 km
Number of laps:	57
Most wins:	3 – Sebastian Vettel (2011, 2012, 2013)

THAILAND

With Alexander Albon racing with a Thai competition licence, the country has its first F1 driver for fully seven decades.

Prince Birabongse Bhanudej, known in racing circles as 'B Bira' was an exotic face on the grids of post-war Grands Prix, initially in an ERA car that was a twenty-first birthday present from cousin and guardian Prince Chula. As the level of competition increased with the start of the World Championship in 1950, Bira raced on with less success until the end of 1954, peaking with two fourth-place finishes. His name lives on as the Bira Circuit near Pattaya opened as Thailand's first road course in 1985. Thailand's only other permanent racing facility, the Chang International Circuit at Buriram, opened in 2014 and it has proved to be a popular venue for GTs and MotoGP.

Alexander Albon, with a British father and a Thai mother, is now Thai fans' great hope, and he has impressed since stepping up to F1 in 2019. He had been a star in F2 against title rivals George Russell and Lando Norris and earned his promotion with Scuderia Toro Rosso. Better still, he was then moved up to Red Bull Racing later in the year before being dropped again after 2020 yielded just two third places. It has been his form with struggling Williams since then that has impressed more, proving that he could be a winner in a competitive car.

COUNTRY FACTS

Formula One drivers:	2
World champions:	0
Grand Prix circuits:	0
Grands Prix hosted:	0

UNITED ARAB EMIRATES

Dubai led the way in attracting top sports to the region, but it was senior emirates partner Abu Dhabi that brought in F1.

Having observed how Dubai used the hosting of sporting events to promote itself and give itself a global brand, Abu Dhabi responded once it had considered how F1 would give it an even more global jewel in its crown.

Although Dubai had hosted a race for international stars on a temporary street circuit in the early 1980s, there was no motor-sport heritage to build on in Abu Dhabi as the island emirate was too small to have hosted the rally raids popular in the region, but Abu Dhabi's ruling family reckoned that there were enough local people who liked fast cars and F1. So, showing its determination to build a top sports resort, the 2,550-hectare Yas Island to the east of Abu Dhabi's main island was provided as the setting for the F1 circuit in a facility that would also include the Ferrari World theme park, several golf courses and, of course, the marina. That, it was decided, was how to do things properly. Work started in 2008 and the Yas Marina Circuit made its bow in 2009, with the standard of its facilities blowing the F1 teams away. This was a money-no-object project in every way and the level of finish was first class.

The second Abu Dhabi GP proved to be the most memorable to date as it was a four-way title decider between Ferrari's Fernando Alonso, Red Bull Racing's Sebastian Vettel and Mark Webber and McLaren's Lewis Hamilton, with pole helping title outsider Vettel to both victory and the title.

Yas Marina Circuit

Hermann Tilke's ideas seem to be good ones when he designed the Yas Marina Circuit, with two lengthy straights leading into trademark combinations of tight

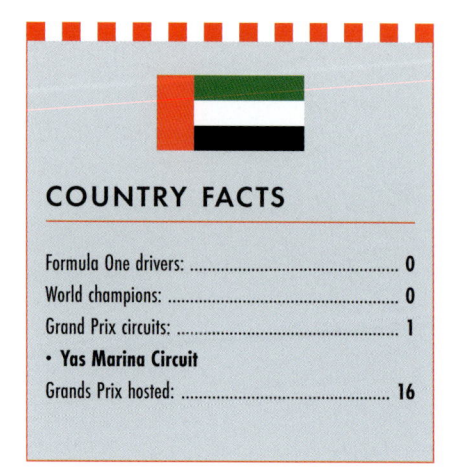

COUNTRY FACTS

Formula One drivers:	0
World champions:	0
Grand Prix circuits:	1
• Yas Marina Circuit	
Grands Prix hosted:	16

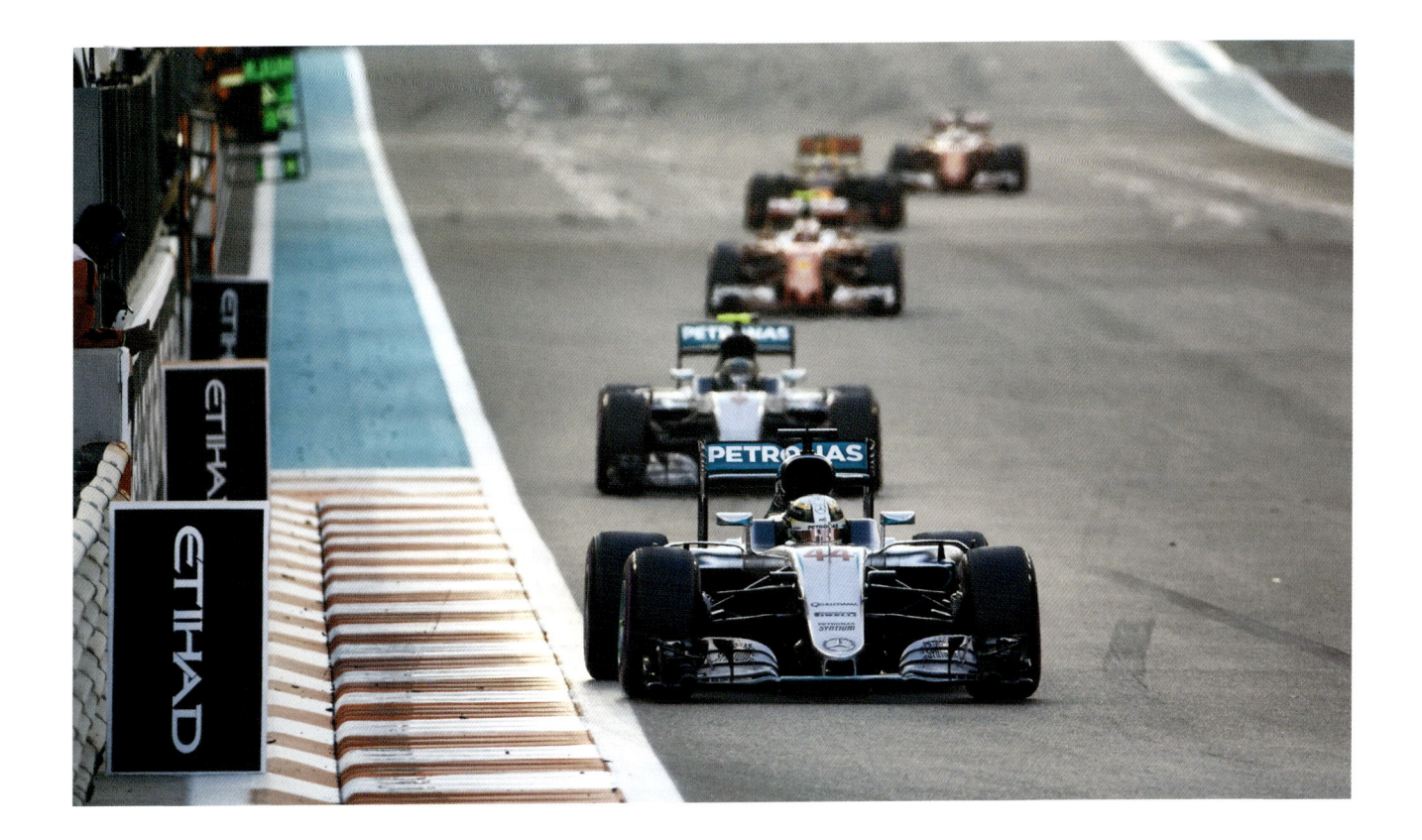

corners. Yet, the theory that this format ought to produce plenty of overtaking simply didn't work and eventually had to be changed.

The lap begins with an open left-hander that feeds into three sweeping turns. Initially, this brought the drivers to a left-right chicane, but this has been replaced with a direct run to the hairpin. The reason for the change is that cars tend to be closer together without the chicane and so run more as a pack down the straight that follows, giving them more of a chance of making an overtaking move at the end of the long straight that runs down to Turn 6.

The format of the following section of the circuit is similar, and this too was modified recently with the chicane at the end of the second straight removed. Although it's certainly not Monaco, the next section of the lap is around the marina, with the middle of this sector made spectacular by running under a linking bridge between two parts of the Yas Victory Hotel that is illuminated for this day-to-night race. The lap then completes its course with a high-speed right-hander and then a tighter one onto the start-finish straight.

Above: Lewis Hamilton battles with teammate and title rival Nico Rosberg in 2016.

Opposite: Max Verstappen and Sergio Pérez lead the field on the first lap in 2022.

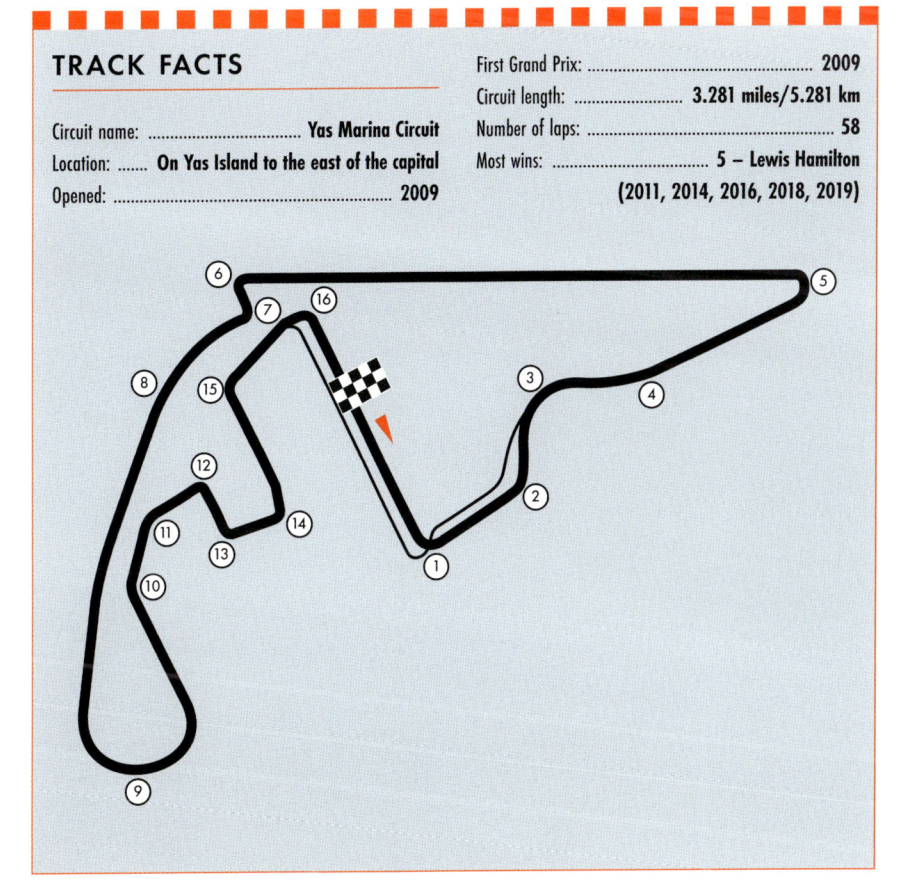

TRACK FACTS

Circuit name: .... **Yas Marina Circuit**
Location: .... **On Yas Island to the east of the capital**
Opened: **2009**
First Grand Prix: **2009**
Circuit length: .... **3.281 miles/5.281 km**
Number of laps: **58**
Most wins: .... **5 – Lewis Hamilton**
(2011, 2014, 2016, 2018, 2019)

UNITED ARAB EMIRATES | 227

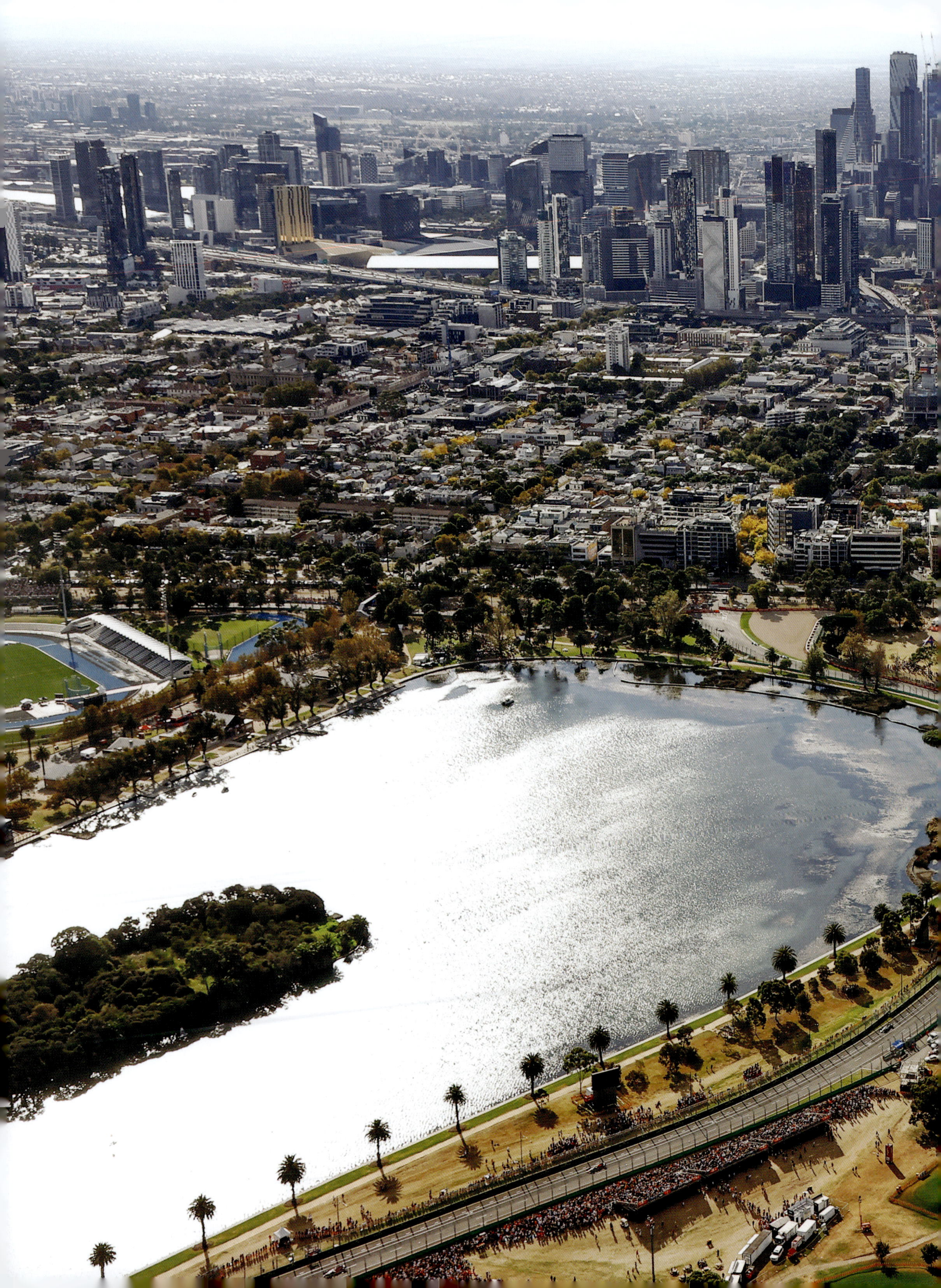

OCEANIA

Being so far from racing's European heartland, it took decades before the World Championship visited the Antipodes. F1 teams and drivers had raced there in the European winters of the 1960s in a championship spread between Australia and New Zealand known as the Tasman Series. Yet even though Australia produced three-time world champion Jack Brabham, who starred in the late 1950s and through the 1960s, and New Zealand produced his marque-founding Cooper teammate Bruce McLaren, it took until 1985 before Australia was able to host its first World Championship round. New Zealand is still waiting.

Adelaide stole a march on Sydney then Melbourne, but by 1996 Melbourne had taken over the Grand Prix. Australia also possesses a fabulous circuit at Bathurst and an impressive new facility called The Bend, but they are better suited to GT and touring-car racing, with national series hampered by the huge distances that competitors need to travel.

New Zealand has had an amazing decade in producing driving talent, with Earl Bamber and Brendon Hartley winning the Le Mans 24 Hours, Mitch Evans and Nick Cassidy being Formula E front runners in recent years and Liam Lawson one of the sport's new stars. Hampton Downs and Taupo are its newest circuits, marking a changing of the guard as long-standing favourite Pukekohe has closed. A series now called Formula Regional Oceania is held across New Zealand's five circuits and it's a championship that current F1 racers Lando Norris and Lance Stroll, plus new face Lawson, all contested in their early racing days.

AUSTRALIA

Australia held a Grand Prix from 1928 until 1984 before it attained World Championship status for its races in Adelaide then Melbourne.

Australia might have felt far removed from racing's two key centres in Europe and North America in the pre-war and post-war years, but it has always had a strong racing scene of its own, albeit the huge distances that need to be covered to contest a national championship have always been prohibitive.

The early days of its Grand Prix were focused on the wonderful clifftop Phillip Island circuit south of Melbourne, but from 1937 the race went walkabout around the country, visiting a host of circuits, but including current GT and touring-car mecca Bathurst, Tasmania's fast and frightening Longford, the joint horse and car racing venues at Sandown Park near Melbourne and Warwick Farm near Sydney. Eventually, after a spell in the 1970s of being run for F5000 cars, the Australian GP turned to Formula Pacific (like Formula Atlantic) and hosted four races in succession at Calder.

Then, finally, in 1985, its big race was given World Championship status and F1 came to town. Its first stop was Adelaide, but sporting capital Melbourne's muscle told and it took over the Grand Prix from 1996. Sydney has long wanted to get some F1 action, but all plans to date have failed.

Whatever the state of F1, a huge number of Australian fans still consider the Bathurst 1000 as their annual treat. The strict divide of Ford versus Holden with their Australian-built Falcon and Commodore V8s are gone, but the passion remains, although the annual Bathurst 12 Hours for GT3 cars attracts considerably more international involvement.

Opposite: Mark Webber won nine Grands Prix for Red Bull Racing but never the title.

Below: This aerial shot shows the pit buildings, Albert Park's lake and parched golf course and the Melbourne suburbs stretching away.

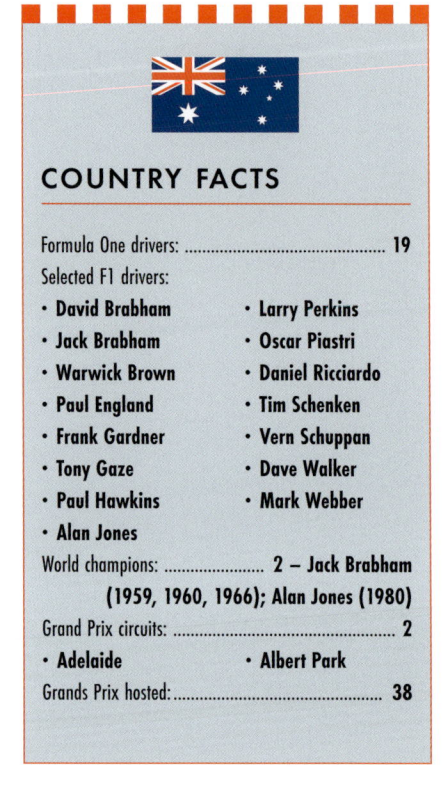

COUNTRY FACTS

Formula One drivers: 19
Selected F1 drivers:

- David Brabham
- Jack Brabham
- Warwick Brown
- Paul England
- Frank Gardner
- Tony Gaze
- Paul Hawkins
- Alan Jones

- Larry Perkins
- Oscar Piastri
- Daniel Ricciardo
- Tim Schenken
- Vern Schuppan
- Dave Walker
- Mark Webber

World champions: .... 2 – Jack Brabham (1959, 1960, 1966); Alan Jones (1980)
Grand Prix circuits: 2
- Adelaide
- Albert Park

Grands Prix hosted: 38

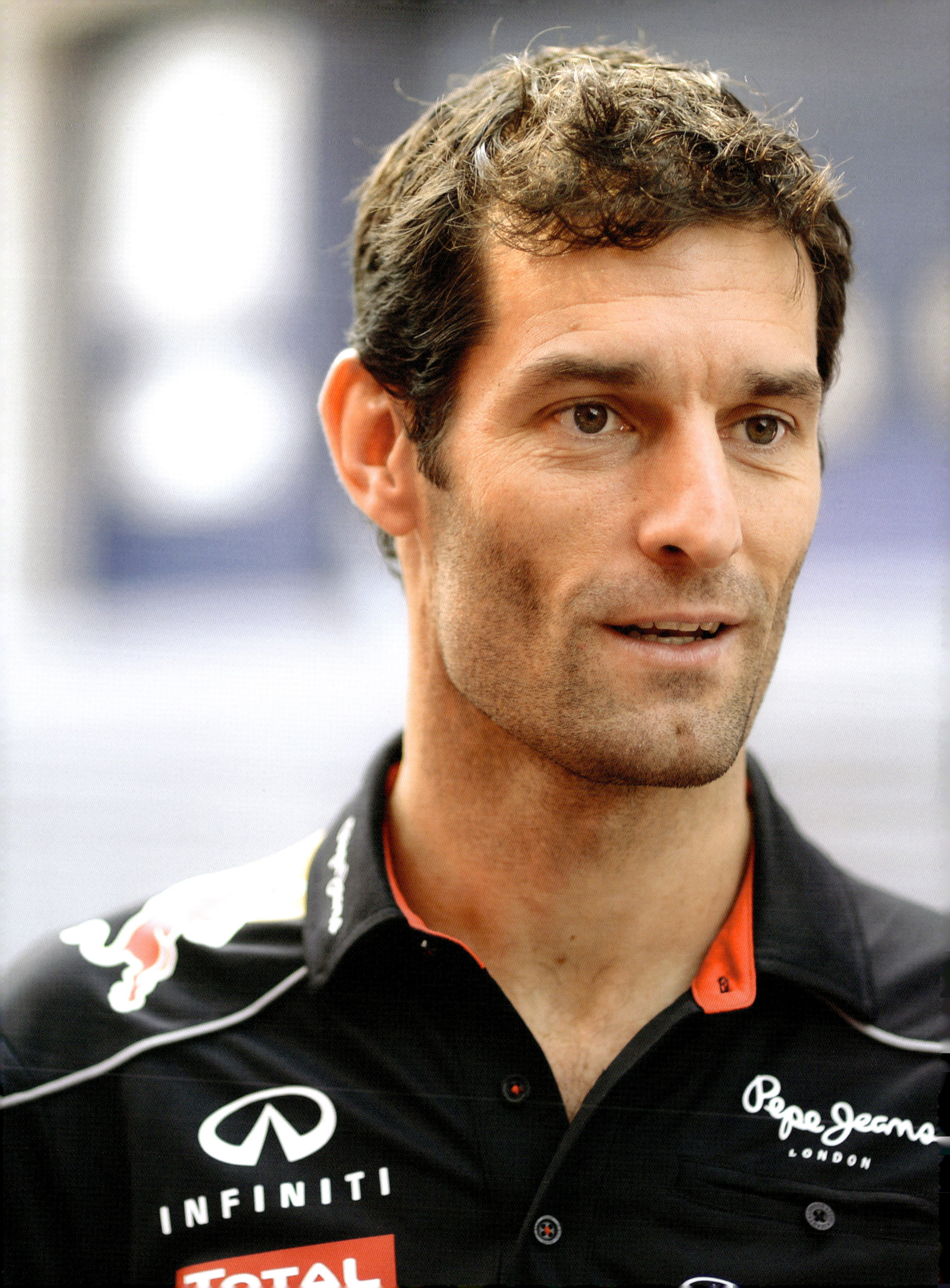
INFINITI
Pepe Jeans
LONDON

DRIVERS

World beaters in cricket, Australians took a while to burst onto the world racing scene, but Jack Brabham led the way and Alan Jones followed.

Tim Schenken

When Tim based himself in Britain in the early stages of his single-seater career, he claimed a staggering forty-two Formula Ford wins in 1968. Strong form in F3 and then F2 encouraged Frank Williams to give him his F1 break in a de Tomaso after Piers Courage's death in the Dutch GP. Ron Tauranac signed him to race for Brabham in 1971 and Tim came third in the Austrian GP. However, a move to Surtees was not a success. He started with fifth in Argentina, but it went downhill from there. Fortunately, his year was saved when he won the Nürburgring 1,000kms for Ferrari.

Mark Webber

Mark impressed at the 1995 Formula Ford Festival to land a works drive for 1996 and took second in the British championship. With promotional help from rugby great David Campese, Mark stepped up to F3, but his career took an unexpected turn as Mercedes signed him for its GT programme. After two years in F3000, Paul Stoddart gave him his F1 break with Minardi. Two years with Jaguar followed, then two at Williams. Red Bull Racing was on the up and Mark took his first F1 win at his 147th attempt at the 2009 German GP at the Nürburgring and he would add eight more.

Daniel Ricciardo

Living in Perth meant Daniel had to travel huge distances to race, so heading to Europe in 2007 was easy, Daniel stepped up from Formula Renault to win the British F3 title in 2009. He was second in Formula Renault 3.5 in 2010 then, midway through 2011, the HRT Team gave Daniel his F1 break. Red Bull placed him at Scuderia Toro Rosso in 2012 and promoted him to Red Bull Racing in 2014, with Daniel taking the first of his eight wins in Montreal. He moved to Renault in 2019, then McLaren in 2021, winning at Monza, but losing his mojo, before returning with AlphaTauri.

Alan Jones

Alan's father won the Australian GP in 1960 and he followed in his wheeltracks as soon as he could. By 1973, he was a front runner in F3, but the DART Team folded. Alan tried Formula Atlantic in 1974 and stepped up to F1 in 1975 in Harry Stiller's Hesketh, but the team folded. Alan got his break with Surtees in 1976. In 1977, he took a surprise win for Shadow, before a move to Williams took him to another level. After three wins in 1979, he stormed to the 1980 title. Alan's F1 career ended with an uncompetitive drive with Team Haas in 1986.

Jack Brabham

This no-nonsense Australian has a record that will surely never be equalled: he won the F1 World Championship in a car bearing his own name. After winning the 1955 Australian GP, he travelled to Europe and found glory when he won the F1 drivers' title with Cooper in 1959 and 1960. Jack then elected to build his own cars in 1962, but it was teammate Dan Gurney who took Brabham's first win in 1964. A change of rules doubled F1 engine size to 3,000cc in 1966 and Jack hit the jackpot with Repco engines as he won four rounds to take his third title. In 1967, teammate Denny Hulme became champion to help give Brabham its second constructors' title. After a competitive 1970 season, Jack sold the team to designer Ron Tauranac in 1971, who then sold it to Bernie Ecclestone, who guided Nelson Piquet to drivers' titles in 1981 and 1983.

CIRCUITS

The downtown Adelaide street circuit led the way, but Melbourne's Albert Park circuit is the one that has held sway since 1996.

Albert Park

When Melbourne took over the running of the Australian GP from Adelaide in 1996, its circuit could not have been more different. Whereas Adelaide's street circuit had a serrated outline as it ran around city blocks before opening out onto some straights across the Victoria Park Racecourse, Melbourne's new venue had more flow to it and an entirely parkland setting.

Albert Park is an urban park just a mile and a half from downtown Melbourne, centred on a sailing lake surrounded by a golf course and assorted sporting facilities. It had its first taste of racing in the 1950s when it twice hosted the then non-championship Australian GP, the second of which was won by Stirling Moss in 1956.

Apart from the modernisation of the facilities for the arrival of the World Championship in 1996 with the inclusion of proper kerbs and temporary pit buildings, the main change from the original circuit was the direction of flow, with the F1 track running in a clockwise direction.

The lap starts with a right-left combination feeding onto a short straight into a tight right. An open left follows past a sports stadium before the track runs under an avenue of trees. There is a definite change of pace after Turn 6, as the lap starts its middle sector. This is now a series of increasingly fast sweepers between the golf course and the lake, all the faster since a tightish right, the Clark Chicane, was removed. Cars can now hit 195 mph (313.8 kph) before having to brake heavily for Turn 13. This marks the final sector of the lap, and it mirrors the first sector, with a run under the trees and a series of tight turns in front of the grandstands leading the cars back to the start-finish straight.

There was some initial protest about the race being held in the park, but this has ebbed away and the city supports its race like few others, with the hospitality venues packed for all three days of the meeting and few gaps in the activity as the Australian GP invariably has more support races than any other Grand Prix. In so many ways, this is a model Grand Prix, even down to the way that most people arrive and leave on public transport.

The fact that the fans are enthusiastic and knowledgeable really adds to the atmosphere.

Opposite: Lake and path are separated from the track only by barrier and debris fencing.

Following pages: The 1991 Australian GP at Adelaide was one of the wettest of all time, with Ayrton Senna splashing clear for McLaren.

TRACK FACTS

Circuit name:	Albert Park
Location:	1.5 miles (2.4 km) south of central Melbourne
Opened:	1953
First Grand Prix:	1996
Circuit length:	3.280 miles/5.278 km
Number of laps:	58
Most wins:	4 – Michael Schumacher (2000, 2001, 2002, 2004)

234 | AUSTRALIA

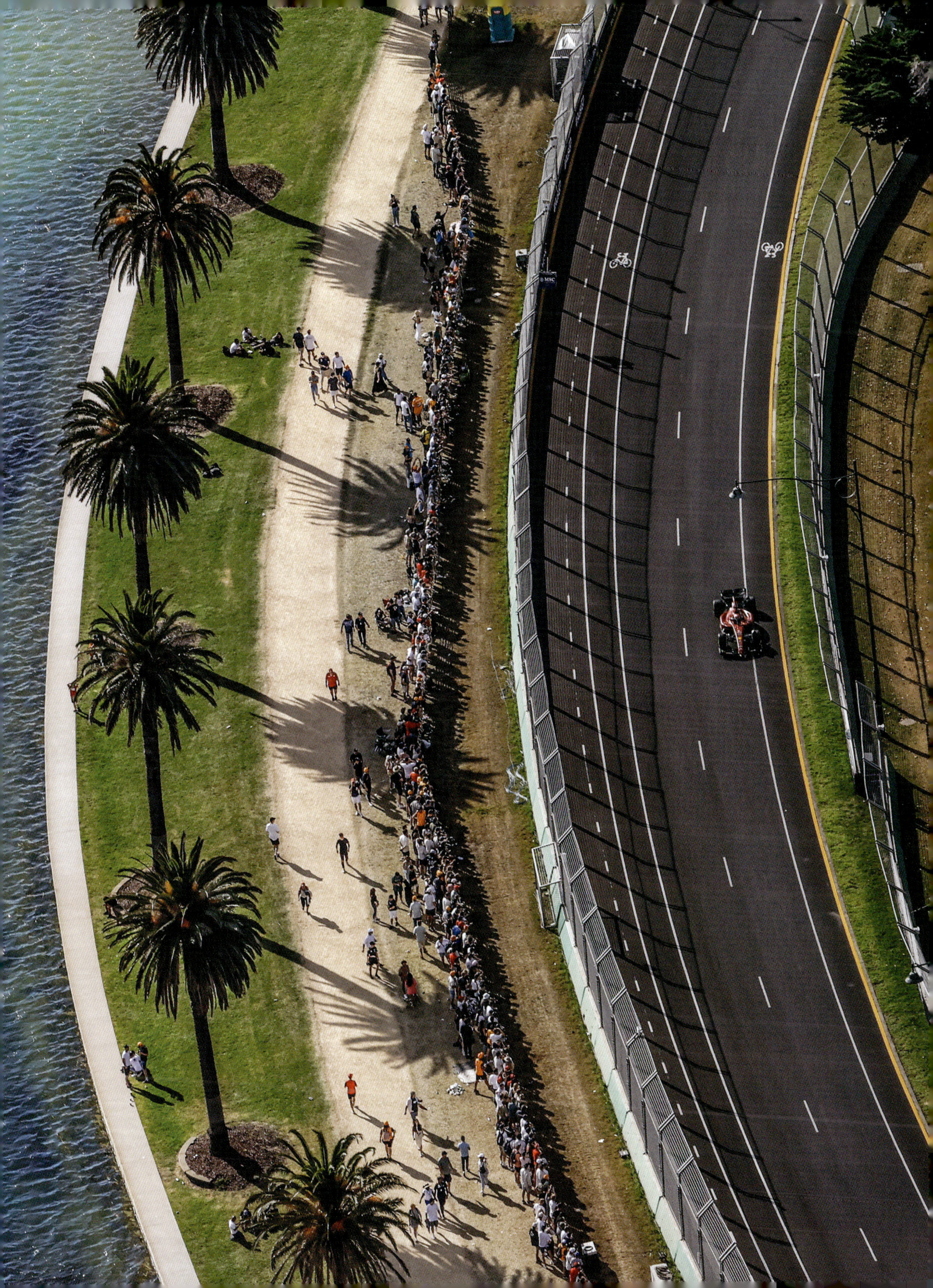

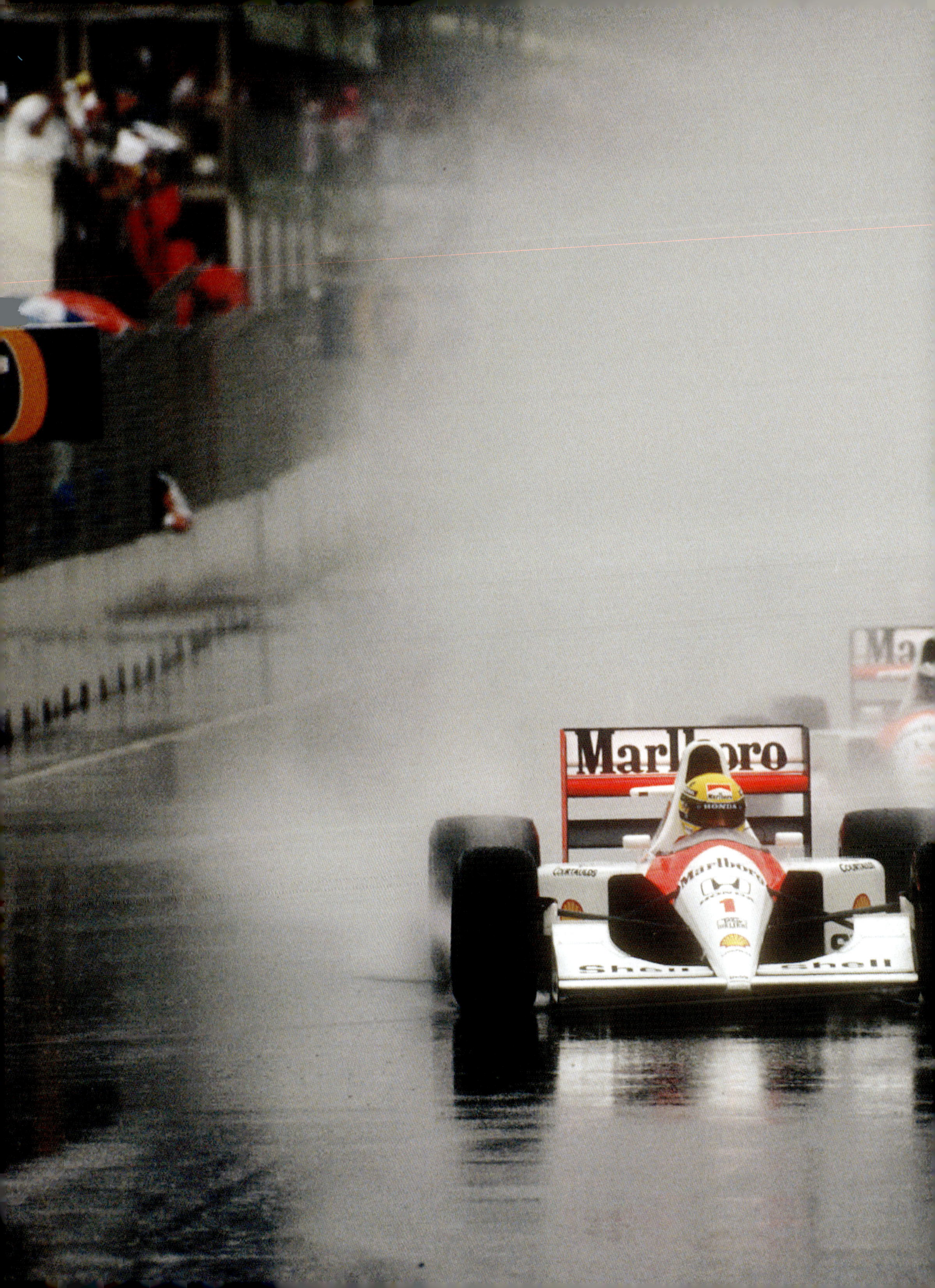
Marlboro
Marlboro
HONDA
1
Shell
Shell

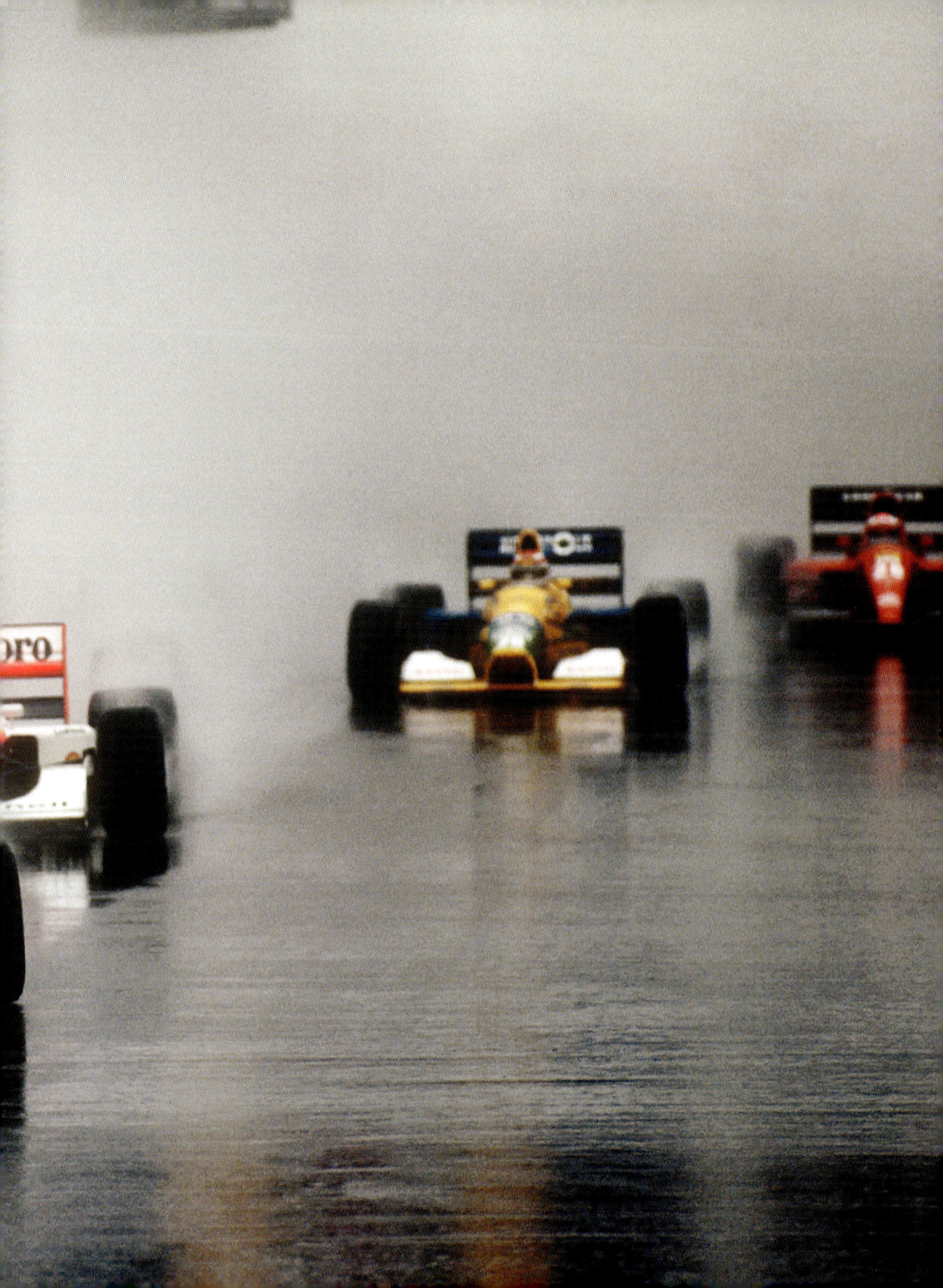

MOMENTS

Sometimes the opening race of the season, sometimes the last, Australian GPs have seldom been short on action and incident.

Charles Leclerc wins on F1's return

The World Championship circus arrived in Melbourne in 2020 and practice got underway, but the meeting was scratched as COVID surfaced and everyone was sent home. So, it was with extra excitement that the fans greeted the teams when they next turned up in 2022 and Ferrari's Charles Leclerc seized the moment by dominating proceedings. He led away from pole and his lead increased when Max Verstappen retired for the second time in three races. Red Bull Racing did still manage to claim the points for second as Sergio Pérez dropped behind the Mercedes duo but fought back past them, with George Russell taking third when Lewis Hamilton was caught out by the timing of a safety car.

Ayrton Senna walks on water

Every now and again, extreme weather hits a Grand Prix and the 1991 Australian GP was one such occasion. The major problem was that the Adelaide street circuit lacked the drainage of purpose-built circuits, with the drivers all but powerless to prevent their cars from aquaplaning. Ayrton Senna started from pole ahead of McLaren teammate Gerhard Berger, but it was Nigel Mansell who gave chase until he spun his Williams and brought out the red flag after fourteen of the eighty-one laps. After a long wait, with no improvement, it was decided that enough was enough. As only a fraction of the planned distance had been run, half points were awarded for the first time since 1984.

Coulthard hands win to Häkkinen

McLaren arrived for the 1998 season opener in impressive form as F1 adopted grooved tyres and a narrower car width, with Mika Häkkinen taking pole ahead of David Coulthard. Michael Schumacher's Ferrari was the best of the rest, fully 0.7 seconds slower. So, it came as no surprise that the MP4/13s raced clear. Midway through the race, though, Häkkinen called at the pits when not expected after misunderstanding a radio message. He was sent straight back out. Then, with two laps to go, Coulthard slowed to let him through to win, as McLaren had made its drivers agree that, in order not to squander their performance advantage, whichever driver led into the first corner should win, so the Scot simply honoured that.

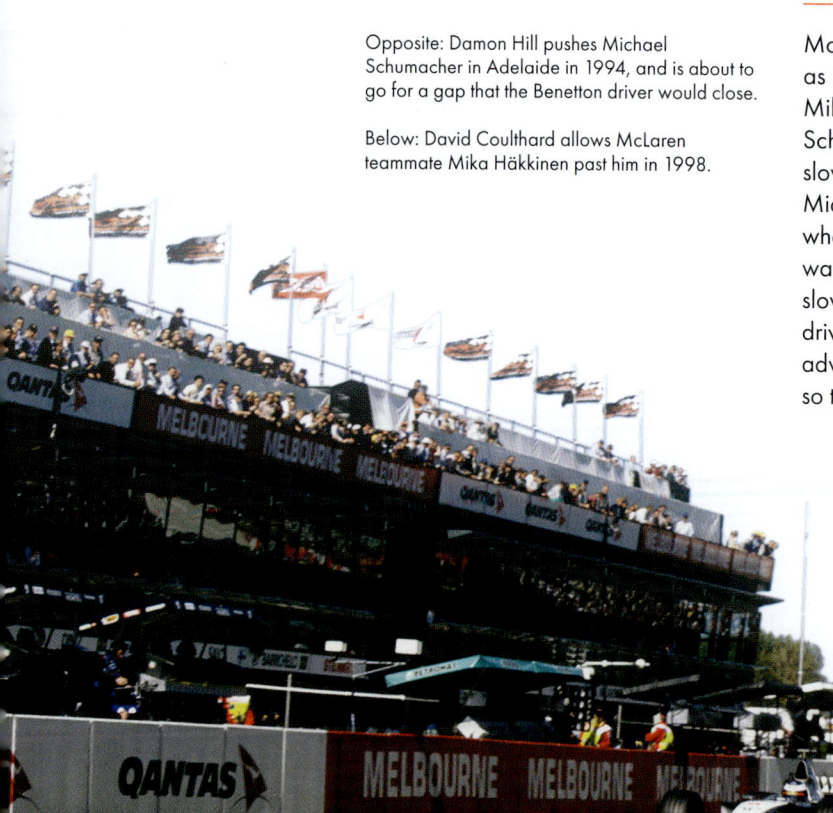

Opposite: Damon Hill pushes Michael Schumacher in Adelaide in 1994, and is about to go for a gap that the Benetton driver would close.

Below: David Coulthard allows McLaren teammate Mika Häkkinen past him in 1998.

Michael Schumacher drives into Damon Hill

This shoot-out in Adelaide in 1994 was shaping up to be an epic scrap as Michael Schumacher and Damon Hill really went at it. Schumacher led, but pressure from Hill's Williams was mounting as they neared half distance. Having started the day with a one-point lead, the drivers knew that whichever of them won would become champion. Then it happened: Schumacher skimmed a wall causing damage to his Benetton's suspension. Having not seen the impact, Hill dived up the inside into the next corner, only to be chopped by a desperate Schumacher. Schumacher was out on the spot and Hill's left front wishbone was wrecked. The title went to Schumacher, but the race win to Nigel Mansell in the second Williams.

NEW ZEALAND

New Zealand is a country whose sportspeople punch above their weight, and it is one of the select few that can claim a world champion.

Small in number but big of heart is a good way to describe New Zealand's sports stars. Rugby is by far their biggest sporting export, but motor racing can claim to be next, as it has a world champion and a Grand Prix winner who went on to create F1's second most successful team. These are, respectively, Denny Hulme and Bruce McLaren.

Being located as far as possible from the European centre of motor racing meant that New Zealand has always been out on a limb and its drivers had to take the make-do-and-mend approach to keep their machinery in trim.

Like neighbouring Australia, it held its own non-championship Grand Prix for years, in this case from 1950, chiefly at the Ardmore airfield circuit and then purpose-built Pukekohe, but what attracted most attention in the 1960s was the Tasman Cup, which caused the European F1 drivers to leave the northern hemisphere behind them to travel down and compete in a series of races on either side of the Tasman Sea. McLaren was the first champion in 1964, Jim Clark won it three times and it continued until 1975. As well as swinging the spotlight onto New Zealand, it also led to new cars being sold to local enthusiasts, improving the bloodline.

Chris Amon and Howden Ganley followed McLaren and Hulme to F1, with Brendan Hartley and Liam Lawson doing the same decades later.

While Pukekohe closed recently, there are modern venues at Highlands Motorsport Park, Hampton Downs and Taupo that host rounds of the Formula Regional Oceania for young talent.

Denny Hulme

Denny travelled to Europe to try his hand at Formula Junior and F2 in what were dangerous days, with the other winner of the Driver to Europe scholarship, George Lawton, being killed. Working as a mechanic at Brabham, he impressed his boss with his form in F2 and so joined Brabham in F1 in 1965. After a strong season in 1966, when Brabham found a performance advantage, Denny won the 1967 title by taking his first two wins. After moving on to McLaren, Denny won twice in 1968 and was a consistent challenger for the next six years, adding six more wins.

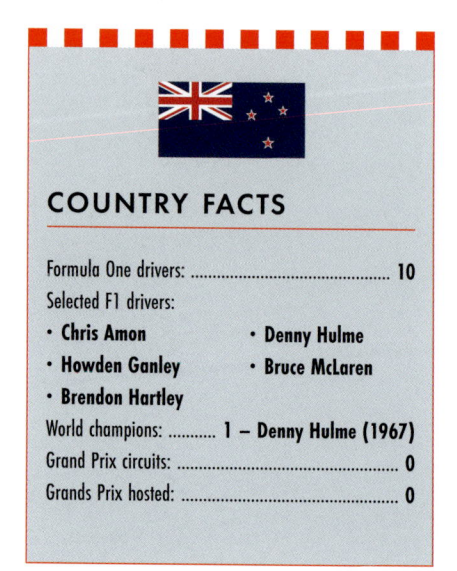

COUNTRY FACTS

Formula One drivers:	10
Selected F1 drivers:	
• Chris Amon	• Denny Hulme
• Howden Ganley	• Bruce McLaren
• Brendon Hartley	
World champions:	1 – Denny Hulme (1967)
Grand Prix circuits:	0
Grands Prix hosted:	0

Right: New Zealand's champion, Denny Hulme, heads to victory in the 1967 German GP.

Bruce McLaren

Bruce began his career doing beach races, but soon headed to Europe and made an instant impact in F2. F1 with Cooper followed in 1959 and he became the then-youngest F1 winner when he rounded out the year with a win at Sebring at the age of twenty-two. A win in Argentina helped him to rank second behind teammate Jack Brabham in 1960, but Cooper lost form and he started his own team in 1966. Success wasn't immediate, but he started winning in 1968 as well as taking lucrative Can Am titles in 1967 and 1969, before he died in a test at Goodwood in 1970.

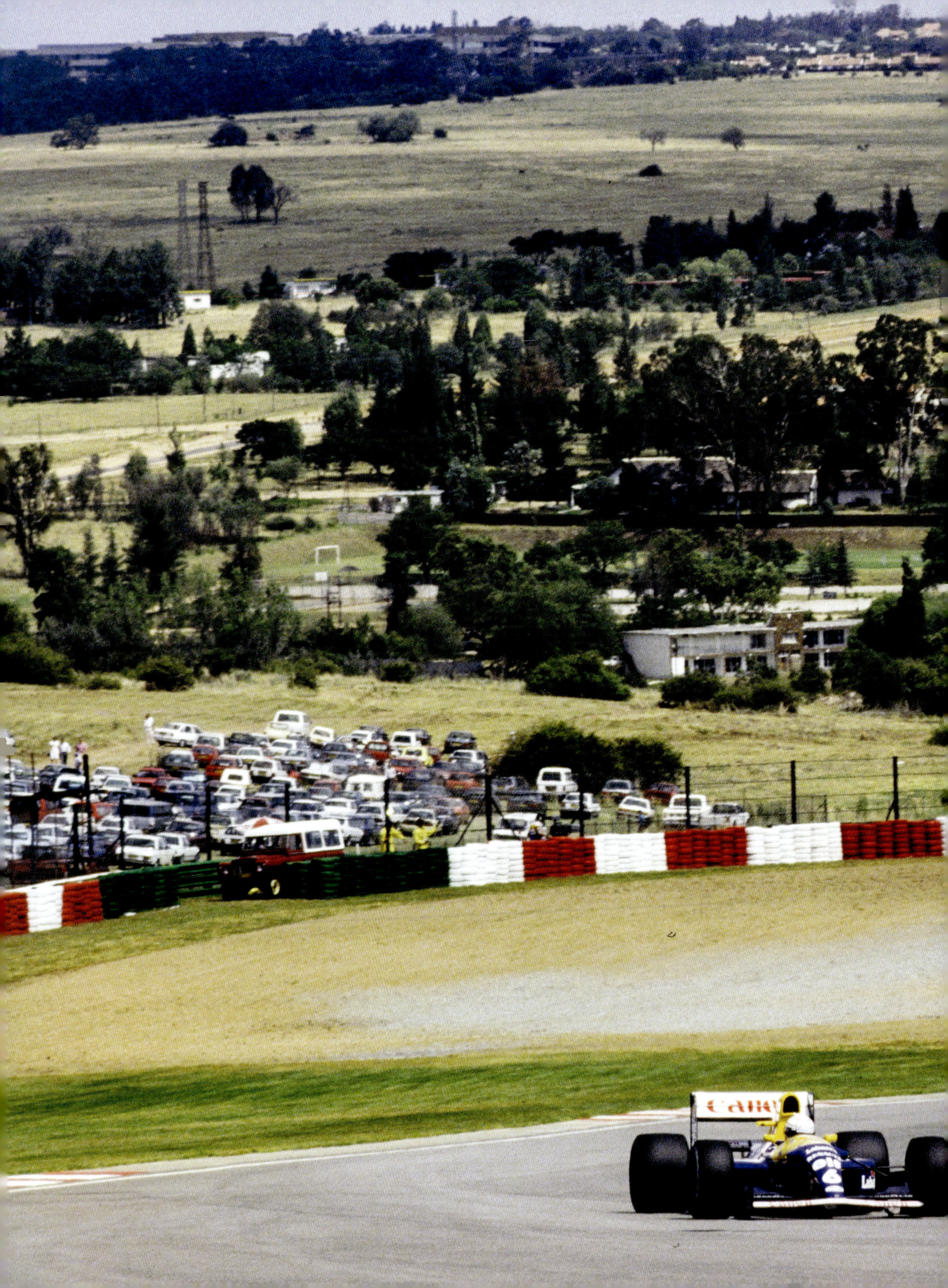

AFRICA

Africa remains a continent that is still short on international motor racing. Grand Prix racing took place at Mellaha in Libya in the 1930s and Morocco hosted a Grand Prix in 1958 and more recently a street circuit on the outskirts of Marrakech has been used by Formula E. However, almost all the racing has been at the southern end of the continent. South Africa has inevitably led the way in this, hosting a Grand Prix at two venues, East London and Kyalami, before its apartheid policy made the country unacceptable in the sports world. There is now a desire for South Africa to host F1 again at Kyalami, but a financial agreement needs to be met first.

The South African racing scene gained in strength through the 1960s, and it even ran its own F1 championship, usually with slightly outdated cars, and drivers from Zimbabwe would also compete in that. In time, the national championship was downgraded in the late 1970s as F1 machinery became too expensive for the local teams, but fans had a circuit in every province at which to watch racing, with touring cars becoming predominant from the 1980s.

In the 1960s, other countries in the region also got to see the international stars, with the Springbok sportscar series holding rounds not only in South Africa but also on temporary street circuits or airfield circuits in Angola, Mozambique and Rhodesia (now Zimbabwe), giving European drivers a place to race in the sun through the northern hemisphere winter.

Rwanda is now looking to build a circuit to welcome the World Championship back to the continent.

MOROCCO

Morocco made an appearance in the World Championship in 1958 with a circuit made up of public roads near Casablanca.

There was motor racing in Morocco as early as the 1920s, initially on a street circuit in Casablanca and then at Anfa, a temporary street circuit in the city's western suburbs. This hosted the Casablanca GP in 1931 and 1932, with Marcel Lehoux starring in the first then winning the second. Renamed as the Moroccan GP in 1933, victory went to Louis Chiron in his Alfa Romeo.

Although street races continued after Morocco's days as a French colony, in Agadir and Tangier as well as in Casablanca, the Suez crisis in 1957 led to racing in Europe being threatened and so the Royal Automobile Club of Morocco and King Mohammed V acted with speed to create a road circuit. This was Ain Diab. After holding a non-championship F1 race in 1957, which was won by Jean Behra in a Maserati, it was in a position to hold a World Championship round the following year. However, this was a one-hit wonder and afterwards the final round of the World Championship was moved to Sebring as the USA took over this coveted position for the first time. In 1958, Stirling Moss won for Vanwall.

Then the Moroccan racing scene dwindled, but it has been revived in the past decade by hosting a round of the Formula E on a temporary circuit just outside the walls of Marrakesh.

No Moroccan drivers have climbed the single-seater ladder, but Mehdi Bennani went well in the World Touring Car series, then won the European TCR title in 2020.

COUNTRY FACTS

Formula One drivers:	2
World champions:	0
Grand Prix circuits:	1
• **Ain Diab**	
Grands Prix hosted:	1

Below: Stirling Moss at speed in his Vanwall as he heads to victory in 1958, but it wasn't enough to stop Mike Hawthorn taking the title.

André Guelfi

André was one of two French nationals who raced under a Moroccan licence in the 1950s along with Robert La Caze, but is the more Moroccan of the pair as he was born there. He made a name for himself driving a Delahaye in Agadir's sportscar race in 1953, then partnered Jean Behra in the Casablanca 12 Hours. André finished a class-winning sixth with Jacques Pollet in a Gordini in the Le Mans 24 Hours in 1954, then in 1955 was national champion. He had his first taste of single-seaters at Pescara in 1954 and after an impressive run to second in an F2 race at Montlhery in 1958, André entered a similar Cooper in the 1958 Moroccan GP, ending up fifteenth, ahead of Graham Hill's delayed Lotus, but one place behind La Caze.

Ain Diab

The Ain Diab circuit wasn't all new when it opened in 1957, as a section of its 4.7-mile (7.56-km) lap had been used for a sportscar race in 1953. The lap started on the coast road, turned right away from the sea by the Ain Diab suburb and then right again to get to the lap's highest point at which they turned onto the desert road. This slightly snaking straight was the main road from Casablanca to Azemmour and lasted a good mile and a half before the third right-hander on this roughly rectangular temporary circuit took the course back down to the coast road. The track received praise for being smother than expected.

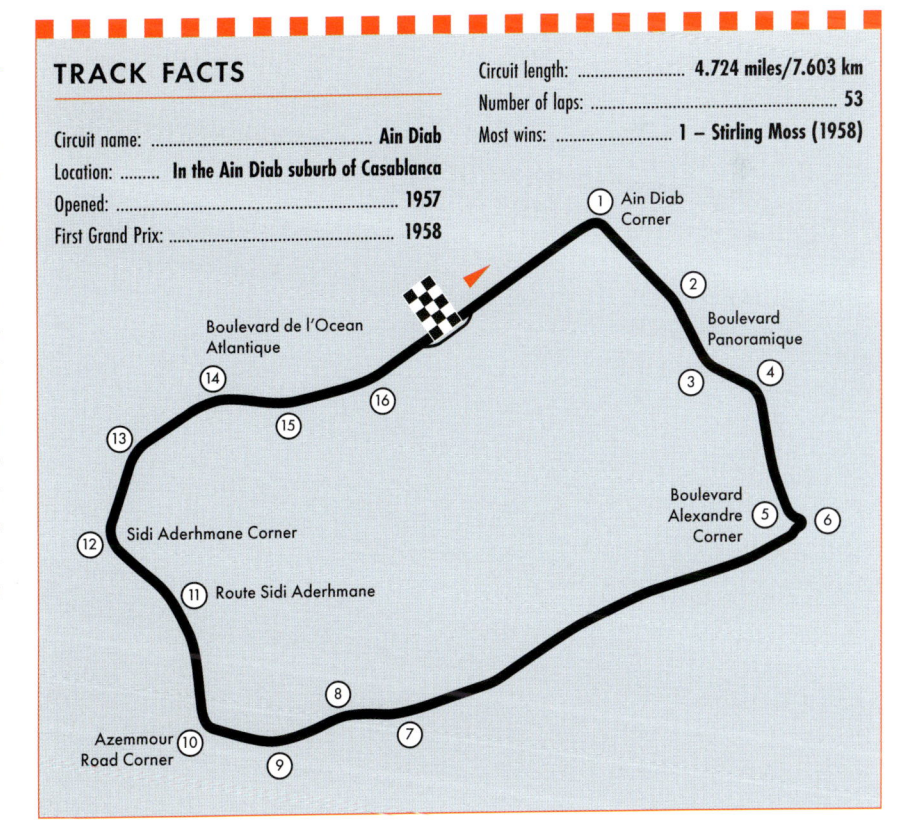

TRACK FACTS

Circuit name:	Ain Diab
Location:	In the Ain Diab suburb of Casablanca
Opened:	1957
First Grand Prix:	1958
Circuit length:	4.724 miles/7.603 km
Number of laps:	53
Most wins:	1 – Stirling Moss (1958)

Corners:
1. Ain Diab Corner
2. —
3. —
4. Boulevard Panoramique
5. Boulevard Alexandre Corner
6. —
7. —
8. —
9. —
10. Azemmour Road Corner
11. Route Sidi Aderhmane
12. Sidi Aderhmane Corner
13. —
14. —
15. —
16. Boulevard de l'Ocean Atlantique

MOROCCO | 245

ZIMBABWE

Motor racing had pretty much petered out by the time the country gained independence, but it very nearly produced an F1 winner.

COUNTRY FACTS

Formula One drivers:	4
World champions:	0
Grand Prix circuits:	0
Grands Prix hosted:	0

Racing in Rhodesia, as the country was called until 1980, was chiefly on airfield circuits in the 1950s, but also on the Marlborough stadium dirt circuit near the capital, plus the Belvedere street circuit.

In the early 1960s, it advanced to holding its annual Grand Prix on the Kumalo airfield circuit. This was at a level way below World Championship Grands Prix on a circuit far short of the required standard, but it was the big race of the national scene.

At the end of the decade, the country gained its first purpose-built circuit just outside its second city, Bulawayo. The Breedon Everard Raceway became best known for its Three Hour sportscar race, a round of the Springbok series that was largely based in South Africa but which also included this race, one in Lourenço Marques in Mozambique and one on a street circuit in Luanda, the capital of Angola.

The list of Zimbabwean F1 drivers is limited to Mike Harris, John Love, (non-qualifier) Clive Puzey and Sam Tingle. However, Love almost pulled off one of F1's all-time shocks when he led the 1967 South African GP until seven laps before the finish, but then had to pit his privately entered Cooper for fuel and ended up second.

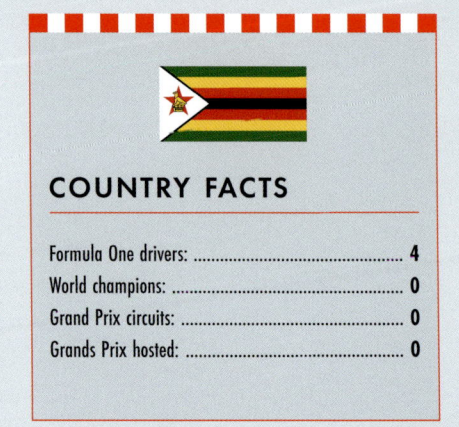

Below: John Love was all smiles on the Kyalami parade in 1968 a year after he almost won.

246 | ZIMBABWE

SOUTH AFRICA

South Africa has long wanted to host a Grand Prix again, but each plan fails, which is a shame as the country has a strong racing history.

The first South African GP was a race held on a 15-mile (24-km) loop of roads outside the city of East London. This was in 1934 and victory went to Whitney Straight in a Maserati. The Prince George circuit was then cut down to 11 miles (17.7 km) for subsequent races. East London created a new circuit in 1959 and it hosted a round of the World Championship for the first time in 1962, when BRM's Graham Hill took on Lotus' Jim Clark in a title battle.

The South African Motor Racing Club wanted to move its race closer to its main centre of population, Johannesburg, and so the Kyalami circuit was built there. This hilly circuit hosted a round of the World Championship each year from 1967 to 1985 except 1981 when F1's internal power struggles rendered it a non-championship event. Pressure was mounting on the teams not to continue going in 1985 because of opposition to apartheid and F1 returned in 1992 and 1993 only after apartheid had ended.

The South African racing scene lives in a degree of isolation due to it being so far from the heart of the racing world. However, the country enjoyed its own F1 championship in the 1960s and 1970s, often using cars that had been retired by the teams contesting the World Championship.

South African fans also enjoyed the Springbok sportscar series that attracted international entries in the early 1970s, but their diet today is squarely GT and touring-car racing.

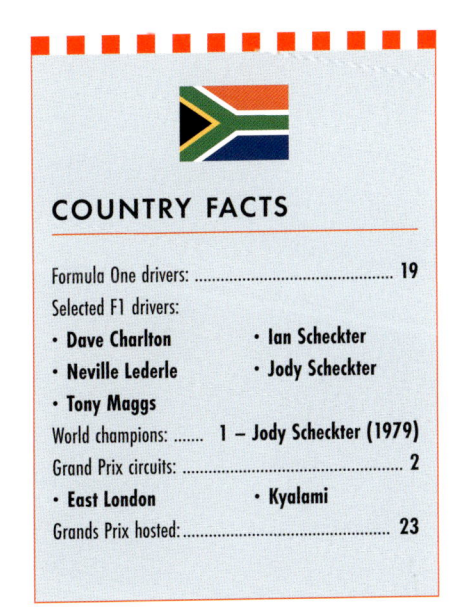

COUNTRY FACTS

Formula One drivers: 19
Selected F1 drivers:
- Dave Charlton
- Ian Scheckter
- Neville Lederle
- Jody Scheckter
- Tony Maggs

World champions: .... 1 – Jody Scheckter (1979)
Grand Prix circuits: 2
- East London
- Kyalami

Grands Prix hosted: 23

Below: Lotus's winner Ronnie Peterson holds off Carlos Reutemann and Alan Jones in 1978.

Jody Scheckter

Jody was a quick but wild driver. After winning a prize to race in England, he vaulted quickly to F3 in 1971, with McLaren signing him for its F2 team for 1972. A win at Crystal Palace was a highlight before he was given his debut at the US GP. McLaren entered Jody in a third car in 1973, and he certainly made an impression, with his mistake at the end of lap one at Silverstone triggering an accident that left nine drivers unable to continue. However, Jody matured and became a Grand Prix winner at Anderstorp in 1974 for Tyrrell. More wins followed before a move to Wolf in 1977 saw him win first time out. It was with Ferrari, though, that he blossomed, landing the 1979 title ahead of teammate Gilles Villeneuve. He had planned to do just one more year and still wishes he hadn't as Ferrari was uncompetitive in 1980.

DRIVERS

Jody Scheckter stands clear of all his compatriots who reached F1 as he was the only one to win a Grand Prix and also a drivers' title.

Dave Charlton

Dave was the gold standard on South Africa's domestic racing scene for more than a decade. He took the battle to John Love through the 1960s, then won six titles on the trot from 1970, first with a Lotus and then with a McLaren, with his best season being in 1972 when he took nine wins. He also entered the South African GP most years through until 1970, before trying the Dutch and British GPs with Lotus in 1971. In 1972, he tried three more, with a self-entered Lotus 72, but was slowed by an ear infection that gave him double-vision.

Ian Scheckter

The older brother of Jody, Ian also moved from Formula Ford in South Africa to try his luck on the British racing scene. This was in 1972, but no doors opened, so he returned home and began a successful spell of competing in the South African F1 series. Team Gunston entered Ian for his home Grand Prix in 1974, a race he entered again in 1975 and 1976, before he landed a full-season ride with March in 1977 that yielded a tenth place among a string of retirements. Ian won the South African drivers' title six times after it changed from F1 to Formula Atlantic machinery.

Neville Lederle

Neville was a driver of obvious talent who never got the breaks he deserved. Instantly a pacesetter on the national scene in his Lotus 18, he traded up to a Lotus 21 and finished sixth in his home Grand Prix, also making his name by winning the South African drivers' championship title. A broken leg suffered when he crashed in practice for the Rand 9 Hours wrecked his 1963 season and it took so long to heal that it affected the start of 1974 too. Neville had a final shot but failed to qualify his old Lotus for the 1965 South African GP.

Tony Maggs

Tony was the first South African to try his hand at F1. He showed his promise in 1959 and 1960 and was signed by Ken Tyrrell for his Formula Junior team for 1961 and ended the year as co-champion with Jo Siffert. Two solid outings in F1 in Louise Bryden-Brown's Lotus earned him a works Cooper drive for 1962 and Tony was fifth first time out, at Zandvoort, then peaked with a second-place finish in the French GP at Rouen. He was second in France again in 1963. Tony's career ended abruptly when he killed a boy standing in a prohibited area during a race at Pietermaritzburg.

CIRCUITS

People associate the South African GP with Kyalami, but it joined the World Championship with a far more spectacular circuit in 1967.

Kyalami

Kyalami was built on a hillside to afford spectators a good view and because it was just off the main road between Johannesburg and Pretoria. With the aim of attracting the World Championship, the circuit hosted a non-championship Grand Prix in 1961 that was won by Jim Clark for Lotus. The circuit was popular for its flow, notably through Jukskei Sweep and its flat-out run from Leeukop Bend to Crowthorne Corner.

Kyalami was reconfigured in 1987 as the top half of the plot was sold to become an industrial estate and the circuit used only the lower section combined with a new loop further down the hill.

The lap starts with a straight into an esse, after which it immediately starts a climb up a slope to where it hits the old circuit at Jukskei, turning left to take Sunset Bend in reverse direction to the original. A climb from here takes the cars to the tight left at Clubhouse Bend and then it feeds into an esses, cuts away from the old circuit and kicks up a steep slope to a hairpin before plunging down through a quick left to a tight right. The lap is completed with a chicane and a 150-degree left.

East London

The circuit was created in a hollow overlooking the Indian Ocean. It is roughly triangular in shape, with an uphill straight to its highest point, the open right called Potters Pass Curve. A kinked run then took the cars down to Cocobana Corner, where the drivers would have had a view of the ocean before turning hard right to run parallel with the cliff edge. A four-corner infield loop slowed the return leg, then took the track back to the cliff edge before a righthand hairpin, Beacon Bend, brought the cars back to the start-finish straight. Gusts of wind were known to blow cars off-line.

Opposite: Jackie Stewart pulls clear in 1973 after rising from sixteenth to the lead in seven laps.

TRACK FACTS

Circuit name:	Kyalami
Location:	15 miles (24 km) north of Johannesburg
Opened:	1961
First Grand Prix:	1967
Circuit length:	2.648 miles/4.262 km
Number of laps:	72
Most wins:	4 – Jim Clark (1961, 1963, 1965, 1968)

250 | SOUTH AFRICA

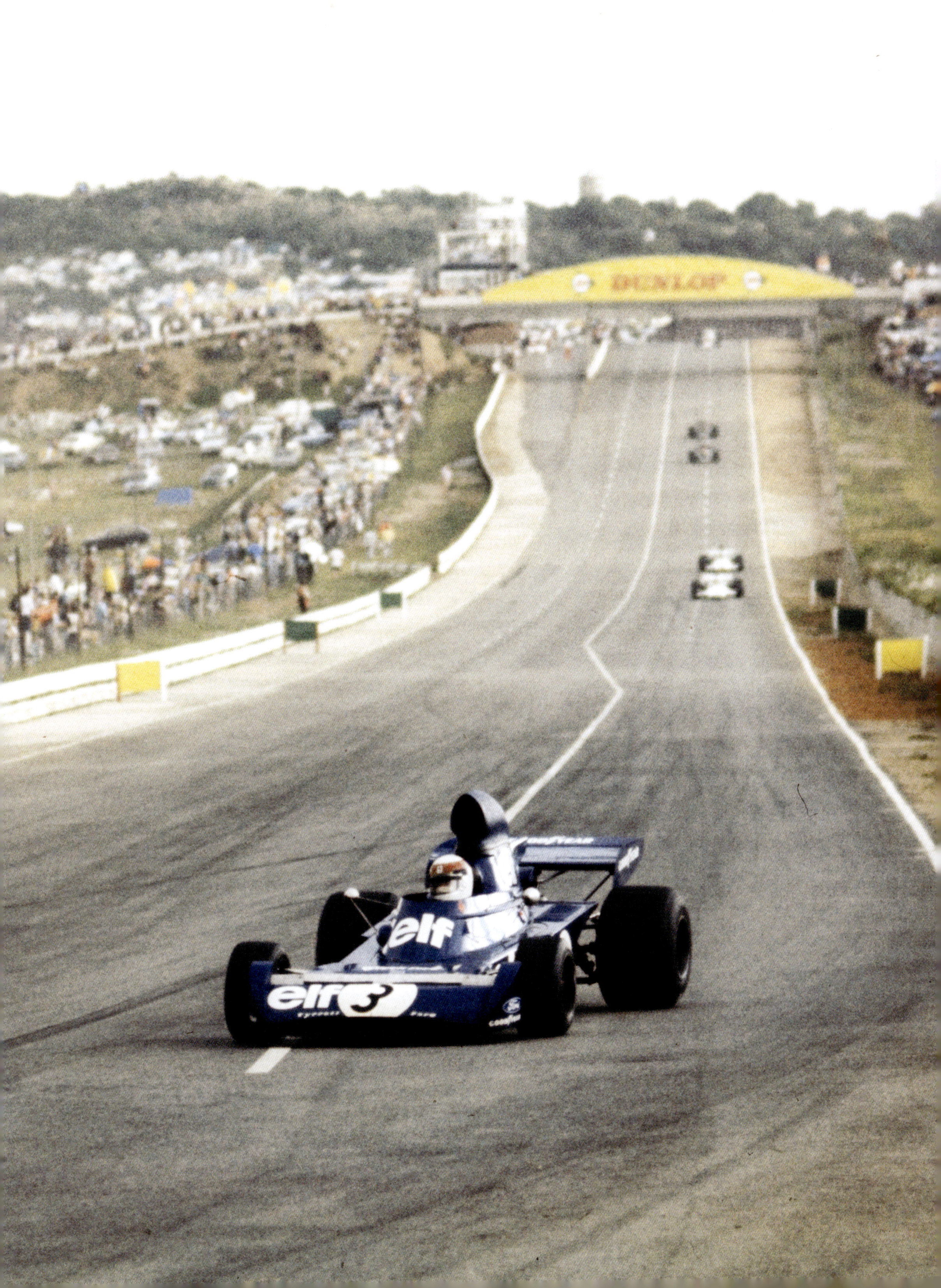
DUNLOP
elf
elf 3

MOMENTS

Sometimes the first race of the World Championship, sometimes the last, the South African GP has never lacked drama.

Winning on his Ferrari debut

Mario Andretti had every reason to like Kyalami when he made his first visit in 1971, as this was his first outing for Ferrari, the team he had revered when growing up in Italy before emigrating to the United States. The Indycar ace qualified fourth and drove cautiously at first before climbing from seventh as he picked off those ahead, including teammate Clay Regazzoni. After moving past John Surtees into second, he set about catching Denny Hulme's McLaren and was within four seconds with four laps to go when the New Zealander's suspension began to come apart. This caused him to run wide and Mario did not need a second invitation and went on to win by twenty seconds from Jackie Stewart.

Opposite: Lotus boss Colin Chapman chats to Jim Clark in the East London pits in 1962, a race that the Scot would control but lose.

Below: Ayrton Senna leads Alain Prost and Michael Schumacher past the pit in 1993.

An unnecessary double disaster

If only the story of the 1977 South African GP was as simple as Niki Lauda advancing from third on the grid to win for Ferrari. Sadly, it is remembered for an unnecessary moment that led to a most unfortunate outcome. Renzo Zorzi's Shadow pulled off with engine failure and, unaccountably, two marshals chose to cross the track to stop the minor blaze. Unfortunately, Zorzi's teammate, Tom Pryce, was fighting for position with March's Hans Stuck and he had no chance of avoiding marshal Jansen van Vuuren and was hit in the helmet by van Vuuren's fire extinguisher and was killed as well. Pryce's car then continued down to the next corner where it took out Jacques Laffite's Ligier.

Prost returns to F1 in style

Alain Prost, Ayrton Senna, and Michael Schumacher had a good scrap in the final Grand Prix held at Kyalami in 1993. This season opener marked Prost's return after a sabbatical and he put his Williams on pole from Senna's McLaren. However, he was beaten away at the start and even fell behind Michael Schumacher's Benetton. It took Prost thirteen laps to get past before he could chase after Senna, hitting the front on the twenty-fourth lap. Senna's MP4/8 was slowed by a suspension problem and so it fell away from Prost and into the sights of Schumacher. The young German challenged Senna, but was overambitious: they collided and the rising star was out as Prost eased to victory.

All good until a puff of smoke

Jim Clark would dominate the 1963 and 1965 South African GPs at East London, but the World Championship's first visit to the clifftop circuit in 1962 had more at stake, as there was a championship battle between Graham Hill for BRM and Jim Clark for Lotus. They had three wins each, but Clark's Lotus 25 had been less reliable, so he trailed by a few points. The Scot blasted into the front and pulled away to build a lead of half a minute. Victory would have given him the title, but it wasn't to be as his engine's oil pressure was falling which left Hill to sweep by to take victory by fifty seconds from Cooper's Bruce McLaren and the title in his P57.

INDEX

A

ABB FIA Formula E World Championship 81
Abu Dhabi Grand Prix 226–7
Ain Diab circuit 245
Aintree circuit 132
Alastaro circuit 35
Albert Park circuit *230, 234, 234*
Albon, Alexander 225
Alboreto, Michelle 29, 69, *70*
Algarve International Circuit 99, 102
Alguersuari, Jaime 111
Alonso, Fernando 29, 110, *115, 118,* 210
Amon, Chris 26
Anderstorp circuit 121
Andretti, Mario 88, *182,* 215, 252
Angelis, Elio de 20
A1 GP Series 206
A1-Ring circuit 16
Ardennes circuit 22
Ards circuit 65
Argentinian Grand Prix 140–9
Arnoux, René 29, 41, *50, 51*
Ascari, Alberto 69
Asian Le Mans Series 205
Aspern circuit 12
Athy circuit 65
Australian Grand Prix 37, 54, 90, 209, 215, 229, 230–9
Austrian Grand Prix 12–21, 41, 88
Autodromo Las Vizcachas circuit 173
Autodromo Ricardo Mejia circuit 174
Avus circuit *52, 52,* 59, 62
Azerbaijan Grand Prix 198–9

B

Bahrain Grand Prix 200–1
Bahrain International Circuit 200
Baku City circuit *198, 198*
Balaton Park circuit 64
Bandini, Lorenzo 12, *177*
Barcelona-Catalunya circuit 112
Barrichello, Rubens 16, *153, 157*
Beaufort, Carel Godin de 90
Belgian Grand Prix 22–33
Beretta, Olivier 82
Berger, Gerhard 15, *16,* 70
Bhanudej, Prince Birabongse ('B Bira') 225
Bottas, Valtteri 35, *202,* 210
Boutsen, Thierry 22, 25
Brabham, Jack 50, 86, 96, 233
Brambilla, Vittorio 20
Brands Hatch circuit 131, 136
Brazilian Grand Prix 150–61
Breedon Everard Raceway circuit 246
Bremgarten circuit 122
British Grand Prix 124–37
Brooks, Tony 52
Buddh International Circuit *204,* 205
Buenos Aires circuit 144
Button, Jenson *172,* 173

C

Caesars Palace circuit 69
Canadian Grand Prix 162–73
Cantoni, Eitel 194, *194*
Capelli, Ivan 42
Caracas circuit 195
Carrera Panamericana 175
Cecotto, Johnny 195, *195*
Cesaris, Andrea de 86
Cevert, François 38, *56*
Chang International Circuit 225

Chapman, Colin 252
Charade circuit 38
Charlton, Dave 249
Chile 173
Chimay circuit 22, 25
Chimeri, Ettore 195
Chinese Grand Prix 202–3
Chiron, Louis 82
Circuit Gilles Villeneuve 166
Circuit of the Americas (COTA) 138–9, 188
Clark, Jim *97, 126, 132,* 252, *253*
Clermont-Ferrand circuit 38, 42
Codasur F2 173
Colapinto, Franco 140
Colombia 174
Copenhagen Grand Prix 34
Coulthard, David *128,* 238
Czechoslovakian Grand Prix 34

D

Danish Grand Prix 34
Depailler, Patrick *187*
Detroit circuit 193
Dijon-Prenois circuit *50,* 51
Donington Park circuit *124,* 136
Donohue, Mark 183
DTM (Deutsche Tourenwagen Masters) 90
Dundrod circuit 65
Dutch Grand Prix 88–97

E

East London circuit *250, 252*
Eaton, George 164
Ecclestone, Bernie 59, 104, 233
Eläintarha circuit 35
Enna-Pergusa circuit 66
Estoril circuit *102, 102*
European Le Mans Series (ELMS) 99, 205
European Touring Car Championship 34

F

Fabi, Teo 16
Fangio, Juan Manuel *45, 50, 50,* 66, 122, 143, 148, *149*
Farina, Giuseppe *45,* 69
Fédération internationale de l'automobile (FIA) 74, 81, 82, 214
Fédération Internationale du Sport Automobile (FISA) 78
Ferihegy circuit 64
Ferrari, Enzo *70*
FIA GT 34
Finnish Grand Prix 35–7
Fisichella, Giancarlo 69
Fittipaldi, Emerson 22, 32, *153,* 160, *161*
Formula 3000 83, 90, 100, 124, 153, 194, 208, 217, 232
Formula Atlantic 36
Formula E 81, 122, 173, 194
Formula Easter (Forma Easter) 64, 104
Formula Ford 65, 69, 90
Formula Junior 98
Formula Nippon 54
Formula Pacific 36
Formula Super Vee 36
Formula Three (F3) 15, 25, 36, 41, 65, 69, 80, 82, 83, 90, 91, 99, 174, 175, 194
Formula Two (F2) 12, 15, 24, 25, 34, 35, 36, 41, 59, 69, 83, 90, 174, 175, 225
French Grand Prix 38–51, 80, 82
  first-ever (1906) 11
Frentzen, Heinz-Harald 46, 52, 62
Frère, Paul 22, 25

G

Gasly, Pierre *78, 190,* 218

Gendebien, Olivier 25
German Grand Prix 52–63
Gethin, Peter *78*
Ginther, Richie 183
GM Lotus Euroseries 36
González, José Froilán 142
González, Óscar 194
Gordon Bennett Trophy 65
Grand Prix Masters 218
Grands Prix Two (GP2) 54
GP2 Asia 218
Gregory, Masten 52
GT racing 82, 99
Guanyu, Zhou 203
Guelfi, André 245
Gurney, Dan 46, 132, 183

H

Hailwood, Mark 78
Häkkinen, Mika 35, 36, 238
Hämeenlinna circuit 35
Hamilton, Lewis 29, 99, *127, 136, 137, 150, 154,* 160, *177, 188,* 202, 216, 218, 227
Harris, Mike 246
Haryanto, Rio 206
Hawthorn, Mike 50, 244
Hill, Damon 215
Hill, Graham 126
Hill, Phil 183
Hockenheim circuit 59
Hulme, Danny *240, 240*
Hungarian Grand Prix 64–5
Hungaroring circuit 65
Hunt, James *97, 131, 187,* 215

I

Ickx, Jacky 24, 162, 172
Imola circuit 73
Indian Grand Prix 204–5
Indianapolis 500 11
Indonesian Grand Prix 206
Interlagos circuit *154,* 160
International Trophy (BRDC) 36
Irish Grand Prix 65
Istanbul Park circuit *8,* 123
Italian Grand Prix 66–79

J

Jacarepaguá circuit 157
Japanese Grand Prix 207–15
Jarama circuit *108,* 115
Jeddah Corniche circuit 220
Jerez circuit *108, 108,* 118
Jones, Alan *184, 192,* 232, *247*
Jyllandsringen circuit 34

K

kart racing 36, 54, 83, 91
Karthikeyan, Narain 205
KAVO (Korea Auto Valley Operation) 224
Keimola circuit 35
Kemora circuit 35
Korea International Circuit 224
Korean Grand Prix 224–5
Kubica, Robert 98, *172, 172,* 210
Kumpen, Sophie 91
Kvyat, Daniil 106
Kyalami circuit 250

L

Laffite, Jacques 38, *41,* 118, 252
Lammers, Jan 92
Lamy, Pedro 100
Las Vegas circuit 190
Latifi, Nicholas 164
Lauda, Niki *14, 14,* 32, 97

Lausitzring circuit 69
Le Mans 24 Hours 11, 15, 24, 25, 34, 41, 69, 82
    first-ever (1923) 38
Le Mans-Bugatti circuit 38, 42
Leclerc, Charles 38, 66, 83, 87, 200, 222, 238
Lederle, Neville 249
Liechtenstein 80
Ligier, Guy 46
Long Beach circuit 187, 195
Lourenco Marques circuit 246
Love, John 246, 246
Luanda circuit 246
Lusail International Circuit 218
Lwów circuit 98

M
Maarsbergen, Ecuri 90
McLaren, Bruce 132, 241
Maggs, Tony 249
Magny-Cours circuit 38, 46, 50
Mairesse, Willy 25
Malaysian Grand Prix 216–17
Maldonado, Pastor 195
Mansell, Nigel 8, 33, 112, 118, 126
Marimón, Onofre 142
Marina Bay circuit 222
Marlborough circuit 246
Mass, Jochen 108
Massa, Felipe 153, 154
Menditeguy, Carlos 142
Mexican Grand Prix 175–9
Mexico City circuit 178
Miami circuit 190, 191
Misano circuit 66
Modena circuit 11
Monaco Grand Prix 81–7
Mondello Park circuit 65
Monsanto Park circuit 99
Monte Carlo circuit 81, 84
Montjuich Park circuit 108
Montoya, Juan Pablo 174, 174
Montreal circuit 166
Monza circuit 66, 70, 70, 78
Moroccan Grand Prix 244–5
Mosport Park circuit 169
Moss, Stirling 140, 148, 244
Moto GP 218
Mugello circuit 74, 74
Munkkiniemi circuit 35

N
Nakajima, Kazuki 208
Nakajima, Satoru 209
NASCAR 37, 139, 184
Nepliget Park circuit 64
Netherlands 88–97
New Zealand Grand Prix 240–1
Newey, Adrian 50
Nivelles-Baulers circuit 22, 29, 32, 32
Norris, Lando 74, 104
Nürburgring circuit 56, 59

O
Ocon, Esteban 64
Olympic Winter Games 104
Opel, Rikky von 80
Oranje, Prince Bernhard van 92
Osella 90
Osterreichring circuit 12, 16, 20
Oulton Park circuit 11

P
Pace, Carlos 150
Padborg Park circuit 34
Panis, Olivier 46
Paris-to-Rouen race (1894) 38

Patrese, Riccardo 68
Paul Ricard circuit 38, 38, 42, 50
Pedralbes circuit 108
Pérez, Sergio 84, 176, 178, 200, 227
Pescara circuit 66, 74
Peterson, Ronnie 88, 121, 247
Phoenix Park circuit 65
Piquet, Nelson 8, 153, 157
Piriapolis circuit 194
Pironi, Didier 41, 73
Playa Ramirez circuit 194
Poland 98
Porsche Supercup 81
Porto circuit 102
Portuguese Grand Prix 99–103
Poznań circuit 98
Prost, Alain 8, 38, 40, 42, 124, 192, 214, 215, 252, 252
Punta del Este circuit 194
Puzey, Clive 246

Q
Qatar Grand Prix 218–19

R
Räikkönen, Kimi 8, 35, 37
rallying 37
Red Bull Ring circuit 16
Regazzoni, Clay 32, 131, 187
Reims circuit 45
Reutemann, Carlos 142, 144, 148, 148, 247
Rhodesia, see Zimbabwe
Ricard, Paul 11, 46
Ricciardo, Daniel 74, 87, 198, 232
Rindt, Jochen 15, 136, 136
Ring Djursland circuit 34
Rodríguez, Gonzalo 194
Rodríguez, Pedro 176
Rosa, Pedro de la 111
Rosberg, Keke 20, 36
Rosberg, Nico 52, 54, 127, 227
Roskilder Rin circuit 34
Rothengatter, Huub 90
Rouen circuit 11
Rouen-Les-Essarts circuit 46, 50
Russell, George 150, 190
Russian Grand Prix 104–7, 104

S
Sainz, Carlos, Jr 70, 79, 84, 87, 108, 111, 180
Sakhir Grand Prix 83, 176, 200
Salazar, Eliseo 173
Salzburgring circuit 12
San Marino Grand Prix 66, 73, 78
Sato, Takuma 208
Saudi Arabian Grand Prix 220–1
Scheckter, Ian 249
Scheckter, Jody 144, 248
Schenken, Tim 232
Schumacher, Michael 16, 32, 35, 46, 55, 102, 108, 118, 140, 148, 215, 239, 252
Schumacher, Ralf 15, 54
Second World War 64, 66, 69, 82, 88, 98, 124, 128, 140, 144, 154, 194
Seinäjoki circuit 35
Senna, Ayrton 8, 38, 84, 101, 101, 112, 124, 136, 152, 160, 160, 177, 180, 192, 193, 214, 215, 234, 238, 252
Sepang International Circuit 217
Shanghai International Circuit 203
Silverstone circuit 128
Singapore Grand Prix 222–3
Slovakia 34
Snetterton circuit 11
Sochi Autodrom circuit 107
South African Grand Prix 68, 247–53
South Korean Grand Prix 224–5

Spa-Francorchamps circuit 26
Spa 24 Hours 22
Spanish Grand Prix 108–19
sportscar racing 12, 139
Springbok series 246
St Jovite circuit 172
Stewart, Jackie 56, 126, 136, 136, 250
Stroll, Lance 164, 169
Styrian Grand Prix 16
Surtees, John 132, 177
Suzuka circuit 35, 210, 215
Suzuki, Aguri 208
Swedish Grand Prix 120–1
Switzerland 122
Syracuse circuit 11

T
Targa Florio 25, 66
Testut, André 82
Thailand 225
Theodore Racing 92
Three Hour 246
Tingle, Sam 246
Trintignant, Maurice 38, 41
Trips, Wolfgang von 54
Trulli, Jarno 66
Tsunoda, Yuki 207, 208
Tulln-Langenlebarn circuit 16
Turkish Grand Prix 123
Tuscan Grand Prix 74

U
United Arab Emirates (UAE) 226–7
United Kingdom (UK), see British Grand Prix
United States Grand Prix 180–93
Uria, Alberto 194
Uruguay 194

V
Valencia circuit 108
Vallelunga circuit 66
Venezuela 195
Verstappen, Jos 90
Verstappen, Max 12, 66, 87, 88, 91, 127, 160, 162, 175, 180, 190, 216, 222, 227
Vettel, Sebastian 54, 59, 74, 87, 204, 224
Vila Real circuit 99
Villeneuve, Gilles 50, 51, 73, 115, 164, 169, 172, 184
Villeneuve, Jacques 102, 108, 118, 165, 166

W
Watkins Glen circuit 184
Watson, John 192, 192
Webber, Mark 230, 232
Wharton, Ken 194
World Championship:
    covid-19 effect on 8, 66, 73, 74, 74, 92, 99, 102, 123, 197, 202, 218, 238
    first-ever (1950) 11, 22, 38, 45, 45, 66
World Endurance Championship (WEC) 22, 70
World Rally Championship (WRC) 35, 99, 123
World Series 98
World Sports-Prototype Championship 175
World Touring Car 100, 218, 244
Wurz, Alex 15

Y
Yas Marina circuit 226–7
Yoong, Alex 217

Z
Zakspeed 90
Zandvoort circuit 92
Zeltweg circuit 12, 12
Zimbabwe 246
Zolder circuit 22, 29

PICTURE CREDITS

The publishers would like to thank the following sources for their kind permission to reproduce the photographs and artwork in this book.

GETTY IMAGES: El Grafico 146-147; Intercontinentale / AFP 50, 149; Adam Pretty / Formula 1 12

GRAPHIC NEWS: 16, 26, 29 bottom right, 42, 45 bottom right, 46 bottom left, 56, 59 bottom right, 65, 70, 73 bottom right, 74 bottom left, 84, 92, 102, 107 bottom right, 112, 115 bottom right, 121 bottom, 122, 123, 128, 131 bottom right, 132 bottom left, 144, 154, 157 bottom right, 166, 169 bottom right, 178, 184, 187 bottom right, 188 bottom left, 190 top, 191 bottom, 198, 200, 203 bottom, 205 bottom, 210, 217 top, 218, 220, 222, 225, 227 bottom, 234, 245 bottom, 250

MOTORSPORT IMAGES: 5 top right, 8-9, 14, 17, 24, 25, 27, 30-31, 46-47, 48-49, 86, 88, 93, 113, 114-115, 118, 124, 125, 129, 233, 242-243; Sam Bagnall 4 left, 10-11; Carl Bingham 111, 203 top; Sam Bloxham 4 right, 52, 109, 138-139, 180, 230; Charles Coates 64, 238; Ercole Colombo / Studio Colombo 68, 145, 152; Glenn Dunbar 60-61, 87, 137, 155, 191 top, 221; Steve Etherington 90, 99, 188-189, 204, 211, 227 top; Andrew Ferraro 6-7, 158-159, 173; Simon Galloway 83, 127; Honda Motor Company 110; Andy Hone 5 bottom left, 66, 85, 91, 223, 228-229, 235; JEP 134-135; LAT Photographic 13, 15, 21, 22, 28-29, 36 top left, 39, 43, 44-45, 57, 67, 69, 71, 72-73, 78, 80, 82, 96, 121 top, 136, 140, 143, 150, 156-157, 164, 168-169, 176 top left, 177, 181, 183, 185, 186-187, 192, 193, 194, 195, 208, 232, 236-237, 239, 240, 244, 245 top, 247, 249, 252, 253; Charly Lopez 81; Zak Mauger 38, 76-77, 170-171, 175, 176 bottom right, 207, 216, 219; David Phipps 130-131, 132-133, 148, 161, 215, 246, 251; Photo4 18-19; Rainer Schlegelmilch 33, 41, 63, 100 bottom left, 116-117, 153, 182, 241; Alastair Staley 89; Sutton 20, 32, 35, 36 bottom right, 37, 40, 51, 54, 55, 58-59, 62, 97, 98, 100 top right, 101, 103, 104, 108, 119, 120, 126, 141, 142, 160, 163, 165, 167, 172, 174, 205 top, 206, 209, 212-213, 214, 217 bottom, 231, 248; James Sutton 5 top left, 196-197, 226; Mark Sutton 23, 79, 105, 106-107, 151, 162, 179, 190 bottom, 201, 202; Michael Tee 53; Steven Tee 74-75, 94-95, 107 top right, 199, 224

Every effort has been made to acknowledge correctly and contact the source and/or copyright holder of each picture. Any unintentional errors or omissions will be corrected in future editions of this book.